20 Questions

about Youth & the Media

PETER LANG
New York • Washington, D.C./Baltimore • Bern
Frankfurt am Main • Berlin • Brussels • Vienna • Oxford

20 Questions
about Youth & the Media

EDITED BY
Sharon R. Mazzarella

PETER LANG
New York • Washington, D.C./Baltimore • Bern
Frankfurt am Main • Berlin • Brussels • Vienna • Oxford

Library of Congress Cataloging-in-Publication Data

20 questions about youth and the media / edited by Sharon R. Mazzarella.
p. cm.
Includes bibliographical references.
1. Mass media and youth—United States. 2. Mass media and children—
United States—Government policy. 3. Violence in mass media.
4. Parenting—United States. 5. Mass media—Social aspects—United States.
I. Mazzarella, Sharon R. II. Title: Twenty questions about youth and the media.
HQ799.2.M35A17   302.23083—dc22   2006022705
ISBN 978-0-8204-8864-6 (hard cover)
ISBN 978-0-8204-6334-6 (paperback)

Bibliographic information published by **Die Deutsche Bibliothek**.
Die Deutsche Bibliothek lists this publication in the "Deutsche
Nationalbibliografie"; detailed bibliographic data is available
on the Internet at http://dnb.ddb.de/.

Cover design by Lisa Barfield

The paper in this book meets the guidelines for permanence and durability
of the Committee on Production Guidelines for Book Longevity
of the Council of Library Resources.

To Rich, whose companionship nurtures the child in me.

Contents

Acknowledgments

As I write this on September 8, 2006, it is hard to believe that it was a mere 18 months ago that I began this project by approaching an impressive group of youth and media scholars, asking them to share their expertise with me and with the intended student audience for the book. Seeing the merit in the project, and despite my rigid stylistic/content guidelines and deadlines, they enthusiastically joined in. This finished product is a testament to their intellectual expertise, dedication to the study of youth and media, and commitment to educating the current generation of college students. It has been a genuine pleasure to work with each and every one of them.

While I pulled this project together, the initial idea belonged to Damon Zucca, my editor at Peter Lang Publishing. When Damon first contacted me about this project way back when, he did so, he said, to pick my brain about what I thought such a book should look like and whether I could recommend someone who would make a good editor for it. After giving him some ideas about the book's content, I excitedly told him that I would make a great editor! All these months later, I am left wondering if that was Damon's evil plan from the beginning—to get me excited enough about the project so that I would volunteer to take it on. Well, it worked, and I could not be happier.

Thank you to Amy Jordan for granting permission to reprint her educational strength scale in chapter 12 (Jordan & Woodard, 1997) and to Eric D. Carlson, Executive Editor of *STS NEXUS*, for granting Christine Bachen permission to use all or part of her 2001 *STS NEXUS* article in chapter 16. Thanks also to Angharad N. Valdivia for granting permission for me to use or adapt portions of a chapter appearing in her *Media Studies Companion* in chapter 3.

A project such as this could not be accomplished without the support of one's educational institution. I am fortunate to have the support and encouragement of my colleagues in the Communication Studies Department at Clemson University, and especially that of my chair, Katherine Hawkins. Everyone should work in such a nurturing and academically stimulating environment.

Finally, no book on youth and media would exist without young people themselves. They are the reason we study what we do.

REFERENCES

Bachen, C. (2001). The family in the networked society: A summary of research on the American family. *STS NEXUS*, 1(1). Retrieved November 20, 2006, from http://www.scu.edu/sts/nexus/winter2001/BachenArticle.cfm.

Jordan, A. B., & Woodard, E. (1997). *The state of children's television report: Programming for children over broadcast and cable television* [Report No. 14]. Philadelphia: University of Pennsylvania, Annenberg Public Policy Center.

Mazzarella, S. R. (2003). Constructing youth: Media, youth and the politics of representation. In A. N. Valdivia (Ed.), *Media studies companion* (pp. 227-246). Malden, MA: Blackwell.

Where Have We Been and Where Are We Going?

ELLEN WARTELLA

As I sit here in summer 2006 reflecting on where we as youth and media scholars have been and where we are going, I am struck, after all these years, by the continuing public concerns about youth and the media. Over the course of the past year, for example, there have been legal attempts to prohibit video stores from distributing violent video games in Illinois (SafeGamesIllinois.org, n.d.); there has been a major national report from the National Academy of Sciences examining the strong relationship between food marketing practices and the diets of children and youth (McGinnis et al., 2006); and there has been public controversy over a new twenty-four-hour cable channel called BabyFirstTV directed at children under the age of two (BabyFirstTV, 2006), as well as the marketing of new baby-oriented videos called *Sesame Beginnings* (Sesame Workshop, 1998–2006), as two examples of the commercialization of infants. *Plus ça change, plus c'est la même chose.*

When I entered the field of communication in the early 1970s, public attention to youth and media (specifically television) was quite extensive in terms of (1) its potential influence on violence, (2) its educational potential, and (3) the ethical implications of advertising to children. The 1970s turned out to be a busy decade for public discussion of and research studies on children and media. In what follows, I will briefly address each of these issues as well as the role of communication scholars in that public discussion.

Television Violence

Following the spate of violence on the streets of U.S. cities and the assassinations of public figures such as Robert Kennedy and Martin Luther King, Jr., in the late 1960s, concern about television violence and its alleged effects on violent behavior was high on the public agenda, a concern seen in the first study of the Surgeon General's Scientific Advisory Committee on Television and Social Behavior (1972). At that time, studies of the effects of television violence were not just the focal point of media and youth concerns, they colonized *all* considerations of media influences on youth. To study media effects on youth was to study violence—period. I remember trying to distance myself from such research by introducing myself as a children and media researcher—not a media violence researcher. Gradually, however, spaces opened for other kinds of studies of media influences on children and youth, and eventually the spaces opened wide enough to enable scholars to ask questions beyond those related to media effects and influences.

Educational Television

During the 1970s, two groups helped to expand the conversation about media and youth: the Children's Television Workshop's (CTW) production of *Sesame Street* demonstrated the educational potential of television for children, while Action for Children's Television (ACT) launched an advocacy campaign to decommericalize children's television. Two spokeswomen became synonymous with the movement for quality children's television: Joan Ganz Cooney, of CTW, and Peggy Charren, of ACT. At the same time, researchers of media and youth began to work in the television industry to help produce quality children's television and to become active in the policy arena. (I will return to a discussion of ACT in the next section.)

We really cannot underestimate the influence *Sesame Street* had, not only on the production of children's television in the United States but also on how families, academics, and policymakers viewed what children's television could and should be. *Sesame Street* demonstrated the educational potential of television for preschoolers and, in time, gave U.S. parents evidence that not all television was bad for children. By marrying research on how preschool children understand and learn from television with the production of a program whose goal was to teach an age-appropriate educational curriculum, *Sesame Street* demonstrated that well-designed and age-targeted educational television could be both entertaining and beneficial for children. Content matters, and content that takes into account the age and developmental needs of the child audience can be a very powerful educational tool. And in the early 1970s, the successful marriage of researchers and producers in developing *Sesame Street* opened up new career avenues for those researchers interested in putting their knowledge to work in producing children's television. It has become a regularly accepted practice to have a children's television expert either as a consultant or on the production staff of a children's educational program. My ten years as a trustee of Sesame Workshop, which produces *Sesame Street,* has demonstrated to me the powerful voice researchers now have in the production of educational programming for children.

The success of *Sesame Street* led, by the 1980s, to children's cable networks like Nickelodeon and Disney and a wide range of children's programs with educational content as parents, over time, learned to trust not only *Sesame Street* but also, gradually, other educationally oriented programs for their children. In the 1990s, the Children's Television Act inscribed the public understanding and belief in the power of planned educational television for children by requiring broadcasters to program and identify three hours a week of children's programs that are informational and educational. That broadcasters had an affirmative obligation to schedule quality programming for children and that such content could be identified and assessed became an accepted standard of television production practice. Joan Ganz Cooney's vision of using television as an out-of-school informal educational tool is now an industry standard, in particular as it applies to programming for preschoolers.

Advertising to Children

ACT came along somewhat simultaneously with the growth of planned educational programming for children and raised awareness of the commercialization of children's television and the potential harmful impact of advertising directed at children. As the spokeswoman for and public face of ACT, Peggy Charren testified at a variety of Federal Communications Commission (FCC), Federal Trade Commission (FTC), and Congressional investigations into children's television advertising practices. In 1970 ACT petitioned the FCC with a request that it assume responsibility in the area of children's television and more specifically that practices such as having children's hosts also sell products during the children's program be banned. At both the FCC and the FTC there was considerable activity around children's advertising issues, resulting first in the FTC investigations into the fairness of children's television advertising, which began in 1978 (the investigations were dropped), and ultimately in the establishment of advertising time limits in the Children's Television Act of 1990. It is interesting to ponder how different children's lives might be today if the 1978 proposal from the FTC staff to place restrictions on the advertising of heavily sugared cereals and other foods to children and to ban all TV advertising to children too young to understand advertising's persuasive intent had gone into effect.

Of course, no such restrictions ever did go into effect; rather, self-regulatory groups such as the Better Business Bureau's Children's Advertising Review Unit were set up to continually monitor advertising practices to ensure that they are consistent with children's developmental understanding of advertising claims. Had rules been implemented regarding advertising of heavily sugared foods to children in the 1970s, we would be having a very different public conversation today about factors contributing to the current epidemic of childhood obesity. The environment, however, has changed, I believe, in terms of what U.S. parents expect of food marketers, and there are examples of several different food companies promoting healthier foods to children via advertising. Given the high-profile nature of the current concerns about childhood obesity, it will be interesting to see how children's television programmers, food marketers, and even the federal government respond (if they do at all) to these concerns.

It seems clear to me that, starting with ACT's petitions to the FCC and the FTC in the 1970s, a whole new range of public questions about television's influence on children (beyond the violence issue) required researchers' expertise and involvement in the public arena. As pointed out in several chapters in this book, there have been a variety of different hearings before the FCC, FTC, and Congress since the middle of the twentieth century, and academic researchers with specific expertise in the area of youth and media have regularly been invited to testify and to report on the current academic understanding of how youth use and/or are influenced by media. As a scholar in this area, I have found it particularly gratifying to do research on media and youth because it enables me to apply my knowledge to work in the public arena.

Thirty Years Later and Beyond

While the conversational spaces for dialogue have opened, there remain ongoing concerns about media violence and its impact on children. While I tried to distance myself from that research area early in my career, I entered the conversation as a coprincipal investigator on the National Television Violence Study in the late 1990s (Wartella et al., 1997; Whitney et al., 1998). That project, the largest content analysis of American television to this day, was an exciting and rewarding experience. We found a formula for how television portrays violence—by glamorizing, sanitizing, and trivializing it—that is of particular concern when children are in the audience. While attention has shifted from concerns specific to *television* violence to an inclusion of other forms of media violence such as that found in video games, the special nature of children as an audience continues to be a focal point, and the contribution that media violence (along with other contributing factors) makes to youth violence is still a hot political issue. No amount of consensus among social scientists who study media violence effects (not unanimity but consensus) will appease the naysayers' rejection of the conclusions from the vast number of studies of violence effects. It seems that the public debate will continue.

In looking forward, it is clear that interactive, digital technologies such as the Internet, cell phones, and iPods have brought to studies both old questions of how children and youth use these media (how often and to what ends and with what impact on the user and the family), as well as newer questions about the power of a networked media world in which children and youth have more agency and control of the content and their response to it. The power of interactivity and networking is not yet well understood. Moreover, it is not at all clear to me whether these newer media will challenge some of the fundamental understandings I know I have acquired in the study of youth and media: that children are a special audience different from adults and that they have special needs at different ages and that content matters. And how might these media have an influence on children's real lives around the world—can they be used to increase children's health and well-being?

These are just some of the issues I have been particularly interested in over the course of my career, and this volume demonstrates that the topic of youth and media is a robust area for research as well as an ongoing site of public discussion and debate.

Twenty Questions about Youth and the Media

As an introduction to the research on media and youth, this volume clearly lays out both the ongoing public concerns and some newer issues. Designed with the classroom in mind, this book brings together leading experts in the field of youth and media to address a range of pressing topics, including the commercialization of youth culture, the effects of media violence, how young people actively use media and technology in their lives, and the internationalization of youth culture. The chapters, each of which features end-of-chapter questions and exercises, are organized into three sections, in order to facilitate classroom use and student learning.

The book begins with a section identifying the major players in the discussions about youth and media (corporations, government, parents, child advocacy organizations, and scholars). Chapter 1 revisits the earliest days of radio and motion pictures and continues through to today's digital, multimedia environment in order to understand how the kids' media industry has evolved. In this chapter, J. Alison Bryant examines media creators, distributors, advertisers, and toy companies in order to enable students to see the complex, dynamic, and interconnected relationships among these stakeholders and to understand how today's children's media came to be.

Since the early years of the twentieth century, but especially since the 1950s, the U.S. government has had an interest in youth media, and it is this topic that is taken up in chapter 2. In this chapter, Alison Alexander and Keisha L. Hoerrner take the reader on a fifty-year journey through the evolution of youth media regulation, focusing specifically on the fine line between protecting the young and protecting the rights laid out in the First Amendment. As a result, the authors contend, we've experienced fifty years of both "action and inaction" with the U.S. government more likely to threaten to institute regulations than to actually create or enforce new regulations. Over the past fifty-plus years, such threats of government regulation of media and culture have been generated in response to one or another moral panic about youth and media and culture.

In chapter 3 Sharon R. Mazzarella asserts that the way in which we have come to define youth in the United States—as innocent and needing protection—is, in part, responsible for the proliferation of these panics manifested by various adult constituencies including parents, journalists, educators, the clergy, politicians, and so on. Focusing specifically on three example of such panics—the 1950s comic-book scare, the public outcry over popular music in the 1980s, and the more recent concerns about youth and the Internet—Mazzarella identifies their defining common characteristics, notably the role of the news media in perpetuating public concerns. As Mazzarella points out, many moral panics often generate extensive media publicity and governmental action despite a lack of concrete research evidence presented by those lay "experts" raising the concerns. The next two chapters, however, address how academic experts employ both theory and research in studies of youth and media. In chapter 4, Cyndy Scheibe discusses how various developmental theories have influenced youth and media research over the previous several decades. Highlighting social-learning, cognitive-developmental, and information-processing theories, Scheibe shows how the formal study of youth and media from such psychosocial perspectives has been highly influential in the field of youth and media scholarship.

While Scheibe focuses on one category of theories and scholarship guiding youth and media scholars, Dafna Lemish, in chapter 5, outlines a wide range of approaches informing such studies. She begins by addressing the difficulties researchers face when studying the young and then identifies the two primary schools of thought guiding much of the research—a more quantitative approach (such as that addressed in chapter 4) that Lemish describes as focused more on "the becoming child," as well as a more qualitative and cultural approach that she describes as focused more on "the being child." While acknowledging what seems to be an unbridgeable gap between these two approaches in terms of topics, theories, and methods, Lemish closes her chapter with a call for scholars to "integrate the knowledge" gained from each of the perspectives so as to more fully round out our understanding of the topic.

Research and theory related to youth and media are not limited to the academy. In chapter 6, Katharine E. Heintz-Knowles examines how youth advocacy organizations use media research to provide evidence for their claims and initiatives. What makes this chapter so compelling is that Heintz-Knowles discusses her firsthand experiences as a researcher working for such advocacy organizations as Action for Children's Television, Children Now, the Frameworks Institute, and the Kaiser Family Foundation.

Following from Lemish's discussion of the two strains of theory and methodology guiding much of the scholarship on youth and media, the next two sections of the book each focus on one strain. The second section addresses the concerns about and research in the areas of media use, content, and effects primarily from a more quantitative, empirical tradition.

In chapter 7 Nancy A. Jennings discusses the research on the effects of advertising on children. Beginning with a discussion of how children are socialized as consumers, Jennings goes on to thoroughly examine the research on both the content of children's advertising as well as the effects of this content on their behavior, knowledge of consumerism, and attitudes and beliefs about advertising. She concludes with a call for increased "parental involvement, governmental oversight, and ethical marketing practices" in order to help children navigate the ubiquity of marketing messages targeted to them.

Chapters 8 and 9 take on what arguably has been the most controversial and studied issue related to youth and media: media violence. Asking, "Should we be concerned about media violence?" in chapter 8, Erica Scharrer compellingly explains the wealth of recent research on violence in television, video games, and films. Her goal is to provide the reader with answers to questions related to how media violence is defined; how much violence there is in media; what its effects are; why it exists; and why it is so appealing to the audience. While Scharrer focuses primarily on the recent wave of studies on media violence, John P. Murray, in chapter 9, takes a more historical and methodological approach, showing how the topic has been studied over the previous five-plus decades, concluding with a discussion of the direction in which future scholarship on this topic is moving—including ongoing research at the Harvard Medical School and Children's Hospital in Boston related to children's neurological responses when viewing media violence. Based on decades of research, both Scharrer and Murray conclude their chapters on cautionary notes, asserting that we should be concerned about the potential effects of violent content on the young.

One of the most prolific research programs in the past three decades has been the Cultural Indicators Project, founded by the late George Gerbner at the University of Pennsylvania's Annenberg School. A primary theoretical tenet of this program's cultivation analysis is that people learn from the stories they are told and that the media (notably television) function as the primary storytellers in our culture. It is from this perspective that two of the project's leading scholars, Michael Morgan and Nancy Signorielli, write in chapters 10 and 11. In his chapter asking what young people learn about the world from watching television, Morgan begins by outlining the theoretical and methodological assumptions of cultivation research. He then goes on to show how this research program has been able to document what the media teach young people about violence, gender roles, occupations, families, "deviant" behaviors, and a range of other topics. He concludes by showing how such mediated learning plays out on an international scale.

The beginnings of cultivation analysis are found in in-depth content analysis of various aspects of media content, such as how characters of specific demographic backgrounds are portrayed. In chapter 11, Signorielli looks at how prime-time television programs portray young people and why this is significant. Comparing recent studies with those conducted in the 1980s, Signorielli documents what she describes as a "limited and static image of children and adolescents" over the past thirty years. Despite the fact that a large proportion of television content is targeted to the young, Signorielli argues that these portrayals result in a devaluing of childhood and adolescence that has far-reaching consequences.

While cultivation analysis is concerned with what young people learn from media that are not explicitly intending to teach them, one of the most prolific areas of research on media and the young has focused on media content that is intentionally educational. In chapter 12, Deborah L. Linebarger and Deborah K. Wainwright look at decades of scholarship on educational television in order to understand whether the idea that children can have positive learning experiences while viewing is an "urban myth or dream come true." Completing the section on media uses, content, and effects is chapter 13, on media literacy effects and efforts to help young media consumers become more critical of and less vulnerable to the media messages they consume. In this chapter W. James Potter and Sahara Byrne begin by defining media literacy effects as different from other types of media effects—specifically the nature of the former as focusing on proactive, intentional, and positive effects. The authors go on to document the growing body of research on media literacy effects and research identifying opportunities for intervention in helping young people become more media literate.

The second broad category of research on media and young people discussed by Lemish in chapter 5 is more qualitative and cultural research. As Lemish notes, such scholarship is characterized by an attempt to understand the role media and culture play in the lives of the young, not necessarily to document the effects it has on them. The remaining chapters in the book all take just such an approach. Beginning with chapter 14, in which Susannah R. Stern and Taylor J. Willis ask, "What are teenagers up to online?," we can see that the goal is not so much to document any potential negative effects computer technology might have on youth, but rather, as the title suggests, to explore how young people are using this technology. Focusing on such uses as instant messaging (IM), blogs, Web pages, and social networking spaces such as Myspace.com, the authors pay particular attention to adolescence as a distinct life stage and then address how and why the Internet can have particular appeal and utility during this stage.

One aspect of youths' media use that emerges from chapter 14 is the role the technology plays in identity development and expression. Following up on this, JoEllen Fisherkeller in chapter 15 asks, "How do kids' self-identities relate to media experiences in everyday life?" Grounded in the qualitative and ethnographic fieldwork of her own research and that of others, Fisherkeller documents how young people negotiate their self-identities—including aspects related to gender, sexuality, class, race, ethnicity, regionality, and nationality through interaction with various forms of media and other cultural artifacts. Reminding us that kids' relationships with media are not straightforward, Fisherkeller compellingly provides the reader with a glimpse into the complexities inherent in these relationships.

If young peoples' relationships with media are complex, the complexity only increases when we focus on the role of communication technologies in family life. Christine M. Bachen begins chapter 16 with the acknowledgment that this complexity is due both to changes in family structures as well as to the evolution and proliferation of communication technologies. While questions about the role of media and family emerged in the 1950s with concern over whether television displaced other family activities, today the issues range from the ubiquity and variety of various communication technologies in U.S. homes, the negotiation of rules and roles related to newer technologies in the home, as well as the blending of home life and work life facilitated by these technologies. Bachen concludes her chapter with a call for more ethnographic research to better understand these new family scenarios.

The authors of the previous chapters in this section remind us that there is no such thing as one monolithic definition of "youth," and that there is a range of complicating factors mediating young people's relationship with mass culture. One such factor is gender. Indeed, one of the most prolific subtopics within media studies of youth has proven to be "girls' studies," a field often considered to be an offshoot of women's studies. In chapter 17, Mazzarella shows us how scholars within the field of girls' studies address three components of girl culture: (1) mediated representations of girls and girl culture, (2) how girls themselves have come to actively negotiate and resist the hegemonic cultural messages that surround them, and (3) how girls have actively appropriated newer communication technologies in order to become active producers of their own culture.

The next two chapters deal with the commercialization of youth culture. In chapter 18 Matthew P. McAllister asks, "Just how commercialized is children's culture?" Focusing on the controversial Bratz dolls as an example of this commercialization, McAllister traces the historical evolution of licensing and media tie-ins within kids' culture. Arguing that the reason U.S. kids' culture seems so hypercommercialized is that this is a trend that pervades *all* culture in the United States now; he goes on to show how recent marketing trends such as aggressive advertising, the proliferation of mega-media corporations, and the growth of new media (the latter creating new outlets for commercial messages) have contributed to this phenomenon of which the Bratz are but the most recent example. Following from McAllister, Stephen Kline in chapter 19 ponders whether children are victims of consumer culture, empowered consumers, or consumers-in-training. Beginning with a historical perspective on the changing definition of childhood and the evolution of the child as consumer, Kline argues that children are, from birth, consumers-in-training, with parents, peers, media, and schools all playing a role in this training and socialization.

Finally, grounded in a large body of international research, Katalin Lustyik in chapter 20 seeks to address whether youth today live "in a shared world culture." Specifically, she addresses this broad issue by introducing a number of subtopics: globalization and youth cultures, the targeting of youth by transnational media conglomerates, and young people's appropriation of such commercialized, global artifacts. She concludes by acknowledging that answering the chapter's title question necessitates that we as scholars include an analysis of issues related to national and cultural identity, cultural imperialism, increasing media conglomerations and globalization, as well as how young people consume media and cultural artifacts.

Indeed, the role not only of new media but also of old media in the lives of children and youth is a recurring topic. In fact, what is most impressive about this book is that it locates the current issues regarding media in a historical context and examines them with an eye to the future. It deals with both where we have been and where we are going. That has not always been the case.

REFERENCES

BabyFirstTV. (2006). *About us*. Retrieved July 25, 2006, from http://www.babyfirsttv.com/content.asp?xml_id=1612.

McGinnis, J. M., Gootman, J. A., & Kraak, V. I. (Eds.). (2006). *Food marketing to children and youth: Threat or opportunity?* Washington, D.C.: National Academies Press.

SafeGamesIllinois.org. (n.d.). *Governor Blagojevich's initiative that bans minors from buying violent and sexu-*

ally explicit videogames. Retrieved July 25, 2006, from http://www.safegamesillinois.org/proposal.php.

Sesame Workshop. (1998–2006). *Sesame beginnings*. Retrieved July 25, 2006, from http://www.sesame workshop.org/sesamebeginnings/new/.

Surgeon General's Scientific Advisory Committee on Television and Social Behavior. (1972). *Television and growing up: The impact of televised violence*. Washington, D.C.: United States Government Printing Office.

Wartella, E., Whitney, D. C., Lasorsa, D., Danielson, W., Olivarez, A., Klijn, M., Lopez, R., Jennings, N., & Klijn, M. (1997). Television violence in reality programs, year II results. In Center for Communication and Social Policy, University of California, Santa Barbara (Ed.), *National television violence study, 1995–96* (pp. 205–266). Thousand Oaks, CA: Sage.

Whitney, D. C., Wartella, E., Lasorsa, D., Danielson, W., Olivarez, A., Jennings, N., & Lopez, R. (1998). Television violence in reality programs, year III results. In Center for Communication and Social Policy, University of California, Santa Barbara (Ed.), *National television violence study, 1996–97* (pp. 221–284). Thousand Oaks, CA: Sage.

The Players

Corporations, Government, Parents,
Child Advocacy Organizations, and Scholars

CHAPTER ONE

How Has the Kids' Media Industry Evolved?

J. ALISON BRYANT

The kids' media industry has changed dramatically over the last eight decades. From silent films to massive multiplayer online role-playing games, the ways in which children and adolescents can spend their leisure time have expanded exponentially. With this increase in choice has come an increase in the complexity of creating, distributing, and financing children's media. This chapter looks at what goes on "behind the curtain" in the kids' media industry and how that affects the media that kids have and use. This chapter will follow the children's media industry from the early days of film and radio to today's multimedia environment to look at the coevolution of the industry and the technology. In particular, it will look at the relationships among distributors, content creators, toy companies, and advertisers as children's media has changed over time and will delve into the shifting dynamics among these organizational actors.

Early Days of Film and Radio (1920s–1940s)

The first two mass media to capture the eyes and ears of youth were motion pictures and radio programming. In the 1920s movie theaters became a major form of entertainment for kids, with the average child attending 1.6 movies per week in 1929 (Cressey, 1934). For young film viewers, the Saturday-afternoon matinee became a social ritual. Although originally these matinees were primarily short films and newsreels, once studios saw the revenue coming from their younger crowds, they began producing family films (Mitroff & Herr Stephenson, 2007). The first company to delve into this market is probably not a surprise to anyone today, since it continues to dominate the family-film genre. Disney released *Snow White and the Seven Dwarfs* in 1937 to great commercial success (Paik, 2001).

As film was gaining wide popularity in the 1920s, radio was still in its infancy. But by the 1930s, radio had firmly established itself as a kid-friendly medium. By 1930, 46 percent of American families had radios in their homes, and by 1940, 80 percent did (Paik, 2001). This in-home, easily accessible medium soon began to give film a run for its money—literally. As children curbed their cinema attendance, they greatly increased their radio listening time. By the mid-1930s, tweens (nine- to twelve-year-olds) were listening to two to three hours of radio a day, and in the New York City area alone there were fifty-two radio programs for kids (DeBoer, 1937; Eisenberg, 1936; Jersild, 1939; Paik, 2001).

As radio gained popularity and status as the new family "hearth," there was a shift in the commercial interest paid to the medium. This shift manifested itself in two ways. First, networks were established in order to lure advertisers with the promise of larger audiences and to share costs, thus establishing the network model that would later be adopted by television (Alexander & Owers, 1998; Mitroff & Herr Stephenson, 2007). Second, advertisers began to see radio as an important medium, especially for reaching children (Pecora, 1998). Companies such as General Mills, Ovaltine, and Jell-O began to sponsor radio programs for kids (for example, *Jack Armstrong*, *Little Orphan Annie*, and *Wizard of Oz*, respectively) (Pecora, 1998; Summers, 1971). This form of radio sponsorship remained relatively unchanged until the 1950s, when television began to supplant radio as the kids' medium of choice.

TV Reigns Supreme (1950s–1970s)

In the 1940s and early 1950s, the purpose of television programs for children was to create the vision of the television as the new family hearth and to therefore sell television sets to parents (Calabro, 1992; Melody, 1973; Schneider, 1987). The first daily thirty-minute program designed specifically for children, *Small Fry Club*, went on the air in 1947 (Mitroff & Herr Stephenson, 2007). It was soon followed by advertiser-sponsored shows such as *Kukla, Fran and Ollie*, and *Howdy Doody*, which were created by the broadcast networks, shown during prime-time hours, and meant to be entertaining for both children and adults. Although NBC, CBS, the now-defunct DuMont, and later ABC provided children's television programming as part of their lineup, for the most part programming for children was concentrated at the local level and was generally inexpensively produced live local programming, *Popeye* cartoon reruns, and old *Hopalong Cassidy* movies (Schneider, 1987). During this time period, NBC surpassed the other networks on a national level in the amount of children's programming it aired (Melody, 1973).

The advent of children's television programming and advertising as we know it today, however, occurred in the mid-1950s. In late 1954, ABC partnered with Disney to create *Disneyland*, an hour-long, high-quality program for children in which Disney was allowed to fully promote the new Disneyland amusement park and the collection of Disney films (Melody, 1973). This program met both ratings and critical success and quickly became the model for children's programming—Hollywood studio programming sponsored through advertisements and program sponsorships. Disney's next venture, *The Mickey Mouse Club*, solidified this model. In November 1955, Walt Disney's *Mickey Mouse Club* became the first show to be aired every weekday during the child-targeted after-school time (Schneider, 1987). "No other show before it reached as many children with as much frequency. And no other show before it was used as effectively by advertisers of children's products" (Schneider, 1987, p. 12). In addition, *Captain Kangaroo*,[1] which was until recently the longest-running children's program, was introduced that year by CBS.

This new advertising model provided a wonderful opportunity for toy companies to take a strong position in children's television advertising. Mattel's Burp Gun became the first toy featured in a television commercial when it aired during *The Mickey Mouse Club* (Cross, 1997; Schneider, 1987). For the first season of *The Mickey Mouse Club*, the cost of advertising sponsorship for the program was $500,000 per year (Schneider, 1987). For this amount, Mattel was given fifteen minutes to show three toy commercials. These commercials aired Wednesday evenings from 5:30 to 5:45, during *The Mickey Mouse Club*. At that time, there were no toy-industry giants as we know them today (such as Hasbro, Fisher-Price, or Mattel), so this was a sizeable investment for a toy manufacturer. The wild success of the show proved to be worth the outrageous price tag. Sales of the Mattel Burp Gun, for example, doubled the company's entire previous annual profit in the few weeks between Thanksgiving and Christmas, 1955 (Schneider, 1987).

In 1958 Mattel introduced its first girl-directed toy, the Barbie doll. "Each commercial [for Barbie] was treated as a mini-episode in Barbie's glamorous life"; the advertising campaign was so successful that the television exposure of the doll had to be immediately cut back due to a demand for the doll that far outweighed the supply (Schneider, 1987, p. 30). The Barbie doll was soon followed by an array of tie-in products, such as the Barbie newsletter, Barbie magazine, and Barbie books, and the formation of the Barbie Fan Club. These tie-ins were extremely successful, and the Barbie Fan Club became the second-largest girls' organization in the world (the largest was the Girl Scouts) (Schneider, 1987). These early successes for Mattel solidified the notion that commercials within children's programming were highly effective. By 1962, Hanna-Barbera, following this new model, was making over a million dollars from tie-in products alone (Barnouw, 1970, qtd. in Melody, 1973).[2]

Non-toy advertising directed to children also began to emerge en force in the mid-1960s. Products such as Cheerios, Twinkies, Karo Syrup, Tootsie Rolls, Fiddle Faddle, Cocoa Puffs, Hostess Ding Dongs, and Star Brite Toothpaste all found their place in children's television programming (*Kid's Commercials*, 2003). One of the first, and most obvious, manifestations of this new advertising model was General Foods' creation of programs as vehicles for the spokescharacters for their cereals (Schneider, 1987). In 1964 CBS premiered *Linus the Lionhearted*, which included shorts for Linus and for Sugar Bear (Kurer, 2003). The show was a coproduction of Ed Graham Productions and General Foods, and the cartoon characters became sponsors for General Foods cereals (Kurer, 2003).

During this period, advertising agencies began to specialize in the children's market and to understand the relative economic status and buying power of children within the household (Melody, 1973). Ogilvie and Mather, for example, represented products such as Rolos (Hershey's), Burger Chef (General Foods), Kool-Aid (General Foods), Cookie Crisp (Ralston), and Aim toothpaste (Lever) (Schneider, 1987). In addition, the first advertising agencies specializing in the children's market began to appear, with Helitzer, Waring, and Wayne opening in 1963 (Pecora, 1998).

Shortly after the advent of advertising-driven children's programming, two related but disparate forces changed the face of kids' programming. First, the homogenous viewing audience for television programming, which up to this point had been comprised of both adults and children, began to segment (Mitroff & Herr Stephenson, 2007). Programming watched by adults during prime hours became very lucrative for networks because it could command high advertising rates. This prompted the networks to relocate children's television in the 1960s to Saturday morning, a heretofore financially dismal time slot (Melody, 1973). Concurrently, the relative commercial success, now synonymous with advertising revenue, of shows like *The Mickey Mouse Club* made the networks recognize the untapped potential of the children's market. They began to pack this Saturday-morning time with inexpensive animated programming and extensive advertising (twice as much as in prime-time programming) (Melody, 1973). Stations began to realize huge profits from this new programming, due to the inexpensive costs of acquiring such programming coupled with the increases in advertising revenues from companies eager to put their products in front of the increasing number of child viewers (Schneider, 1987).

In the mid-1960s, Fred Silverman, a twenty-six-year-old executive for CBS, decided to revisit what had become very formulaic, low-production-cost Saturday-morning programming (Schneider, 1987). Silverman introduced new production techniques and new higher-quality cartoons to network television and quickly put CBS in the number-one spot for children's programming. (CBS had been third.) These new cartoons, such as *The Jetsons*, garnered larger audiences than the old shows and quickly became indispensable avenues of advertising for toys and other child-oriented products. ABC and NBC obviously took notice and quickly followed suit, creating a ratings war for Saturday mornings similar to that of prime time. If a program was not getting the ratings, it was quickly replaced (Schneider, 1987).

In the late 1960s, a new player entered the children's television broadcasting market— the Public Broadcasting System. Concurrent with the formation of PBS was the creation of Children's Television Workshop (CTW), whose program *Sesame Street* quickly became a highly heralded and highly watched educational program. The show was originally created to improve basic knowledge and social skills in preschool children, particularly minority and inner-city youth. The success of *Sesame Street* paved the way for an increase in educational programs on PBS in the 1970s. *The Electric Company* came on the scene in 1971, and over the next several years other shows, including *Zoom*, *Big Blue Marble*, *Villa Allegre*, and *Vegetable Soup*, were created (Simensky, 2007). Most of these programs were relatively short-lived, however, in part due to their expensive, research-intensive live-action production costs. (See chapter 12 for a thorough discussion of educational television programming.)

In the 1970s, the networks focused on animation instead. The production-distribution system began to change during this period. Large production companies, such as Hanna-Barbera, created relationships with the networks, entered into production contracts, and often won contracts based on the ideas of smaller firms that had been bought by the networks. Small independent firms were often required to create an entire season of programming (in finished form) before they could sell it to one of the networks, whereas the larger companies often garnered contracts based simply on storyboards. To highlight this inequality, in the 1972–73 season, three large production houses, along with a few smaller companies, provided the twelve hours of Saturday-morning programming on the networks (Melody, 1973).

Another change in the production-distribution system came when toy manufacturers entered the mix. Mattel was, again, the groundbreaker in this arena, entering into an alliance with ABC to create the first children's television program focused around a specific toy. *The Hot Wheels* show, created in 1969 by Mattel and programmed on Saturday mornings on ABC, was a thirty-minute program devoted to the product through the storylines (Schneider, 1987). It became the first in the genre of the "program-length commercial." The program did not air for long, but its influence would resurface again in the 1980s.

Although such barefaced toy tie-ins in entertainment programming were taboo in the 1970s, licensing of program-related products took off in the late 1970s (Pecora, 1998). In particular, licensing related to *Sesame Street* became an important archetype for providing for program longevity. Although originally funded by governmental bodies and philanthropic organizations, the program's producer, CTW, soon received pressure from the funders to find alternative sources of revenue to support the exorbitant production costs of the program (J. G. Cooney, personal communication, April 3, 2003). They quickly turned to licensing revenue and partnered with the Jim Henson Production Company, which had created characters that were easily turned into plush, cuddly toys (Cross, 1997; J. G. Cooney, personal communication, April 3, 2003). Although it took several years for the licensing model to begin generating substantial revenue, by the mid-1970s licensing revenue was a major source of funding for the nonprofit organization (Pecora, 1998; J. G. Cooney, personal communication, April 3, 2003).

In addition to toy tie-ins, advertising for other children's products continued to move heavily into children's programming. By the early 1970s, Kellogg, Mattel, and General Mills accounted for 30 percent of all advertising revenues on the networks (Pearce, 1972). Moreover, the fast-food wars, between Ronald McDonald and the Burger "King," had begun in full force (McNeal, 1992).

TV Still Rules, but Pac-Man
Begins to Gobble up Kids' Time (1980s)

Throughout the 1970s, children's television continued to consist mostly of inexpensive cartoons. In the 1980s, animation continued to dominate, but the organizations creating those cartoons changed to some extent. The deregulatory atmosphere of the Reagan administration, along with changes in the technological environment of television (specifically the marked increase in cable channels), provided an environment in which a new programming and sponsorship model for entertainment content arose. (See chapter 2 for a complete history of the regulation of children's media in the United States.) In the 1980s, "program-length commercials" resurfaced and became the children's television standard.

> It is at this point that the line between sponsorship and program became blurred as producers, looking to spread the risk of program production costs, turned to toy manufacturers, and toy manufacturers, wanting to stabilize a market subject to children's whim and fancy, turned to the media. Shows were developed with the consultation, and in some instances, financial backing, of toy manufacturers and licensing agents. . . . The cost of producing the program could be spread between program producers and product manufacturer or licenser, and recognition of either the product merchandise or the program increases sales and ratings. (Pecora, 1998, p. 34)

Programs from the benign *Smurfs*, *Rainbow Brite*, and *My Little Pony* to the brutish *Transformers*, *He-Man*, and *Thundercats* proliferated in this environment. In many cases, content creators during this decade were so tightly aligned with toy manufacturers that it was hard to tell where one organization began and the other ended in the production of the programs. Two particularly telling examples show how this blurring of organizational boundaries occurred: *The Smurfs* and *He-Man and the Masters of the Universe* (Pecora, 1998).

The U.S. licensing rights to the Smurfs, which were created by the Belgian author Peyo, were held by Wallace Berrie Company, which had bought the rights from the Belgian media firm SEPP (Greene & Spragins, 1982; Pecora, 1998). President of NBC Fred Silverman commissioned a cartoon based on the toys, to be produced by Hanna-Barbera, and put them in the NBC lineup in 1981 (Greene & Spragins, 1982; Pecora, 1998). Before the Smurfs reached the air, there were forty licenses for Smurf products (Pecora, 1998). The airing of *The Smurfs*, which boosted NBC to number one in the Saturday-morning time slot, doubled the number of licenses annually for the first four years of the program ("How they keep the Smurfs," 1983; Pecora, 1998). Under this arrangement, the production boundaries were drawn so that Wallace Berrie owned the licensing rights, "SEPP owned the idea, NBC supplied the outlet, and Hanna-Barbera supplied the animated program" (Pecora, 1998, p. 67). As the cartoon moved into syndication, these organizational boundaries began to blur (Pecora, 1998). Hanna-Barbera held the syndication rights to the animation, and those independent stations owned by Hanna-Barbera's parent company, Taft, were given first right of refusal of the program (Pecora, 1998; "Smurfs now bartered for '86," 1984).

The creation, financing, distribution, and licensing of *He-Man and the Masters of the*

Universe is an extreme example of how the organizational boundaries blurred in the 1980s (Pecora, 1998). Filmation and its parent company, Group W, created and financed *He-Man* in conjunction with Mattel, with creative control remaining in Mattel's hands (Mattel, 1984; Pecora, 1998). Financially, Mattel retained all licensing rights for *He-Man* products and Filmation/Group W retained syndication rights (Pecora, 1998). With regard to programming outlets, the cartoon was shown on independent stations, which reaped the benefits of the show in both ratings and product cost (Pecora, 1998). In addition, the direct relationship between Mattel and the stations was mutually beneficial: "Stations had a guaranteed commitment of advertising revenue from Mattel; Mattel, on the other hand, had up-front assurances of advertising time from the stations" (Pecora, 1998, p. 71). A barter relationship was created between the two: the stations provided the time and Mattel provided the programming.

The amazing financial success of *He-Man* for all companies involved provided the example for the creation, financing, distribution, and licensing of toy-based entertainment programming for children throughout the decade. Instead of characters being created through television or movies and then licensed to toy manufacturers, many of the most popular characters of this decade were created by toy companies and then turned into television shows (Cross, 1997). *He-Man and the Masters of the Universe* and *She-Ra: Princess of Power* (Mattel), *G.I. Joe* and *Transformers* (Hasbro), *Gobots* (Tonka), *Thundercats* (Rankin-Bass), *Ghostbusters* (Filmation), *Strawberry Shortcake* (General Mills/American Greetings/Those Characters from Cleveland, Inc.), *Rainbow Brite* (Mattel/Hallmark), and *Care Bears* (Bernie Loomis/Those Characters from Cleveland, Inc.) are all examples of this type of character-program relationship (Pecora, 1998; Schneider, 1987). In the 1983–84 season alone, there were fourteen program-length commercials on television (Cross, 1997). A few of these characters (for example, Strawberry Shortcake, the Care Bears, and Rainbow Brite) were the products of collaborative partnerships specifically focused on creating licensable characters (Schneider, 1987). Content creators, such as Filmation, Marvel, and DIC, entered into creative partnerships with toy companies to create these programs (Cross, 1997). DIC alone created 330 hours of toy-based programming on contract from toy manufacturers in 1987 (Cross, 1997). To highlight the extent of this trend toward toy-based programming, between 1980 and 1987 the percentage of toys sold in the United States that were based on licensed characters increased from 10 percent to 60 percent (Cross, 1997).

The licensing frenzy of the 1980s also brought to light an important benefit of the relationship among toy manufacturers, content creators, and broadcasters—"by linking toys to television, the longevity of a product line can be enhanced" (Pecora, 1998, p. 51). In return, consumption of the licensed product reinforces demand for the television program, both in original and syndicated form. This cycle has been particularly productive for some of the licensed characters of the 1980s, such as the Care Bears and Strawberry Shortcake, which have very recently been acquired by new production companies, revamped for the new generation of television viewers, and rereleased on television and in the toy marketplace (A. Heyward, personal communication, March 26, 2003).

In addition to the change in the type and quality of children's programming being broadcast by the major networks, the 1980s also brought the launch of a fundamental change in the television landscape—the rise of cable. By 1983, "cable supplied almost 70% of children's programming hours" (Pecora, 1998, p. 82). By 1987, half of America had cable, so access to cable programming for children was a reality for half of American families (Calabro, 1992). Two major cable organizations, Nickelodeon and the Disney Channel, entered the children's television community during this time and were responsible for most of this dramatic change in children's television programming.

Nickelodeon, created as the program *Pinwheel* in 1979 and evolving into a cable channel by 1982, was the first cable channel aimed entirely at a child audience (Pecora, 1998). Although the channel was originally commercial free, in 1983 it moved to an advertising-sponsored model (Calabro, 1992; Mifflin, 1999; Pecora, 1998; R. Weisskoff, personal communication, April 2, 2003). The programs were targeted to the six- to twelve-year-old set, and Nickelodeon successfully set its brand identity as the anti-adult channel (Tracy, 2002; D. F. Meir, personal communication, March 28, 2003). As the decade wore on, Nickelodeon expanded both its reach, through the expansion of cable, and its audience share. Although Nickelodeon's programming, which was mostly original, live-action productions, did not necessarily lend itself to the type of licensing found with the program-length commercials and Disney model (described below) during the same time period, Nickelodeon did begin to license products, such as green slime shampoo, in the late 1980s (Pecora, 1998). In addition, Nickelodeon used the public broadcasting underwriting model on some programs and product sponsorship on several of their programs, particularly live-action game shows (Pecora, 1998).

Soon after Nickelodeon hit the cable lines, Disney launched a channel based on its megabrand (Kalagian, 2007). Unlike Nickelodeon, the Disney Channel began as a premium channel. Like Nickelodeon, the Disney Channel focuses on children, although 15 to 30 percent of its viewers are families without children (Pecora, 1998). Unlike Nickelodeon, however, the channel began with a strong footing because of the Disney conglomerate and its sheer reach throughout the children's media and products. The channel was used to capitalize on the larger Disney brand image, and although the channel is technically commercial free, the entire set of programming, from regular programs to movies to interstitials, was "one long advertisement for the Walt Disney empire" (Pecora, 1998, p. 84). Considering the vast holdings of the Walt Disney company, this "advertisement" had a large effect on the licensing of products, from theme park tickets to plush dolls, related to the programming (Pecora, 1998).

These new cable venues provided even more airtime for children's product advertising. In 1984 there were more than seventy-five corporations in the United States that provided services or products for children nationally, including "General Foods, General Mills, Kellogg's, Quaker, and Ralston; Coleco and Mattel; Hershey's, Mars M&Ms, and Nabisco Brands; American Greetings and Hallmark; Walt Disney, Hanna-Barbera, and Warner Communications; Burger King and McDonalds" (Schneider, 1987, p. 7). These companies were spending over $500 million on advertising annually, most of which was concentrated on television advertisements (Schneider, 1987).

While television continued to flourish, a new medium began to gain ground in the lives of kids. Although arcade games had been around since the 1970s, it wasn't until the 1980s that video-game consoles for home use became commonplace. The Atari 2600, which was released in 1977, suddenly exploded in popularity with the release of *Pac-Man* in 1980 (McDonald, 2005). Über-hits based on popular arcade games, like *Donkey Kong* and *Q*Bert*, soon followed. By 1981, video-game consoles were a billion-dollar industry (Hart, 2000). After flourishing for a couple years, the video-game industry floundered until 1985, when Nintendo released its Nintendo Entertainment System (NES).

> The [NES] would become the highest selling system in history, and also the most notorious. Nintendo would be involved in the intimidation of retailers, competing companies, and even licensed "partners." They would have countless lawsuits brought up against them, and fill the gaming community with inaccurate rumors and "vapor-ware"[3] for the sole purpose of detracting public attention away from competitors. Ultimately, Nintendo would be brought up on charges of monopolizing, price fixing, and anti-trust violations by District Attorneys from all fifty states, and lose. (Hart, 2000, n.p.)

Even with its litigation problems, Nintendo managed to dominate the video-game industry. A huge game catalogue, including *Super Mario Bros.*, *Legend of Zelda*, and *Final Fantasy*, secured Nintendo's dominance until the mid-1990s. The release of the Nintendo GameBoy in 1988 changed family road trips forever, with kids now able to take their video games with them anywhere.

The Decade of Consolidation (1990s)

The 1990s began with major changes in strategy by two key broadcasters that had a significant effect on the children's television community. The first transformation was PBS's revamping of its educational programming lineup. In 1991 PBS responded to the doldrums of children's programming by scheduling *Barney & Friends*, *Shining Time Station*, and *Lamb Chop's Play-Along*. *Barney*, in particular, was a huge success, and PBS took steps to add more programming. In 1992, through the Ready-to-Learn Act,[4] PBS furthered its goal of providing a significant amount of educational programming by implementing its Ready-to-Learn (RTL) programming block (S. Petroff, personal communication, April 7, 2003). PBS's RTL combines eleven hours of educational programming throughout the day with community and parent outreach and resources, to address social and emotional development, physical well-being and motor development, approaches to learning, language skills, cognitive skills, and the general knowledge of two- to eight-year-olds. In order for a program to be part of RTL, it must have curriculum goals, as well as a formative and summative research plan, either in- or out-of-house.

In 1994, partly in response to RTL and partly out of the recognition that preschool-age children were still underserved, Nickelodeon made a major organizational change, deciding to invest $60 million and six hours a day in Nick Jr., a channel-within-a-channel focusing on educational programming for preschoolers (Andersen, 1998; Tracy, 2002). This foray into preschool educational programming got off to a stellar start, and *Blue's Clues*, the first in-house Nick Jr. production, was a financial coup for Nickelodeon. Nick Jr.'s successful model of educational production, channel branding, and product licensing became the gold standard in children's programming.

The success of Nickelodeon spurred several other large media corporations to take the plunge into children's television. The Cartoon Network by Time-Warner; Fox Kids Network by Fox; Noggin, a joint venture in educational television by CTW and Nickelodeon (which is now wholly owned by Nickelodeon); Discovery Kids by Discovery Channel; and the Kids Channel by PBS are examples of the very recent boom in cable channels entering the population of children's television content programmers. This has fundamentally altered the content programming landscape. In 1997, for example, basic cable provided 40 percent of children's programming; PBS provided 22 percent; premium channels provided 19 percent; small networks (FOX, UPN, WB) provided 17 percent; and the Big Three provided only 2 percent (Jordan & Woodard, 1997).

The larger industry trend toward vertical integration in the 1990s affected those organizations that program content for children. ABC, for example, became saturated with programming from its owner, Disney, and WB was able to program any Warner Bros. cartoons from its vast archive—and all at a huge profit margin. In addition, media conglomerates began to use their in-house resources to provide the educational and informational programming required by the Children's Television Act of 1990. For instance, CBS began airing programming from its Viacom sister-company, Nick Jr, and NBC began using Discovery Kids programming.

In addition to consolidation within and among media companies, the relationship between toy manufacturers and content creators remained strong in the 1990s. Programs such as *Teenage Mutant Ninja Turtles*, *Mighty Morphin Power Rangers*, and *Pokémon* continued the trend of successful licensing and toy-driven media products (Cross, 1997). A similar development was seen in the renewed and amplified fervor of successful licensing relationships between toy manufacturers and educational content. *Barney*, *Sesame Street*, and *Blue's Clues* all had phenomenally successful merchandising ventures (A. Cahn, personal communication, April 3, 2003; Pecora, 1998; M. Williams, personal communication, March 31, 2003). The Tickle-Me Elmo doll produced by Fisher-Price/Mattel in 1996 became a legend in merchandising history (Byrne, 2003; Fisher-Price, 2003). In 1998 *Teletubbies* generated $800 million in licensed product sales (Mifflin, 1999). In essence, toy licensing became a major factor (if not *the* major factor) in measuring the success of any children's television program.

Although this decade was a triumphant time for toy companies with regard to their position in the children's television community, it was also a very turbulent time for the toy industry with regard to mergers and acquisitions. In the 1980s Hasbro had merged with Milton Bradley and acquired Playskool, and Binney Smith had been acquired by Hallmark (Cross, 1997; Pecora, 1998). By 1985, the top three toy manufacturers (Hasbro, Mattel, and

Coleco) controlled 35 percent of the market ("Battle of the fun factories," 1985). The trend continued in the 1990s, with the acquisition of Fisher-Price and Tyco by Mattel (Fisher-Price, 2003; Mattel, 2003). As in many other industries, the trend became for larger companies to simply buy up any smaller companies that create successful products (T. Conley, personal communication, April 4, 2003; T. Bartlett, personal communication, April 3, 2003). By the end of the century, the three largest toy companies (Hasbro, Mattel, and LEGO) controlled nearly 85 percent of the marketplace (T. Conley, personal communication, April 4, 2003; T. Bartlett, personal communication, April 3, 2003).

Advertisers also saw an enhanced relationship with media companies during the 1990s. The most noteworthy change in the television landscape from the advertisers' perspective was the segmentation of the children's market by age and gender (McNeal, 1992). With more than a thousand hours of children's programming a week on network and cable channels, and programming being targeted to smaller niche age groups, audience fragmentation increased dramatically (Alexander & Owers, 2007). This fragmentation, in turn, gave advertisers greater choice in where to place their advertising, but made it harder to reach a large kids audience. From 1996 to 1999, the amount of advertiser revenue increased "at a double-digit rate annually, and it exceeded $1 billion for the 1998–99 season" (Mifflin, 1999, ¶4). The major players in advertising, however, remained the same: Hasbro, Mattel, Kraft, General Foods, and Kellogg (Alexander & Owers, 2007).

Just as the television audience grew fragmented because of an increase in programming choices, so did the market for video games in the 1990s. Although Nintendo entered the decade with a stranglehold on the market, for the first time it faced real competition. With the release of the Sega Genesis in 1989, Sega gained a foothold in the console market and had sold 1 million units by 1991 (Hart, 2000). Nintendo, realizing that its position of power was quickly waning, responded with the release of the Super Nintendo system. Although this system secured Nintendo's primacy in the market for the next few years, it was clear that the video-game industry was changing. The competition between Nintendo and Sega helped to increase the popularity of video games for two reasons. First, both companies were under pressure to offer their customers a seemingly unending number of titles. This compelled them to partner with content-creation companies, such as Electronic Arts, and therefore altered the licensing structure of the industry (Hart, 2000). Second, the struggle for kids' eyeballs and thumbs played out in the television advertising arena. Both Sega and Nintendo spend enormous amounts of money trying to sell their brands to kids (Hart, 2000; Sheff, 1993).

By the second half of the decade, the race for the most powerful gaming system and the largest share of the market had quickened. Sony entered the contest with their PlayStation in 1995, just as Sega was reentering the market with the Saturn. Nintendo countered by releasing the Nintendo 64 in 1996. At the close of the decade, Sega got in a final jab with the release of the Dreamcast system.

While console gaming systems flourished, another medium was beginning to compete for kids' attention—online games. As personal computers became more commonplace in homes, and the Internet extended its reach, kids and companies began to explore the possibilities of gaming that was also socially interactive. Although this type of gaming did not really catch on until the next century, the potential for combining the popularity of gaming with the power of the Internet was becoming clear.

Everything's Multimedia (2000 and Beyond)

The media world of today's youth is marked by simultaneous consumption of multiple media (Roberts et al., 2005). The media industry is marked by similar multiplicity. Continuing on a wave of industry consolidation and cross-industry partnerships, the many media that kids are using are becoming more and more integrated and interrelated. In order to pitch a product for the children's entertainment market, you must have thought about the viability of the product, licensable figure, or brand in other media.

> The increasingly integrated marketing of media products means that a "children's program" is almost never considered apart from concerns about merchandising and licensing; ancillary sales of videos, games, and music; book and movie tie-ins; international production and sales; creation of stars to be promoted; and branding of the network to name only a few. The real profit in children's television is in the production/distribution arena, where ancillary marketing, aftermarkets, and international co-ventures and distribution are a multi-billion dollar industry. (Alexander & Owers, 2007)

A continued increase in the number of television channels, especially in light of the move to digital television, coupled with new technologies that give audiences more agency over their viewing, such as video-on-demand and digital video recorders (such as TiVO), have fundamentally changed the advertising model that the industry has been accustomed to since the 1950s. Other new technologies and Internet applications, such as MP3 players, instant messaging, and broadband video streaming, are also competing for kids' attention. (See chapters 14 and 15 for thorough discussions of how young people use the Internet and other digital technologies.) In response, advertisers and the broadcasters that depend on their revenue are searching for new alternatives to the traditional ways of making money.

Product placement in every medium, from television to film to video games, has been one popular solution to this issue of advertising. Another solution that has been highly discussed, and contested, is the use of interactive advertising. This type of advertising is already being used extensively on the Internet, through vehicles such as "advergames" that highlight specific products (Pereira, 2004). On television, interactive advertising may come as Internet capabilities are integrated into digital television. With the click of a remote-control button, kids can go from a program on Nickelodeon to Nick.com to play games or buy products. Although this opportunity for advertisers and broadcasters is being highly contested by advocacy groups, the final form that interactive advertising takes remains to be seen.

From a content and programming perspective, there has been a trend toward embracing the dissolution of boundaries between the media and focusing on cross-platform branding as a means of hooking and reeling in kids' attention. The cross-platform branding reifies the multimedia conglomerates, particularly those that are well integrated horizontally. Megaliths like Viacom, ABC/Disney, and AOL/Time Warner can work from their vast libraries of content and characters to produce products in every medium in which they have a stake. From television to film to home video to publishing and beyond, what becomes important is licensing rights. This issue has become particularly clear recently as companies begin to alter their licensing agreements for digital rights to their content (Castleman, 2005). As media converge and companies consolidate, maintaining control over one's product, and making a profit, becomes increasingly problematic. Various "modes of digital distribution such as VOD, mobile and broadband are making inroads with consumers and threatening to supplant linear network broadcast in the coming decade" (Castleman, 2005, p. 93). The same program can be shown on broadcast, on demand, online, and on mobile phones (such as via Verizon's new VCast service). Ironically, this means that kids' have more access to less content, which is what we've seen happen with television in the era of mergers and acquisitions (Children Now, 2003).

Similar issues are arising on the video-game side of the children's media industry. In 2001 three video-game consoles were released—Microsoft's Xbox, Nintendo's GameCube, and Sony's PlayStation 2—with the Xbox being the first console to integrate online gaming capabilities. Online gaming, both console- and computer-based, has also taken hold, especially massive multiplayer online role-playing games, such as *Everquest* and *World of Warcraft*. Although originally many of these games were developed and distributed through smaller companies, we are beginning to see a trend toward consolidation within the large media conglomerates like Sony and Microsoft. Moreover, alternate revenue-generation methods—product placement and advertising in games, for example—are becoming commonplace. Finally, other media tie-ins, such as character licensing for film and television, although not new to video gaming, are becoming a more integrated part of the game-creation and product-license process.

In addition, with the release of Sony's PlayStation Portable (PSP), we have seen further integration of media technologies. The PSP can play video games, either as a standalone portable console, or online (player-to-player) through its wireless capabilities. In addition, it can play movies using a new compact storage media. As a new generation of video-game consoles are released—Microsoft's Xbox 360 in 2005 and Sony's PlayStation 3 and Nintendo's Revolution in 2006—the lines between the media will continue to be blurred.

The next several years will provide a challenge to those creating and providing media content to children and adolescents. As media converge, industry norms and practices that have been revered for decades will have to change. Right now, the children's media industry is in the middle of a transformation. Although there is a lot of speculation as to what the technology and the industry will look like in ten years (or even two years), it is likely that the actual evolution of the industry will look very different from the predictions.

EXERCISES

1   Create a timeline of the children's media industry. Make sure to include both changes in technology as well as the major players in the industry during each period. What have been the most interesting changes? What surprises you as remaining relatively constant?

2   Imagine you are Sony, a global media corporation with a huge consumer products base. What is your next move within the children's media industry? Come up with a business plan for the next five years. What partnerships within the industry would you try to forge? Which competitors will you have to worry about? How will you deal with the converging media environment?

3   Imagine that you are Disney. You own the rights to one of the largest catalogues of children's media content in the world. Come up with a business plan for the next five years. How would you go about capitalizing on your content? What have you learned from your experiences over the past eight decades that will inform your decision-making?

4   Imagine that you are an advertising agency in today's media environment. You've just landed a major account with Kellogg to completely revamp its advertising strategies. What would be your pitch? Make sure to reflect on the issues raised in the chapter, such as branding and the challenges to advertising in the new environment of converging media.

NOTES

1   *Captain Kangaroo* was introduced on CBS in 1955 and ran until 1984. The show featured Bob Keeshan as Captain Kangaroo, a jovial character who taught preschool children through sketches, stories, songs, and cartoons with the help of friends like Mr. Green Jeans and Mr. Moose.

2   Some of the most popular Hanna-Barbera licensed characters were Tom and Jerry, Scooby Doo, the Flintstones, Yogi Bear, and Huckleberry Hound.

3   "Vapor-ware" is software or hardware that is announced by a company during its development but is never actually released.

4   The Ready-to-Learn Act provided funding to PBS, through the Secretary of Education, to create television programming to improve school-readiness in young children and to develop and distribute support materials for parents, child-care providers, and educators.

REFERENCES

Alexander, A., & Owers, J. C. (1998). *Media economic theory and practice*. Mahwah, NJ: Lawrence Erlbaum.

Alexander, A., & Owers, J. C. (2007). *The economics of children's television*. In J. A. Bryant (Ed.), *The children's television community*. Mahwah, NJ: Lawrence Erlbaum.

Andersen, D. R. (1998). Educational television is not an oxymoron. *Annals of the American Academy of Political and Social Science, 557*, 24–38.

Barnouw, E. (1970). *A history of broadcasting in the United States, vol. 3: The image empire*. New York: Oxford University Press.

Battle of the fun factories. (1985, December 16). *Time*, 44–46.

Byrne, C. (2003). *Toys: Celebrating 100 years of the power of play*. New York: Toy Industry Association.

Calabro, M. (1992). *Zap! A brief history of television*. New York: Four Winds.

Castleman, L. (2005, October). Digital deal making: Between a right and a hard place. *KidScreen*, 93–97.

Children Now. (2003). *Big media, little kids: Media consolidation and children's television programming*. Oakland, CA: Children Now.

Cressey, P. (1934). The motion picture as informal education. *Journal of Educational Sociology, 7*, 504–515.

Cross, G. (1997). *Kids' stuff: Toys and the changing world of American childhood*. Cambridge, MA: Harvard University Press.

DeBoer, J. J. (1937). The determination of children's interests in radio drama. *Journal of Applied Psychology, 21*, 456–463.

Eisenberg, A. (1936). *Children and radio programs*. New York: Columbia University Press.

Fisher-Price. (2003). *About us*. Retrieved April 15, 2003, from http://www.fisher-price.com/us/hr/aboutus.asp#story.

Greene, R., & Spragins, E. (1982, November 8). Smurfy to the max. *Forbes*, 67–70.

Hart, S. N. (2000). *A brief history of home video games*. Retrieved December 15, 2005, from http://www.geekcomix.com/vgh/.

How they keep the Smurfs under control. (1983, December 5). *Sales and Market Management*, 63–64.

Jersild, A. T. (1939). Radio and motion pictures. In G. M. Wipple (Ed.), *The thirty-eighth yearbook of the National Society for the Study of Education* (pp. 153–160). Bloomington, IL: Public School.

Jordan, A. B., & Woodard, E. H. (1997). *The 1997 state of children's television report: Programming for children over broadcast and cable television* (no. 14). Philadelphia: University of Pennsylvania, Annenberg Public Policy Center.

Kalagian, T. (2007). Programming children's television: The cable model. In J. A. Bryant (Ed.), *The children's television community*. Mahwah, NJ: Lawrence Erlbaum.

Kid's Commercials. (2003). Retrieved December 15, 2005, from http://www.tvdays.com/Merchant2/merchant.mv?Screen=CTGY&Store_Code=VRA&Category_Code=kids.

Kurer, R. (2003). *Linus the Lionhearted*. Retrieved April 16, 2003, from http://www.toontracker.com/linus/linus.htm.

Mattel. (1984). *Annual report*. El Segundo, CA.

Mattel. (2003). *Mattel history*. Retrieved April 15, 2003, from http://www.mattel.com/about_us/history/.

McDonald, G. (2005). *GameSpot presents: A brief history of video game music*. Retrieved December 15, 2005, from http://www.gamespot.com/gamespot/features/video/vg_music/index.html.

McNeal, J. U. (1992). *Kids as customers: A handbook of marketing to children*. New York: Lexington Books.

Melody, W. (1973). *Children's television: The economics of exploitation*. New Haven, CT: Yale University Press.

Mifflin, L. (1999, April 19). A growth spurt is transforming TV for children. *New York Times*, p. A1.

Mitroff, D., & Herr Stephenson, R. (2007). The television tug-of-war: A brief history of children's television programming in the United States. In J. A. Bryant (Ed.), *The children's television community*. Mahwah, NJ: Lawrence Erlbaum.

Paik, H. (2001). The history of children's use of electronic media. In D. G. Singer & J. L. Singer (Eds.), *Handbook of children and the media* (pp. 7–28). Thousand Oaks, CA: Sage.

Pearce, A. (1972). *The economics of network children's television programming* (staff report). Washington, D.C.: Federal Communications Commission.

Pecora, N. (1998). *The business of children's entertainment*. New York: Guilford.

Pereira, J. (2004, May 3). Junk-food games: Online arcades draw fire for immersing kids in ads; Ritz Bits wrestling, anyone? *Wall Street Journal*, p. B1.

Roberts, D. F., Foehr, U. G., & Rideout, R. J. (2005). *Generation M: Media in the lives of 8–18 year-olds*. Menlo Park, CA: Kaiser Family Foundation Report.

Schneider, C. (1987). Children's television: The art, the business, and how it works. Lincolnwood, IL: NTC Business Books.

Sheff, D. (1993). *Game over: How Nintendo zapped an American industry, captured your dollars, and enslaved your children*. New York: Random House.

Simensky, L. (2007). Programming children's television: The PBS model. In J. A. Bryant (Ed.), *The children's television community*. Mahwah, NJ: Lawrence Erlbaum.

Smurfs now bartered for '86; only Taft stations get first dibs. (1984, March 21). *Variety*.

Summers, H. (1971). *A thirty year history of programs carried on national radio networks in the United States, 1926–1956*. New York: Arno.

Tracy, D. (2002). *Blue's Clues for success: The 8 secrets behind a phenomenal business*. Chicago: Dearborn Trade Publishing.

CHAPTER TWO

How Does the U.S. Government Regulate Children's Media?

ALISON ALEXANDER & KEISHA L. HOERRNER

There's no question that children are avid consumers of media content. National data show that the average American child consumes more than six hours of media each day, combining and often multitasking with television, the Internet, video games, and other forms of mass media (Rideout et al., 2005). The love affair between media and its youngest audience members has been a staple of electronic media, especially television. While "children's television" refers to programs targeted primarily to children and designed to attract a majority of viewers who are children, it is only a small part of the total viewing of television by children. A popular prime-time situation comedy may attract many more child viewers than a "children's program" does, despite the fact that it is not targeted primarily to children, and children are not a majority of the audience.

Children's enjoyment of television began when the first television sets entered homes in the 1950s—often called the Golden Age of Television, when television became the most popular source of entertainment seemingly overnight. At that time, children played an integral role in television's popularity. They were fascinated with the visual images and were drawn in to shows, like *Howdy Doody,* that were developed just for them. Programs were even used as marketing tools for television manufacturers, whose advertisements told parents to purchase TVs for the benefit of their children (Alexander et al., 1998).

Children's enjoyment of television in the 1950s influenced more than just electronics sales. It sparked governmental concern about possible negative effects of children's viewing of television and ignited a debate over what role, if any, government should have in regulating television, especially content that reached the child audience. This debate has raged for more than fifty years.

This chapter will summarize the complex set of legal concepts, players, and social issues that have defined this debate. You might find that the intense discussion of government regulation over the last fifty years has actually led to more questions than answers. Politicians, regulators, parents, advocacy groups, and media critics struggle to reach consensus on the following questions: Should the government regulate children's media? If so, how? If not, why not? After reading this chapter, decide how you would answer those questions.

First Amendment versus Vulnerable Audience: The Foundational Legal Concepts

Before delving into the specific issues of regulation and children's media, it is important to step back and briefly summarize broadcast regulation in general. All forms of mass media enjoy a certain degree of protection from governmental interference because of the First Amendment, which was added to the U.S. Constitution in 1791. Those forty-five words, which include "Congress shall make no law . . . abridging the freedom of speech or of the press," ensure that U.S. media outlets are not owned by the government, that they do not face daily censorship from government officials, and that they can criticize the government without facing onerous sanctions.

On the surface, the First Amendment sounds quite simple. Congress, and thereby the government, is prohibited from interfering with media content. But that's not how the First Amendment has been interpreted by the federal courts, especially when it comes to broadcasting. "No law" has never been interpreted as a complete prohibition on governmental regulation of broadcasting. Broadcast regulation experts Thomas Krattenmaker and Lucas Powe (1994) note that broadcasting has been treated differently by legislators and judges since its inception. It is the only form of mass communication, in fact, that faces direct content control by the federal government. Print media and even the Internet enjoy significantly stronger constitutional protection than radio and television.

The genesis for that control precedes the development of television. Beginning with the Radio Act of 1927, Congress has sought some control over broadcasting through the government's ownership of the electromagnetic spectrum. Reliance on spectrum space makes radio and television distinct from other forms of media and provides a ready rationale for governmental involvement in private industries. The Communications Act of 1934, which was overhauled extensively in 1996, provides Congress with a permanent justification for broadcast regulation.

Both the 1927 and 1934 acts explicitly stated that broadcasters must operate in the "public interest" in order to maintain their licenses for using the electromagnetic spectrum. Part of serving the public interest is to serve specific categories of audience members. One of those is children. Beginning in 1960, broadcasters have had a special obligation to serve their child audiences, ruled by regulators to be a vulnerable audience. A 1978 U.S. Supreme Court decision made it clear that "broadcasting is uniquely accessible to children, even those too young to read" and it is "uniquely pervasive," so it required closer scrutiny by the government, which has traditionally protected vulnerable members of society utilizing laws and regulations. The child labor laws are but one illustration of Congress's concern for children. (See chapter 3 for an explanation of the cultural definition of childhood that has led to such concerns and legislation.)

It is clear, then, that government regulation of broadcasting requires a balancing act between protection of First Amendment rights and protection of vulnerable members of the audience. A complex group of governmental and private entities struggles to maintain the balance.

The Broadcast Policy-Making Spectrum: The Major Players

In their influential work *The Politics of Broadcast Regulation*, Erwin Krasnow, Lawrence Longley and Herbert Terry (1982) explain the complex web of entities that determine broadcast regulation. They broadly categorize these entities into six groups: the Federal Communications Commission (FCC), the federal courts, the White House, Congress, the industry, and citizens' groups. It is useful to add the Federal Trade Commission (FTC) when specifically discussing children and television issues. Following is a brief explanation of each of these groups.

- The FCC is a regulatory agency developed by Congress in 1934 to oversee broadcasting, telegraphs, and telephony. It now oversees cable, satellite, and digital communication. The FCC has five commissioners and thousands of employees.
- The federal courts, or the judicial branch of the government, hear challenges to FCC and FTC regulations as well as congressional legislation. The D.C. Circuit Court of Appeals reviews numerous cases involving the FCC and FTC.
- The White House, or executive branch of the government, both directly and indirectly influences broadcast regulation. Of course, the president must choose whether or not to sign any legislation that impacts broadcasting. That's a direct influence. More often, though, the president indirectly influences regulation by choosing to highlight or ignore issues related to media content.
- Congress, or the legislative branch of the government, can also directly and indirectly influence regulation. It can pass laws that direct agencies such as the FCC and FTC to develop specific regulations. It can also hold hearings to investigate

issues, even though no legislation results from those hearings.

■ The broadcasting industries are composed of individual station owners, corporate conglomerates, media professionals, and large trade organizations such as the National Association of Broadcasters (NAB).

■ Citizens' groups are generally advocacy organizations. Groups of parents, educators, and critics band together for a specific purpose. Action for Children's Television (ACT), which formed in 1968 and disbanded in 1996, was the most influential citizens' group in terms of children and media issues. (See chapter 6 for a further discussion of the role of research in supporting the efforts of such organizations.)

■ The FTC is a regulatory agency that oversees commercial speech, or advertising. It ensures that the public is not misled by false or misleading advertising and promotes fair competition among advertisers.

Strolling through History: A Decade-by-Decade Review of Social Issues and Their Impact on Regulation of Children's Television

An examination of television's major changes by decade gives an overview of media development, social concerns, and public policy in the United States. (See chapter 1 for a more detailed decade-by-decade history of the evolution of children's television content.)

The 1950s

This decade is defined not only by poodle skirts and Edward R. Murrow. It is the decade of the first congressional hearings concerning the possible negative effects of television on children. These hearings served as the template for congressional inquiries into the issue for the next four decades.

In 1950, 9 percent of American homes had television sets; by decade's end, sets existed in 87 percent of homes (Alexander et al., 1998). During this pivotal decade, television advertising aimed at children also achieved maturity as advertisers and television executives alike searched for appropriate ways to fashion advertising messages. What worked (and what did not) was clearly demonstrated in the commercials aired during that time. Programs for children ranged from *Green Hornet*, a holdover from radio, to *Roy Rogers*, *Kukla, Fran & Ollie*, and *The Mickey Mouse Club*. Shows targeting a child audience were shown not only in the morning hours but in the afternoon and even prime-time hours in the 1950s. At the decade's beginning, these shows often had one sponsor that underwrote the entire program, or dual (shared) sponsorship, with noncompeting advertisers rotating sponsorship. By the end of the decade, the thirty- to sixty-second spot announcements familiar today had replaced sole or dual sponsorship.

There was no regulation specifically targeting children's shows in the 1950s. The FCC was primarily concerned with stations' overall service to the "public interest." Congress, however, decided to grapple with the subject of television's impact on children, something it knew little about. In 1952 the House opened hearings to investigate "immoral and otherwise offensive matter" in radio and television programs. After hearing testimony from industry representatives, teachers, members of the clergy, and a representative of the National Grand Lodge of the International Order of Good Templars (who was really more concerned with beer sponsorship of adult-oriented programs than offensive material in children's shows), the House subcommittee issued a report that said that "the television industry was in too great a state of flux to 'pass any conclusive judgment' upon it" (*Investigation*, 1952, p. 10).

The Senate took up the issue of television violence in 1954 and 1955. Actually, a Senate subcommittee was investigating causes and effects of juvenile delinquency. Two brief statements by witnesses turned the subcommittee's attention to television as one of the causes (Hoerrner, 1999a). Senator Estes Kefauver, a Democrat from Tennessee, who had hopes of a presidential run in 1956, sparred with industry representatives over the negative effects of television crime and violence. No legislation was passed as a result of the Senate hearings, however, because there was little research to substantiate either side's claims. Industry representatives repeatedly invoked the First Amendment as a protection against governmental interference in television content while at the same time promising to self-regulate and reduce the amount of violence. In response to these early hearings, the NAB adopted a Television Code noting industry responsibility to the child audience. (See chapter 3 for further discussion of these hearings and their investigation of what role, if any, comic books had on juvenile delinquency.)

The results of congressional interest in negative effects of television content on child audiences were not laws or directives to the FCC. Instead, they were increased national publicity for Kefauver, who used the attention effectively during his run for the presidency in 1956, which resulted in his selection as Adlai Stevenson's running mate that same year. There were also results for the industry, researchers, and Congress as a whole. "Unwritten guidelines" were developed in these hearings that were utilized numerous times. Keisha Hoerrner (1999a) refers to it as the development of a win-win situation: "The politicians scored points with their constituents for showing concern and outrage at any factor that contributed to crime and violence. The industry kept the government out of its daily affairs, allowing it to program the shows that would generate the greatest audience and result in more revenue."

The 1960s

During the 1960s children's programming became an extremely lucrative business. By the end of the decade, most children's programs were broadcast on Saturday mornings, a previously unprofitable time slot. By 1968, 86 percent of all children's programs were animated. Popular programs included *The Bullwinkle Show*, *The Jetsons*, *Spiderman*, and *Space Ghost*.

Famous educational programs such as *Sesame Street* and *Mister Rogers' Neighborhood* also debuted during this decade and were popular alternatives to many of the animated cartoons. Advertising minutes on Saturday-morning shows were high, up to sixteen minutes per hour in the early part of the decade (Kunkel & Wilcox, 2001), and advertisers increasingly recognized the importance of children as a potentially lucrative audience to whom they could sell toys, cereal, snacks, candy, and ultimately fast food.

In 1960 the FCC identified children's programs as one of fourteen program types usually necessary in order for broadcasters to meet their public-interest obligation (Kunkel & Wilcox, 2001). This was the first time the FCC had identified children as a "special audience" that deserved attention. Stations had to provide evidence that they were serving this special audience to facilitate the license renewal process, which had to be completed every eight years.

Congress was also paying attention to children and television in the 1960s. Five Senate hearings were held in that decade, led by Senator Thomas Dodd (a Democrat from Connecticut) and Senator John Pastore (Democrat of Rhode Island). The 1969 Pastore hearings resulted in substantive action; the Secretary of Health, Education, and Welfare accepted the Senate subcommittee's request for a scientific study to determine whether a causal link existed between television violence and children's behaviors. The Surgeon General was asked to oversee this multiyear, million-dollar project. The results from this study were the subject of their own congressional hearings in the early 1970s.

The White House was also intrigued about the possible link between television violence and real-life crime following the assassinations of Robert Kennedy and Martin Luther King, Jr., in 1968. President Lyndon Johnson created the Commission on the Causes and the Effects of Violence. The commission's report contained a chapter on media violence, although no causal connection was established. (See chapters 8 and 9 for a thorough investigation into the research on media violence.)

The 1970s

The decade of the 1970s can be encapsulated as the "public advocacy decade." While concerned-citizens' groups were finding new ways to advocate for better children's programming, the industry seemed content to provide more of the same. Saturday morning remained the major programming block for children. Some popular series included *Super Friends*, *Scooby's All Star Laff-a-Lympics*, and *The Bugs Bunny/Road Runner Hour*. Educational inserts became popular during this decade. These short, commercial-like educational and information sketches focused on such things as news, grammar, math, nutrition, and civic understanding. Cable also became a part of the television landscape for children, with Nickelodeon debuting in 1979. Advertising to children continued unabated, and thirty-second spots dominated. The four categories of advertising to children (candy and snacks, cereals, toys, and fast food) continued to represent the majority of ads. (See chapter 7 for more information on the products advertised to children.)

A group of mothers in Massachusetts banded together to promote better programming options for children. Formed in 1968 and headed by Peggy Charren, Action for Children's Television (ACT) was among the most vocal of citizens' groups calling for governmental action. ACT sought to change current programming and advertising practices by going directly to the governmental regulators charged with oversight of electronic media and the advertising industries, the FCC and the FTC (Clark, 2004).

ACT petitioned the FCC in the early 1970s to protect children from commercial persuasion and promote educational programming (Enis et al., 1980). The FCC responded in 1971 by issuing a notice of inquiry (NOI) and a notice of proposed rulemaking (NPRM), two official requests for public feedback on the issues. The FCC proposed to require stations to program at least fourteen hours a week of educational programming. In 1974 the FCC instituted guidelines stating that each broadcaster was required to make a meaningful effort to provide programming for both preschool and school-aged children and that programs were to air during both weekday and weekend periods when children were likely to view. The goal of the FCC was to limit the "Saturday-morning ghetto" and promote child-targeted programs throughout the week. There were no firm requirements put in place, however, like a minimum number of hours or a list of sanctions that could be employed if stations chose not to comply.

The FCC did require broadcasters to maintain a "clear separation" between program content and commercial speech in order to simplify recognition of advertising messages. This meant that program-length commercials, shows designed to sell products like a new toy, were prohibited. Host selling, which occurs when a character on a show promotes a product during the program or in spot advertisements shown during the program, was also banned. "Bumpers," such as the familiar "We'll be back after these messages," were required. Finally, the FCC endorsed NAB amendments to its code limiting the amount of advertising during children's programs to twelve minutes per hour on weekdays and nine and a half on weekends (Kunkel & Wilcox, 2001).

When the FCC assessed compliance with the 1974 guidelines in 1979, the agency found three areas of concern: (1) total time devoted to children's programming was insufficient; (2) too little educational, informational, or age-specific programming was on the air; and (3) children's programs were still concentrated in a few time periods. The FCC promised to work on these concerns in the 1980s, but a change in leadership brought a change in the agency's focus (Alexander & Hoerrner, 2006).

ACT's next move was to petition the FTC to ban all commercials during children's programs. The FTC sent tremors through both the networks and advertisers in 1978 when it seemed to agree with the group. Because the FTC has congressional authority to protect consumers against unfair, deceptive, and fraudulent advertising, the regulators argued that children were being unfairly targeted by the ads they were too young to understand. In an unprecedented show of lobbying power, the television and advertising industries derailed the proposal by getting Congress to pass a law that specifically prohibited the agency from adopting the children's advertising rules (Alexander & Hoerrner, 2006).

While the FCC and FTC were imposing specific restrictions on programming and advertising targeting children, the Senate was concerned with broader "kidTV" issues. In 1972 the Report to the U.S. Surgeon General (widely known as the Surgeon General's Report) was released, cautiously linking children's violent behavior with television viewing. The Senate held hearings to discuss the report and its implications. Various proposals were explored, including the idea of rating television programs, but no legislative action resulted from the hearings.

Changes in programs targeting both children and adults were instituted in 1975 as a result of the "family viewing hour" agreement. All the television networks agreed to keep the first hour of prime-time programming free of violence or other content not suitable for the entire family. The FCC did not initiate the "family viewing hour," but the FCC chairman Richard Wiley did call all the network presidents together in a meeting that resulted in the agreement. Some members of Congress felt that any FCC involvement in the agreement constituted a violation of broadcasters' First Amendment protections. In the end, Congress took no action on the "family viewing hour," neither endorsing nor opposing it. It was dropped by the networks in 1976 after the Writers Guild and other constituencies in the television industry sued them for antitrust violations (Martin, 2003).

The federal courts also had an impact on indecent content in television programs during this decade. The U.S. Supreme Court issued a ruling in 1978 that said that the FCC had every right to enforce a "safe-harbor" restriction on content that met the agency's definition of "indecency."[1] The safe-harbor restriction kept programs with indecent content off the radio and television airwaves from 6 A.M. to 10 P.M., times when children were most likely to be in the audience. The courts and the FCC felt this was acceptable under the First Amendment because the government wasn't seeking to ban indecent content, just move it to hours when adults could view it but children were most likely to be asleep.

The 1980s

The 1980s have been characterized generally as the "deregulation decade," and that is certainly true in the area of children's television regulation. The marketplace was supposed to separate quality programs from junk, and it was supposed to punish advertisers who unfairly targeted children with deceptive messages. At least that was the opinion of the FCC under its new chairman, Mark Fowler.

Children were watching a variety of programs on an increasing number of channels in the 1980s. Popular titles included *He-Man and the Masters of the Universe*, *My Little Pony*, *Teenage Mutant Ninja Turtles*, *Fraggle Rock*, and *Inspector Gadget*. Children were perceived as the primary consumers not only for shows but for a variety of products. They were also influential in their family's purchase of other products and services. Character licensing and the growth of specialty stores such as Toys 'R' Us expanded the range of products available, and competition for the eyeballs of young viewers was intense. There was segmentation of the child market, with an enhanced definition of "tweens," ten- to thirteen-year-olds who were interested in "teen" products but not yet as independent as their older counterparts.

The decade began with ACT expecting the FCC to work on quality educational programs for children and the diversification of time slots for children's shows. Those expectations would not be fulfilled when President Ronald Reagan appointed Fowler. Under his leadership the FCC removed time restrictions on advertising content during children's programming and redefined program-length commercials more narrowly as programs that include ads for the same characters as those shown in the program (Kunkel & Wilcox, 2001). Basically, the FCC kept the prohibition on program-length commercials simply by redefining them as examples of host selling, a practice the FCC had prohibited for years. As part of the streamlined licensing process, the FCC significantly reduced the information stations had to provide about how they served the public interest and their special audiences. Under Fowler's leadership, license renewals were quite easy to secure (Kunkel & Wilcox, 2001).

In 1982 a consent decree dictated by the federal courts eliminated the National Association of Broadcasters' self-regulatory advertising guidelines; the program guidelines were later abandoned. There was now less self-regulation and governmental regulation dictating programming content (Kunkel & Wilcox, 2001).

Congress, however, was still debating its role in broadcast regulation and how it could promote and/or mandate a reduction in the amount of inappropriate material on television. Senator Paul Simon (Democrat of Illinois) led the charge for the government to act to reduce both sexual and violent content. Simon and his like-minded colleagues authored five bills in the 1980s seeking to create an antitrust exemption for the television industry so representatives of the major networks, independent stations, local affiliates, cable channels, and trade organizations could develop industry-wide guidelines to reduce inappropriate content (Hoerrner, 1998). Simon's rationale was that one network would never take the risk of reducing violence in its shows, for example, because of the potential loss of viewers to other networks. If all the players in the industry worked together to develop specific guidelines that they all employed at the same time, they would be willing to adhere to them. Simon, who was quite conscious of the First Amendment implications of any governmental regulation on media content, saw the antitrust exemption as promotion of self-regulation among broadcasters. None of the bills was passed in the 1980s, but Simon did get his antitrust exemption in 1990. Simon, like Kefauver and Pastore before him, also got national publicity for his efforts to reduce television violence. That publicity served him well when he ran for the presidency in 1988 (Hoerrner, 1998).

The 1990s

The 1990s could clearly be categorized as the "decade of reckoning." The FCC changed leadership, and Congress changed its stance from simply talking about regulating television to actually passing laws that did just that. In fact, seventeen bills specifically designed to reduce violence on television were introduced in Congress between 1990 and 1996, a 150 percent increase from the prior forty years combined (Hoerrner, 1999b).

While children were busy watching *Captain America, The Powerpuff Girls, Bill Nye, the Science Guy,* and *Barney & Friends,* legislators and regulators were trying to ensure that there was less violence and other problematic content on adult-oriented shows that children also viewed. They also mandated educational programs for children, rather than just hoping broadcasters would provide quality shows for young audiences.

The Children's Television Act of 1990 was the crowning achievement for ACT's years of work to push the government to improve the value of shows children were viewing (Kunkel & Wilcox, 2001). It mandated time restrictions on advertisements in children's programming, and it obligated stations to air educational/informational (E/I) programs for children under the age of eighteen. The first piece of legislation to actually regulate children's television content, the act focused on limiting the number of advertisements children were exposed to while increasing programming choices that furthered their cognitive learning and social/emotional needs. The act affected only traditional broadcast television, not the numerous cable channels that also aired popular programs for children (Kunkel, 1998).

The FCC designed the exact specifications for both the advertising and content rules. It quickly developed the advertising limits, requiring stations to show no more than ten and a half minutes of ads per hour on the weekend and twelve minutes per hour during the week for programs with a primarily child audience. Product placement is also prohibited during children's shows as a result of these advertising limitations (Kunkel, 1998).

After years of wrangling over how much programming and what type of programs met the E/I requirements of the act, the FCC issued a report in late 1996 that specified stations should air three hours of educational programming each week. Stations are required to keep logs of those programs that can be viewed by the public and utilized by the FCC during license renewals. Shows that are designed to meet the educational requirements of the act are designated with a special E/I rating shown at the beginning of the show. (See chapter 12 for a thorough examination of educational television.)

The Telecommunications Act of 1996 was the largest piece of legislation to impact broadcast regulation. A major legislative package that rewrote the 1934 Communications Act, its primary focus was on opening competition within the industry, but it also included provisions requiring the adoption of a ratings system and the integration of a V-chip into television sets (Hoerrner, 1998). The V-chip, an electronic monitoring device that uses ratings to block specific programs, had been discussed in Congress for years but came to the forefront in the 1990s as a technological tool to empower parents to limit objectionable content. It was hailed by its chief sponsor, Representative Edward Markey (Democrat of Massachusetts), as a "balance between parents who feel overwhelmed by the 200-channel television world of the future and those who believe the First Amendment denies government any role in managing television" (Hoerrner, 1998, p. 117).

The V-chip cannot operate without a ratings system for television programming. Although a voluntary ratings system developed by the broadcast industries is called for in the legislation, there's also language that empowers the FCC to appoint an advisory board to assist in the establishment of a system should the industry choose not to do it on its own ("Telecommunications," 1996). In an interesting case of arm-twisting that did not implicate First Amendment concerns, the industry chose to voluntarily develop a ratings system, thereby negating the need for the FCC advisory board.

First age-based ratings were developed, which mirrored the ratings scheme for motion pictures (Rice & Brown, 1996). These six ratings were unveiled in December 1996 and took effect in January.[2] Several members of Congress spoke out immediately, charging that age-based ratings were not specific enough to provide parents with the information they needed to make informed programming choices (Fleming, 1997). A few months later, content designations were added to the ratings system. Those include "FV" for fantasy violence (a designator used for many animated children's cartoons), "V" for violence, "S" for sexual content, "L" for adult language, and "D" for suggestive dialogue. Most networks and most cable channels were using age and content ratings by the end of 1997, although NBC and BET remained notable holdouts on the use of content ratings (Albiniak, 1997).

On March 13, 1998, the FCC gave its official approval of the ratings scheme and, in a separate report, approved the Electronics Industry Association standards for implementation of the V-chip technology.[3] It seemed that the issue over the V-chip and ratings had finally reached a political conclusion, even though the FCC issued another notice of inquiry in July 2004 to gain comments on the effectiveness of the program.

At the end of the decade, a tragedy brought video-game violence to the center of America's attention. In April 1999 the nation was stunned by the Columbine High School shootings, in which twelve high school students and a teacher were killed by two classmates. Several media reports noted that the two killers played the first-person shooter game *Doom* extensively, even constructing a shooting environment that bore many resemblances to their high school. The Entertainment Software Ratings Board (ESRB) rating system that had been in effect since 1994, and operated much like the MPAA system for film, could not shield the video-game industry from public outcry that constant exposure to violent video games, particularly those first-person shooter games, was blurring the distinction between real and fantasy violence. Since that time, a handful of states have tried to enact laws banning the purchase of violent or sexual video games to minors (Gledhill, 2005). The debate this tragedy engendered was a prelude to the concerns for privacy, decency, and safety that have recently been the subjects of intense public and political concern.

This Decade: Same Song, New Verse

With the decade incomplete and without the benefit of hindsight, it is difficult to characterize the early years of the twenty-first century. Certainly the first half of the decade shows continued congressional interest and public concerns about an ever-expanding array of attractive media choices and their content. The concerns seem to showcase a "same song, new verse" way of summarizing political interest: Congress, the FTC, and the FCC have been busy investigating issues of indecency, violence, and educational programming (Shields, 2006).

By 2000, when it was signed into law, the CIPA (Children's Internet Protection Act) was the third attempt by Congress to create legislation to protect children from indecent material on the Internet. This act required schools and libraries that receive federal funding and discounts for computer access to install filtering software and to enact policies regarding children's use of Internet. The previous 1996 Communications Decency Act (CDA), which prohibited posting indecent material on the Web, and the Child Online Protection Act (COPA), which prohibited the Internet transmission of material deemed harmful to minors for commercial purposes, were ruled unconstitutional by the Supreme Court. CIPA, however, was upheld by the Supreme Court. Also still in force is COPPA—the Children's Online Privacy Protection Act, enforced by the FTC—which applies to the online collection of personal information from children under thirteen. These rules outline requirements for a privacy policy, when and how to seek verifiable consent from a parent, and the responsibilities of a Web site operator to protect children's privacy and safety online.

In 2000 the FTC issued a report exploring two issues involving marketing to children: Do the industries promote products that they themselves acknowledge warrant parental caution in venues where children make up a substantial percentage of the audience? In addition, are these advertisements intended to attract children and teenagers? The report found that "for all three segments of the entertainment industry, the answers are plainly 'yes'" ("FTC Report," 2000). The report found that film, video-game, and music industries routinely target children under seventeen, despite content rating identifying the content as inappropriately violent. The FTC recommended additional self-regulatory behaviors by the industry.

In late 2004 the FCC issued a report making it clear to broadcasters that educational programming for children must remain part of the programming options as they move to digital broadcasting. Essentially, the FCC wanted to make it clear that the core requirements of the Children's Television Act—the three-hour minimum, the minimum length of the programs, and the E/I rating—transferred to the digital environment. The FCC's report also specified that the advertising limits remain intact in a digital world ("FCC Report," 2004).

The 2004 Super Bowl halftime show ignited a firestorm of protest when Justin Timberlake ripped the outfit of Janet Jackson, exposing her breast. The debate raised the old question of whether there should be some measure of control exerted over sexually provocative material. Defenders of the media say the First Amendment gives them wide latitude to broadcast sexually provocative material, which simply reflects changing contemporary mores. However, critics of today's radio and television content say sexually oriented broadcasting can harm society, especially children, and that in order to increase viewership television and radio are constantly pushing the bounds of taste into the realm of indecency.

This social debate turned serious for the networks when Congress became involved. In June of 2006, President Bush signed a bill which raised the ceiling on indecency fines from $32,500 to $325,000 per incident. The law allows cumulative fines of $3 million per day for multiple violations (Ahrens, 2006).

DISCUSSION

So how could you summarize the government's regulation of children's media? More than five decades of action—and inaction—have shown that Congress, the White House, and governmental agencies take cautious steps toward doing something about media content likely to be consumed by children, while not wanting to appear to infringe on First Amendment rights. It's almost like a parent threatening a child. Congress wants to persuade the film, video-game, and television industries (especially the latter) to protect children, but they really want the industries to make the decision to "do the right thing" on their own. They threaten legislation more than they actually produce it, hoping that the mere threat will prompt corrective action.

Media industries can issue their own threats, however. They can threaten to appeal a congressional act, or an FTC or FCC regulation, to the federal courts, prompting a discussion of First Amendment rights and governmental interference. Court appeals can stall governmental initiatives, because laws and regulations are generally not enforced while the case is working its way through the court system.

Both the government and the media industries are at times more concerned with the court of public opinion than with the court of law. Americans seem to be concerned about the safety and privacy of children, but they are also reluctant to support governmental actions that seem to infringe on hallowed free press and free speech rights. Both sides can use those social concerns to their benefit, and they often do.

It's these seemingly conflicting societal concerns that lead to a great deal of talk but very little action regarding regulation of children's media. Certainly, the U.S. Supreme Court has made it clear that television and radio enjoy less First Amendment protection than other forms of mass media, a declaration that has not changed even with the development of cable, satellite, and other new methods of broadcast transmission. The few Court decisions regarding the Internet have provided that medium with almost the same level of First Amendment protection that newspapers and other printed media enjoy. Because a video-game case has yet to reach the Supreme Court, there's no determination on First Amendment protections for this and many other forms of mass media. Practically all media industries that call children their consumers have learned from watching the film, television, and radio industries interact with Congress and the courts. They push the notion of self-regulation to avoid governmental interference whenever possible. Thus far, the strategy seems to have worked.

DISCUSSION QUESTION

1   Are children a "special" audience in need of regulatory protection? Why or why not? What age group are you referencing when you think of "children"? Should media content directed at different age groups be regulated more or less stringently than others?

EXERCISES

1   Before you begin reading, consider who should regulate content. Write as many arguments as you can for and against government regulation, self-regulation by media industry bodies, and parental control.

2   Divide the class into groups, with each assigned to watch at least three children's programs on a selected broadcast or cable network. Have each group report to the class about the content and advertising that they see. Compare these shows to the programs watched by the students when they were young children. Groups may also want to look at content and advertising in prime-time programs that children view regularly.

3   Do an in-home observation of a child watching television or video, or playing video or computer games. Note the level of attention and engagement (rapt or wandering attention), amount of time spent with the media, and any interaction with you or others about the media. What have you learned about children and media? How does the way children react to media compare to adult consumption patterns?

4   What type of media content, if any, seems to warrant more parental attention: television shows, movies on VHS/DVD, or video games? Why? Should Congress also be more concerned about one type of media content than another? Provide a rationale for your argument.

NOTES

1   The Supreme Court's *FCC v. Pacifica Foundation* (1978) decision upheld the FCC's definition of "indecency," which is "language or material that, in context, depicts or describes, in terms patently offensive as measured by contemporary community standards for the broadcast medium, sexual or excretory organs or activities."

2   The ratings were TV-Y (all children), TV-Y7 (older children), TV-G (general audience), TV-PG (parental guidance suggested), TV-14 (parents strongly cautioned), and TV-M (mature audiences only).

3   For specific information regarding the technological standards approved by the FCC on March 13, 1997, visit http://www.fcc.gov/Bureaus/Engineering_Technology/Orders/1998/fcc98036.html.

REFERENCES

Ahrens, F. (2006, July 11). Six-figure fines for four-letter words worry broadcasters. *Washington Post*, p. A01.

Albiniak, P. (1997, October 6). NBC hangs tough on ratings. *Broadcasting & Cable*, p. 16.

Alexander, A., & Hoerrner, K. (2006). Children's advertising. In J. Ciment (Ed.), *Social issues: An encyclopedia of social issues, histories, and debates*, (pp. 37–44). Armonk, NY: M. E. Sharpe.

Alexander, A., Benjamin, L., Hoerrner, K., & Roe, D. (1998). "We'll be back in a moment": Evolution of children's television advertisements in the 1950s. *Journal of Advertising, 27*(3), 1–10.

Clark, N. (2004). The birth of an advocacy group: The first six years of Action for Children's Television. *Journalism History, 30*(2), 66–76.

Enis, B. M., Spencer, D. R., & Webb, D. R. (1980). Television advertising and children: Regulatory vs. competitive perspectives. *Journal of Advertising, 9*(1), 19–42.

FCC report and order (M. M. Docket 00–167), on children's television obligations of digital television broadcasters (2004). November 23.

Fleming, H. (1997, January 13). TV ratings opponents get busy. *Broadcasting & Cable*, p. 6.

FTC report on marketing violent entertainment to children. (September 2000).

Gledhill, L. (2005, December 23). Judge blocks ban on sale of violent video games to minors. *San Francisco Chronicle*, p. A1.

Hoerrner, K. (1999a). The forgotten battles: Congressional hearings on television violence in the 1950s. *Web Journal of Mass Communication Research, 2*(3). Retrieved March 12, 2006, from http://www.scripps.ohiou.edu/wjmcr/v0102/2–3a.htm.

Hoerrner, K. (1999b). Symbolic politics: Congressional interest in television violence from 1950 to 1996. *Journalism & Mass Communication Quarterly, 76*(4), 684–698.

Hoerrner, K. (1998). Symbolic politics: An historical, empirical and legal discussion of congressional efforts and the issue of television violence. Unpublished dissertation, University of Georgia.

Investigation of radio and television programs. (1952). 82nd Cong., 2nd sess., 1952. H. Rept. 2509. U.S. Congress. House. Committee on Interstate and Foreign Commerce.

Krasnow, E., Longley, L., & Terry, H. (1982). *The politics of broadcast regulation*, 3rd ed. Gordonville, VA: Palgrave-Macmillan.

Krattenmaker, T. G., & Powe, L. A. (1994). Regulating broadcast programming. Blue Ridge Summit, PA: National Book Network.

Kunkel, D. (1998). Policy battles over defining children's educational television. *Annals of the American Academy of Political and Social Science, 557*: 39–63.

Kunkel, D., & Wilcox, B. (2001). Children and media policy. In D. S. Singer & J. L. Singer (Eds.), *Handbook of children and the media* (pp. 589–604). Thousand Oaks, CA: Sage.

Martin, K. J. (2003). Family-friendly programming: Providing more tools for parents. *Federal Communication Law Journal, 55*(3), 553–563.

Rice, L., & Brown, R. (1996, December 30). Networks rolling out TV ratings. *Broadcasting & Cable*, p. 7.

Rideout, V., Roberts, D., & Foehr, U. (2005). *Generation M: Media in the lives of 8–18 year-olds.* Menlo Park, CA: Kaiser Family Foundation. Retrieved March 12, 2006, from http://www.kff.org/entmedia/7251.cfm.

Shields, T. (2006, January 2). Forecast 2006: Regulation. *Mediaweek*, p. 18.

Telecommunications Act of 1996. (1996). Public Law No. 104–104.

CHAPTER THREE

Why Is Everybody Always Pickin' on Youth?

Moral Panics about Youth, Media, and Culture[1]

SHARON R. MAZZARELLA

Why is it that only the forms of popular culture that apparently have some sort of direct effect on audiences are the dangerous ones? No one seems to believe that more Meg Ryan movies will transform the United States into a land of sweetly perky romantics, yet the sort of virtual violence depicted in The Matrix *could be cited as "obvious" inspiration for the very real violence that took place at Columbine in 1999.*
—Gilbert Rodman

In seeking to answer the question posed by its title, this chapter first examines the way in which "youth" functions as a cultural construct enabling journalists, politicians, and parents to invest it with their own definitions—definitions often contributing to the seemingly endless cycle of moral panics raging over youth and culture since the early years of the twentieth century. It then briefly outlines examples of various twentieth-century moral panics, concluding with a discussion of the role of media in perpetuating such panics.

Following Joe Austin and Michael Nevin Willard's (1998) lead, "youth" in this chapter refers to young people roughly between the ages of twelve and twenty-four. It is this age group upon whom I predominantly focus; however, often I will discuss children of a younger age. This is not to imply that children and "youth" are one and the same, but rather is an acknowledgment that, at times, the issues related to their mediated representations and cultural constructions do overlap. I will return to the discussion of moral panics and the role of the press in fueling their flames later in this chapter, but in order to understand these phenomena, we first must understand the changing construction of childhood and adolescence that occurred in the United States during the late nineteenth and early twentieth centuries (see, for example, Aries, 1962; Hawes & Hiner, 1985), a change that created a climate in which adults could easily lapse into moral panic about youth culture.

Youth as a Construct

Quite simply, childhood and adolescence are socially constructed phenomena. The child, according to Lyn Spigel (1993, p. 259), is a "cultural construct, a pleasing image that adults need in order to sustain their own identities. Childhood is the difference against which adults define themselves." Yet while the sociocultural construct of youth works toward defining adult identities, according to Henry Giroux (1996, p. 10), it also "has become indeterminant, alien, and sometimes hazardous to the public eye." How did we get to this point?

Prior to the late nineteenth and early twentieth centuries, children were not necessarily considered as a distinct social group, but rather as miniature adults who, in all but upper-class families, played specific and vital economic roles within the family structure. In most rural families, for example, boys learned their fathers' trades at a young age, and girls learned domesticity from their mothers. As a result, with the exception of bourgeois children, most children did not attend school beyond just a few years. With industrialization and urbanization, the structure of families began to change. Families were no longer self-sufficient; we became a nation of consumers rather than producers. As a result, children ceased to fill the same productive economic role within families, leaving them with more time on their hands, not to mention more things to consume.

Deriving from these changes in the construction of childhood was a belief in the innocence and naiveté of children. According to Spigel (1993, p. 261), since the beginning "of industrialization, children have been conceptualized as blank slates upon whom parents 'write' their culture." As a result of this belief, the early years of the twentieth century witnessed the designation of children as a group meriting the attention and intervention of reformers and activists (Wartella & Mazzarella, 1990). Specifically, it was at this time that public education was institutionalized. In fact, gradually across the decades of the last century, an increasing percentage of youth stayed in school for longer and longer periods of time, a phenomenon that immersed them in a world dominated by peers and kept them further out of their parents' control. Moreover, children and adolescents (by this time also defined as a distinct group) became the focus of scientific study and inquiry. It was around this time that G. Stanley Hall (1904) founded the discipline of adolescent psychology, advancing his now-discredited belief that all adolescents go through a period of "storm and stress." Accompanying this inquiry were assorted pieces of federal legislation (for example, child labor laws and mandatory schooling laws) designed to "protect" innocent children. Giroux (2000, p. 5) argues that this "myth of childhood innocence" continues to this day to be at the heart of adult concerns about youth and mass culture. In fact, David Buckingham (2000, p. 15) takes issue with such characterizations of children as "pre-social individuals," as this construction of children "effectively prevents any consideration of them as social beings, or indeed as citizens. Defining children in terms of their exclusion from adult society, and in terms of their inability or unwillingness to display what we define as 'adult' characteristics, actively produces the kinds of consciousness and behaviour which some adults find so problematic."

Paralleling the social construction of childhood innocence, another factor contributing to moral panics over youth and youth culture was a shift over the course of the twentieth century in the leisure behaviors of society at large and of children in general—notably the tendency of the young to quickly embrace each new communication technology introduced during the last century (Wartella & Mazzarella, 1990). Several major studies and reports (see, for example, Hurt, 1924; Walter, 1927) were issued early in the twentieth century documenting that youth were spending their newfound leisure time in questionable and "unworthy" pursuits (that is, hanging out with friends, going to the movies, and so on). These reports called for the need to institutionalize leisure through such adult-sanctioned and supervised activities as scouting. These studies, according to Wartella and Mazzarella (1990, p. 177),

> articulate the Progressive era's concern about adolescent youth's leisure time. In general, young people of fourteen to eighteen were seen as having too much time simply to hang around with their peers, unsupervised, or to spend in commercial activities, like the movies, that were thought to have questionable moral standards. Child savers were concerned that such ill-spent leisure would lead to moral degeneration, particularly in the absence of control by family, church, and school. The reformers argued that unless young people occupied their leisure more constructively, leisure could become a hazard, breeding delinquency and crime outside the home.

In the midst of this leisure revolution and its attendant public outcry, a new youth culture was born. "By the 1940s, high school students as a group were labeled, identified, and the subject of popular attention and concern" (Wartella & Mazzarella, 1990, p. 181). The label "teenager" first appeared in a 1941 issue of the magazine *Popular Science* (Hine, 1999), and *Seventeen* magazine was founded in 1944 as one of many attempts to exploit and capitalize on the newly emergent postwar middle-class youth culture and its vast disposable income (Palladino, 1996). It was, at this time, according to Kathleen Knight Abowitz (n.d.), that "adolescents became a 'generation,' recognized more by their common experiences of age than by the class, racial, or ethnicity-based differences that separated them." According to Larry Grossberg (1994, p. 26), "the very existence of youth, at least in the twentieth century, is intimately tied to the media and vice versa: we might say that, perhaps more than any other social identity, youth always exists, as a style, with and within the media."

Comics and Music and the Web, Oh My!

In 1985 Ellen Wartella and Byron Reeves conducted an exhaustive literature review of the research done on children and media during the first half of the twentieth century. They found that the introduction into U.S. society of each of the major electronic technologies of film, radio, and television was accompanied by considerable public discussion and debate over their perceived impact on audiences, in particular youth. John Springhall (1998) has shown this also to have been the case in Great Britain as well. The arguments and debates identified by Wartella and Reeves recurred throughout the twentieth century and, indeed, continue today. The same concerns we hear now about gangsta rap (see, for example, Lipsitz, 1998), goth, the Internet, and video-game violence (see, for example, Jenkins, 1999) were expressed in the 1920s about movies, in the 1930s about radio, in the 1940s and 1950s about comic books, in the 1950s about rock 'n' roll and television, and so on. The recurrence of these debates is directly linked with the way in which society at a given time defines youth and constitutes what James Gilbert (1986, p. 4) calls an "episodic notion." For example, Wartella and Mazzarella (1990) point out that many of the concerns expressed about children and television during the late twentieth century were reminiscent of concerns expressed in the 1920s about college students—the first youth culture. Drawing on the work of Paula Fass (1977), Wartella and Mazzarella (1990, pp. 178–179) report that "The moral panic [in the 1920s] arose out of the fact that adolescents were developing an autonomous peer-oriented leisure-time culture, a culture independent of adults, outside the home, unsupervised, and increasingly commercialized. Indeed, the late 1920s established a pattern of public concern about all children's use of media for leisure time that would continue in succeeding decades."

Moral Panic Defined

Given the cultural belief in the "innocence" of children and of the role of parents in "molding" the values of their children as well as "shielding" them from harmful messages, it is no wonder that mass culture historically has been fodder for moral panics. As defined by Springhall (1998, pp. 4–5), a moral panic occurs "when the official or press reaction to a deviant social or cultural phenomenon is 'out of all proportion' to the actual threat offered." Stanley Cohen (1980, p. 9) goes on to elaborate that a moral panic occurs when

> a condition, episode, person or group of persons emerges to become defined as a threat to societal values and interests; its nature is presented in a stylized and stereotypical fashion by the mass media; the moral barricades are manned by editors, bishops, politicians and other right-thinking people; socially accredited experts pronounce their diagnoses and solutions; ways of coping are evolved or (more often) resorted to; the condition then disappears, submerges or deteriorates and becomes more visible.

Further, Angela McRobbie (1994, p. 199) argues "that at root the moral panic is about instilling fear in people and, in so doing, encouraging them to try and turn away from the complexity and the visible social problems of everyday life." In the case of child and youth culture, moral panic has resided along generational fault lines. In fact, as McRobbie (1999, p. 199) notes, such panics over youth culture serve as "a means of attempting to discipline the young through terrifying their parents," a phenomenon she describes as "a powerful emotional strategy." As can be seen in the examples to be discussed in this chapter, moral panics over youth culture are characterized by all or most of the following:

- adults' fears of losing control over "vulnerable" youth;
- the need to find a simple solution to a complex problem involving youth (whether real or perceived);
- the perceived link to popular culture often grounded in a focus on manifest content of media/culture (for example, song lyrics);
- little or no actual evidence of a link between this content and the perceived problem of youth;
- claims made by "elites" (doctors, politicians, and the like);
- a wave of often exaggerated press coverage;
- government hearings to investigate the so-called problem; and
- media-industry fears of government regulation leading instead to voluntary self-regulation.

In the sections that follow, I examine how these characteristics were manifested in three specific instances of moral panic: the comic book/juvenile delinquency scare of the 1950s, the controversies over popular music (heavy metal and hip-hop) in the 1980s and 1990s, and the panic over the rash of school shootings, notably Columbine High School, in the 1990s. In each case, as noted by Abowitz (n.d., n.p.), "moral panics often increase the level of social control upon youth. Judicial, legislative, and administrative responses to moral panics over youth are quite common."

Juvenile Delinquency in the 1950s

The media-centered youth culture came to full fruition during the 1950s, as did the contradictory belief in the "innocence" of children and the necessity for parents to "mold" their children (Spigel, 1993). The clash between these two beliefs led adults who witnessed youths' new look, argot, and leisure to label such behaviors as delinquent, with the result that the decade produced a massive moral panic over juvenile delinquency and the alleged contribution of mass culture (for example, television, comic books, and rock 'n' roll). (See, for example, Beaty, 2005; Gilbert, 1986; Spigel, 1993; Springhall, 1998).

In the 1950s, according to Spigel (1993, p. 268), "The anxieties about television's effects on youth were connected to more general fears about its disruption of generational roles, particularly with regard to power struggles over what constituted proper children's entertainment." Spigel argues that the primary concern in this struggle was that the innocence of children was at stake. "At the heart of the advice on children and television was a marked desire to keep childhood as a period distinct from adulthood. Critics of the medium feared that television might abolish such distinctions by making children privy to adult secrets" (Spigel, 1993, p. 271).

While Spigel is specifically referring to the early panic over children and television, there was, at the time, an even bigger moral panic—one focusing on the role of comic books in promoting juvenile delinquency, and equally related to adult fears of losing control. "Most historians of the comic book trace the birth of anti-comic book concern to a single influential 8 May 1940 editorial in the *Chicago Daily News*, 'A National Disgrace,' written by Sterling North and widely reproduced" (Beaty, 2005, p. 113). Throughout the 1940s and into the 1950s, concern over the relationship between comic books and youth violence grew, in part, in response to the changing nature of their content—focusing more and more on crime and horror—and in part in response to their increased popularity: comic books reached a sales peak in 1953 and 1954, "by which time a staggering 75 million 10-cent copies were being bought and traded" each month (Springhall, 1998, p. 124).

Indeed, it was the immense popularity of these crime and horror comics that provided the fodder for the claims of psychiatrist Frederic Wertham, whose 1954 book, *Seduction of the Innocent*, put forth the unsubstantiated claim that such comics were a direct "contributing factor" in the perceived rise of juvenile delinquency. A psychiatrist counseling youth offenders, Wertham offered as evidence the fact that the majority of youth with whom he worked were avid readers of comic books. Wertham himself conducted no controlled studies systematically isolating what, if any, influence such comics had on "normal" youth and instead relied solely on his interviews with youth in treatment for various psychological, social, and criminal problems (Gilbert, 1986). By the time the book had been condensed in *Reader's Digest*, a publication that made his claims more accessible to the general public, these claims had created "an exaggerated fear among American parents of what was lurking behind the covers of the comic books read so avidly by their children" (Springhall, 1998, p. 125). While it's easy to look back now and dismiss Wertham's conclusions based on lack of concrete evidence, it is important to understand the climate of the United States in the 1950s—a climate described by Springhall (1998, p. 121) as characterized by "McCarthyism, intellectual hostility to mass culture, and the cult of domesticity," making it easy for parents, politicians, educators, clergy, and so on to be easily convinced by the "reductionist causal link between comic books and crime" (Springhall, 1998, p. 125) made by such a respected expert on youth as Dr. Wertham.[2] "A pervasive social anxiety about the spread of juvenile delinquency, amplified by the mass media and politicians, lent support to Wertham's unsubstantiated allegation that the parallel phenomenon (sic) of rising crime figures and rising sales of 'horror comic' books were somehow causally related" (Springhall, 1998, p. 135).

It was within this cultural and political climate that the Senate Subcommittee to Investigate Juvenile Delinquency was formed in 1953. While charged with investigating a range of potential causes of juvenile delinquency including substandard schools and families, "the mass media held center stage [as a potential cause] from 1954 through 1956" (Gilbert, 1986, p. 143). Indeed, between 1953 and 1955, the committee received more than

fifteen thousand unsolicited letters from citizens, some 75 percent of which expressed concerns about the link between juvenile delinquency and mass media (Springhall, 1998).
During the course of these hearings, numerous representatives from various media industries, including comic-book publishers (notably EC Comics's Bill Gaines), as well as so-called
violence experts, testified for or against the belief that comic books were harmful.

When the political and media circus was over, the subcommittee rejected "Wertham's
monocausal model of juvenile delinquency" (Springhall, 1998, p. 139), opting instead to
identify comic books as one factor in a greater social problem and choosing not to undertake any kind of federal government legislation against the medium, while at the same time
warning that the industry should undertake responsible self-regulatory means. At the
same time, however, in eighteen states, local ordinances restricting the sale of crime and
horror comics were passed (Springhall, 1998). In response, a group of comic-book publishers formed the Comics Magazine Association of America in late 1954, a group responsible for creating and administering the newly created Comics Code. Based on the
self-regulations imposed by the Comics Code, "all scenes of horror, excessive bloodshed,
gory or gruesome crimes, depravity, lust, sadism, and masochism . . . walking dead, torture,
vampires, ghouls, cannibalism and werewolfism" were forbidden, as were titles containing
the words *horror* or *terror* (Springhall, 1998, p. 140). Publishers had to submit their books
to code authorities who, if they approved, issued a seal of approval that would ensure distribution to retail outlets. The end result of the code was that numerous comic-book titles
and publishers were forced out of business since they could not comply with code guidelines and still produce the content they had become known for. Without the code's
endorsement, it was all but impossible to distribute and sell comic books.[3]

Gilbert (1986, p. 7) describes the 1950s debate over youth culture as "a struggle in which
the participants were arguing over power—over who had the right and responsibility to
shape American culture." Those same power arguments recurred some thirty years later in
the form of a public outcry about popular music.

Popular Music in the 1980s and '90s

In the mid-1980s, the Parents' Music Resource Center was placed in the "expert" role that
Wertham took on in the 1950s by leading the campaign against what some called "porn
rock." Formed in May 1985 and headed by a group of prominent Washington, D.C.,
wives—Tipper Gore (wife of then-senator Al Gore), Susan Baker (wife of then–treasury
secretary James Baker), and Peatsy Hollings (wife of then-senator Ernest Hollings), among
others—the group got its start, in part, in response to Gore's shock upon first hearing the
Prince song *Darling Nikki*, a song referencing masturbation. Focusing primarily on heavy-
metal rock, the PMRC advocated for warning labels and/or printed lyrics on controversial albums so as to warn parents that the content was inappropriate for children. Using
as an example a hit list of songs they identified as "The Filthy Fifteen" (including songs
by Sheena Easton, Judas Priest, Madonna, Prince, and Def Leppard, among others), they

proposed a rating system whereby offending albums would be rated V (violence), X (sexually explicit), O (occult), D/A (drugs and alcohol), or S (suicide).

Beginning in September 1985, a series of hearings were held before the Senate Commerce Technology and Transportation Committee, hearings featuring testimony by the PMRC on one side, and a strange-bedfellows mixture of musicians including Frank Zappa, Dee Snyder (Twisted Sister), and John Denver on behalf of the music industry. The end result was a November 1985 agreement on the part of the Recording Industry Association of America (RIAA) to "encourage" its members (representing 85 percent of U.S. record companies) to place warning labels on controversial albums or to print the lyrics on the album cover (Heins, 1993, p. 84; Chastagner, 1999). Between January 1986 and August 1989, 49 out of the 7,500 albums released contained a warning label, despite the fact that the PMRC had deemed 121 albums to be offensive (Chastagner, 1999).

But, as Marjorie Heins notes, the closure of the hearings and the RIAA's agreement did not take the issue out of the public eye. In 1988 the PMRC went on to create and market an inflammatory video for parents called *Rising to the Challenge: A Revealing Look at the Pied Pipers of Today's Rock 'n' Roll*, a video produced by Bob DeMoss of the fundamentalist group Focus on the Family (Chastagner, 1999) and described on its back cover as "an eye-opening educational video for parents." The video, intended to warn parents about what their children were listening to and seeing on album covers and in music videos, offered graphic visual and lyrical evidence of what was categorized as the dangerous content of popular music, notably heavy metal. What is notable about the video is that it employed the same tactics used by the PMRC throughout its campaign. Like Wertham, they offered no scientific or controlled evidence that there was a link between the music and the resulting effects they warned about: adolescent drinking, drug use, sexual promiscuity, rape, and suicide. Contrary to their promotional claims, that this was "33 minutes of carefully documented evidence sure to change the way you and your children listen to music" (video case back cover), the evidence in the video was far from "carefully documented." Instead, the video offered a wealth of frightening and compelling statistics on such phenomena as the rise in youth violence, drinking, and suicide, which were then linked to music by focusing on the manifest content of various song lyrics. But the video presented no research evidence to document or support a cause-and-effect relationship between the music and any of these phenomena. At a time when the country was undergoing a conservative and reactionary turn in the mid- to late-1980s, and when adult fears of youthful transgressions were again peaking, the video spoke to already existing fears and offered a simple solution to the alleged problem with youth.

By 1990, some eighteen states were considering legislation related either to music labeling or censorship (Heins, 1993), a fact that led the RIAA to follow a longstanding trend (seen, for example, in the creation of the Comics Code in the 1950s) and opt for industry self-regulation to avoid the threat of government regulation. In 1990 the RIAA adopted the "Parental Advisory/Explicit Lyrics" label we have all become so familiar with. Most of the major company members of the RIAA adopted the label, although, unlike in the case of the Comics Code seal, each individual company made the decision about which albums would carry the label. There were neither centralized industry-wide guidelines nor a board overseeing the use of the label as there was in the case of the Comics Code or as there is in the case of the Motion Picture Association of America (MPAA) movie ratings. Yet, as in the case of the Comics Code, there was an effect on sales, although not to the same extreme, as some retailers, notably Wal-Mart, have refused to carry stickered albums.

But this was far from the end of the story as the cycle continued into the 1990s with a new public outcry over a different genre of music—rap. In the early 1990s, there were a series of obscenity prosecutions throughout the United States in which either rappers themselves or record store owners or clerks were charged, arrested, and/or prosecuted under U.S. obscenity statutes.[4]

While law enforcement and individual states/counties/cities engaged in obscenity prosecutions related to rap, other elites and the federal government again got involved in the debates, notably in the form of what George Lipsitz (1998) has called the "hip hop hearings"— federal government hearings held in response to concerns raised by C. Dolores Tucker of the National Political Congress of Black Women. The 1994 hearings, held at the urging of Senator Carol Mosley Braun and Representative Cardiss Collins, focused on critiquing "the music as obscene, misogynous, and a threat to decency within Black communities" (Lipsitz, 1998, p. 402). Tucker had argued that gangsta rap was the reason "why so many of our [Black] children are out of control and why we have more black males in jail than we have in college (qtd. in Lipsitz, 1998, p. 396). In her testimony before the committee, Tucker labeled such music "'pornographic smut,'" and went so far as to argue for a total ban on rap music on the grounds that it is harmful to Black communities. As in previous examples, or moral panics, an elite individual or group—in this case, Tucker as a representative of the National Political Congress of Black Women—raised concerns that resulted in the federal government holding hearings to investigate the issues. Tucker, like Wertham and the PMRC before her, offered no scientific evidence to support her claims, in Tucker's case that rap "glamorized violence, degraded women . . . incited violence, and seduced young people into a life of crime" (Lipsitz, 1998, p. 402). Why, then, did such claims spark so much interest and governmental involvement? Lipsitz (1998) compellingly demonstrates that the moral panics over hip-hop in general and gangsta rap in particular have served to blame the music for problems (crime and violence, for example) that are more appropriately attributed to broader social, political, and economic causes. According to Lipsitz (1998, p. 404),

> Like most conservative mobilizations over the past two decades, the crusade against rap music identifies real problems in people's lives. . . . [But it] takes these social realities out of history. . . . The crusade against rap music suppresses social memory by claiming that only culture counts, that history—in this case deindustrialization, economic restructuring, white backlash against the civil rights agenda, and neoconservative politics—has nothing to do with social disintegration in our society.

Taking Aim at the Causes of School Shootings

Some fifty years after the juvenile delinquency/comic-book hearings, the arguments remained the same. The aftermath of the April 20, 1999, Columbine High School shootings, in which two male students, Dylan Klebold and Eric Harris, killed thirteen others at the school before taking their own lives, provides an example of the moral panic about youth violence in general, school shootings in particular, and the alleged role of mass culture in contributing to both.

While 71 percent of adults polled shortly after the incident believed "a school shooting was 'likely' to happen in their community," research conducted by the Justice Policy Institute found that a child's chance of being killed in school is a mere 1 in 2 million (Brooks et al., 2000, p. 6). This discrepancy, the report argues, is due, in part, to the media coverage of shootings such as Columbine, coverage that results in American adults being "exponentially misinformed" (p. 30). The report goes on to call for an end to the "hyperbole that too often follows school shootings" and for the media to "add more context" to their coverage of such events (p. 30).

In looking at the post-Columbine news coverage, Giroux, in his book *Stealing Innocence* (2000), isolates how our culture's belief in childhood innocence comes into play in news coverage of youth. Specifically, he points out that childhood innocence is generally applied only to White, middle-class youth, a phenomenon that became painfully clear from such Columbine headlines as "If It Could Happen Here, Many Say, It Could Happen Anywhere" or questioning "How Could This Happen?" The implication being how could this happen *here* (that is, in White, middle-class suburbia)? Moreover, other articles quoted sources exclaiming, "They were good" (that is, White, middle-class suburban) "kids." Implicit in such statements is the belief that this kind of behavior is to be expected of urban, poor, and/or African-American and Latino youth, but that these kinds of things just don't happen in White suburbia. Giroux exposes this bias, arguing that "white middle-class children often are protected by the myth of innocence and are considered incapable of exhibiting at risk behavior" (p. 8). When they do exhibit such behavior, as in the case of Columbine, it is accompanied both by a wave of "soul searching" (p. 8) and the need to identify outside causes (for example, popular culture) "well removed from the spaces of 'whiteness' and affluence" (p. 8).

Indeed, in the ensuing moral panic and national soul searching, hundreds of articles were published addressing the "causes" of this tragedy, a significant proportion of which singled out media and popular culture. In their content analysis of Columbine coverage, Erica Scharrer, Lisa Weidman, and Kimberly Bissell (2003, p. 81) document the manner in which the press "quickly came to focus on popular-culture and entertainment-media products as causal contributors to the massacre." It didn't take long—only until the next day, in fact—for the press to start looking for causes (Scharrer et al., 2003). In this case, some of the most frequently mentioned causes were movies (for example, *The Matrix* and *The Basketball Diaries*), video games (*Doom* and *Quake*), the Internet, the goth subculture, and popular music (Marilyn Manson and the German band KMFDM). More than any other alleged cause, it was Manson who bore the brunt of attacks, prompting him to publish an eloquent response in *Rolling Stone* (1999) in which he wrote of the post-Columbine "witch hunt": "Man's greatest fear is chaos. It was unthinkable that these kids did not have a simple black-and-white reason for their actions. And so a scapegoat was needed" (Manson, 1999).

As in the case of other moral panics about youth culture, extensive media coverage was accompanied by government hearings to investigate both the shootings in general and the role of media and popular culture in contributing to them. In this case, the hearings were held before the Senate Commerce Committee. As a well-respected scholar on video games (although not a supporter of the belief that video games cause youth violence), Henry Jenkins was called to testify along with others whom he describes as "anti-popular culture types, ranging from Joseph Lieberman to William Bennett" (Jenkins, 1999), and high-profile military psychologist and anti–video game crusader David Grossman, as well as industry spokespeople. Jenkins realized he "would be the only media scholar who did not come from the 'media effects' tradition and the only one who was not representing popular culture as a 'social problem,'" a fact he worried was a "setup" (Jenkins, 1999). In a reflection piece he posted on the Internet shortly after the hearings, Jenkins described the circuslike atmosphere of the hearings, which included displays consisting of "massive posters" of ads for "some of the most violent videogames on the market," "professional witnesses" with accompanying staffs, "props," "professionally-edited videos," and out-of-context clips from movies such as *The Basketball Diaries* (Jenkins, 1999). In the end, Jenkins likened the experience to a "national witch hunt" (Jenkins, 1999). According to Jenkins, both the senators and the press covering the hearing clearly had their minds made up in advance about the causes—popular culture such as video games, music, and the Internet—and he, as the only scholar speaking from outside of the media effects tradition, was attacked and dismissed. "The press," Jenkins (1999) reports, "swarmed around the anti-violence speakers but didn't seem to want to talk to me." Clearly, according to Jenkins, the government and the press in this example had an agenda to deliver to the U.S. public, a particular message and a predesignated enemy—popular culture. Jenkins's views simply did not support the plan, so he was silenced.

The Role of the Press in Constructing Youth as a Problem

One of many common components in the cycle of moral panics has been the role of the press in perpetuating and fueling public concern with the panic du jour, although it's more accurate to point out that the moral panics discussed in this chapter are individual moments in a larger, ongoing moral panic that has raged for the past several decades—a panic identifying youth itself as a problem.

According to sociologist Donna Gaines (1994, p. 231), recent popular media "misrepresentation(s)" of youth often include "images of kids as 'thugs,' 'animals,' drive-by shootouts, gangsters and teenage crack moms rocking in the free world, jock gang rapists, parricide perps, low math and science scorers, zombies without morals." Gaines is neither the first nor the only scholar to expose the media's war on kids. (See, for example, a theme issue of the magazine *Extra!* titled "Media Take Aim at Youth" [1994].) A wave of scholars has begun to examine the "representational politics" (Giroux, 1998, p. 28) guiding media constructions of youth. In addition to Gaines, scholars including Henry Giroux, Henry Jenkins, Larry Grossberg, Mike Males, Kathleen Knight Abowitz, and others have turned their attention to the role of media, in particular the press, in perpetuating what Giroux (1996, p. 36) calls "an essentialist representation of youth." The coverage has been described as characterized by a "mean spirited discourse" (Giroux, 1996, p. 30), further evidence of the "adolescent apocalypse" (Males, 1999, p. 7), part of the larger crisis discourse that dominates the conversations about youth (Abowitz, n.d.), and, in general, evidence of an overall "crisis in representation" of the young (Giroux, 1998, p. 30).

Like Lipsitz (1998), Abowitz argues that this crisis discourse "leads to certain readings of the problems of youth as problems of *individual* youth rather than systematic, structural, or cultural problems at large (Abowitz, n.d.). In other words, it denies the need to focus on broader social, economic, and cultural factors affecting youth (for example, poverty), a denial she argues is rooted in a "conservative ideology" (Abowitz, n.d.).

In his aptly titled book *Framing Youth*, Mike Males (1999) deconstructs the press coverage of teenagers in the United States and compellingly shows how the press consciously and systematically distorts the facts about youth, whom he calls "the officially designated scapegoat of the 90s" (p. 288). This phenomenon is even more pronounced when covering youth of color (Binder, 1993; Dixon & Azocar, 2005; Giroux, 2000). According to Giroux (2000, p. 20), "Current representations of youth—which range from depicting kids as a threat to society or as defenseless against the corrupting influence of the all-powerful popular culture—often work to undermine any productive sense of agency among young people, offering few possibilities for analyzing how children actually experience and mediate relationships with each other or with adults." Moreover, youth are rarely, if ever, given the opportunity to speak for themselves in news coverage about them (Children Now, 2001; Edwards, 2005; Hartley, 1998; Jackson, 1994; Mazzarella & Pecora, 2007; Tucker, 1998). Instead, journalists rely on various "official," adult sources: law enforcement, researchers, social workers, educators, psychologists, and so on. This phenomenon, what Jackson (1994, p. 14) calls "constricted sources," is typical of press coverage of youth.

What's the Big Deal?

Why does it matter that as a culture we've devoted so many newspaper pages, government hearings, and sleepless nights to the relationship between youth and popular culture? One hallmark of moral panics is that they focus attention and direct resources toward simple solutions to complex problems and often serve as smokescreens enabling us as a society to ignore larger, more troubling problems. These misdirected panics take attention away from the real problems confronting youth in our society (Abowitz, n.d.; Giroux, 2000; Lipsitz, 1999; Males, 1999)—notably the dramatic decline in government funding of education, the reduction in social services for children, the disappearances of noncommercial public spaces for the young, and the increasing commercial and sexual exploitation of children, not to mention the epidemic of adult-perpetrated violence against children, a crisis that is powerfully, statistically documented by Males (1999). Moreover, our deeply entrenched cultural belief in the need to protect children from the "harmful" outside influences of mass culture (for example, video games, goth music, the Internet) has had powerful ramifications for how we conceive of the relationship between youth and media. According to Jenkins (1999), we have became so caught up in our concerns about what media has been doing to kids that have failed to understand what "our children are doing with media." This failure is due in part, according to Jenkins (1999), to the fact that adults fear adolescents; they also fear new technologies, in part because they lack the knowledge and expertise to incorporate these technologies into their own lives; and youth culture has grown increasingly visible, making it harder than ever to ignore. "We are afraid of our children. We are afraid of their reactions to digital media. And we suddenly can't avoid either" (Jenkins, 1999).

DISCUSSION QUESTIONS

1   When you were growing up, how did the warning labels on recorded music affect you? Did your parents forbid you to purchase stickered music? Did a record-store clerk ever refuse to sell you a stickered CD? Did the sticker ever make you want the CD more (the "forbidden fruit" argument)?

2   What grade were you in when the Columbine school shooting took place? How did the aftermath of the shooting affect your school in terms of increased security, fear, or profiling of goth or other outsider kids?

3   This chapter begins with a quotation from Gilbert Rodman. The full quote from his article on rapper Eminem reads as follows:

Why is it that only the forms of popular culture that apparently have some sort of direct effect on audiences are the *dangerous* ones? No one seems to believe that more Meg Ryan movies will transform the United States into a land of sweetly perky romantics, yet the sort of virtual violence depicted in *The Matrix* could be cited as "obvious" inspiration for the very real violence that took place at Columbine in 1999. Few people seem willing to claim that popular computer games like *The Sims* will produce a world of brilliant and creative social planners, but it's almost a given that graphically violent games like *Mortal Kombat* will generate armies of murderous superpredator teens bent on terror and mayhem. *The Cosby Show* . . . was unable to usher in an era of racial harmony and tolerance, but edgy cartoons like *South Park* will supposedly turn otherwise angelic, well-adjusted children into foul-mouthed, misbehaving delinquents. (1999, pp. 98–99).

To paraphrase Rodman's opening questions, why is it that we as a culture believe that the only forms of popular culture that affect youth are the "dangerous" ones?

EXERCISES

1   Take one of the examples mentioned in the above excerpt, *The Matrix, Mortal Kombat,* or *South Park* (or even a currently controversial movie, TV program, musician, or the like) and study newspaper coverage of the controversies. Using the Lexis-Nexis database, search for articles published during the relevant time period for your specific topic.

What concerns were raised about your chosen content or performer? What evidence/proof is offered? Who is making the claims (and/or quoted in the articles)? Are young people quoted or interviewed?

NOTES

1   Portions of the first section of this chapter first appeared in S. R. Mazzarella (2003), "Constructing youth: Media, youth and the politics of representation," in A. N. Valdivia (Ed.), *Media studies companion* (pp. 227–246) (Malden, MA: Blackwell), and have been adapted/reprinted with permission of the editor.

2   Despite his legacy as a conservative, anti-comics, anti–popular culture crusader, recent books examining Wertham's writings and other works have revealed him to have been a progressive thinker whose ideas were appropriated by conservative social critics in support of the move to regulate the comic-book industry and mass culture in general (Beaty, 2005; Nyberg, 1998).

3   The Comics Code is still in existence today, although, as a result of new distribution outlets and the growth of underground comics, its influence is minimal. In fact, according to *Wikipedia* (Comics Code Authority, n.d.), the only major publishers still submitting works to the Comics Code Authority for approval are DC Comics (only some of their lines) and Archie Comics. The code was modified twice in its fifty-year existence. In 1971 the code was revised to allow for the depiction of narcotics provided it was to show drug use as bad, and in 1989 the code revision provided for nonstereotyped portrayals of gay and lesbian characters. For a compelling and detailed examination of the anti-comics movement and the Comics Code itself, see Nyberg (1998).

4   While pornography (sexually explicit content) is not illegal, obscenity is. As defined by the landmark *Miller v. California* (1973) U.S. Supreme Court case, content that meets all of the three following criteria is deemed legally obscene, and therefore not protected by the First Amendment (Miller Test, n.d.):

   a   Whether the average person, applying contemporary community standards, would find that the work, taken as a whole, appeals to the prurient interest,
   b   Whether the work depicts/describes, in a patently offensive way, sexual conduct specifically defined by applicable state law,
   c   Whether the work, taken as a whole, lacks serious literary, artistic, political, or scientific value.

   A discussion of the obscenity prosecutions applied to rap music is beyond the scope of this chapter, but for an excellent and thorough accounting of these incidents, see Heins (1993).

REFERENCES

Abowitz, K. K. (n.d.). *Discourses on youth: Youth in crisis?* Retrieved July 18, 2004, from http://www.nits.muohio.edu/edulead . . . ses/334/334_discourse_on_youth.html.

Aries, P. (1962). *Centuries of childhood: A social history of family life.* (R. Baldick, Trans.). New York: Vintage.

Austin, J., & Willard, M. N. (Eds.). Introduction: Angels of history, demons of culture. In J. Austin & M. N. Willard (Eds.), *Generations of youth: Youth cultures and history in twentieth-century America* (pp. 1–20). New York: New York University Press.

Beaty, B. (2005). *Frederic Wertham and the critique of mass culture.* Jackson: University Press of Mississippi.

Binder, A. (1993). Constructing racial rhetoric: Media depictions of harm in heavy metal and rap music. *American Sociological Review, 58,* 753–767.

Brooks, K., Schiraldi, V., & Ziedenberg, J. (2000). *School house hype: Two years later.* Washington, D.C.: Justice Policy Institute. Retrieved July 18, 2004, from http://www.prisonsucks.com/scans/jpi/shh2.pdf.

Buckingham, D. (2000). *After the death of childhood: Growing up in the age of electronic media.* Cambridge U.K.: Polity.

Chastagner, C. (1999). The Parents' Music Resource Center: From information to censorship. *Popular Music, 18*(2), 179–192.

Children Now (2001). *The local television news media's picture of children.* Retrieved March 2, 2004, from http://www.childrennow.org/newsroom/news-01/pr-10-23-01.cfm

Cohen, S. (1980). *Folk devils and moral panics: The creation of the mods and rockers.* New York: St. Martin's.

Comics Code Authority. (n.d.). *Wikipedia.* Retrieved April 8, 2006, from http://en.wikipedia.org/wiki/Comics_Code_Authority.

DeMoss, R., Jr. (Executive Producer), & Norwood, J. (Writer). (1988). *Rising to the challenge: A revealing look at the pied pipers of today's rock 'n' roll* [videotape]. Arlington, VA: Parents Music Resource Center.

Dixon, T. L., & Azocar, C. L. (2005). The representation of juvenile offenders by race in Los Angeles area television news. *Howard Journal of Communication, 17,* 143–161.

Edwards, L. Y. (2005). Victims, villains, and vixens: Teen girls and Internet crime. In S. R. Mazzarella (Ed.), *Girl wide web: Girls, the Internet, and the negotiation of identity* (pp. 13–30). New York: Peter Lang.

Fass, P. (1977). *The damned and the beautiful: American youth in the 1920s.* New York: Oxford University Press.

Gaines, D. (1994). Border crossing in the U.S.A. In A. Ross & T. Rose (Eds.), *Microphone fiends: Youth music and youth culture* (pp. 227–234). New York: Routledge.

Gilbert, J. (1986). *A cycle of outrage: America's reaction to the juvenile delinquent in the 1950s.* New York: Oxford University Press.

Giroux, H. A. (1996). *Fugitive cultures: Race, violence, and youth.* New York: Routledge.

Giroux, H. A. (1998). Teenage sexuality, body politics, and the pedagogy of display. In J. S. Epstein (Ed.), *Youth culture: Identity in a postmodern world* (pp. 24–55). Malden, MA: Blackwell.

Giroux, H. A. (2000). *Stealing innocence: Corporate culture's war on children.* New York: Palgrave.

Grossberg, L. (1994). The political status of youth and youth culture. In J. S. Epstein (Ed.), *Adolescents and their music: If it's too loud, you're too old* (pp. 25–46). New York: Garland.

Hall, G. S. (1904). *Adolescence: Its psychology and its relation to psychology, anthropology, sociology, sex, crime, religion, and education.* Engelwood Cliffs, NJ: Lawrence Erlbaum.

Hartley, J. (1998). Juvenation: News, girls and power. In C. Carter, G. Branston, & S. Allan (Eds.), *News, gender and power* (pp. 47–70). New York: Routledge.

Hawes, J. M., & Hiner, N. R. (Eds.). (1985). *American childhood: A research guide and historical handbook.* Westport, CT: Greenwood.

Heins, M. (1993). *Sex, sin and blasphemy: A guide to America's censorship wars.* New York: The New Press.

Hine, T. (1999, September) The rise and decline of the teenager. *American Heritage,* pp. 71–82.

Hurt, H. W. (1924). *Boy facts: A study from existing sources.* New York: Boy Scouts of America.

Jackson, J. (1994). The "crisis" of teen pregnancy: Girls pay the price for media distortion. *Extra!, 7*(2), 13–14.

Jenkins, H. (1999). *Professor Jenkins goes to Washington.* Retrieved July 16, 2001, from http://web.mit.edu/21fms/www/faculty/henry3/profjenkins.html.

Lipsitz, G. (1998). The hip hop hearings: Censorship, social memory, and intergenerational tensions among African Americans. In J. Austin & M. N. Willard (Eds.), *Generations of youth: Youth cultures and history in twentieth-century America* (pp. 395–411). New York: New York University Press.

Males, M. (1999). *Framing youth: Ten myths about the next generation.* Monroe, ME: Common Courage Books.

Manson, M. (1999, May 28). Columbine: Whose fault is it? *Rolling Stone.* Retrieved March 15, 2005, from http://www.rollingstone.com/news/story/5923915/columbine_whose_fault_is_it

Mazzarella, S. R., & Pecora, N. (2007). Girls in crisis: Newspaper framing of adolescent girls. *Journal of Communication Inquiry, 31*(1), 6-27.

McRobbie, A. (1994). The moral panic in the age of the postmodern mass media. In *Postmodernism and popular culture* (pp. 198–219). New York: Routledge.

Media take aim at youth. (1994, March/April). *Extra! 7*(2).

Miller Test. (n.d.). *Wikipedia.* Retrieved March 5, 2006, from http://en.wikipedia.org/wiki/Miller_Test.

Nyberg, A. K. (1998). *Seal of approval: The history of the Comics Code.* Jackson: University Press of Mississippi.

Palladino, G. (1996). *Teenagers: An American history.* New York: Basic.

Rodman, G. R. (2006). Race . . . and other four letter words: Eminem and the cultural politics of authenticity. *Popular Communication, 4*(2), 95–121.

Scharrer, E., Weidman, L. M., & Bissell, K. L. (2003). Pointing the finger of blame: News media coverage of popular culture culpability. *Journalism & Communication Monographs, 5*(2).

Spigel, L. (1993). Seducing the innocent: Childhood and television in postwar America. In W. S. Solomon (Ed.), *Ruthless criticism: New perspectives in U.S. communication history* (pp. 259–290). Minneapolis: University of Minnesota Press.

Springhall, J. (1998). *Youth, popular culture and moral panics: Penny gaffs to gangsta rap, 1830–1996.* New York: St. Martin's.

Tucker, L. (1998). The framing of Calvin Klein: A frame analysis of media discourse about the August 1995 Calvin Klein jeans advertising campaign. *Critical Studies in Mass Communication, 15*(2), 141–157.

Walter, H. R. (1927). *Girl life in America.* New York: National Committee for the Study of Juvenile Reading.

Wartella, E., & Mazzarella, S. (1990). A historical comparison of children's use of leisure time. In R. Butsch (Ed.), *For fun and profit: The transformation of leisure into consumption* (pp. 173–194). Philadelphia: Temple University Press.

Wartella, E., & Reeves, B. (1985). Historical trends in research on children and the media, 1900–1960. *Journal of Communication, 35*(2), 118–133

CHAPTER FOUR

Piaget and Power Rangers

What Can Theories of Developmental Psychology Tell Us about Children and Media?

CYNDY SCHEIBE

There is now a growing body of evidence detailing how people use different forms of media, and how the media—primarily television, films, and video games—are likely to affect them. Much of this research shows that children of different ages use and are affected by the media differently (Dorr, 1986; Kundanis, 2003; Van Evra, 2004). Theories of developmental psychology can help us interpret this evidence by identifying the potential mechanisms explaining why those effects may occur, and by guiding our predictions about which children are most at risk for specific effects. They also help to explain how children make sense of media content, and how their understanding of the media changes with age. Finally, in the absence of a credible mechanism or theoretical explanation for how two variables are related, developmental theories can help to separate real causal relationships from spurious ones.

Generally speaking, developmental theories can be organized into three main categories: those that emphasize the development of acquired *behaviors*, those that emphasize the development of *cognition* (that is, attention, learning, memory, understanding, and judgments), and those that emphasize the development of *personality and emotions* (including the psychoanalytic theories of Freud and Erikson). Other theories that are typically part of a developmental approach include *neurobiology* theories (emphasizing brain functioning and responses), and *ecological* theories (emphasizing the multiple and interactive environments in which a child develops and functions).

Which theoretical approach you use to explain a given set of data or observations depends partly on your own view of human development and partly on the nature of the question under consideration. Theories differ in their emphasis on cognition, for example. If you are interested in how children understand (or misunderstand) what they see on television, then all of the cognitive theories will be very applicable to that question; many other theories (for example, behaviorism or Freud's psychosexual theory) have little to say about thinking or understanding. In addition, some developmental theories describe qualitative changes that occur during specific and predictable stages of development (for example, Piaget's theory), whereas others portray a more gradual process of changes that occur with age (for example, social learning and information-processing theories). Finally, some theories emphasize the importance of innate, biological, or unconscious influences ("nature"), while others stress the importance of environmental influences ("nurture"); the latter are more useful for studying children and media.

Theories and Learning

One of the key issues of interest in the study of children and media has to do with learning—*how* do children learn a given behavior, idea, or piece of information, and what factors play a role in whether a given child *will be likely to* learn something from a particular media example? Generally speaking, there are four basic ways in which children can learn, and a "key issue" that affects the likelihood of learning for each.

1   *Direct experience.* This reflects learning through *operant conditioning*, where the child actually has to *do* the behavior. If they are rewarded (reinforced), then they should be more likely to repeat the behavior again; if they are punished, then they should be *less* likely to repeat the behavior again. The key issue has to do with the nature of the reward or punishment—what will work for this particular individual? Effective reinforcers for young children are usually different from those that work for older children or teens. For example, young children are likely to be heavily influenced by praise or criticism from their parents and other family members, while teens might be more heavily influenced by feedback from their peers.

2   *Observational learning.* This involves learning by watching someone else do the behavior and then imitating them (or deciding *not* to imitate that behavior because of the consequences experienced by that person). Here the key issue involves the extent to which you identify with the person observed, see yourself as similar to them, and/or want to be like them. Again, this is likely to vary for children of different ages (and different genders); younger children typically identify with and look up to their same-sex parents and older siblings, while teens often model their behavior after peers and figures from popular culture.

3   *Symbolic learning.* For older children, adolescents, and adults, most of our learning comes through written or spoken language; we are often told to do (or not to do) something, and why. The key issue in this case has to do with the credibility of the source: How much do you trust them or believe that they are telling the truth?

4   *Cognitive learning.* In this case learning is based on information that the child already has and his or her overall understanding of the issues involved. With cognitive learning, there are a number of key issues that come into play, including developmental age, cognitive ability, and prior information available.

How do these four ways of learning relate to children and media? Learning through direct experience has only limited application, because the media don't directly reinforce (reward or punish) children for their behaviors. However, positive or negative responses from parents and/or peers to something a child does (or says) after learning it on TV might well influence the likelihood that the child will do (or say) that again. Children are also likely to draw conclusions about what they see on television, depending on whether the characters are rewarded or punished for their actions; numerous content analyses have noted that violent actions often go unpunished and are sometimes even rewarded, making it more likely for children to conclude that aggression is a good thing (Bushman & Huesmann, 2001). And of course parents may also, intentionally or unintentionally, reward certain kinds of media use (for example, reading) and punish or set restrictions on other kinds (TV or video games).

Observational learning easily applies to the influence of media on children and is discussed in the section on social learning theories below. Symbolic learning and cognitive learning also apply, especially with respect to children's use of media for information (for example, *Sesame Street,* the news, or the Internet) and to developmental differences in children's interpretation of media messages and their understanding of the media in general. These are both important mediators in media effects and are discussed in the sections on cognitive-developmental theories and information processing theories below.

Social Learning (Social Cognitive) Theories

Developed by Albert Bandura, *social learning theory* was initially grounded in traditional behavioral theories, emphasizing behaviors that children could and would imitate from observing role models in their social environment and a gradual, continuous process of developmental change (Bandura, 1977). Unlike traditional behaviorist theorists, however, Bandura believed that behavior was due to more than just the influence of the environment; it also reflected children's observations and interpretations of what they saw and who they identified with most strongly. Social learning theory predicts that children are more likely to imitate people they admire, those who are rewarded for their actions, and so on.

Over time, Bandura has increasingly emphasized the importance of cognition, including the roles of individual choice, personality, and interpretation in determining a person's modeled behaviors. His approach is now called *social cognitive theory* (Bandura, 2002), and while it is not a stage theory of development (like Piaget's, which is described in the next section), it does include the concept that social cognitive processes change with age. The role models for young children are not the same as those for adolescents, and while young children often directly and immediately imitate what they see, adolescents and adults are more likely to observe and remember a given behavior that can be demonstrated later if the appropriate situation arises. Both children and adults may also learn what *not* to do from observing the behaviors of others, especially by paying attention to the consequences of their actions in the situation observed.

Before television and movies, children's role models were limited to people they saw in their everyday lives (parents, older siblings, other family members, people in the neighborhood, teachers, and so on). Now television and other audiovisual media provide a wide range of exciting and intriguing role models for children and teens, including real people, characters who are played by live actors, cartoon characters, and superheroes like the Power Rangers. Once television became part of children's daily lives, the potential for social cognitive learning through observation and imitation of the behaviors of others skyrocketed.

But *would* children imitate mediated portrayals of behaviors in the same way they did behaviors they saw performed by real people in their own world? Bandura's earliest and most famous series of studies on this topic (Bandura et al., 1963) demonstrated that they could and would imitate specific aggressive behaviors shown on television (for example, kicking a bobo doll) as much as they would for live people, and that their imitation of a "cartoon" character (in this case, a person dressed as a cat) was almost as high as imitation of a real person. This is a particularly important finding, given children's frequent viewing of cartoons, and it has been supported by subsequent studies of imitation of cartoon violence (Bushman & Huesmann, 2001). (For complete discussions of children and media violence, see chapters 8 and 9.)

Social cognitive theory would also predict that children will learn prosocial behaviors from viewing media portrayals as well as antisocial behaviors, and indeed that is supported by research (Dorr et al., 2002). It also means that children may learn what *not* to do from cartoons and other fictional TV programs. However, such learning may only be effective if there are realistic consequences shown for an action; if the Coyote is fine again after falling off a cliff or being hit on the head with an anvil on the Road Runner cartoons, then children may well be drawing inaccurate conclusions about what they have observed.

An important tenet of social cognitive theory involves the relationship between the observer (child) and the observed (media character), especially the extent to which the child identifies with the character and sees him or her as a role model. By the age of three or four, children have developed gender awareness and gender constancy (that is, understanding that gender is permanent regardless of changes in hair, clothing, or activities), after which gender will be an important mediator of social cognitive learning. Research has shown that boys are much more likely to choose role models who are male (especially powerful ones), while girls are more likely to select both male and female role models (Anderson & Cavallaro, 2002). The same studies have found that African-American and White children were most likely to pick role models of the same race as themselves, while Latino and Asian-American children were most likely to pick White role models (possibly because there are fewer portrayals of Latino and Asian characters on children's television).

Cognitive-Developmental Theories

While Swiss psychologist Jean Piaget actually died long before *The Mighty Morphin Power Rangers* debuted in 1993, his *cognitive-developmental theory* has important applications for the study of children's understanding of media, especially regarding the limitations in cognitive reasoning abilities of young children. Piaget's theory argues that children actively construct their understanding of the world through the ongoing processes of *assimilation* (incorporating new information into existing knowledge) and *accommodation* (reorganizing ways of understanding to take into account new information) (Flavell, 1963).

Unlike social cognitive theory, cognitive-developmental theories describe children's development as occurring in a series of stages, with dramatic and abrupt shifts in the quality of children's thinking as they move from one stage to the next. As children develop, their understanding of the world doesn't just gradually improve; it is qualitatively *different* at different ages. Piaget believed that this process unfolded naturally, and that all children proceed through these stages in the same order and at roughly the same ages. While his approach reflects many biological concepts of maturation, he did not believe that cognitive development was genetically based, occurring on a predetermined timeline that is wired into the human brain; instead he emphasized the child's own role in developing cognitive *schemes* (ways of knowing or action patterns) by actively exploring, manipulating, and making sense of his or her environment (Crain, 2000).

While Piaget himself wrote primarily about children's developmental stages in terms of understanding the *physical* world, his theory can also be applied to the understanding of *social* information provided by the media, and predictable age differences in children's interpretations of media content. Piagetian theory includes four stages of cognitive development that always occur in the same sequence (Singer & Revenson, 1996), although the age at which children move from one stage to the next may vary:

1   The *sensori-motor stage* (birth to two years), in which infants and toddlers get information through their senses and manipulation of objects; by age two, children have developed an internal representation of schemes including the capability for deferred imitation, an understanding of object permanence, basic grasp of cause and effect, the beginnings of language, and self-awareness.

2   The *preoperational stage* (two to seven years), during which there is rapid growth and reorganization of understanding and symbolic thought, but the child's thinking is illogical and his or her approach to problem-solving is unsystematic; during the early part of this stage, the child's thinking is often *egocentric* (marked by an inability to take into account other perspectives than his or her own) and *animistic*

(attributing human motivation and characteristics to inanimate objects), the child's judgments reflect *centration* (focusing on one central characteristic of an object or person to the exclusion of others), and the child has difficulty distinguishing between fantasy and reality; even after age four, children typically base their conclusions on intuitive rather than logical thought.

3   The *concrete operational stage* (seven to twelve years), in which children can demonstrate the ability to mentally manipulate objects and are able to take into account more than one dimension of an object and perspectives of it, but are still limited to applying this understanding to concrete (rather than abstract) examples.

4   The *formal operational stage* (twelve years and older), in which most adolescents can demonstrate abstract thinking, hypothetical-deductive reasoning, and systematic approaches to problem-solving.

Most of the media research using a Piagetian framework has focused on the cognitive limitations of preoperational thinking, especially for children under the age of four or five who have a difficult time fully grasping the nature of television and its content. One study showed that two- and three-year-old children often believe that the TV characters lived inside the TV set (Noble, 1975), while another found that three-year-old children interpreted a television image of a glass of water as more similar to real life (where the water would spill out if you turned it upside down) than to a photograph of a glass of water (where it wouldn't) (Flavell et al., 1990).

Research on children's understanding of fantasy versus reality shows that while children as young as two or three can both engage in fantasy play and understand that it is only pretense, they are much more confused by whether something is real or only fiction on television (Davies, 1997). This has been explored in a number of important realms, including children's consumer behavior (Valkenburg & Cantor, 2001) and the impact of media violence (Comstock & Paik, 1991). Research on media and children's fears shows that young children are most afraid of characters and scenes that *look* scary (like monsters and witches), while older children are more afraid of realistic scenes and situations (portraying things that could actually happen) (Cantor, 2001).

Other preoperational limitations are reflected in the study of children's *theory of mind*, their understanding of their own mental processes and those of other people (Flavell et al., 1995; Flavell, 2004). Preschoolers tend to believe that other people know and see what they know, and have difficulty understanding concepts like *false beliefs* (believing something that is not actually true) or *dreams* (which are often believed to be real). They also have difficulty with what is known as the *appearance-reality distinction* (understanding the difference between what something seems to be and what it actually is. It is not surprising, then, that young children may be confused by media storylines that emphasize different characters' understanding of something that happened, or include characters who appear to be good (or look nice on the outside) but are really bad, and vice versa.

Piaget also proposed stages of moral reasoning that are relevant to the understanding of media effects (Crain, 2000). During the preoperational stage, children's reasoning reflects moral *heteronomy*, which is grounded in blind adherence to rules that are immutable, a sense of immanent justice (that is, that wrong-doers will always be caught and punished), and judgments of right and wrong that focus on the consequences of the action. Older children, especially after the age of ten, exhibit moral *autonomy*; they understand that rules can be changed and that wrong-doers might not be discovered, and base moral judgments more on the individual's *intentions* rather than the consequences of the action. Young children, then, may easily misinterpret the moral lessons found in media stories that are centered on judgments about an actor's intentions, or when someone breaks the rules in order to achieve a more positive and just outcome.

Information Processing

Information-processing theories focus on the processes of memory and attention (using a computer-based model of data input, output, and storage), and while they do not predict unique ways of processing information by children of different ages, developmental studies have shown that younger children do attend to and remember information differently than older children. For example, young children are less likely to pay attention to the central or important information, and instead will often attend to irrelevant or idiosyncratic aspects of a situation (Santrock, 2006). They are also less likely to be able to recall detailed information about something they have been taught or experienced.

Studies of children's attention to and comprehension of television confirm the importance of these developmental limitations (for example, Anderson & Burns, 1991; Collins, 1981). Young children often miss the salient information that's important for the story to make sense and may recall only unrelated pieces of information that were interesting to them rather than the main points of the story. They are also more likely to attend to unusual auditory or visual features (for example, special visual effects, funny voices, sound effects) even when they are unrelated to the main story.

Information-processing theories also emphasize the importance of information that is already available to the individual (from learning and prior experience) as a mediator of understanding and interpretation; using the computer model, an individual can only process information in the context of information he or she already has stored. Interpretation of a TV storyline, then, will be influenced by *explicit knowledge*: what the child already knows about the common structure of stories, the "formal features" of television (that is, the meaning of special visual or auditory effects), and the characters in the program. It will also be influenced by the child's *implicit knowledge*: knowledge about the real world and inferences drawn about interscene relationships and character motivations. It is this latter category that often puts children at a disadvantage (Collins, 1981; Condry, 1989).

Information processing also helps to explain how children develop beliefs and ideas (including erroneous ones) about a topic. Their beliefs are likely to be based on inaccurate sources such as advertising or fictional media stories; children are less likely to question fictional stories because they don't have the training or real-world knowledge to judge their credibility. This is similar to cultivation theory in communications (Gerbner et al., 1994), which predicts that heavy viewers who "mainstream" themselves into the world of television are more likely to incorporate information from television (even fictional television) into their beliefs about the real world. (See chapter 10 for a thorough explanation of cultivation theory and research.) It is also reflective of cognitive script theory (Valkenburg, 2004), which deals with the ways children develop expectations about how to act in certain situations based on "scripts" they have seen in real life and the media.

In the context of gender development, information processing is reflected in gender schema theory emphasizing children's organization of information and perceptions about the categories of male and female based on sociocultural standards and stereotypes (Martin & Ruble, 2004), including those reflected in the media. Research shows that children's TV programs continue to portray stereotypical gender roles, especially with respect to appearance, relationships, and occupations (Signorielli, 2001).

Information-processing theory also helps to explain children's learning of educational content from television. Some children's television producers, such as Sesame Workshop, carefully base their program content on research about children's learning. The importance of reinforcing concepts and understanding by using explicit and concrete examples with sufficient repetition, for example, has been demonstrated by research on the effectiveness of programs like *Sesame Street* (Fisch & Truglio, 2001). (Refer to chapter 12 for a look at educational television.) These same techniques are beginning to be used in media literacy curricula aimed at improving children's understanding of the purpose of TV commercials and misleading messages about nutrition (Scheibe et al., 2005). (See chapter 13 for a discussion of media literacy.)

Other Developmental Theories

There are a number of other developmental theories that have been applied to the study of children and media, including *psychoanalytic theories* linking media influences to personality development (Aschbach, 1994), identity (Huntemann & Morgan, 2001), and fantasy play (Bettleheim, 1976). Urie Bronfenbrenner's (2000) *ecological theory* emphasizes the concentric "systems" in which children develop; television could be considered part of both the microsystem (early and immediate influences in the home) and the broader macrosystem (culture in which a child develops). Recent *neurobiology theories* have begun to be applied to research on brain responses to media violence (Murray, 2001), and some theorists have speculated that there may be a "sensitive period" during which the effects of media violence are most powerful (Eron & Huesmann, 1986). (See chapter 9 for an explanation of this line of research.)

Lev Vygotsky's *sociocultural-cognitive theory* has not really been applied to studies of children and media, despite its emphasis on how social interaction and culture combine to influence children's learning and development (Crain, 2000). His concepts of scaffolding and a "zone of proximal development" (within which children have the capacity to learn something with help from a more experienced child or adult) certainly have potential applications for both educational television and media literacy education.

Summary and Conclusions

In 1978 former FCC commissioner Nicholas Johnson said, "All television is educational television. The question is: what is it teaching" (Quotations about Television, 2006)? Developmental theories are key to answering this question, because they go beyond simply analyzing the content shown to include the unique nature of the child who is being taught. Media effects often depend on the age of the child as well as the amount of time they spend with each medium and the content to which he or she has been exposed (Condry, 1993). Thus developmental psychology and media studies should go hand in hand. Developmental textbooks are finally starting to include media influences in discussions of cognitive development and other topics (for example, Berk, 2004; Santrock, 2006), not just focusing on the effects of TV violence on aggression in the chapter on early childhood (as was typically the case until a few years ago). Communication textbooks may well follow the same path, providing those who study media and those who produce it an increasing appreciation for the application of developmental theories in their work.

DISCUSSION QUESTIONS

1   Which developmental theories could be used to explain the influence of the Power Rangers on children's beliefs, behaviors, and emotions, and what would each one predict?

2   Think about one other effect of media content on children involving learning that you have heard about or is described elsewhere in this text. Which of the four ways in which children learn would be most applicable to explaining this effect, and why? How would the "key issues" help to determine whether a given child would be likely to learn that behavior or information from a particular media portrayal?

3   Based on the developmental theories presented in this chapter, what types of media might have the strongest impact on children's aggression and other behaviors, on their knowledge and beliefs, and on their feelings? How will this vary depending on the child's age?

4   Do you think there might be a "sensitive period" during which children are most strongly influenced by television? If so, when would it occur and how would it reflect developmental theories? Might there be other sensitive periods for other types of media?

EXERCISES

1   Watch two half-hour children's TV shows, one from PBS or Nick Jr. that is educational or emphasizes prosocial lessons, and one that consists of action adventure (live or cartoon) that features good guys and bad guys. Identify which characters might be role models for children's viewing, including whether they would be more appealing to boys or girls, and/or children from a particular age group. What behaviors might children be likely to imitate from these programs, and why?

2   Watch several TV programs or movies that are aimed at children and young teens. Take notes on the gender messages that are included (including those in the commercials shown during the TV shows). Based on the set of messages you have seen, what kind of gender schema might children develop about what it means to be a boy or a girl?

REFERENCES

Anderson, D. R., & Burns, J. (1991). Paying attention to television. In J. Bryant & D. Zillmann (Eds.), *Responding to the screen: Reception and reaction processes* (pp. 3–25). Hillsdale, NJ: Lawrence Erlbaum.

Anderson, K. J., & Cavallaro, D. (2002). Parents or pop culture? Children's heroes and role models. *Childhood Education, 79*, 161–168.

Aschbach, C. (1994). Media influences and personality development: The inner image and the outer world. In D. Zillmann, J. Bryant, A. & Huston (Eds.), *Media, children, and the family: Social scientific, psychodynamic, and clinical perspectives* (pp. 117–128). Hillsdale, NJ: Lawrence Erlbaum.

Bandura, A. (1977). *Social learning theory*. Englewood Cliffs, NJ: Prentice-Hall.

Bandura, A. (2002). Social cognitive theory. *Annual Review of Psychology*, vol. 52. Palo Alto, CA: Annual Reviews.

Bandura, A., Ross, D., & Ross, S. A. (1963). Imitation of film-mediated aggressive models. *Journal of Abnormal and Social Psychology, 63*, 3–11.

Berk, L. (2004). *Development through the lifespan* (3rd ed.). Boston: Allyn and Bacon.

Bettleheim, B. (1976). *The uses of enchantment: The meaning and importance of fairy tales*. New York: Vintage.

Bronfenbrenner, U. (2000). Ecological theory. In A. Kazdin (Ed.), *Encyclopedia of psychology*. New York: Oxford University Press.

Bushman, B. J., & Huesmann, L. R. (2001). Effects of televised violence on aggression. In D. G. Singer & J. L. Singer (Eds.), *Handbook of children and the media* (pp. 223–254). Thousand Oaks, CA: Sage.

Cantor, J. (2001). The media and children's fears, anxieties and perceptions of danger. In D. G. Singer & J. L. Singer (Eds.), *Handbook of children and the media* (pp. 207–222). Thousand Oaks, CA: Sage.

Collins, W. A. (1981). Schemata for understanding television. In H. Kelly & H. Gardener (Eds.), *Viewing children through television* (pp. 31–45). San Francisco: Jossey-Bass.

Comstock, G., & Paik, H. (1991). *Television and the American child*. San Diego, CA: Academic Press.

Condry, J. (1989). *The psychology of television*. Hillsdale, NJ: Lawrence Erlbaum.

Condry, J. (1993). Thief of time, unfaithful servant: Television and the American child. *Daedalus, 122*(1), 259–278.

Crain, W. (2000). *Theories of development: Concepts and application* (4th ed.). Upper Saddle River, NJ: Prentice-Hall.

Davies, M. M. (1997). *Fake, fact, and fantasy: Children's interpretations of television reality*. Mahwah, NJ: Lawrence Erlbaum.

Dorr, A. (1986). *Television and children: A special medium for a special audience*. Beverly Hills, CA: Sage.

Dorr, A., Rabin, B. E., & Irlen, S. (2002). Parents, children, and the media. In M. H. Bornstein (Ed.), *Handbook of parenting*, vol. 5 (2nd ed.). Mahwah, NJ: Lawrence Erlbaum.

Eron, L. D., & Huesmann, L. R. (1986). The role of television in the development of prosocial and anti-social behavior. In D. Olweus, J. Block, M. & Radke-Yarrow (Eds.), *The development of antisocial and prosocial behavior: Research, theories, and issues* (pp. 285–314). New York: Academic Press.

Fisch, S. M., & Truglio, R. T. (2001). Why children learn from *Sesame Street*. In S. M. Fisch & R. T. Truglio (Eds.), *"G" is for growing: Thirty years of research on children and Sesame Street* (pp. 233–244). Mahwah, NJ: Lawrence Erlbaum.

Flavell, J. (1963). *The developmental psychology of Jean Piaget*. Princeton, NJ: Van Nostrand.

Flavell, J. H. (2004). Theory-of-mind development: Retrospect and prospect. *Merrill-Palmer Quarterly, 50*, 274–290.

Flavell, J. H., Flavell, E. R., Green, F. L., & Korfmacher, J. E. (1990). Do young children think of television images as pictures or real objects? *Journal of Broadcasting & Electronic Media, 34*(4), 399–419.

Flavell, J. H., Green, F. L., & Flavell, E. R. (1995). Young children's knowledge about thinking. *Monographs of the Society for Research in Child Development, 60* (1, serial no. 243).

Gerbner, G., Gross, L., Morgan, M., & Signorielli, N. (1994). Growing up with television: The cultivation perspective. In J. Bryant & D. Zillmann (Eds.), *Media effects: Advances in theory and research* (pp. 17–41). Hillsdale, NJ: Lawrence Erlbaum.

Huntemann, N., & Morgan, M. (2001). Mass media and identity development. In D. G. Singer & J. L. Singer (Eds.), *Handbook of children and the media* (pp. 309–322). Thousand Oaks, CA: Sage.

Kundanis, R. M. (2003). *Children, teens, families, and mass media: The millennial generation*. Mahwah, NJ: Lawrence Erlbaum.

Martin, C. L., & Ruble, D. (2004). Children's search for gender cues. *Current Directions in Psychological Science, 13*, 67–70.

Murray, J. (2001, April). Children's brain response to TV violence: Functional magnetic resonance imaging (FMRI) of video viewing in 8–13 year-old boys and girls. Poster presented at the biennial meeting of the Society for Research in Children Development, Minneapolis, MN.

Noble, G. (1975). *Children in front of the small screen*. London: Constable.

Quotations about television. (2006). Retrieved August 29, 2006, from http://www.quotegarden.com/television.html

Santrock, J. W. (2006). *Life-span development* (10th ed.). Boston: McGraw-Hill.

Scheibe, C., Gagnon, N., & Tennis, A. (2005, April). Using media literacy to improve young children's understanding of nutrition. Poster presented at the biennial meeting of the Society for Research on Child Development, Atlanta, GA.

Signorielli, N. (2001). Television's gender role images and contributions to stereotyping: Past, present, future. In D. G. Singer & J. L. Singer (Eds.), *Handbook of children and the media* (pp. 341–357). Thousand Oaks, CA: Sage.

Singer, D. G., & Revenson, T. A. (1996). *A Piaget primer: How a child thinks.* New York: Plume.

Valkenburg, P. M. (2004). *Children's responses to the screen: A media psychological approach.* Mahwah, NJ: Lawrence Erlbaum.

Valkenburg, P., & Cantor, J. (2001). The development of a child into a consumer. *Journal of Applied Developmental Psychology, 22*(1), 61–72.

Van Evra, J. (2004). *Television and child development* (3rd ed.). Mahwah, NJ: Lawrence Erlbaum.

CHAPTER FIVE

How Do Researchers Study Young People[1] and the Media?

DAFNA LEMISH

As researchers, parents, educators, legislators, and so on, we have many questions regarding children, youth, and the media. These questions are diverse, exciting, and challenging. But do we have adequate tools in our "kit" to investigate them? Often, the methods we choose for research are as important as the questions themselves, as they reveal a great deal about our perception of who kids are, what they are capable of doing and willing to share with us, the value of our findings, and the interpretations we make of them.

Throughout the long history of research on children, youth, and media, a diverse array of methodologies have been applied. One reason for this is that a broad range of researchers from a variety of disciplinary homes have contributed to our knowledge base: media specialists; developmental psychologists; sociologists studying childhood and leisure; cultural studies scholars concerned with children's popular culture, identities, and globalization processes; educators working in the field of media literacy; health professionals specializing in children; professionals engaged in the production of texts for children; and policymakers concerned about children's well-being. In fact, most of these perspectives are represented by the various chapters in this book. These various scholarly and applied populations have worked within the research traditions familiar to them; that is, those perceived as legitimate and "scientific" within their own epistemological[2] communities. As a result, a wide range of methodologies available for studying social and psychological phenomena has been applied to the study of children and media: experimental designs, surveys, field studies, ethnographies, interviews, life histories, artwork, content and critical analyses, and the like.

The Challenges: Children
as Unique Research Participants

While many of the methodological concerns raised in this chapter are shared by scholars across disciplines, several have discussed the unique challenges we face given our particular interest in children and media (Buckingham, 1993; Götz et al., 2005; Graue & Walsh, 1998; Hodge & Tripp, 1986; Livingstone & Lemish, 2001; Mahon et al., 1996). In summarizing these concerns, we should recall that children are a very special group of people to study: they develop and change at a rate and intensity unparalleled in the human life cycle. As a result, what may be an appropriate method for studying adults (such as filling in a questionnaire) may be completely inappropriate for young children. For example, the use of language (such as the wording of specific questions) needs to be tailored differently for children even a few years apart. This makes studies that compare children of different ages particularly tricky. Furthermore, the study of young children raises a host of ethical concerns: the need to guarantee anonymity, not to exploit their naiveté and trust of adults, to make them aware that their own words can be used against them, and the like.

The gap that exists between their abilities (that is, mental skills, knowledge, comprehension) and their linguistic performance, too, means that young children's explanations may well be unsatisfactory, as we cannot assume that language is a clear indicator of the child's actual inner world. For example, in a study of kindergartners' understanding of television (Lemish, 1997a), I found that the interviewees often failed to represent their understanding due to shyness. Indeed, one child resorted to producing strings of "I don't know" in response to various questions concerning his favorite cartoon. A less persistent or inexperienced interviewer might have concluded that the child "really doesn't know." However, later in the interview, when the child was involved in a different chain of thought, other stimuli prompted the same child to suddenly produce complicated and sophisticated responses referring directly to the issue previously avoided. In other cases, children produced more complicated talk than they were actually able to understand, using concepts and terms in a mistaken or irrelevant way. For example, in the aforementioned study one child used the term *audience* to refer to a specific person, most likely the director of a television show.

Children and media researchers are also required to pay particular attention to the social context in which their study is conducted, as from a very young age many children adapt to the social expectations of the environment and learn to behave in accordance with what they perceive to be both their social role (for example, a pupil at school or the family's "baby" at home) as well as their gender role (that is, in ways appropriate for boys or girls). For example, studies conducted in schools or with research assignments that require children to "think," "explain," "write," and the like, often elicit a school-related behavior that may facilitate cognitive achievements but not necessarily spontaneous sharing of feelings and attitudes (Buckingham, 1993). Studies conducted at home may induce more free talk, but also anxieties due to "impression management"[3] of the family and their socioeconomic and class status. Similarly, the gender of the participants is often a central dimension of context, as children react differently in unigender situations in comparison with mixed groups. Further, this tendency takes different forms and shapes at different stages of their development, as their relationships with the opposite gender change.

As a result of all of the above, studying children and media often requires designing and employing creative research methods that engage children in pleasurable activities that can optimize their cooperation and facilitate a more valid understanding of their inner worlds. Given this broad survey of the nature of the world of children and research, the purpose of this chapter is to present some of the central methodological approaches that have been applied to our field, to highlight their major advantages and disadvantages, and to raise questions about how knowledge of the world of "kids" is obtained by applying certain research methodologies. This chapter presents the two methodological traditions that are central in our field, discusses their underlying assumptions and the primary methodologies they utilize, and gives examples of the types of questions they have sought to answer in specific research projects. The chapter will conclude with a brief presentation of an emerging trend, in which various methods are combined to foster our understanding of the role media have in the lives of children and youth around the world.

The Grand Divide

The literature published in our field in academic journals and books is characterized by a binary discourse between what are most commonly referred to as "quantitative" and "qualitative" methods. Other names you might find in the literature contrast "positivist" studies with "ethnographic" ones; "American logical empiricism" with "European cultural studies"; and more. While these terms are unsatisfactory, they are widely used, and for lack of better terms, I will apply them here, too, in order to discuss the central concern of this chapter: How have these two methodological schools of thought been applied in the study of children and media?

The "Becoming" Child: The Quantitative Approach

Traditionally, studies of children and media that embrace developmental theories in cognitive psychology have centered on the individual child. (See chapter 4 for a detailed explanation of the application of developmental psychology in the study of youth and media.) Accordingly, this approach views children as in the process of "becoming" an adult. Their abilities and skills are tested and measured in comparison to the ideal model of the adult thinker. This approach has been often named "the deficiency model" (for example, Lemish, 2006), as it assumes that the child is "deficient" in comparison to the adult. Thus, for example, the development of children's ability to distinguish between fantasy and reality has been studied from this perspective (for example, Fitch et al., 1993), as well as children's understanding of narrative (for example, Collins & Wellman, 1982), their moral judgments of characters on television (for example, Rosenkoetter, 2001), their computer-literacy skills (for example, Brown, 2001), their naive trust of advertisements (for example, Macklin & Carlson, 1999), and their emotional reactions to disturbing news (Smith & Wilson, 2002).

This approach has been advanced by a research paradigm with roots in various stimulus-response models in psychology, as well as effects studies in communication, whose main goal is to find correlations between media content and child behavior, cognition, and emotions, and even argue for causal relationships between, for example, television violence and aggressive behavior (for example, Paik & Comstock, 1994), heavy use of Internet pornography and distorted attitudes (for example, Wartella et al., 2000), and viewing of educational television and learning and prosocial behaviors (for example, Fisch, 2004).

Research applying this approach has been conducted primarily through "quantitative" methods, such as experimental designs, where children are brought into a study setting and presented with various tasks. In most cases, such studies quantify predefined activities. Thus, for example, the researcher counts the number of times the child behaves in a specific manner in response to viewing television (for example, says something aloud, sings a song, imitates a behavior, and the like), or tests the child on specific skills acquired (for example, new vocabulary, a concept, a piece of information). The major strength of studies conducted in such a manner is that they can isolate and control the issues selected for study and place each child in a comparable situation. For example, they can control the kind of television material to which the child is exposed during the experiment, the skills tested, the toys available in the room, and the like. Researchers assume that such a context has a greater chance of attaining more specific information, as well as causal explanations. For example, they can determine that specific content in an educational program can elicit a certain behavior, while a violent program does not. There are many examples for this line of research, but most come from the study of television: for example, researchers measure children's learning of a specific prosocial behavior, new vocabulary, or knowledge after having been presented with an educational program (for example, Fisch, 2004); measure children's attention to specific television formal features[4] (for example, Meyer, 1986); measure children's behavior following exposure to violent content (for example, Bandura et al., 1963) or their choice of snack following different food commercials (for example, Borzekowski & Robinson, 2001). (See chapter 12 for a discussion of the research on the effectiveness of educational programs; chapters 8 and 9 for a synthesis of fifty years of research into the effects of media violence on youth; and chapter 7 for a discussion of the effects of children's advertising.)

Many questions can be raised regarding the type of activities selected for coding or the cognitive and behavioral skills measured. Most of the reservations, however, are made regarding the suitability of the unnatural experimental setting for studying children's media-related behaviors: Is the way children behave under research conditions indicative of their everyday behavior? Does the short-term effect measured in such a situation last beyond that particular time?

In correlation studies, another often-applied research format, everyday media-related behaviors are measured through responses to questionnaires and correlated with other cognitive skills, emotions, attitudes, and behaviors. For example, children's exposure to news in the various media is measured as well as their knowledge about the political and social world (for example, Chaffee & Yang, 1990; Smith & Wilson, 2002). The responses are correlated, suggesting, for example, that those who are heavier users of printed news media are better informed about current events than those more heavily dependent on television news. (See, for example, chapter 10 for a thorough summary of the correlational research approach known as "cultivation.") A different correlation study may correlate between young people's exposure to pornography in the media (viewing pornographic programs, playing pornographic computer and video games, surfing pornographic Web sites, reading pornographic magazines, and so on) and their self-report of their attitudes toward women, intimacy, sexuality, and sexual crimes (for example, Malamuth & Impett, 2001). Such a study, for example, might present evidence that adolescents who are heavy consumers of pornography in the media hold more stereotypical attitudes toward women and have a more callous attitude toward sexual crimes in comparison to those who are not exposed regularly to such content.

The major strength of this research method is its ability to examine long-term, accumulative influences of media use on a very large number of children and to offer insights that can be generalized to other situations. There are many variations on this method, including longitudinal studies that follow a group of children over time (such as some of the studies presented in chapters 8 and 9 of this book). Those might involve asking a question such as the following: Is heavy viewing of television in the early years related to lower achievement scores in school (for example, Hancox et al., 2005)? Are heavy consumers of violent content more involved in aggressive incidents as young adults (Huessman & Miller, 1994)? While such longitudinal studies are few and far between, due to among other reasons their costly nature, they usually attract a great deal of attention and controversy. The central focus of concern here is the question of causality: Is it possible to infer from correlation studies a causal direction? Is it possible to suggest that behavior at a young age is indeed the reason for behavior at a later stage? Or could it be the other way around; that an early predisposition or tendency leads to the media-related behavior in the first place? For example, are children who consume a lot of violent content attracted to it in the first place for personal or social reasons? Could it be that children who are exposed to computers at an early age are being raised in a family that prioritizes technological education and/or encourages competitiveness? Naturally, different studies handle these issues in different ways.

The "Being" Child: The Qualitative Approach

The "qualitative" research tradition observes children in their own familiar settings as they express or articulate their inner worlds in their talk, play, drawing, or other art forms, including producing media products themselves (such as videos, Web sites, and blogs). These are usually small-scale studies that take place in the natural environments—homes, schools, playgrounds, as well as on the Internet—where children engage in and reveal the role of media in their lives spontaneously. Researchers who apply ethnographic (Lindlof & Taylor, 2002) methods observe as well as talk to children, and try to make sense of what they do and say. They focus on seeing children as "beings" in their own right, at each individual stage of their development. (See, for example, the research discussed in chapter 15.)

In studies conducted through the qualitative approach, children are presumed to act subjectively in meaningful ways that express their own perspectives, worldviews, and self-image. Researchers approach children as socially competent, autonomous individuals who actively make sense of—indeed, construct and express meanings for—the world around them as they interact with it. What is perceived as central or important in a medium or a text for adults is not necessarily so for children; thus the comparison with adults as a central criterion to evaluating children's cognitive, emotional, or behavioral worlds is perceived as misleading. Such studies concentrate on "the meaning media have for children" and "what children do with media," rather than on "how children's comprehension of media is deficient in comparison to adults'" and "what media do to children." A case in point is a study of how children understood the controversial issue of television violence and the pleasures they derived from it (Tobin, 2000); or how preadolescent girls employed the all-female pop group the Spice Girls in their gendered-identity struggles (Lemish, 1998).

To understand how children evaluate characters, judge their morality, or identify with them requires understanding the social context of the child. The epistemological implications are that this approach assumes that the use of media, understanding of texts, and the pleasures derived from them, are by definition both individualized as well as contextualized experiences. Like adults, children, too, have a gender, a race, a social class, a religion, a culture, a political view. They live in very diverse cultures all over the world. Therefore, ethnographic studies investigate how children who live in different contexts comprehend media texts and develop different explanations and models of such comprehension. Such studies, for example, documented how children from various social classes and ethnicities interpreted television series differently (Buckingham, 1993); how Native-American girls made sense of the Disney movie *Pocahontas*, which features a Native-American heroine (Aidman, 1999); or how South Asian immigrant girls in the United States used the media to construct their sexuality and diaspora identity (Durham, 2004).

Given the assumptions and ambitions of this approach as well as the complexities involved in studying children, there is a need to design creative methods to complement traditional approaches to ethnography that are based on the participant observation; for example, observing babies' behaviors around television in their homes (Lemish, 1987); observing children's free media-related play at home and in school playgrounds (Jenkins,

1993); combining roles of teacher-researcher as a participant observer in schools or community centers (Seiter, 2005); and in-depth interviews with children, individually or in focus groups (for example, Buckingham, 1993; Lemish, 1997a; Mazzarella & Pecora, 1999). There are many possibilities for applying creative methods: interpreting children's drawings and artwork; allowing them to videotape themselves as they go about their daily routines and to tell us about them; studying their bedroom possessions (including various media, wall posters, memorabilia, clothes, toys, and games); designing role-playing situations; setting up imitations of popular programs; having them, or their parents, fill in diaries; and more (for example, Buckingham & Sefton-Green, 1994; Fisherkeller, 2002; Götz et al., 2005; Tobin, 2000).

This research tradition has been enriched by the development of feminist theory and research (for example, hooks, 2000; Rakow, 1986; Van Zoonen, 1994), which is particularly sensitive to the social construction of gender, as well as the conditions of individual children and youth, diversified by race, class, sexual orientation, religion, ethnicity, and disability. Much of this form of research rejects binary oppositions such as public/private (for example, school versus home use of media), rational/emotional (for example, what children learn from media versus how they feel about it), nature/culture (for example, what children bring with them genetically versus what they acquire socially and culturally), and the like. Rather, it shifts research interests to the previously devalued and ignored domains of the private sphere, the emotional realm, and the taboos surrounding bodily functions and sexuality. Its ethics are particularly sensitive to individuality and diversity, and to the power hierarchies in the research situation, particularly those existing between the children studied and the privileged positions of the usually middle-class, well-educated researcher who is often from a majority ethnic group (see, for example, Reinharz, 1992).

However, this approach is not without its own weakness. Such in-depth studies are almost always very limited in the number of children studied and therefore their findings cannot be generalized to larger populations of children (of the same socioeconomical class, culture, age, or other central demographics). This, of course, is a thorny issue, as researchers would like to be able to make claims that enable us to speak about experiences and understandings that extend beyond a specific group of children. In addition, they do not claim to be able to provide causal explanations, as they nearly always posit that there are multiple qualities of children when they are involved with the multiple characteristics of any medium.

Epistemological Terms of the Debate

The debate between the two approaches in the social sciences, presented above succinctly, has been long, complicated, and not without serious implications for both research and researchers engaged in it. It is important to realize that this is not a trivial debate, as it is deeply rooted in the most central questions regarding what science and the production of knowledge are all about (consult, for example, the following resources: Deacon et al., 1999; Lindlof & Taylor, 2002; Reinard, 1998; Watt & van den Berg, 1995; Wimmer

& Dominick, 1997). These can be summarized, in a purist and oversimplified form, around the following four main issues as they become relevant to the study of children and media.

The goals of science. The first concern is for the goal of science and our research activities. "Quantitative" research sets out to confirm specific hypotheses[5] that have been deducted from a more general theory. Its goal is to be able to make predictions according to certain rules. For example: to make a prediction that children who are heavy players of violent computer games will become more violent in their everyday behaviors; or that girls who are heavy consumers of television programs depicting a particular thin-beauty model will be more prone to developing eating disorders. As a result, this research tradition emphasizes the need for random sampling[6] that will reveal the unifying rules and overcome problems of deviations from them.

"Qualitative" research, on the other hand, is inductive. Being mainly concerned with understanding phenomena, it seeks to discover rather than to prove. Qualitative research dismisses representative sampling as representing a form of objectivity, as it argues that such sampling has a different built-in bias: it assumes that all children are equal, when in reality they are not. For example, it will try to understand the kinds of pleasures and meanings that children get from violent computer games or the processes of adoration or identification that girls engage in with their female role models.

The difference between the social and the physical worlds. The second central issue concerns the understandings of the difference between the social and physical worlds and, as a consequence, between the social and natural sciences. On the whole, "quantitative" researchers argue that "the scientific method"[7] as applied in study of the physical/natural sciences should be emulated in studying the social world. Further, they argue that since the social sciences are relatively young in comparison to the natural ones, they have not as yet had the chance to develop accurate measures and methods for studying human phenomena, but that, with time, their sampling methods, research tools and measures, statistical programming, and applied mathematical models will be perfected. The differences between the social and natural sciences are mostly perceived as differences in degree, and not in kind. For example, while it is true that we are dependent on children's cooperation for examining their surfing behaviors on the Internet, we can design research tools that follow and map their movements in virtual reality and provide us with comprehensive accounts of all of their activities, and thus bypass the need to count on children's cooperation and subjective self-reporting.

In contrast, "qualitative" researchers assume that the differences between the two realms of inquiry are differences of kind and not of degree. Children, like all people, are unpredictable individuals, and their media-related behaviors, understandings, pleasures, and influences can be neither predicted nor generalized. Research in itself is perceived to be a form of human activity and, like all forms of behaviors, it is dependent on the views, training, and experiences of individual researchers, academic fashions and institutions, and economical and political constraints. Therefore, the research orientation applied to study the social world requires a very different methodology. Accordingly, such researchers may have little interest in the sophisticated mapping of children's online activities, as they may argue that it does not help us unveil the meaning of these activities.

The subject-object distinction. In a related matter, "quantitative" research distinguishes clearly between the thinking, feeling "child-subject" and the media objects around him or her (for example, a television set, a pop-music CD) and tries to create objective knowledge that is independent of the subject. For example, a survey or an experiment on children's attitudes and emotional reactions toward news reporting of a major terror event will include a set of questions and clear instructions for the interviewer not to divert from the wording, not to express emotions or opinions, and not to interact with the child in any way that might influence responses. All children will be approached through the same research terms, asked the very same questions in the same manner, while the researcher is assumed to be uninvolved in the process or in the reality she or he is studying.

"Qualitative" research, on the other hand, assumes that there is no meaningful independent existence of the object outside of the child-subject that experiences it; that is to say, there is no one or universal meaning to a love affair on a soap opera in and of itself, and no such agreed-upon meaning to an action-adventure cartoon, but only meaning constructed in the experience of the child viewing it. Furthermore, it dismisses the possibility of distinguishing between researcher and researched, as both are involved in the research interaction that affects both of them. Research, accordingly, can never be neutral or objective, in that it always stems from a point of view, an ideology, a perspective on life. As a result, "qualitative" research encourages researchers not to erase their subjective individuality but, on the contrary, to make use of it for digging deeper into understanding of the underlying meanings of the phenomenon studied.

The role of everyday experience. Finally, the fourth major difference relates to the way both traditions evaluate the role of our everyday knowledge and experiences. "Quantitative" research is based on the claim that researchers should not count on their own personal experiences and common sense or on those of the children they study since it is only in the symbolic realm of rational thought that it is possible to understand reality. Consequently, children's personal accounts of their media pleasures, for example, are not deemed "truthful" or "true to life," as they are not based on rational analysis of data we call "facts" (for example, the number of hours spent viewing television; list of Web sites accessed last night; names of popular celebrities).

"Qualitative" research, on the other hand, assigns great importance to those taken-for-granted, everyday experiences, including those happening in the private sphere of the child's own bedroom or those belonging to the world of emotion that reading comic books or listening to pop music evokes. It also supports the researcher's employment of his or her own everyday experience in making sense of these phenomena, such as a researcher using her mothering skills to interview a reluctant child, or to compare her own family's television viewing habits in an attempt to make sense of somebody else's.

Bridging the Divide?

Is it possible to bridge such differences? Can researchers from both traditions learn from each other, even cooperate? To date, those seeking to confront such dilemmas in relation to conducting research on children and media are working with two general approaches. Some researchers, from both traditions, believe that the two are so fundamentally and philosophically different that there is no way to bridge the gap or to compromise between them. You are either with "us" or with "them": you conduct research purely according to your chosen research tradition, you publish it in appropriate outlets, and you do not incorporate knowledge created within the opposing tradition in your own work. The opposite approach accepts that each research tradition has its advantages and disadvantages, that each contributes to our accumulating knowledge in different ways, and that therefore both should be used according to the type of research question, the characteristics of the children studied, the different stage of the research, the personal preference of the researcher, and other considerations.

Aside from various proclamations, it is also instructive to see how some research projects have attempted to combine methods from both traditions. For example, a study of children and their changing media environment in twelve European countries (Livingstone & Bovill, 2001) combined personal in-depth interviews with large-scale surveys. In this case, the data collected in the interviews preceded the distribution of the survey and provided insights into the building of the latter research tool. A different combination was practiced in a study of the effects of television wrestling programs on elementary-school children in Israel: the study included unstructured phone interviews with school principals, structured questionnaires filled out by children, and individual in-depth interviews with a sample of both populations (Lemish, 1997b). There are many possibilities for "mix and match," given that researchers find that they can bridge the underlying theoretical underpinnings of the two approaches.

Indeed, I would like to make a "proper disclosure" and suggest that my personal perspective is that these two approaches should be treated as complementary rather than competitive, and that we should seek to integrate the knowledge gained from both traditions into a fuller and more comprehensible understanding of the role of media in children's lives. In my view, it is possible to accept that children lack the skills and knowledge that adults have developed as they have matured, but at the same time to respect the meanings they produce from media as worthwhile in their own right. We can consider each child's individual development, but at the same time integrate our understanding of this development as embedded in complicated social contexts. We can seek to reach generalizations that will allow us to predict some of children's reactions, yet at the same time also pursue attaining in-depth understandings of individual and unique experiences that provide us with insights into larger phenomena. The particular path we choose to follow, as individual researchers, will say much about the questions we ask and the kind of knowledge we produce, but it will also say much about who we are as researchers.

EDITOR'S NOTE

*   This book has been structured purposely to include both quantitative and qualitative scholars as well as those working to bridge the divide. Only by including a range of voices can we fully understand the topic of youth and media.

DISCUSSION QUESTIONS

1   How does the kind of research method used affect the kind of knowledge it produces?

2   Do you have a preference for either one of the research traditions? Explain your reasoning. Is there anything in your particular academic education that may have influenced this preference?

3   Based on this chapter, what do you think are appropriate criteria for evaluating whether a study is a "good" one?

EXERCISES

1   Review a number of chapters in this book and make a list of methods used in the studies they discuss. Which categories, quantitative, qualitative, or mixed, do they fall into? Note for each study the main research question. Review your list: Is there anything in common among the research questions asked in each of the three categories?

2   Select two different studies described in various chapters in this book, one study from each of the two main research traditions: quantitative and qualitative. Suggest a complementary method for each from the second tradition that will investigate the same research question.

3   Check the library at your institution for journals that publish work on children and media. Flip through the pages of current issues. Can you find some systematic patterns in the type of research traditions they represent?

NOTES

1   In this chapter, I use the phrase "young people" to refer to anyone under the age of 18.

2   Epistemology refers to the study of knowledge including how knowledge is produced, evaluated, organized, and re/presented.

3   "Impression management" describes the various forms of behavior of individuals who wish to convey a special impression of themselves (for example, the way they dress, move, and talk, their facial expressions, the accessories they use, and the like).

4   A medium's formal features refer to structural elements of the codes of conventions it uses, including, for example, visual elements (camera movements, sharp cuts from one angle to another, slow or fast motion, and the like) as well as audio ones (such as unusual noises, music, sound effects, and the like).

5　A hypothesis is an expectation based on some theory about particular phenomena or relationships between variables.

6　Random sampling is a procedure of selecting cases from a population to be studied in such a way that each case (here, a "case" is a child) has an equal and known chance of being included in the sample. As a result, the sample drawn for the purpose of the particular study is presumed to represent the entire population of interest (in this case children).

7　The scientific method refers to the various means scientists use in making claims, answering questions, and drawing conclusions.

REFERENCES

Aidman, A. (1999). Disney's Pocahontas: Conversations with Native American and Euro-American girls. In S. R. Mazzarella & N. Pecora (Eds.), *Growing up girls: Popular culture and the construction of identity* (pp. 133–158). New York: Peter Lang.

Bandura, A., Ross, D., & Ross, S. A. (1963). Imitation of aggression through imitation of film-mediated aggressive models. *Journal of Abnormal and Social Psychology, 67*, 601–607.

Borzekowski, D. L. G., & Robinson, T. N. (2001). The 30-second effect: An experiment revealing the impact of television commercials on food preferences of preschoolers. *Journal of the American Dietetic Association, 101*(1), 42–46.

Brown, J. A. (2001). Media literacy and critical television viewing in education. In D. G. Singer & J. L. Singer (Eds.), *Handbook of children and the media* (pp. 681–697). Thousand Oaks, CA: Sage.

Buckingham, D. (1993). *Children talking television: The making of television literacy.* London: Falmer.

Buckingham, D., & Sefton-Green, J. (1994). *Cultural studies goes to school: Reading and teaching popular media.* London: Taylor and Francis.

Chaffee, S. H., & Yang, S-M. (1990). Communication and political socialization. In O. Ichilov (Ed.), *Political socialization, citizenship education and democracy* (pp. 137–157). New York: Teachers College Press.

Collins, W. A., & Wellman, H. M. (1982), Social scripts and developmental patterns in comprehension of televised narratives. *Communication Research, 9*(3), 380–398.

Deacon, D., Pickering, M., Godling, P., & Murdock, G. (1999). *Researching communications: A practical guide to methods in media and cultural analysis.* London: Arnold.

Durham, M. G. (2004). Constructing the "new ethnicities": Media, sexuality and diaspora identity in the lives of South Asian immigrant girls. *Critical Studies in Media Communication, 21*(2), 140–161.

Fisch, S. (2004). *Children's learning from educational television: Sesame Street and beyond.* Mahwah, NJ: Lawrence Erlbaum.

Fitch, M., Huston, A. C., & Wright, J. C. (1993). From television forms to genre schemata: Children's perceptions of television reality. In G. L. Berry & J. K. Asamen (Eds.), *Children and television in a changing socio-cultural world* (pp. 38–52). Newbury Park, CA: Sage.

Fisherkeller, J. (2002). *Growing up with television: Everyday learning among young adolescents.* Philadelphia: Temple University Press.

Götz, M., Lemish, D., Aidman, A., & Moon, H. (2005). *Media and the make believe worlds of children: When Harry Potter met Pokémon in Disneyland.* Mahwah, NJ: Lawrence Erlbaum.

Graue, M. E., & Walsh, D. J. (1998). *Studying children in context: Theories, methods and ethics.* Thousand Oaks, CA: Sage.

Hancox, R. J., Milne, B. J., & Poulton, R. (2005). Association of television viewing during childhood with poor educational achievement. *Archives Pediatrics and Adolescent Medicine, 159,* 614–618.

Hodge, B., & Tripp, D. (1986). *Children and television: A semiotic analysis.* Cambridge, U.K.: Polity.

hooks, b. (2000). *Feminism is for everybody: Passionate politics.* Cambridge, MA: South End.

Huessman, L. R., & Miller, L S. (1994). Long term effects of repeated exposure to media violence in childhood. In L. R. Huessman (Ed.), *Aggressive behavior* (pp. 153–186). New York: Plenum.

Jenkins, H. (1993). "Going bonkers!" Children, play and *Pee-wee.* In C. Penley & S. Willis (Eds.), *Male trouble* (pp. 157–182). Minneapolis: University of Minnesota Press.

Lemish, D. (1987). Viewers in diapers: The early development of television viewing. In T. Lindlof (Ed.), *Natural audiences: Qualitative research of media uses and effects* (pp. 33–57). Norwood, NJ: Ablex.

Lemish, D. (1997a). Kindergartners' understandings of television: A cross cultural comparison. *Communication Studies, 48*(2), 109–126.

Lemish, D. (1997b). The school as a wrestling arena: The modeling of a television series. *Communication: European Journal of Communication Research, 22*(4), 395–418.

Lemish, D. (1998). Spice Girls' talk: A case study in the development of gendered identity. In S. A. Inness (Ed.), *Millennium girls: Today's girls around the world* (pp. 145–167). New York: Rowman and Littlefield.

Lemish, D. (2006). *Children and television: A global perspective.* Oxford: Blackwell.

Lindlof, T. R., & Taylor, B. C. (2002). *Qualitative communication research method.* Thousand Oaks, CA: Sage.

Livingstone, S., & Bovill, M. (Eds.). (2001). *Children and their changing media environment: A European comparative study.* Mahwah, NJ: Lawrence Erlbaum.

Livingstone, S., & Lemish, D. (2001). Doing comparative research with children and young people. In S. Livingstone & M. Bovill (Eds.), *Children and their changing media environment: A European comparative study* (pp. 31–50). Mahwah, NJ: Lawrence Erlbaum.

Macklin, M. C., & Carlson, L. (Eds.). (1999). *Advertising to children: Concepts and controversies.* Thousand Oaks, CA: Sage.

Mahon, A., Glendinning, C., Clarke, K., & Craig, G. (1996). Researching children: methods and ethics. *Children and Society, 10,* 145–154.

Malamuth, N. M., & Impett, E. A. (2001). Research on sex in the media: What do we know about effects on children and adolescents? In D. G. Singer & J. L. Singer (Eds.), *Handbook of children and the media* (pp. 269–287). Thousand Oaks, CA: Sage.

Mazzarella, S. R., & Pecora, N. (Eds.). (1999). *Growing up girls: Popular culture and the construction of identity.* New York: Peter Lang.

Meyer, M. (Ed.). (1986). *Children and the formal features of television.* Munich: K. G. Saur.

Paik, H., & Comstock, G. (1994). The effects of television violence on antisocial behavior: A meta-analysis. *Communication Research, 21*(4), 516–546.

Rakow, L. (1986). Rethinking gender research in communication. *Journal of Communication, 36*(4), 11–26.

Reinard, J. (1998). *Introduction to communication research.* Boston: McGraw-Hill.

Reinharz, S. (1992). *Feminist methods in social research.* Oxford: Oxford University Press.

Rosenkoetter, L. I. (2001). Television and morality. In D. G. Singer & J. L. Singer (Eds.), *Handbook of children and the media* (pp. 463–473). Thousand Oaks, CA: Sage.

Seiter, E. (2005). *The Internet playground: Children's access, entertainment, and miseducation*. New York: Peter Lang.

Smith, T. L., & Wilson, B. J. (2002). Children's comprehension of and fear reactions to television news. *Media Psychology, 4*, 1–26.

Tobin, J. (2000). *"Good guys don't wear hats": Children's talk about the media*. New York: Teachers College Press.

Van Zoonen, L. (1994). *Feminist media studies*. London: Sage.

Wartella, E., Scantlin, R., Kotler, J., Huston, A. C., & Donnerstein, E. (2000). Effects of sexual content in the media on children and adolescents. In C. von Feilitzen & U. Carlsoon (Eds.), *Children in the new media landscape: Games, pornography, perceptions* (pp. 141–153). Göteborg University: UNESCO International Clearinghouse on Children and Violence on the Screen.

Watt, J. H., & van den Berg, S. A. (1995). *Research methods for communication science*. Boston: Allyn and Bacon.

Wimmer, R. D., & Dominick, J. R. (1997). *Mass media research: An introduction* (5th ed.). Belmont, CA: Wadsworth.

CHAPTER SIX

Who's Looking out for the Kids?

How Advocates Use Media Research to Promote Children's Interests

KATHARINE E. HEINTZ-KNOWLES

During graduate school in Boston, I had my first taste of media advocacy: a one-semester internship with Action for Children's Television (ACT). It was 1984, and ACT was working to drum up support for the Children's Television Education Act, a bill designed to require broadcast stations to air a minimum weekly number of hours of educational programming for children. (See chapter 2 for a complete history of the regulation of children's media.) I worked with ACT president Peggy Charren on informational brochures to send to the members of the U.S. Congress. It was exhilarating to see my accumulating knowledge put to real-world use. I left Boston to pursue further graduate study, feeling confident that I would make a difference in the children's television world if I could only become a better researcher.

I was fortunate to continue my graduate studies with a mentor who believed in using research to address social problems.[1] Together we worked on projects that advanced discussions of children and media both inside and outside the "Ivory Tower." As a graduate research assistant, I worked on a survey report that was used by the Federal Communications Commission (FCC) in its decision-making process regarding broadcast deregulation (Wartella et al., 1990). Those early experiences of putting academic research to use for the public good whet my appetite for continuing to form relationships with advocates and others interested in improving children's media.

For over a decade I have been working with nonprofit organizations interested in improving the quality of media for children. Some organizations advocate for change in media policy; others provide information and education for the public and/or media creators. But the one thing they have in common is the need for research. According to Patti Miller, director of the Children and the Media Program at Children Now, an Oakland, California–based advocacy organization, "Without research, you have no credibility. It's irresponsible to ask for change without evidence to back up your requests" (personal communication, October 2005).

In a review of the history and effectiveness of children's advocacy groups, Laurie Trotta (2001) outlined the various methods used for initiating change in children's media: working within government channels to effect policy change; providing information and/or positive reinforcement (that is, awards) for entertainment-industry personnel; sponsoring independent research on media use and effects; working with the media industries as consultants or technical experts; developing media literacy programs and materials; and organizing protests, campaigns, and boycotts to pressure broadcasters, advertisers, or decision-makers. These methods can be employed singly or in combination, and the most influential groups practice virtually all of these strategies to target three main audiences: policymakers, industry decision-makers, and the public.

How effective are advocacy groups at influencing the content of children's media? According to Trotta (2001, p. 701), "The advocacy movement has had an effect on building awareness of issues, motivating and inspiring industry professionals, and utilizing government processes to lobby for change." As evidence of this, she cites the results of a 1999 survey of senior-level creative executives in children's programming: 40 percent said that advocacy groups provide a valuable contribution to the children's TV industry; 60 percent said they had received useful information from advocates; and half believed advocacy groups were actually making an impact. Those are pretty powerful numbers, and are a testament to the role played by "watchdogs" in our commercial media environment.

In this chapter I will describe three strategies taken by different organizations to effect change in children's media. In the first example, I describe an effort by Children Now to influence regulatory policy regarding television station ownership. They submitted evidence to the FCC indicating that relaxing ownership rules could negatively impact children. The second example describes how the Frameworks Institute, based in Washington, D.C., used media research to demonstrate that public opinion is influenced by media content. They used this evidence to argue that reframing youth issues in the media can change public opinion. Finally, I describe current efforts by the Kaiser Family Foundation to impact media content through the development of partnerships with media companies.

Influence on Media Policy

In September 2002 the FCC issued a notice of proposed rulemaking (NPRM) announcing its biennial review of the commission's broadcast ownership rules. One issue addressed during this review was whether or not to relax or eliminate the limitations on a single corporation's ownership of multiple television stations in one market. Prior to 1999, corporations were limited to just one station in any market area. These restrictions were considered necessary to preserve three goals: (1) diversity (of viewpoints and program genres), (2) competition (among outlets to best serve the audience), and (3) localism (based on the assumption that local owners are more responsive to the needs of the local community) (FCC, 2002).

In 1999, however, the FCC determined that the growth in the number and variety of media outlets in most markets provided sufficient competition and substantial public service benefits. They reasoned that the restrictions on ownership to just one station were unnecessary and modified the rule to allow ownership of two stations in the same market (FCC, 1999). The 2002 NPRM suggested that the mandated review of the ownership rules could result in further modification or even elimination of the ownership limits. But in order to make a well-informed decision, the FCC commissioned a number of studies (through their Media Ownership Working Group) and invited other organizations to provide empirical evidence as well.

Children Now objected to the proposed elimination of ownership restrictions. The organization believed that children's interests were short-changed when ownership diversity was not mandated. They were concerned that concentration of station ownership would reduce the amount and diversity of children's programs available, and they wanted to remind the FCC that children are an important part of the public, whose interest broadcasters are mandated to serve. Essentially, the argument Children Now wanted to make was that relaxing or eliminating the ownership rules would negatively impact children in two ways: (1) by reducing the amount of time devoted to children's programming and (2) by reducing the diversity of children's programs available. But Children Now needed evidence to back up their claims. Because the time allowed to file comments with the FCC is limited, the organization was under pressure to design and conduct a study on a very tight schedule. I had the opportunity to work on this study with Children Now.

In order to support its claims, Children Now needed to be able to show that when one corporation owns more than one station in a single market, the co-owned stations air fewer hours of children's programming overall, and fewer different programs than the independently owned stations. This meant finding a market with both co-owned and independently owned stations so the programming schedules could be compared. It turns out that the FCC had previously allowed News Corporation (in 2001) and Viacom (in 2002) to purchase second stations in the Los Angeles market, creating two duopolies in this market.[2]

This situation made Los Angeles the perfect market for a comparative case study. We could compare program offerings *over time* as well as *between stations*. First, we could examine the amount and types of children's programs available *prior* to the creation of the duopolies and compare it with the amount and types available *after* the creation of the duopolies. We could look specifically at the stations that were previously independent and see if the amount and number of children's programs aired on these stations changed with the conglomeration. Second, we could compare the programming offered by the duopoly stations with that provided by independently owned stations. We hypothesized that the duopoly stations would have fewer hours of children's programs and less diversity among their program offerings than the independently owned stations.

We decided to compare the program schedules of the commercial broadcast stations in L.A. during one week in February, with a five-year period between samples. We chose the month of February because it was neither summer nor a holiday season, so it should be representative of the stations' "normal" schedules. One week of the schedule was considered adequate for comparison since there is little variation in weekly children's programming schedules. The five-year period was chosen because it allowed us to sample from the year just prior to the FCC's initial modification of the ownership rules and to sample from the then-current schedule. We did need to be careful to ensure that this time period allowed us to isolate the creation of the duopolies as *the only possible explanation* for predicted changes in programming. Since ownership or network affiliation of the nonduopoly stations did not change and there were no relevant changes in the Los Angeles media market in that time, we were confident that we could argue that any differences discovered were a result of concentration of ownership.

The information we needed was easy to find. We obtained copies of *TV Guide* for the Los Angeles market for the two sample weeks. To make sure we identified all of the children's programs available in the market, our sample included all programs that met at least one of the following criteria: (1) they were listed in *TV Guide* with a TV-Y or a TV-Y7 rating[3]; (2) they were listed in *TV Guide* with a descriptor such as "children," "cartoon," "teenager," or "educational"; or (3) they were listed in a station's FCC Children's Television Programming Report.[4]

Once the sample was collected, we analyzed the data and made three important discoveries. First, the number of children's series broadcast in Los Angeles decreased by nearly half between 1998 and 2003. Most of the decreases in the number of children's series in Los Angeles were from three of the four stations that are part of duopolies. Second, the number of hours devoted to children's programming each week decreased by more than 50 percent between 1998 and 2003. The largest decreases in programming hours came from stations that are part of media duopolies. Third, children's programs were almost four times more likely to be repurposed (shown on more than one station in the same market) in 2003 than in 1998. All of the repurposing occurred between broadcast and cable outlets that were owned by the same media companies. (For example, all of the children's programs that aired on the local CBS affiliate were also available locally on Nickelodeon. CBS and Nickelodeon are both owned by the same parent company, Viacom.)

Children Now filed the report with the FCC and asked the commission to make three accommodations: (1) prohibit duopoly stations from sharing children's programming, (2) require a minimum amount of original programming, and (3) conduct further research on the impact of media consolidation on children.

When the commission released its report and order on July 2, 2003, it did indeed modify the ownership rule, relaxing the restrictions on multiple station ownership in the same market. However, the report submitted by Children Now was referenced multiple times *and resulted in a significant stipulation.* According to the report and order (FCC, 2003):

> We share the concern of Children Now that the diversity of children's educational and informational programming could be reduced if commonly owned stations in the same market air the same children's programming. . . . We therefore clarify that where two or more stations in a market are commonly owned and air the same children's educational and informational program, only one of the stations may count the program toward the three-hour processing guideline.

So while the FCC did make major changes that benefit station owners, they also acknowledged the stations' obligations to children. The FCC chose to act on the issue of repurposing by requiring commonly owned stations to air unique educational/informational (E/I) programs to meet the standards of the Children's Television Act. And the rationale for their decision was a small case study, carefully thought out but quickly conducted, that went right to the heart of the matter. Without this evidence, it is likely that the prohibition of repurposing of E/I programs would never have been included in the 2003 report and order. Children Now's Christy Glaubke summed it up: "This was a small study that didn't cost much, but had an impact on policy. I think it shows that—even on a limited budget and with time constraints—you can conduct really important research and make a difference" (personal conversation, October 2005).

Influence on Public Opinion

In April 2000 I was invited to participate in the White House Conference on Teens, hosted by then First Lady Hillary Rodham Clinton. The invitation was a result of a project I was working on with the Frameworks Institute, an organization committed to helping advocates discuss issues in a way that can change public opinion and, ultimately, public policy.

Decades of research on agenda setting and cultivation have shown that the news and entertainment media are instrumental in shaping the pictures in our heads. Not only do media tell audiences *what issues/topics to think about* (agenda setting), but the ways the issues are framed/presented influence *what audiences know and believe* about the issues/topics (cultivation) (see Bryant & Zillman, 2002). (Refer to chapter 10 of this book for a thorough discussion of cultivation studies of youth.) The folks at the Frameworks Institute had a long history of examining the frames used in news stories and linking those to opinions and beliefs of U.S. adults, but they had yet to apply the concept of framing to entertainment media. The study I conducted for them was the first—and only—such study they've sponsored, and the results continue to inform their work.

The project I was part of was funded by the W. T. Grant Foundation and called "Reframing Youth Issues." The goal for W. T. Grant was to develop a strategy for youth advocates to change the way youth issues are presented in the public arena. In a 1997 editorial in the *Journal of Adolescent Health*, Dr. Karen Hein, president of the W. T. Grant Foundation, offered several examples of public policy initiatives that went directly counter to the scientific evidence regarding adolescent health. For example, although evidence showed juvenile crime on the decline and teens as much more likely to be involved in crime as victims than as perpetrators, the U.S. House of Representatives in 1997 overwhelmingly approved the Juvenile Crime Control Act, to award grants to states that changed their laws to punish juveniles more severely.

This and other actions that directly contradicted both the current conditions and best interests of U.S. youth led Dr. Hein to express concern that most American adults viewed youth as the *source* of problems rather than a *resource* to solve problems. In our increasingly age-segregated society, she rightly acknowledged the role of media as many adults' primary source of information about teens, and called upon youth professionals to work to change public opinion by *reframing* the way youth are talked about (Hein, 1997). To achieve that change, the W. T. Grant Foundation contracted with the Frameworks Institute.

The Frameworks model involves three types of analyses: (1) discover how Americans think about particular issues, (2) examine how media frame these same issues, and (3) discuss the implications these frames of reference have for public policies.

The first part of the "Reframing Youth Issues" project was already well under way when I came on board. Surveys and focus groups were conducted to discover prevailing adult attitudes toward American youth. I was one of the researchers involved in the examination of how media frame youth. In order to get a well-rounded picture of the ways that youth are shown and talked about in media, the project involved examination of both news and entertainment content. I led the team that examined entertainment media, specifically prime-time network television programming.

Because the project was designed to examine whether or not messages about youth in the media were consistent with the opinions that adults hold regarding youth, we started with the information from surveys and focus groups about how American adults think about youth. Some of the highlights (lowlights?) of this research included: (1) adults believe that teens today are more selfish and materialistic than in the past; (2) adults see teens as immature, irresponsible, and lacking self-discipline; (3) adults see kids' problems as a result of irresponsible parenting more than social/economic pressures; (4) adults see teens as lazy and unwilling to give their time to others (Frameworks Institute, 2001).

Taking this information and making it work for a quantitative content analysis was a challenge. For example, how do we quantify the *opinion* that kids today are less motivated and more selfish than they were in the past? How do we observe the *pressures* teens feel? Because we cannot get inside the heads of fictional characters, we designed a study that examined what youth characters *do and say* on television programs and *how they are talked about* by adult characters. We catalogued the *problems* youth characters had—or were reported to have—and the *actions* they took to solve them. We recorded the *activities* youth characters engaged in, and how *competent* they were shown to be in these activities.

For another project, my team had recorded three episodes of every prime-time entertainment series on the six broadcast networks during fall 1999.[5] From this large sample, we were able to identify the subset of programs that contained any youth characters. But, because Frameworks needed this report quickly, we couldn't do the in-depth analysis of all characters in all episodes. Instead, we randomly selected one episode of each program in the subset for further analysis. For purposes of this study, *youth characters* were defined as middle school–aged through college-aged (approximately twelve to twenty-three years old). We examined a total of 163 youth characters in 92 program episodes across the six networks.

The analysis revealed a world in which youth characters were independent and unconnected to family and the larger community. In the world of TV adolescents, problems were mainly social in nature, and caused by teens or their ineffective parents. TV youth did not require anyone's help beyond their small immediate peer group, and were considered immature and childlike by adult characters. These findings were consistent with the survey data showing adults' perceptions of teens as self-absorbed, immature, and interested only in trivial matters. According to Frameworks president Susan Bales (personal conversation, December 2005),

> What is most striking to the audiences who hear about this project is not what is shown in prime time, but what is *not shown*. In this sample, very few youth held jobs or were shown doing chores around the house. While school was a common backdrop for youth characters, they were twice as likely to be shown socializing there than engaging in academic work. And not one single teen character was shown dealing with an issue outside of his or her own experience—like homelessness, poverty, or environmental issues.

This study provided powerful support for Frameworks's contention that the ways that youth are framed in media are consistent with how American adults view youth, but not with the real-world indicators of youth.[6] We can conclude that in the absence of real-world information about teens, people rely on the consistent messages from media to form the pictures in their heads. And those pictures in their heads inform their decision-making about real-world teens. So in order to achieve the goal of changing public opinion, Frameworks proposed that advocates work to change the ways media represent teens.

But is there evidence that changing media frames can change public opinion? Yes. Take, for example, a survey of Minnesota adults conducted by Frameworks in 2001. Two sets of surveys were used with the sample: one in which opinion items were asked with no preliminary questions, and one in which respondents were asked "priming" questions about teens' involvement with sports, arts, or volunteerism prior to the same opinion items. The survey respondents who were exposed to a series of primes to cue an image of teens in sports, arts, or volunteerism had an improved image of teens, a heightened sense of the importance of investing in youth, a greater desire to fund programs for youth, and a greater sense of the importance of a variety of policies to benefit youth (Bostrom, 2002).

These results were so compelling, in fact, that the Minnesota Commission on Out-of-School Time (MCOST), which contracted with Frameworks for the survey research, wrote its culminating report emphasizing the new frame, and have already seen evidence of new thinking in their state. According to Ann Lochner, assistant director of MCOST (personal communication, 2005), University of Minnesota president Brian Bruininks

awarded MCOST a multiyear grant to study the relationship between out-of-school programs and positive youth development. As well, the newly elected mayor of St. Paul made
out-of-school time a key issue in his campaign, promoting himself as the "superintendent
of second-shift learning." Clearly there has been a shift in thinking and talking about adolescents, and this shift can only work to benefit the youth of this state.

Influence on Content Creators

The Kaiser Family Foundation, based in Palo Alto, California, is one of the most active
organizations working to use entertainment media in support of child and adolescent
health. The foundation sponsors research on the uses and content of popular media, and
then uses these results to build public education partnerships with media creators. In the
United States, these partnerships are collaborations between Kaiser and media companies
like MTV, BET, Univision, and Viacom, and involve mutual contributions.

> Kaiser and the media company enter into an agreement to provide financial and substantive expert-
> ise that goes beyond typical public service efforts. Among Kaiser's contributions are issues research;
> briefings for writers, producers, and other media staff; substantive guidance on message develop-
> ment; and funds to support program production and the creation of informational resources for con-
> sumers. The media partner contributes creative and communications expertise; on-air programming
> on the issues addressed by the campaign; and guaranteed placement of the PSAs and other con-
> tent to reach target audiences. (James et al., 2005, p. 856)

The record is impressive. Since beginning the partnership program in 1997, Kaiser has produced or consulted on more than forty original television programs and dozens of ongoing
series, radio and television public service announcements (PSAs), and outdoor advertisements on buses and billboards. Taken together, Kaiser's U.S. campaigns have delivered information about HIV/AIDS and related issues to millions of young people (James et al.,
2005).

In 1996 I worked with the foundation on a study of sexual content in popular daytime
soap operas. They were working in partnership with Population Communications
International on a meeting with soap-opera creative personnel, Soap Summit II, and felt
that a research study documenting how sexual relationships were depicted on soap operas
could facilitate dialogue with content creators on ways to use this medium to present
responsible sexuality.

The soap-opera genre is popular with young people around the world. In fact, the
International Clearinghouse on Children, Youth and Media in 2004 chose for its annual
yearbook the topic of young people, soap operas, and reality TV. The collection of research
articles in the yearbook shows that soap operas (also called telenovelas and serial dramas)
are among the most popular programs for children and adolescents in Europe, Asia, South
America, and the United States (Von Feilitzen, 2004). And these programs are not only
popular internationally, but they are often sources of social learning and identification for
young viewers. Results from studies conducted around the globe show that young viewers

use soaps as an information resource and often believe that soap operas reflect real life. Teens report learning about relationship issues from soaps and comparing their own experiences with soap characters' (Von Feilitzen, 2004). Guided by the theoretical foundations of cognitive social learning and cultivation, Kaiser supported the notion that responsible and healthy depictions of sexual activity on popular programs can positively impact viewers' attitudes and behaviors. The goal was to encourage creators *who were already crafting storylines heavy with sexual content* to incorporate messages related to healthy sexuality.

The first Soap Summit had proven effective at motivating at least one creative team to script an Emmy award–winning story arc about sexual responsibility. According to David Poindexter (1996), president of Population Communications International,

> The best way to describe the first SOAP SUMMIT is to quote some ad lib remarks delivered at the conclusion of the summit by Wendy Riche, Executive Producer, *General Hospital*. "I would like to thank you. I was not aware, and I don't think a lot of us were aware of what we were in for here. I think this group was inspiring and stimulating. We're all sort of chattering about 'we could do this and we could do that.' What it's done is informed us and given us an inspiration to the enormous responsibility that we carry. We appreciate it."
>
> *General Hospital* went to create a six month story line during which one of their young stars became infected with, and finally died of AIDS, and his young wife became HIV positive. *GH* won the EMMY for best daytime serial this year. The episode they chose for screening by the final judging panel was the one during which the AIDS infected actor died.

The second Soap Summit, then, hoped to build on the success of the first and motivate more creative teams to incorporate issues of sexual health and responsibility in their storylines. The content analysis was designed to provide a snapshot of the relational lives of soap opera characters, highlighting opportunities for including more messages about healthy sexuality. Soap operas are a particularly challenging genre to analyze because of the ongoing nature of storylines and the longevity and history of the characters. Soap opera characters tend to have more complicated relational lives than characters in other types of series, due not only to the nature of the genre itself (emphasis on relationships more than action) but also to the longevity of series, where some characters have been developing for decades. It is not unusual for characters to have had prior relationships with many characters, and to be tied to others in a complex web of family relationships. And longtime soap-opera viewers know these character histories and evaluate current behaviors in the context of past behaviors. In this project, then, we attempted to understand the sexual behaviors identified in the larger context of the program rather than as discrete, disconnected behaviors. So the snapshot we wanted to capture might be thought of as using time-lapse photography.

Soap opera storylines build more slowly than those of weekly series. Thus, if we wanted to be able to observe sexual relationships in progress, it was necessary to capture more episodes than we typically examine for a prime-time series content analysis. For this study, my team[7] analyzed ten hours of each of the ten nationally televised daytime soap operas airing over a five-week period in May and June 1996. We analyzed all sexual encounters— identifying discrete verbal and visual behaviors—specifically examining the following: (1)

the type(s) of behavior shown or talked about (ranging from flirting to sexual intercourse); (2) the participants involved, and their relationship to each other; (3) the participants' motivations for sexual activity (such as to establish a relationship, further a career, or achieve pregnancy); (4) the short-term and long-term outcomes of the activity (such as benefiting relationship, breaking up, or feeling guilty); (5) discussion or depiction of planning for and/or consequences of sexual activity (for example, display or discussion of condom use, or waiting).

Our analysis discovered a world where sexual activity was frequent, with an average of six sexual behaviors per program hour. These behaviors were twice as likely to be visual than verbal depictions, although most visually depicted behaviors involved "modest" sexual behaviors like kissing and caressing. Most sexual interactions occurred between participants involved in established relationships with each other and were shown to have positive outcomes for the participants. The few discussions and depictions of planning and consequences were largely confined to a few discrete storylines dealing with consequences (female characters discussing their pregnancies with others).

Instead of using this information to criticize the media, Kaiser and PCI encouraged creators to consider ways of creating the same type of drama through the inclusion of messages regarding sexual health. There was much discussion among network executives and creative personnel as to what would be considered "acceptable" to the networks, and what would interest, and not alienate, the audience. The creators' first priority was making an entertaining program that would attract viewers; the challenge for advocates and educators is providing information that can work with the soaps' production needs.

But is there evidence that health-related messages in entertainment *really* impact viewers? Absolutely. According to Jeffrey Koplan (1999), a survey of regular soap-opera viewers found that nearly half reported that they learned about diseases and how to prevent them from soap operas. In response to health information presented through soap-opera characters, 25 percent of regular viewers had shared the health information with friends and family members, 13 percent had urged someone close to them to take a health-related action, 7 percent had themselves visited a clinic or a doctor, and 6 percent had done something to prevent the problem.

And Kaiser's own research indicates that entertainment education has a strong impact. In a survey designed to assess the reach and effectiveness of its campaign with MTV, the foundation found that a majority of the sixteen- to twenty-four-year-olds surveyed reported having seen the sexual health ads on MTV, and a third reported seeing them multiple times. What's more, nearly two thirds of the young people surveyed said they learned something new, and half reported having made behavior changes as a result of the information they received from the campaign with MTV (Rideout, 2003).

This type of evidence reinforces the partnership goals of the Kaiser Family Foundation. According to Tina Hoff, director of the Partnership Program, "From our research, we know that young people want to know more about issues, like HIV and related topics, so we seek out partnerships with media that reach them to develop appealing public education campaigns. By taking a business approach, we are able to show media that they can both do well commercially and do good, socially" (personal conversation, December 2005).

In the end, designing and conducting research projects for advocates and other organizations is exciting and challenging. It forces the researcher to show why and how the work is useful and important to people outside of academe. And it challenges people who make decisions about media for children and youth to accept responsibility for their actions and acknowledge the power of media. Armed with research evidence to support positive changes in media, groups interested in children can continue to exert pressure on media, the public, and policymakers to do good for kids.

DISCUSSION QUESTIONS

1   Suppose the FCC were considering eliminating the three-hour rule regarding children's educational programming. A children's advocacy organization has asked you to conduct a study that will show the FCC that this type of regulation is necessary. What type of study would you design?

2   There is mounting evidence to support the connection between heavy television viewing and childhood obesity. Suppose you have been asked to make recommendations to media creators about ways to use media to address this issue. What types of media would you target? What types of content? What types of messages would you recommend?

3   Suppose the Frameworks Institute discovered that most American adults believe that young children are spoiled and disrespectful of adults. You have been asked to make recommendations to advocates about how to change that perception. What type(s) of research would you undertake? What type(s) of recommendations would you make?

NOTES

1   Thanks to Dr. Ellen Wartella for her guidance and friendship.

2   A duopoly is created when one company owns two stations in the same market. There were actually three duopolies in Los Angeles, as General Electric owned both KNBC and the local Telemundo station. However, since Telemundo was not one of the primary commercial broadcast stations, it was not included in the study.

3   In response to tremendous growth in the number of television stations available to most U.S. households, and the concern about children's exposure to inappropriate content, the 1996 Telecommunications Act required that all new television sets be equipped with a device allowing parents to block programming they considered objectionable or harmful to their children. The device, called the V-chip, works in conjunction with a rating system developed by entertainment-industry representatives. Beginning in January 1997, broadcast television programs (except news and sports) are labeled with a rating identifying the age-appropriateness of the content. Two ratings specifically apply to children's programs: TV-Y and TV-Y7. According to the TV Parental Guidelines Monitoring Board, TV-Y refers to programs that are considered appropriate for *all children*. Designed for a very young audience, including children ages two to six, these programs are not expected to frighten younger children. The TV-Y7 rating refers to programs directed to children *ages 7 and above*.

Themes in these programs may include mild fantasy violence or comedic violence, or may frighten children under age seven. For more information about TV ratings and the V-chip, visit www.tvguide-lines.org. See also chapter 2 in this book for more information on the ratings.

4   The 1990 Children's Television Act requires commercial broadcast stations to "serve the educational and informational needs of children through its overall programming, including programming designed specifically to serve these needs ('core programming')." To demonstrate compliance, each commercial TV station must complete and file with the Federal Communications Commission quarterly reports regarding their educational programming and make these reports available to the public. These reports must identify the stations' core programming and other efforts to comply with their educational programming obligations. These reports were consulted in case appropriate programs were not labeled or were mislabeled in *TV Guide*.

5   Thanks to Jennifer Henderson and Meredith Li-Vollmer for their work on this project. The programs were originally captured for use in *Fall Colors, 1999* for Children Now (2000).

6   "Real-world indicators" refers to statistics describing the experiences of youth in the United States. Two real-world indicators that are relevant to this study are youth employment and civic involvement. Surveys sponsored by the Frameworks Institute indicated that adults thought that teens today were less involved in their community and less likely to hold a job than in the past. Our analysis showed that prime-time depictions of teens supported this notion, as teen characters were almost never shown volunteering or employed. But, according to national databases and trend analysis, the percentage of youth who work part-time has remained constant or risen a bit since 1970, and the proportions of high school students who volunteer have not changed since 1975 (Frameworks Institute, 2001).

7   Thanks to Kristin Engstrand, Amy Shively, Susannah Stern, and Aaron Delwiche for their work on this project.

REFERENCES

Bostrom, M. (2002). *Creativity, caring, and teamwork: Using positive teen imagery to build support for policy.* A priming survey analysis prepared for the Frameworks Institute, Washington, D.C.

Bryant, J., & Zillman, D. (Eds.). (2002). *Media effects: Advances in theory and research* (2nd ed.). Mahwah, NJ: Lawrence Earlbaum.

Children Now (2000). *Fall colors 1999 prime time diversity report.* Oakland, CA: Children Now.

Federal Communications Commission. (1999). *Report and order* (FCC 99–209).

Federal Communications Commission. (2002). *Notice of proposed rule making* (FCC 02–249).

Federal Communications Commission. (2003). *Report and order and notice of proposed rule making* (FCC 03–127).

Frameworks Institute. (2001). *Reframing youth issues for public consideration and support: A Frameworks message memo.* Retrieved December 1, 2005, from http://www.frameworksinstitute.org/products/reframing.pdf

Hein, K. (1997). Framing and reframing. *Journal of Adolescent Health, 21,* 215–217.

James, M., Hoff, T., Davis, J., & Graham, R. (2005). Grant watch report: Leveraging the power of the media to combat HIV/AIDS. *Health Affairs, 24*(3), 854–857.

Koplan, J. (1999). *Keynote address.* Proceedings of Soap Summit IV. Burbank, CA: Population Communications International. Retrieved December 1, 2005, from http://www.soapsummit.org/transcripts/koplan_ss4_keynote.htm.

Poindexter, D. (1996, September 6). *Welcoming remarks*. Proceedings of Soap Summit II, Burbank, CA: Population Communications International.

Rideout, V. (2003). *Reaching the MTV generation: Recent research on the impact of the Kaiser Family Foundation/MTV public education campaign on sexual health.* Menlo Park, CA: Kaiser Family Foundation.

Trotta, L. (2001). Children's advocacy groups: A history and analysis. In D. R. Singer & J. L. Singer (Eds.), *Handbook of children and the media* (pp. 699–720). Thousand Oaks, CA: Sage.

Von Feilitzen, C. (2004). Introduction. In C. Von Feilitzen (Ed.), *Young people, soap operas and reality TV* (pp. 9–45). Göteborg, Sweden: International Clearinghouse on Children, Youth and Media.

Wartella, E., Heintz, K. E., Aidman, A., & Mazzarella, S. (1990). Television and beyond: Children's video media in one community. *Communication Research, 17*(1), 45–64.

The Concerns

Media Use, Content, and Effects

CHAPTER SEVEN

Advertising and Consumer Development

In the Driver's Seat or Being Taken for a Ride?

NANCY A. JENNINGS

SpongeBob SquarePants. Everywhere you go, there he is. SpongeBob appears on a variety of products including backpacks, comforters, disposable cameras, strollers, watches, portable CD players, and many more items. Indeed, there are 382 products listed for SpongeBob SquarePants in the Nickelodeon Shop (Shop.nickjr.com, n.d.), which does not include the SpongeBob-themed food products available at the local grocery—Kellogg's Pop-Tarts, Kraft Macaroni & Cheese, Oscar Mayer Lunchables, and Nabisco fruit snacks (Kiley, 2005). However, children are no strangers to commercial messages. Children have steadily grown in status as an audience of importance and value since the 1930s (Pecora, 1998). James McNeal (1992), a leading scholar in children's consumer behavior, suggests that marketers have realized that children are three markets in one—they spend their own money (current market), they influence their family's purchases (influence market), and through their own consumer experiences as children they can become brand loyal into adulthood (future market). This chapter will explore how children develop as consumers, looking at the different advertising practices that children encounter during children's television programming and examining the outcomes of an ever-increasingly child-friendly consumer environment. See also chapters 18 and 19 in this book for further discussions of children and consumer culture.

Socialization of the Child Consumer

Children are socialized into a number of roles through their varied life experiences with others, including their role as consumers. Scott Ward (1974, p. 2) defines consumer socialization of youth as "processes by which young people acquire skills, knowledge, and attitudes relevant to their functioning as consumers in the marketplace." This definition implies that there are stages in which a child learns about his or her consumer environment and what role he or she plays in the marketplace. Several scholars have developed theories about how children develop as consumers, acknowledging that children's cognitive and social development has an impact on their consumer knowledge, skills, and interactions (John, 1999; McNeal, 1992; Valkenburg & Cantor, 2001).

Children's consumer socialization starts at a very young age. According to Patti Valkenburg and Joanne Cantor (2001), infants and toddlers are able to express wants and preferences, which is the first stage of consumer development. Moreover, according to McNeal (1992, p. 9), "by the time a child can sit erect, he or she is placed in his or her culturally defined observation post high atop a shopping cart." This perch has been available for developing consumers since 1947, when a child seat was added to the original design of the shopping cart (Wohleber, 2004). However, today a child no longer even needs to sit erect in order to accompany parents to the store. Babies can be nestled in their observational perch with the addition of permanently attached infant carriers to the top of shopping carts (Linsen, 1989). From their observational post, children learn a great deal about different products and stores, enhancing their consumer knowledge and leading to more active consumer behavior. While toddlers begin to ask for products from parents at eighteen to twenty-four months (McNeal, 1992), Valkenburg and Cantor (2001, p. 64) suggest that they should still be considered primarily "*children* of consumers," since they are in the first stages of consumer development.

As children begin to better express themselves in the preschool years (ages two to five), they enter the next phase of consumer development, searching to fulfill their wants and preferences (Valkenburg & Cantor, 2001). As growing consumers, children climb out of the shopping cart and walk through the stores with their parents. Around age three or four, parents start to let their children choose some of their favorite products such as cereal or cookies (McNeal, 1992). Furthermore, around the age of four, children begin to make their own independent purchases in the presence of their parents (McNeal, 1992). Child-friendly shopping carts help make shopping a fun experience for these burgeoning consumers. In August 2001 McCue Corporation introduced the Bean, a shopping cart with an attached child's riding push toy such as a racecar (McCue Corporation, 2005). Children can ride in the car while the parent pushes the cart/car and fills up the basket. While these new carts provide a fun way for parents to harness their children's growing enthusiasm for exploring their consumer environment, McCue Corporation (2005) claims that they also may enhance the store's profits by as much as 20 percent per shopping trip.

In the early elementary years (ages five to eight), children continue to hone their skills as consumers by exercising their purchasing power, the third stage of consumer development (Valkenburg & Cantor, 2001). Between the ages of five and seven, children make their first independent purchase by themselves, without their parents nearby (McNeal, 1992). These years also are particularly important in children's understanding of advertising content. Deborah Roedder John (1999) suggests that most five-year-old children are able to distinguish commercials from other program content even though they may not be able to understand the persuasive intent of advertising. This skill is acquired by the age of seven or eight years. Finally, as children become increasingly aware of the persuasive nature of advertising, they begin to recognize bias and deception in advertising and develop skeptical or negative attitudes in regards to advertising. Therefore, by the age of eight, children are making independent purchases and becoming aware of the nature of advertising with increasing skepticism.

In the later elementary years (ages eight to twelve), children begin to evaluate products and their alternatives, the fourth and final step of consumer development. Around ages seven or eight, children begin "collecting" rather than simply "accumulating" items—that is, they pay more attention to details and draw distinctions between different objects (Acuff, 1997). Furthermore, by around age nine, children make fewer requests for advertised products than seven- to eight-year-olds, and they begin to make requests for useful items such as sport items and school stationery (Buijzen & Valkenburg, 2000). Finally, according to John (1999), in early adolescence (ages eleven to fourteen), children learn about specific advertising tactics and appeals used to persuade, which enhances their understanding of advertising intent. While clearly there is still room for growth, Valkenburg and Cantor (2001) contend that by age twelve, most children have experienced all characteristics of consumer behavior.

Role of Advertising in the Socialization Process

For many children growing up in the United States, childhood is full of media and marketing. Recent research indicates that children ages eight to eighteen spend the equivalent of a full-time job (forty-four and a half hours a week) with media, with television accounting for almost half of this amount (three hours a day, or twenty-one hours a week) (Rideout et al., 2005). Television viewing is also a dominant activity for young children; on average, children under the age of six watch a little over an hour (1:05) of television daily (Rideout et al., 2003). Considering the amount of television children watch, children's exposure to television advertising is potentially quite high. Indeed, estimates based on children's television viewing habits and television commercial frequency indicate that children's exposure to television advertising has been increasing over time, doubling from an average of about twenty thousand commercials per year in the late 1970s (Adler et al.,

1977) to more than forty thousand ads per year in the early 1990s (Kunkel & Gantz, 1992, as cited in Kunkel, 2001). It should come as no surprise, then, that Victor Strasburger and Barbara Wilson (2002) suggest that television advertising is perhaps the easiest way to reach children. Therefore, our discussion of advertising will begin with an exploration of the content of children's television advertising and then focus on children's cognitive, affective, and behavioral response to marketing strategies.

Content Analyses of Advertising Content

Very few content analyses have been conducted on children's advertising. In the early 1970s, F. Earle Barcus documented the state of advertising during children's television programming. His work set a precedent for the examination of nonprogram content and has been replicated and applied to television advertising in the 1980s (Condry et al., 1988), and 1990s (Byrd-Bredbenner, 2002; Kunkel & Gantz, 1992). To reflect on the growth of research in the field beginning in the 1970s, I will examine the nature of advertising during children's television programming since that time.

One of the first questions about children's advertising is: How much advertising do children see? On broadcast stations, the amount of time devoted to commercial content has increased since the 1970s. During the 1970s, Barcus (1975) reported an average of 7.9 minutes (13.2 percent of the viewing hour) per hour for commercials during children's programs on Saturday and Sunday. Advertising time increased slightly to an average of 8.16 minutes (13.6 percent) per hour during the 1980s (Condry et al., 1988) but jumped to 10.08 minutes per hour (16.8 percent) in the 1990s (Kunkel & Gantz, 1992). Some fluctuation was observed in the 1990s, but by the end of the decade advertisements for products accounted for an average of 9.5 minutes (15.8 percent) of the viewing hour (Byrd-Bredbenner, 2002). This may be a reflection of a desire for compliance with the Children's Television Act of 1990, which stipulates that commercial matter during children's programming should be limited to no more than 12 minutes per hour on weekdays and 10.5 minutes per hour on weekends.

Under a proposed ruling, however, the FCC redefined "commercial matter" to include "promotions of television programs or video programming services other than children's educational and informational programming" (FCC, 2004, p. 21). This new definition was to have become effective in spring 2006. However, after Viacom and the Walt Disney Company both petitioned the court to review this, the FCC agreed to postpone implementation of the change. Subsequently, on February 9, 2006, child advocate organizations such as Children Now and various representatives from the industry such as Viacom, the Walt Disney Company, and Fox Entertainment Group submitted a Joint Proposal (FCC-06–33A2) to the FCC which, among other things, suggested changing the promotions rule such that promotions for children's programs or age-appropriate content would not be considered commercial matter (FCC, 2006). Until 1999, time for program promotions hovered between one and two minutes per hour (Barcus, 1975; Condry et al., 1988; Kunkel & Gantz, 1992). However, in 1999 the time for program promotions jumped dramatically to almost five minutes per hour (Byrd-Bredbenner, 2002). Although the FCC has, as of September 2006, yet to announce a final decision regarding the Joint Proposal, it will be interesting to see what transpires during this time of debate about the nature of advertising and promotions directed to children.

This raises the question of what types of items are being advertised to children. Overall, research in the 1970s indicated that four product categories—toys, cereals, candies, and fast-food restaurants—accounted for the lion's share of the types of products advertised to children, 80 percent of all ads (Barcus, 1980). Studies conducted in the 1980s and early 1990s indicated that the four product categories from the 1970s still dominated the field, with some slight variation over time. In the mid-1970s, only about 18 percent of the commercials were for toys, while cereals (25 percent) and sweets (29 percent) accounted for the majority of the products advertised (Barcus, 1975). However, advertisements for toys grew from about 20 percent in 1983 to just over 36 percent of all products advertised in 1987 (Condry et al., 1988). Subsequently, there was less time for commercials for candies and cereals, reaching a low in 1985 of 14.5 percent and 20.5 percent, respectively (Condry et al., 1988). However, in 1990 the distribution of products returned to those found in the 1970s, with more commercials for cereals (31.2 percent) and snacks (32.4 percent), and less for toys (17.3 percent) (Kunkel & Gantz, 1992). Finally, seasonal variations have been noted in the research as well concerning the distribution of products advertised. Research in the 1970s and '80s indicated that during the pre-Christmas season, as early as October, toy ads comprised nearly half or more of the child-directed ads (Barcus, 1980; Condry et al., 1988).

Effects of Advertising on Children

Now that we know what advertising messages children see, what kind of effect might that have on their consumer development? Media researchers historically have analyzed media effects in terms of cognitive (knowledge), affective (attitude), and connotative (behavior) outcomes. Therefore, I will explore how advertising affects children along these lines as well.

Cognitive Effects

Much of the early research on children and advertising focused on understanding how children perceived and understood advertising content. Early research from the 1970s and '80s suggested that the majority of children could correctly label a commercial from program content by the age of five (Blosser & Roberts, 1985; Butter et al., 1981; Levin et al., 1982; Stephens & Stutts, 1982). However, young children made very rudimentary distinctions between commercials and programs. For example, younger children (ages five to eight) indicated length ("commercials are shorter than programs") and placement ("before or after show") as the discriminating factors between commercials and programs, whereas older children (ages nine to twelve) mentioned that "programs are supposed to entertain" and that "commercials sell, make money" (Ward, 1972, p. 40). Other research suggested that some children as young as the age of three years could distinguish between commercials and programs; however, research indicated that this skill improved dramatically with age (Butter et al., 1981; Levin et al., 1982; Stephens & Stutts, 1982).

Being able to distinguish a commercial from a program is just the beginning of understanding advertising. When do children understand that the ad is trying to get them to buy a product? Results of the various survey studies in the 1970s indicated that below age six the vast majority of children could not articulate the selling purpose of advertising (Adler et al., 1977; Bever et al., 1975; Donohue et al., 1978; Meyer et al., 1978; Roberts, 1979; Sheikh et al., 1974; Ward et al., 1977). Between kindergarten and third grade most children could express that advertising was intended to persuade.

As children develop beyond elementary school, a more complete and deeper understanding of persuasive intent and their consumer role develops. Adolescents have a more adult-like knowledge of advertiser tactics (Boush et al., 1994). Teenagers who know more about the marketplace are more likely to recognize persuasion in advertising, and are better able to detect whether ads are truthful or misleading (Mangleburg & Bristol, 1998).

Affective (Emotional) Effects

A consistent finding of the research has been that as children mature, they like commercials less and less. Julian Barling and Clive Fullagar (1983, p. 29) suggest that as children grow older they are "less entertained and more bored and irritated" by commercials. Glen Riecken and Ugur Yavas (1990) found that older children (ages eight to twelve) held a negative opinion of commercials, and most (nearly two thirds) said that commercials were annoying and in poor taste. High repetition of a commercial was also found to be annoying. In one study, boys who were exposed to the same commercial three to five times within a cartoon program tended to make remarks such as "Oh no, not again" or "not another one," indicating annoyance with the repetition (Gorn & Goldberg, 1980, p. 424).

At the same time that they begin to dislike advertising, children tend to grow more skeptical and less trusting of commercials. Very few older children express trust in commercials (Robertson & Rossiter, 1974). Research suggests that fourteen-year-olds were the most cynical, with almost a third (31 percent) indicating that commercials hardly ever tell the truth (Meyer & Hexamer, 1981). Indeed, David Boush and his colleagues (1994) found that by age thirteen children's knowledge of advertiser tactics resembles that of an adult, and this increased knowledge is related to being more skeptical of advertising.

Behavioral Effects

Children use the television as a source of consumer information. Early research indicated that television was a primary source for learning about products such as toys (Donohue, 1975;

Robertson & Rossiter, 1976; Caron & Ward, 1975), particularly for frequent viewers of television (Frideres, 1973). Some research suggested that even children who did not watch a lot of television heard about products advertised during children's programs from their friends (Frideres, 1973). Mothers of young children indicated that their children frequently recognized products they had seen advertised (Burr & Burr, 1977).

Children also seemed to express preferences for advertised products. Children were more likely to express preferences for toys and games following a peak advertising period for such products, such as after the pre-Christmas advertising period (Robertson & Rossiter, 1976). Also, use of premiums can have an impact on children's expressed preferences for products. Children who were exposed to advertising for a cereal that featured a premium indicated a preference for that cereal when given a choice of other advertised cereals (Heslop & Ryans, 1980).

Preferences for products often lead to requests for these products. Early research indicated that advertising can arouse interest in almost all children (over 90 percent) to request a product; however, fewer (only 57 percent) actually made the overt request (Sheikh & Moleski, 1977). Furthermore, research indicated that children are more likely to ask their mother and father together (43 percent) or just their mother (46.5 percent) rather than ask just their father (10.3 percent) for a product (Sheikh & Moleski, 1977). Much of the research regarding children's requests for products focused on their requests for toys during the Christmas season, a period of dramatic increase in toy advertising. A common method of data collection is for researchers to examine children's Christmas wishes in connection to their exposure to television advertising. One consistent finding from this line of research is that heavy exposure to television advertising does have an impact on the types of items children request as Christmas presents (Buijzen & Valkenburg, 2000; Robertson & Rossiter, 1977). A second consistent finding from these studies is that younger children were more likely to request advertised toys than older children (Buijzen & Valkenburg, 2000; Robertson & Rossiter, 1977). Clearly, advertising does have an impact on requests for products, particularly for younger children.

Legal and Ethical Issues in Children's Advertising

Since advertising does have an impact on children's consumer development, this raises ethical questions of advertising to children. Clearly, children are engaging in the consumer environment. McNeal (1999) estimates that children aged four to twelve, as current consumers, spent $35.6 billion in 2000, up from $2.2 billion in 1968, and influenced $290 billion in family purchases in 2000, up from around $50 billion in 1985. Moreover, retailers are trying to attract the child consumer through various practices such as displays at eye level for children, child-sized shopping carts, children's menus, and activities and events to make children feel special. Indeed, in 1991 nearly twice as many retailers (68 percent) had at least one policy or practice targeted toward children compared to 1984, when only 37 percent of retailers were child-oriented (McNeal, 1992). Children are acting as consumers, and retailers are treating them as such.

Yet questions arise as to whether advertising is doing more harm than good for children. As so clearly stated by Debra Goldman (1999, p. 20), "Marketers covet young customers for the same reason child advocates want to protect them: the belief that the young are vulnerable to marketing in a way that adult consumers are not." Indeed, as noted in the research, young children are still developing their consumer skills; therefore, children may be more susceptible to persuasive messages delivered through advertising, particularly when marketers are using strategies to specifically appeal to their target audience.

However, some marketers do seem to recognize the need to strategically appeal to the child yet be wary of deceptive or harmful practices. Marketing consultant Gene Del Vecchio (1997) argues that marketing can be beneficial to parents and children alike but cautions that marketers need to be certain that the benefits of a marketing program outweigh its negative consequences. Similarly, youth marketing consultant Dan Acuff (1997) suggests that it is the duty of those actively involved in the youth-product business to separate themselves from the driving forces of the marketplace and put the interests of the child first by considering whether or not the product or program empowers children. Acuff (1997) distinguishes empowering products or programs as "those which contribute in some significant way toward an individual's positive development" (p. 18) compared to disempowering products or programs that have a substantial negative impact on children. While Acuff (1997) submits that it is rare to find a product that is completely positive or negative, marketers need to examine the ultimate impact of the various aspects of the product or program, taking into consideration children's different stages of development and their cultural experiences.

Measures have been taken to protect children from harmful or deceptive practices. In terms of governmental regulation, the FCC has established public policy regarding children's advertising. In connection with actual content of children's advertising, the FCC has established a "clear separation" principle to mark a distinction between advertising and programming content (FCC, 1974). This "clear separation" principle attempts to address the limited abilities of children to distinguish program from commercial content and encompasses three areas of potentially deceptive practices—bumpers, host selling, and program-length commercials. Bumpers are short video segments shown before and after commercial breaks to indicate a change between program content and commercial content. Host selling is the use of characters from children's programs to promote products either during the program or in commercial blocks adjacent to the program in which they appear. While this was a prevalent practice in the beginning of 1950s, this practice was forbidden by the FCC in the 1970s (Alexander et al., 1999). Finally, although originally conceived as a program with a principal purpose of promoting products (particularly toys) to children, the FCC now defines a program-length commercial as showing a traditional commercial connected to a character during the program in which the character appears. For example, showing a commercial for the Dora Talking House during an episode of *Dora the Explorer* would be considered a violation of the new definition of a program-length commercial. (See chapter 2 for a complete history of the regulation of children's media.)

Self-regulatory steps have also been taken to protect children from deceptive advertising. In 1974 the Children's Advertising Review Unit (CARU) was established to monitor deceptive practices and provide guidelines for responsible advertising to children under the age of twelve (CARU, 2003). These guidelines encourage advertisers to take into consideration the development of the child in order to provide appropriate information and avoid misleading the child. For example, among the numerous suggestions, the guidelines offer procedures for effective use of disclaimers and disclosures and for presentation of premiums.

Disclaimers provide additional information about a product in order to avoid misleading the consumer. However, most disclaimers use adult-oriented language such as "some assembly is required" or "part of a balanced breakfast." Research suggested that children who are eight years old and younger often do not understand the disclaimer and show greater comprehension of the intent of the disclaimer when simpler language is used such as "you must put this together" (Liebert et al., 1977; Palmer & McDowell, 1981; Stutts & Hunnicutt, 1987). Therefore, CARU guidelines suggest that marketers use language that is age-appropriate and understandable for the targeted child audience.

Premiums are prizes that are offered with the target product to sway the consumer to buy the target product. For example, cereals that offer a *Chicken Little* toy inside the box would be enticing the consumer to purchase the cereal to get the toy. Research has found that when premiums were used in ads, they were more likely to be used in commercials for cereals (47 percent) in the 1970s (Barcus, 1975), and fast-food restaurants (36.2 percent) in the 1990s (Kunkel & Gantz, 1992). Research suggests that parents are conflicted about premiums; they indicate that they are likely to buy a product because their child requested the premium offered, but the majority of parents feel that premiums are overemphasized in commercials (Burr & Burr, 1977). In observations of families in the supermarket, very few children (9 percent) actually mentioned the prize as a reason to make a cereal purchase and children who did mention the premium were slightly more likely to get it (69 percent) than those who did not mention the premium (62 percent) (Atkin, 1978). CARU provides clear suggestions in consideration of premiums in advertising. Specifically, CARU indicates that the premium message should be secondary to the primary appeal for the target product and, similar to disclaimers and disclosures, the language used to explain the premium offer should be simple and understandable by young children.

Does self-regulation work? Overall, self-regulation does seem to have a positive impact on limiting deceptive practices in advertising directed toward children. An analysis of more than ten thousand commercials aired during children's programming in 1990 indicated that only 385 (3.7 percent) of the commercials contained violations of the CARU guidelines (Kunkel & Gantz, 1993). Violations relating to premiums accounted for the greatest number of violations (34.6 percent of all violations). The most common violation in regards to premiums was a failure to ensure that the promotion of the premium was clearly a secondary message. While the industry has been making efforts to comply with CARU guidelines, research needs to continue to monitor these actions. Furthermore, compliance does not address the larger questions raised about the very nature of advertising to children.

Future research needs to address these questions in a more contemporary setting as children encounter more and more advertising messages at home, at school, and everywhere in between.

In the Driver's Seat or Being Taken for a Ride?

As developing consumers, children take on many roles. At times, children are passengers, watching the consumer environment from the safety of a stroller or shopping cart. At other times, they are in the driver's seat, selecting items and making purchases. As children transition from passengers to drivers, they encounter persuasive messages and marketing strategies targeted directly to them. Parents need to take an active role in teaching their children the rules of the road to ensure that children don't get taken for a ride. Research has suggested that parents are able to counteract the negative consequences of advertising by being involved with their children (Buijzen & Valkenburg, 2003). While governmental policies and self-regulatory guidelines attempt to make a clear path for the growing consumer, children still need help navigating the marketplace. While it is impossible to clear the road of all hazardous conditions, with parental involvement, governmental oversight, and ethical marketing practices, the path to consumer development should be less treacherous and more easily traveled.

DISCUSSION QUESTIONS

1   Do commercials make children want to buy? What role does advertising play in our society? Does advertising create artificial needs for children?

2   Do you think that advertising should be regulated? If so, what would you propose? If not, who should be held accountable for outcomes from advertising exposure?

3   Do you believe that children are empowered or vulnerable? How does that affect your opinion about the outcomes of children's advertising?

EXERCISES

1   Do a content analysis of children's promotions. How much time is dedicated to nonprogram content? What types of products are advertised during children's programs? Are the program promotions for other children's programs? Are there differences between what you see on cable versus what you see on broadcast stations?

2   Visit a grocery store or shopping center. Is the retailer child-friendly? What types of practices are used to appeal to a child consumer? How does the child respond to these practices? Does the parent or caregiver seem to approve of these practices?

3   Visit a local shopping mall. What are the children wearing? How many children are wearing clothes with media characters or brand names? How many children are carrying toys

or other items that tout media characters? Is there a difference between what girls and boys are wearing and what characters they like? What brand names do you find?

REFERENCES

Acuff, D. (1997). *What kids buy and why: The psychology of marketing to kids.* New York: Free Press.

Adler, R. P., Friedlander, B. Z., Lesser, G. S., Meringoff, L., Robertson, T. S., Rossiter, J. R., & Ward, S. (1977). *Research on the effects of television advertising on children.* Washington, DC: United States Government Printing Office.

Alexander, A., Benjamin, L. M., Hoerrner, K. L, & Roe, D. (1999). "We'll be back in a moment": A content analysis of advertisements in children's television in the 1950s. In M. C. Macklin & L. Carlson (Eds.), *Advertising to children: Concepts and controversies.* (pp. 97–115). Thousand Oaks, CA: Sage.

Atkin, C. K. (1978). Observation of parent-child interaction in supermarket decision-making. *Journal of Marketing, 42*(4), 41-45.

Barcus, F. E. (1975). *Weekend commercial children's television—1975.* Cambridge, MA: Action for Children's Television.

Barcus, F. E. (1980). The nature of television advertising to children. In E. L. Palmer & A. Dorr (Eds.), *Children and the faces of television: Teaching, violence and selling* (pp. 273–285). New York: Academic Press.

Barling, J., & Fullagar, C. (1983). Children's attitudes to television advertisements: A factorial perspective. *Journal of Psychology, 113*(1), 25–30.

Bever, T. G., Smith, M. L., Bengen, B., & Johnson, T. G. (1975). Young viewers' troubling response to TV ads. *Harvard Business Review, 53*(6), 109–120.

Blosser, B. J., & Roberts, D. F. (1985). Age differences in children's perception of message intent: Responses to television news, commercials, educational spots, and public service announcements. *Communication Research, 12*(4), 455–484.

Boush, D. M., Friestad, M., & Rose, G. M. (1994). Adolescent skepticism toward TV advertising and knowledge of advertiser tactics. *Journal of Consumer Research, 21*(1), 165–175.

Buijzen, M., & Valkenburg, P. M. (2000). The impact of television advertising on children's Christmas wishes. *Journal of Broadcasting and Electronic Media, 44*(3), 456–470.

Buijzen, M., & Valkenburg, P. M. (2003). The effects of television advertising on materialism, parent-child conflict, and unhappiness: A review of research. *Applied Developmental Psychology, 24*(4), 437–456.

Burr, P. L., & Burr, R. (1977). Product recognition and premium appeal. *Journal of Communication, 27*(1), 115–117.

Butter, E. J., Popovich, P. M., Stackhouse, R. H., & Garner, R. K. (1981). Discrimination of television programs and commercials by preschool children. *Journal of Advertising Research, 2*(2), 53–56.

Byrd-Bredbenner, C. (2002). Saturday morning children's television advertising: A longitudinal content analysis. *Family and Consumer Sciences Research Journal, 30*(3), 382–403.

Caron, A. H., & Ward, S. (1975). Gift decisions by kids and parents. *Journal of Advertising Research, 15*(4), 15–20.

Children's Advertising Review Unit. (2003). Retrieved December 17, 2005, from http://www.caru.org/.

Condry, J., Bence, P., & Schiebe, C. (1988). Nonprogram content of children's television. *Journal of Broadcasting and Electronic Media, 32,* 255–270.

Del Vecchio, G. (1997). *Creating Ever-cool: A marketer's guide to a kid's heart.* Gretna, LA: Pelican.

Donohue, T. R. (1975). Effect of commercials on Black children. *Journal of Advertising Research, 15*(6), 41–47.

Donohue, T. R., Meyer, T. P., & Henke, L. L. (1978). *Black and White children's perception of the intent and values in specific adult and child oriented television commercials.* Unpublished manuscript, University of Hartford.

Federal Communications Commission. (1974). Children's television programs: Report and policy statement. *Federal Register, 39,* 39396–39409.

Federal Communications Commission. (2004). Report and order and further notice of proposed rulemaking: Children's television obligations of digital television broadcasters. *Federal Register, 70,* 25–38.

Federal Communications Commission. (2006). *Joint proposal of industry and advocates on reconsideration of children's television rules.* Washington, D.C.: Author

Frideres, J. S. (1973). Advertising, buying patterns and children. *Journal of Advertising Research, 13*(1), 34–36.

Goldman, D. (1999). Consumer Republic. *Adweek, 40*(25), 20.

Gorn, G. J., & Goldberg, M. E. (1980). Children's responses to repetitive television commercials. *Journal of Consumer Research, 6*(4), 421–424.

Heslop, L. A., & Ryans, A. B. (1980). A second look at children and advertising of premiums. *Journal of Consumer Research, 6*(4), 414–420.

John, D. R. (1999). Through the eyes of a child: Children's knowledge and understanding of advertising. In M. C. Macklin & L. Carlson (Eds.), *Advertising to children: Concepts and controversies* (pp. 3–26). Thousand Oaks, CA: Sage.

Kiley, D. (2005, February 28). A calorie-conscious SpongeBob. *BusinessWeek,* p. 16.

Kunkel, D. (2001). Children and television advertising. In D. G. Singer & J. L. Singer (Eds.), *Handbook of children and the media* (pp. 375–394). Thousand Oaks, CA: Sage.

Kunkel, D., & Gantz, W. (1992). Children's television advertising in the multichannel environment. *Journal of Communication, 42*(3), 134–152.

Kunkel, D., & Gantz, W. (1993). Assessing compliance with industry self-regulation of television advertising to children. *Journal of Applied Communication Research, 21*(2), 148–162.

Levin, S. R., Petros, T. V., & Petrella, F. W. (1982). Preschoolers' awareness of television advertising. *Child Development, 53*(4),933–937.

Liebert, D. E., Sprafkin, J. N., Liebert, R. M., & Rubenstein, E. A. (1977). Effects of television commercial disclaimers on the product expectations of children. *Journal of Communication, 27*(1), 118–124.

Linsen, M. A. (1989). Rolling with the punches: 50 years of shopping cart development. *Progressive Grocer, 68*(2), 101–106.

Mangleburg, T. F., & Bristol, T. (1998). Socialization and adolescents' skepticism toward advertising. *Journal of Advertising, 27*(3), 11–21.

McCue Corporation. (2005). Retrieved November 11, 2005, from http://www.mccuecorp.com/McCueQ1New/abtHistory.htm.

McNeal, J. U. (1992). *Kids as customers: A handbook of marketing to children.* New York: Lexington.

McNeal, J. U. (1999). *The kids market: Myths and realities.* Ithaca, NY: Paramount Marketing Publishing.

Meyer, T. P., Donohue, T. R., & Henke, L. L. (1978). How Black children see TV commercials. *Journal of Advertising Research, 18*(5), 51-58.

Meyer, T. P., & Hexamer, A. (1981). Perceived truth and trust in television advertising among Mexican-American adolescents: Socialization and developmental consideration. *Journal of Broadcasting*, 25(2) 139–150.

Palmer, E. L., & McDowell, C. N. (1981). Children's understanding of nutritional information presented in breakfast cereal commercials. *Journal of Broadcasting*, 25, 295–301.

Pecora, N. O. (1998). *The business of children's entertainment*. New York: Guilford.

Rideout, V., Roberts, D. F., & Foehr, U. G. (2005). *Generation M: Media in the lives of 8–18 year-olds*. Menlo Park, CA: Kaiser Family Foundation.

Rideout, V. J., Vandewater, E. A., & Wartella, E. A. (2003). *Zero to six: Electronic media in the lives of infants, toddlers, and preschoolers*. Menlo Park, CA: Kaiser Family Foundation.

Riecken, G., & Yavas, U. (1990). Children's general product and brand-specific attitudes toward television commercials: Implications for public policy and advertising strategy. *International Journal of Advertising*, 9, 136–148.

Roberts, D. (1979, January). Testimony before the Federal Trade Commission's rulemaking on children and TV advertising. San Francisco.

Robertson, T. S., & Rossiter, J. R. (1974). Children and commercial persuasion: An attribution theory analysis. *Journal of Consumer Research*, 1(1), 13–20.

Robertson, T. S., & Rossiter, J. R. (1976). Short-run advertising effects on children: A field study. *Journal of Marketing Research*, 13(1), 68–70.

Robertson, T. S., & Rossiter, J. R. (1977). Children's responsiveness to commercials. *Journal of Communication*, 27, 101–106.

Sheikh, A. A., & Moleski, L. M. (1977). Children's perception of the value of an advertised product. *Journal of Broadcasting*, 21(3), 347–354.

Sheikh, A. A., Prasad, V. K., & Rao, T. R. (1974). Children's TV commercials: A review of research. *Journal of Communication*, 24(4), 126-136.

Shop.nickjr.com. (n.d.). Retrieved November 5, 2005, from http://shop.nickjr.com/family/index.jsp?categoryId=1083002&cp=1029093.

Stephens, N., & Stutts, M. A. (1982). Preschoolers' ability to distinguish between television programming and commercials. *Journal of Advertising*, 11(2), 16–26.

Strasburger, V. C., & Wilson, B. J. (2002). *Children, adolescents, and the media*. Thousand Oaks, CA: Sage.

Stutts, M. A., & Hunnicutt, G. G. (1987). Can young children understand disclaimers in television commercials? *Journal of Advertising*, 16(1), 41–46.

Valkenburg, P. M., & Cantor, J. (2001). The development of a child into a consumer. *Applied Developmental Psychology*, 22, 61–72.

Ward, S. (1972). Children's reactions to commercials. *Journal of Advertising Research*, 12, 37–45.

Ward, S. (1974). Consumer socialization. *Journal of Consumer Research*, 1(2), 1–14.

Ward, S., Wackman, D., & Wartella, E. (1977). *How children learn to buy*. Beverly Hills, CA: Sage.

Wohleber, C. (2004). The shopping cart: The invention that made "Giant Economy Size" possible. *American Heritage of Invention & Technology*. Retrieved November 11, 2005, from http://inventionandtechnology.com/xml/2004/1/it_2004_1_dept_objlessons.xml.

CHAPTER EIGHT

Should We Be Concerned about Media Violence?

ERICA SCHARRER

One of the scenarios you frequently encounter when you study media violence, as I do, is the tendency for most people to think of the effects. The underlying implication is that otherwise law-abiding, conscientious, and pacifist children or teens can be incited from a single exposure to a violent media depiction to commit an atrocious act that goes against their nature and flies in the face of societal laws and norms concerning appropriate behavior. I have often found myself fielding this question: "So, you study media violence. Do you really think movies, TV shows, or video games make kids go out and shoot people?" That type of an effect of media violence on an individual's behavior *can* occur. (We know, because we read about those instances in the paper every once in a while. The child who tries out a wrestling move from *WWE* and severely injures a sibling. The suspicion that violent computer games like *Doom* or perhaps the movie *The Matrix* influenced the teens responsible for the Columbine High School shootings.) While these incidents are often tragic and are certainly worthy of attention and concern, the study of media violence is not typically about these extreme and unusual violent copycat crimes, partly because they are impossible to study using social science techniques due to the fact that they have already occurred in "uncontrolled" circumstances in which cause and effect would be impossible to sort out, and partly because they are so rare. Rather, the study of media violence is more often concerned with effects not just on individuals' behavior, but also on their thoughts and attitudes—how they think about various issues, the way they see themselves, others, and the world at large, the fears that they hold, and the things they think of as "normal" or appropriate, as right or wrong. When we do study behavioral effects, most of the behaviors we study are more appropriately characterized as aggression rather than violence, with the former term signifying a wider range of behaviors that vary from the relatively less severe pushing and shoving at the playground to the more serious actions that would put a young person in trouble with the law instead of just in trouble with a parent or the principal.

If we think of the effects of media violence as restricted only to the dramatic and highly antisocial direct duplication of scenes depicted in television, movies, and video games that make the news headlines, it is too easy to dismiss these effects as very uncommon, as occurring only for those who undoubtedly have some deep-seated psychological trauma, or as explained away by some other factor. Most of the research regarding media violence takes a broader and more encompassing view of potential effects, and by taking this view we see that the influence of media violence on the thoughts, attitudes, and behavior of children and teens (as well as adults, although the focus here is on young people) cannot be so readily dismissed.

In writing this chapter, I attempt to address the broad question "Should we be concerned about media violence?" by asking a number of related subquestions, using the research on the topic to provide an answer. I begin with "How is violence portrayed in the media?" because there are a number of ways to show violence, and those variations in depictions can make a substantial difference in the types of media effects we can expect. In the next section, the question "Why is there violence in the media, and what explains its appeal?" is posed, so that we can understand why violent stories have enjoyed such a "starring role" in the media over time. Finally, I ask "What are the effects of media violence?" in order to illuminate the important issues brought up in this introduction and to answer the question posed by the chapter's title.

How Much Violence Is There in the Media, and How Is It Portrayed?

Content analyses—studies that use definitions of concepts applied systematically in order to attempt to "objectively" describe the messages apparent in media content—have provided a great deal of information about how much violence appears in various media forms, and how it is portrayed. With violence most often defined in these studies as one character using physical actions to purposefully attempt to harm or to actually harm another character, researchers have found that many types of media have a great deal of violence. In fact, recent content analyses have shown that violence is frequently depicted in a way that might encourage a negative effect on the audience, such as by not being punished, by being perpetrated by likeable characters who often have a justifiable reason for their actions, and by minimizing pain, harm, regret, grief, and other consequences that would likely attend a violent incident in real life.

Children's Television

The stories designed specifically for children via cartoons and live-action programs in kid-friendly television slots (like weekend mornings) often contain more violence and aggression than any other type of television show. The "violence profile" studies of George Gerbner and his associates have found between eighteen and thirty-two acts of violence per hour in Saturday-morning television, a time slot dominated by cartoons, over the past thirty years (Gerbner et al., 1994). On average, 80 percent of all characters that appear in such programs are involved in violence as either victims or perpetrators (or both). Child characters are slightly more often on the receiving end of violence, with an estimated thirteen to sixteen child victims for every ten child perpetrators.

The National Television Violence Study (NTVS), too, gives cartoons the dubious distinction of containing one of the highest rates of violent acts per hour of any type of programming (Smith et al., 1998; Wilson et al., 1996, 1997). Not only do violent acts occur at a very high rate, but they are often shown in ways that send unrealistic messages about violence and aggression. A comparison of the depiction of violence in programs targeting children aged thirteen and younger to the depiction of violence in general audience programs shows that in children's television, long-term consequences for violence are more rare, violence is more frequently combined with humor, and unrealistically low levels of harm are more likely (Smith et al., 1998). (For low levels of harm, think of Tom being hit repeatedly by an iron frying pan, but showing no signs of stopping his pursuit of Jerry in the classic cartoon *Tom and Jerry*. Or, more recently, think of the Power Rangers getting right back up to resume fighting after experiencing a severe attack.) Overall, children's television contains an astonishing amount of violence, and violence is frequently shown in a manner that detracts from its gravity.

General Audience Television

A study done by Nancy Signorielli (2003) shows an average, between spring 1993 and fall 2001, of 4.5 acts of violence per program during primetime (8 to 11 P.M.), with six out of ten programs containing at least one violent act. About one third of the violent acts are presented as justified, meaning the character using violence has some reason to do so, like revenge, self-defense, or rescuing someone. This type of portrayal can send the message that violence is acceptable if you are provoked and therefore is seen as a negative way to depict violence. Almost two thirds of the violent acts were depicted without accompanying consequences, glossing over pain, harm, regret, or other penalties that might prevent an individual from using violence. Signorielli's comparison of the latest data with those collected over the last thirty-odd years shows only small and sporadic peaks and valleys in an otherwise stable and consistent presence of violence in prime-time television. Thus, although we can claim that changes have occurred over the years in *how* violence is shown on television, the data do not permit us to claim increases in *how much* violence is shown. It may be that TV seems to have become more violent recently because depictions have become more realistic-looking and graphic (Parents Television Council, 2002; Signorielli, 2003).

In year three of the NTVS, a very large and comprehensive content analysis was conducted with a sample that included programming on cable, broadcast, public, and independent stations in all but the wee hours of the night/early morning. This study found that 61 percent of all programs contained at least one violent act. Cable, and especially the movie channels, was found to be more violent than the other types of channels. There was ample evidence that violence is commonly presented in a context that makes it appear rather harmless or as an acceptable way to solve problems. For instance, only 16 percent of programs with violence portrayed long-term negative consequences that might realistically accompany violent actions (like jail time for perpetrators). Almost three quarters of scenes that contained violence (71 percent) depicted no remorse, regret, or "negative sanctions" against violence. About half of all violent interactions showed no pain associated with acts that would cause considerable physical injury in real life. Although in the minority of violent portrayals, 28 percent of all violent interactions stemmed from circumstances considered justifiable by the characters involved and 39 percent were perpetrated by appealing, attractive characters. Violence conducted by "good guys" is more problematic than violence conducted by "bad guys," because young people tend to look up to the former.

Video Games

Violence often takes center stage in video games. Stacy Smith, Ken Lachlan, and Ron Tamborini (2003), in their study of the first ten minutes of game play in the twenty most widely sold games of 1999, found that 68 percent of the games had at least one violent act. Games rated for older audiences (T for teen, M for mature) contained more violence than games with less restrictive ratings. Nevertheless, a full 57 percent of games rated for children or all audiences contained violence. Harm was often shown unrealistically. The majority, 61 percent, depicted little injury or pain in violent interactions, while 41 percent portrayed violence in a humorous context, which could minimize perceptions of the severity of violence.

Kimberly Thompson and Kevin Haninger (2001) studied a sample of E-rated games (E signifies that the game is appropriate for "everyone") and found that in 60 percent of the games it was necessary for one character to intentionally harm another character in order to progress. Almost half (44 percent) of the games that contained violence did not carry a "content descriptor" label warning of its presence. In magazine ads for video-game fans (like *Game Informer* and *Electronic Gaming Monthly*), I found that just over half (55.8 percent) of the ads for video games contained at least one act of violence, and an average of

2.49 weapons, 1.53 violent acts, 2.17 violent words, and 0.85 verbal threats to commit violence appeared per ad (Scharrer, 2004). The genres of games with the greatest amount of violence were action adventure and fantasy/odyssey.

Children's Films

Fumie Yokota and Kimberly Thompson (2000) studied all G-rated animated feature films from 1937 to 1999 that were available on videotape, defining violence as intentional, physical acts with the potential to injure or harm. In a total of seventy-four films, every one had at least one act of violence. Violent scenes took up an average of 9.5 minutes of screen time across the films. Approximately one third of the films (32 percent) contained an explicit message *against* violence. Yet 49 percent contained cheering or laughing about violence, thereby making light of violence. Just over half of all violent acts (55 percent) involved the "good" characters fighting against the "bad" characters, a scenario that may inspire identification and perhaps emulation. We can conclude that violence has a clear and consistent presence in even those films made for the youngest movie viewers.

Why Is There Violence in the Media, and What Explains Its Appeal?

Like all questions about why media producers create the content that they do, one important place to look for answers is the economic structure of the industry. Although violent television programs are not usually the ones to draw the highest ratings, and violent films are not typically the highest grossing (Hamilton, 1998), they do attract audiences that are sizeable and with characteristics appealing to advertisers. James Hamilton (1998) has determined that the largest audience for violent television and film is males eighteen to thirty-four, followed by females eighteen to thirty-four and males thirty-five to forty-nine. The younger groups are attractive to advertisers since people of this age begin to establish brand preferences that may carry through their lifetimes. So advertisers could encourage lifelong consumers through ads positioned during programs that people of this age are likely to see. Economic analyses have also determined that violent films and television shows are likely to bring in revenue through exportation to other countries (Gerbner et al., 1994; Hamilton, 1998). Unlike comedy, which doesn't tend to translate well across language and cultural differences, violence is a universal plot device that is easily comprehended by all.

But this is a book about youth and media, so let's talk specifically about why there is violence in children's media. One explanation is that some children are interested in and drawn to television programs that contain violence. On Saturday mornings, violent television programs tend to get the highest Nielsen ratings (Stipp, 1995). Members of the television industry may think that because children tend to be rather impulsive and because they have so much physical energy, shows with action are the best way to attract them to the television screen, and shows with action often contain violence. Another explanation pertains to the long history of children's stories (in books, nursery rhymes, or the media) that use violence as a way to teach morals. The fate of the "bad guys" serves as a lesson to children, apparently, to be good, even in the face of continuing challenges from "evil." There are also some important differences among children and teenagers that make them more or less likely to enjoy violent media, as well as different features of violent media content that may enhance its appeal (Cantor & Nathanson, 1997).

Gender differences have been found in the research, for instance, with boys more likely to prefer violent video games (Barnett et al., 1997; Funk, 1993; Woodard & Gridina, 2000), violent cartoons, fairly tales, live-action programs like *Mighty Morphin Power Rangers*, and "reality-based" action programs like *Cops* (Atkin et al., 1979; Cantor & Nathanson, 1997; Collins-Standley et al., 1995; Lyle & Hoffman, 1972). Males are also more likely than females to report liking violent and fright-inducing media (Hoffner & Levine, 2005).

Age differences also help determine interest in violent media. The highest level of violence viewing among children has been determined to occur between the ages of seven and nine (Wober, 1988), a scenario likely explained both by developmental changes and the available programming options. Yet there is also evidence that interest in violent media among boys peaks during adolescence (Twitchell, 1989). Joanne Cantor and Amy Nathanson (1997) found a curvilinear relationship between age and interest in cartoons containing violence in a study of those in kindergarten, second, fourth, and sixth grade. Interest was lowest among the youngest and oldest, and highest in the middle age groups.

A range of personality variables also come into play when trying to understand children's interest in violent media. For example, children differ in terms of how aggressive they tend to be, and children with higher *aggressive tendencies* tend to enjoy and seek out violent media more often (Atkin et al., 1979; Blanchard et al., 1986; Cantor & Nathanson, 1997; Diener & DeFour, 1978; Hoffner & Levine, 2005). Another personality variable that predicts preference for violent and fright-inducing media is *sensation seeking* (Hoffner & Levine, 2005), defined as enjoyment of the thrill that stems from taking risks and engaging in adrenaline-producing activities. Further, those scoring low on measures of *empathy* are also more likely to like violent and fright media (Hoffner & Levine, 2005). Moreover, some children like to experience fear from exposure to media violence, because that experience shows them that they can *control their emotions*, and they enjoy the feeling of *reassurance* when everything works out alright in the plot in the end (Bryant et al., 1981; Cantor & Nathanson, 1997; Goldstein, 1986; Zillmann, 1980).

Finally, the presence of labels and ratings warning that media content is appropriate only for older audiences can trigger a *"forbidden fruit" effect* that increases the appeal of that content to the child (Cantor & Harrison, 1996; Christenson, 1992), particularly after the age of eleven and especially for boys (Bushman & Cantor, 2003).

What Are the Effects of Media Violence?

While in the next chapter John P. Murray takes a more historical approach to understanding how fifty years of research on children and television violence has studied the topic—focusing specifically on the variety of methodological approaches used—in this chapter I focus on the three main effects documented from these years of research. Keeping in mind the broad conceptualization of media impact discussed in the introduction to this chapter, research over the last few decades has pointed to three main effects of viewing violence on television: learning aggression, desensitization, and fear (or the mean-world syndrome) (Smith et al., 1998; Wilson et al., 1996, 1997). *Learning aggression* encompasses not only exhibiting aggressive or violent physical acts but also having aggressive thoughts and developing attitudes toward aggression that consider it "normal," acceptable, favorable, or inevitable. *Desensitization* means becoming so used to seeing violence in the media that you no longer have the same reaction to it (for example, being alarmed, upset, concerned, or anxious) as you would have before repeated and prolonged exposure. Finally, *fear* effects are rather self-explanatory—experiencing fright from exposure to violence in the news, in movies, or in other media forms—whereas *mean-world syndrome* effects occur when heavy television exposure shapes an individual's view of the "real world" so that it seems more dangerous, violent, and scary.

Learning Aggression

The first social-science research examinations conducted of whether television violence exposure can lead to aggression in children were published in 1963 by Albert Bandura and his colleagues (Bandura et al., 1963a, 1963b). Bandura and his colleagues (1963a, 1963b) performed experiments that found that aggressive behavior in preschool-aged children as measured by interactions with a bobo doll (a rubberized inflated figure) and other toys was triggered by exposure to a filmed model engaging in aggressive play. In both of the two studies, the preschoolers who had seen the filmed model were more likely to play aggressively with the toys than those in the control group, even when the filmed model was made to look like a cartoon character rather than a typical person (and therefore was less realistic) and especially when the filmed depiction showed the aggressor in the film being rewarded rather than punished. After exposure to the mediated models, the young children performed behaviors and uttered expressions both directly imitative of the aggression they had just seen and also incorporating some of their own original ideas for aggressive play.

Since these early experiments, there have been more than two hundred other studies that have investigated the issue, with the vast majority finding that there is, indeed, a connection between exposure to violence on television and aggression in both children and adults (Comstock & Scharrer, 1999; Potter, 1999). Based on the preponderance of evidence, most of the scholars in the research community concur that the question of whether television violence can cause aggression is an open-and-shut case. Their conviction rests on the size and strength of the research evidence, as well as the fact that despite many variations—including the age of the research participants, the ways that aggression has been measured, the type of depiction to which individuals are responding, and the research methods employed—most studies have led to the same conclusion.

Each research method has its own strengths and limitations, so when a variety of approaches is used and most results agree, we can make claims with much more confidence. Experiments like those conducted by Bandura can be criticized for being rather artificial, possibly not reflecting the way that young people watch and respond to television in real life. To address that limitation, we can turn to the evidence accumulated through surveys. (Field experiments are also helpful in this regard. They use many of the same aspects of lab experimental research—exposure to a stimulus and comparison of treatment and control groups—but collect data in the places where you would naturally find individuals, such as at home or at school, rather than in the lab. Due to space constraints, however, we will focus on surveys rather than field experiments here.)

Surveys. Surveys ask respondents about their thoughts, attitudes, and day-to-day behaviors, which can potentially do a better job of getting at real-life experiences. Data garnered from this approach consist of correlations between the amount of exposure of the child to violent television and the amount of aggression reflected in responses. We don't have the space to discuss the many survey studies conducted on our topic in detail (for reviews, see Comstock & Scharrer, 1999; Potter, 1999), but let's use one as an example.

A very recent study employs not just survey research but *longitudinal* survey research (with data drawn over time instead of as a one-shot deal) to investigate whether exposure to television violence in childhood can contribute to aggression or criminal behavior in adulthood. L. Rowell Huesmann and his colleagues (Huesmann et al., 2003) began their study in the 1970s with a sample of more than five hundred first- and third-graders from the Chicago area, and gathered follow-up data from as many of these individuals as they could find in the mid-1990s, when they were in their twenties. Using this procedure, they reinterviewed almost three hundred of the original research participants fifteen years later. When the participants were children, lists of eighty programs were provided to them, and they reported how frequently they watched each. The programs were then rated for amount of violence. Also when they were children, the participants were asked how much they identified with various characters (defined as how much they acted like or did things like those characters) and how realistic they perceived programs to be. Data regarding the aggressive behavior of the participants in adulthood were gathered from reports from the individuals themselves, reports by others (a close friend, spouse, or significant other), and crime records from the state. Various forms of aggression were studied and together formed a composite measure, including (but not limited to) verbal aggression, indirect aggression (harming another behind the scenes, such as attempting to get other people to dislike someone), aggression against spouse/significant other, aggressive personality, severe aggressive behavior (including threatening to stab or shoot another, or punching, kicking, choking, or beating another), and criminal behavior.

Results of the longitudinal study show that the amount of violence viewing as a child was significantly related to aggression as a young adult fifteen years later. Furthermore, both thinking of television violence as realistic as a child and identifying with same-sex aggressive characters as a child also correlate with adult aggression. The link between early violence viewing and adult aggression remained in place even when statistically controlling for childhood aggression. In other words, early television violence viewing played a role in adult aggression even after the role of childhood aggression in adult aggression had been taken into account. Finally, the possibility of a "reverse hypothesis"—that instead of child violence viewing leading to adult aggression, perhaps child aggression led to adult violence viewing—was tested and ruled out. Correlations were much larger and statistically significant for the former and not the latter.

Meta-analysis. An excellent way to summarize the many studies that have been conducted on the link between television violence exposure and aggression is to perform a meta-analysis. In a meta-analysis, an attempt is made to gather as many studies on a single topic as possible, and then the results of all of those studies are entered into a computer and statistical analysis techniques are used to find patterns. One particular meta-analysis conducted by Haejung Paik and George Comstock (1994) from the television-violence literature collected data from 217 studies that consisted of 1,142 instances in which a relationship between television viewing and aggressive or criminal behavior (referred to collectively as "antisocial behavior") was measured (since many of the studies tested more than one such relationship). Meta-analysis results showed a positive and statistically significant relationship between viewing and antisocial behavior for laboratory experiments, field experiments, and surveys. In other words, examining all studies at once, regardless of the research method they employed, increased television violence viewing was related to increased aggression. The strongest relationships were found when the antisocial behavior examined involved "simulated aggression," which included toy play, self-reporting aggressive tendencies, and using aggression machines where the participant thinks she or he is harming another but is not, and "minor aggressive behavior," which included verbal aggression and relatively minor physical acts against objects and people. A smaller but still positive and statistically significant relationship was found between violence viewing and "illegal and seriously harmful activities" such as burglary, grand theft, and violent acts committed against a person.

Other meta-analyses (Hearold, 1986; Hogben, 1998; Wood et al., 1991) have come to largely the same conclusions. Thus, the additional evidence from meta-analyses, because of their unique ability to summarize large numbers of individual studies, adds considerable strength to our conclusion that television violence can, indeed, stimulate aggression. In fact, the recent report from the U.S. Surgeon General (U.S. Department of Health and Human Services, 2001) on the causes of violence among youth included television violence exposure as a contributing factor that was characterized as a small effect but was of the same magnitude as such clearly important issues as poor performance in school and weak social ties.

Video Games. A much smaller but growing number of studies have been conducted to determine whether playing violent video games can also impact aggression in children and adolescents. These studies are best summarized (especially, again, since we can't get into too
much detail here in this chapter) with meta-analysis. Two meta-analyses have been performed, one by John Sherry (2001) incorporating twenty-five studies and one by Anderson
and Bushman (2001) drawing from thirty-five studies.

Sherry (2001) found a positive relationship between violent video-game playing and
aggression, with an overall effect size (which is just what it sounds like, the mathematical
summary of the relationship between video-game use and aggression taken as a whole from
all of the studies in the meta-analysis) that was statistically significant but smaller than that
found for television viewing and aggression. He also determined that effects sizes have gotten larger over time, presumably due to the more realistic nature of recent games, and that
games featuring human or fantasy violence led to higher effects sizes than sports violence.
Anderson and Bushman (2001) also found a positive and significant relationship between
video-game playing and three different aggression-related outcomes, aggressive behavior,
aggressive thoughts, and aggressive affect (measured by experiencing feelings such as anger
and hostility). The size of the effect was similar for children compared to college-aged adults,
for males compared to females, and for experimental studies and surveys.

Although there have been far fewer studies conducted on the effects of video-game compared to television violence, and some of the early studies on video-game effects were rather
inconclusive, the research evidence that has accumulated in more recent years (as is apparent in both of the meta-analyses) has pointed convincingly to an effect on aggression. The
interactive nature of video games and the possibility for greater identification with characters compared to television exposure has led to speculation that some effects may be heightened in this media form. Players take on the persona of video-game characters and control
characters' actions with their own, which is an unprecedented situation with potentially
important implications for effects.

Desensitization

Desensitization is the least frequently studied of the three major outcomes of violent
media. Yet the studies that do exist demonstrate the ability of exposure to violence in the
media to make individuals become accustomed or even inured to subsequent violence exposure. Desensitization has been measured in many different ways, including physiological evidence of becoming used to violence (for example, initially the subject's heart rate quickens
but with repeated exposure to violence it slows again), lack of empathy for victims of violence, becoming progressively more reluctant to label horror films or other media as "violent" or "disturbing," and willingness or speed with which an individual responds to an
aggressive situation. Each of these measures of desensitization indicates a tendency to perceive violence as no big deal, which is a good way to define this effect.

Even a single exposure to media violence has been shown to lead to an immediate drop
in concern about or sympathy about aggressive acts perpetrated by others (Drabman &

Thomas, 1974a, 1974b; Thomas & Drabman, 1975). Others have found an incremental increase in desensitization with repeated violent media exposure (Thomas, 1982; Thomas et al., 1977). Violent video-game use has been linked to low scores on empathy (Funk et al., 2004). Both violent video-game use (Knapp, 2002) and violent television exposure (Molitor & Hirsch, 1994) also led to a delay in seeking help when a physical fight was believed to have occurred, an indication of a desensitization effect.

Fear and the Mean-World Syndrome

Fear and mean-world syndrome effects are not the same thing, although they are conceptually related. The former is most often studied from the point of view of an immediate (but also potentially lingering) emotional impact of one particular program, news segment, or movie, whereas the latter is a cumulative effect of heavy exposure to the medium of television as a whole rather than to any specific program. For fear responses, a single horror movie, for instance, can trigger anxiety, fright, and perhaps nightmares or other sleep disturbances that are felt instantly and also may last for a while. For the mean-world syndrome, growing up in a television culture in which violence pervades programs gradually shifts perceptions of the "real world" among heavy viewers, so that it is thought of as scary, dangerous, and violent.

Fear. It is quite common for children to experience fear from media exposure. In a survey of a randomly drawn sample of parents from across the country, Douglas Gentile and David Walsh (1999) found that 62 percent of parents reported that their child had expressed fear that something witnessed in a television program or movie might happen to them. In another study, 75 percent of preschoolers and elementary-school-aged children said they had become frightened by something seen on TV or in the movies (Wilson et al., 1987).

Fear is not necessarily a fleeting response, and its effects can be debilitating. In fact, the memory of a fear response to media can endure for quite some time. In studies, nearly all college-aged and older adults were able to remember in vivid detail being frightened as a child by something in the media (Harrison & Cantor, 1999; Hoekstra et al., 1999; Johnson, 1980), with common consequences including sleep disturbances (reluctance to sleep alone, needing a nightlight or lights on, not being able to sleep, having nightmares), eating disturbances (such as loss of appetite), as well as generalized feelings of anxiety and "mental preoccupation."

The age of the child has a tremendously important role in determining what she or he will find frightening on television or in film. The changes from early childhood to adolescence reflect developmental shifts from the more tangible to the more abstract, from fantasy to reality, and from the personal to the social. Cantor (2001, p. 211) explains:

> Children from approximately 3 to 8 years of age are frightened primarily by animals; the dark; supernatural beings such as ghosts, monsters, and witches; and anything that looks strange and moves suddenly. The fears of 9- to 12-year-olds are more often related to personal injury and physical destruction and the injury and death of family members. Adolescents continue to fear personal

injury and physical destruction; in addition, school fears and social fears arise at this age, as do fears regarding political, economic, and global issues.

The effectiveness of various ways of coping with the fear brought on by media exposure also depends heavily on the age of the child (Cantor, 1998, 2001; Wilson & Weiss, 1991). *Noncognitive strategies*, those that do not involve thinking through information provided verbally by others, work best with the youngest children, such as preschoolers. Examples of noncognitive strategies include clutching a cherished object or hiding one's eyes. *Cognitive strategies* that take place when a child is encouraged by an adult to consider the frightening stimulus in a different light work better as children grow older. Examples of cognitive strategies include telling the child that the program or movie is not real or the situation it depicts is very rare or highly implausible or assuring the child that it will all turn out alright in the end.

Mean-World Syndrome. Mean-world syndrome is a key component of cultivation theory, a theory that suggests that heavy exposure to television's ubiquitous and consistent themes helps form viewers' perceptions of the world around them (Gerbner et al., 1980). (An in-depth discussion of cultivation theory as it relates to a range of effects, in addition to violence, can be found in chapter 10.) When it comes to violence, the theory asserts that those who spend large amounts of time witnessing the inflated rates of violent actions on the screen will slowly come to perceive the world around them as mean and violent, will believe that they themselves are more likely to be involved in a crime, and will believe that others are up to no good and cannot be trusted compared to relatively light television viewers (Gerbner et al., 1980).

Evidence of the mean-world syndrome and its attending consequences, often studied in adults, has been found in young viewers as well (Gerbner et al., 1979, 1980). The consequences of this cultivated view of the world for children often overlap with the manifestations we reviewed for fear effects. For example, a survey of more than two thousand third-through eighth-graders found that the more hours of television viewing the child engaged in per day, the more likely she or he experienced anxiety, signs of depression, and symptoms of posttraumatic stress (Singer et al., 1998). In another study of nearly five hundred kindergarten through fourth-graders, amount of television viewing was associated with sleep disturbances like nightmares (Owens et al., 1999). Additional studies have found that rather than overall amount of television exposure leading to a mean-world syndrome outlook, exposure to the news, specifically, appears to stimulate such views among children and teens (Cohen & Weimann, 2000; Wilson et al., 2005).

So, Should We Be Concerned about Media Violence?

The research evidence brings us unambiguously to an answer to the question posed in the title of this chapter. Yes, media violence is a cause for concern. The conclusions from the extensive research on the effects of television violence have less to do with the "copycat crimes" that we read about in the newspaper and more to do with learning aggression, desensitization, and fear or a mean-world syndrome outlook. The term *aggression* encompasses a wide variety of forms, including verbal, indirect, and relatively minor physical expressions, as well as more severe criminal behavior, while the phrase *learning aggression* (adopted here from the National Television Violence Study, Smith et al., 1998; Wilson et al., 1996, 1997) reminds us that thoughts, perceptions, and attitudes about aggression (in addition to behavior) are also important media effects.

Media violence depictions are also a cause of concern. We have seen that violence is now and always has been a pervasive theme in television content. It also is widespread in video games and the ads used to promote them. Violent images have gotten more realistic-looking and more graphic on both television and in video games over time. Children's media stands out as being particularly violent, with a rate of violent acts per hour that is about four times as large as that found in prime-time television. Violence is often depicted in television and video games in a way that the research shows makes negative effects more likely, such as being accompanied by rewards or lack of punishment, occurring with few consequences, being perpetrated by likeable characters that have a justifiable reason for being violent, and in a humorous context that can trivialize violence.

We have also seen that the television industry, and, by extension, the video-game industry, enjoys economic gains that accrue from the characteristics of audience members for violent programming that attracts advertisers and through exportation of programs that contain violence. Yet, in response to pressure from politicians, interest groups, and others (admittedly in a context of an overall "industry-friendly" easing of ownership rules), the Telecommunications Act of 1996 required all new television sets to be equipped with a V-chip that electronically reads newly created labels for television programs, thereby giving parents and caregivers the opportunity to block out programs they deem inappropriate. It is beyond the scope of this chapter to discuss the obstacles that currently stand in the way of the successful operation of the V-chip and use of the labels to make viewing decisions, but I believe there is potential, nonetheless, in these new opportunities. (See chapter 2 for a complete history of the regulation of children's media.)

Two other ways to counter media violence also show great promise, media literacy in schools and parental mediation. The former involves showing young people how to use media (for example, by encouraging them to create their own video projects) as well as how to critically analyze media content, effects, and production processes. (See chapter 13 for more information on media literacy.) The latter encompasses the ways in which parents and caregivers set and explain rules for media use, discuss media depictions and potential effects while co-viewing (or watching video-game play) with children, and generally encourage critical thinking about media. Recent media violence research has attested to the effectiveness of media literacy and parental mediation in creating knowledge and awareness about media violence and reducing the likelihood of experiencing one or more of the three effects.

DISCUSSION QUESTIONS

1   What are the current obstacles involved in using the V-chip and program labels?

2   Do you think media content will get less violent? Why or why not?

3   Is it the government's responsibility to regulate media violence?

4   Besides violent media exposure, what are other causes of aggression and violence?

5   Do you think that other media that may contain violence, like the Internet and popular music, influence violence? Why or why not?

EXERCISES

1   Compare and contrast the experience of playing video games that are violent and watching television programs that are violent. On a sheet of paper, create two columns, one labeled "similarities" and one labeled "differences." Think carefully about how and why individuals use the two media forms. When you have finished filling in the two columns, discuss the implications of the two experiences (playing violent games and watching violent programs) for the possibility of each of the three effects (learning aggression, desensitization, and fear or the mean-world syndrome).

2   Perform your own content analysis of the depiction of violence in your choice of media. First, decide on a medium, such as television, newspapers, video games, or films. Then, if you need to narrow your sample down further, consider choosing a genre or type within that medium, such as soap operas, first-person-shooter video or computer games, top-grossing films, and so on. Gather a small set of that content for your analysis. (If you were doing a full-fledged study, you'd want a large sample, but since this is just an exercise, a smaller sample will do.) Now, you need to come up with your coding scheme. What will you look for? How will you know it when you see it? If you are counting violent acts, come up with a clear definition of a violent act so that you can recognize them consistently. In addition to how much violence there is, think about assessing how violence is presented. Is it rewarded? Done by likeable characters? Justified? For each of these characteristics of violent portrayals, you'll need careful and precise definitions in order to document their presence in your sample.

3   Do you like media violence? If so, why do you find it appealing? If not, why not? Write a one-paragraph essay describing your own attraction (or lack thereof) to violent television programs, movies, and games, as well as your careful and considered assessment of the reasons for that attraction.

REFERENCES

Anderson, C. A., & Bushman, B. J. (2001). Effects of violent video games on aggressive behavior, aggressive cognition, aggressive affect, physiological arousal, and prosocial behavior: A meta-analytic review of the scientific literature. *Psychological Science, 12*, 353–359.

Atkin, C., Greenberg, B., Korzenny, F., & McDermott, S. (1979). Selective exposure to televised violence. *Journal of Broadcasting, 23*, 5–13.

Bandura, A., Ross, D., & Ross, S. A. (1963a). Imitation of film-mediated aggressive models. *Journal of Abnormal and Social Psychology, 66*, 3–11.

Bandura, A., Ross, D., & Ross, S. A. (1963b). Vicarious reinforcement and imitative learning. *Journal of Abnormal and Social Psychology, 67*, 601–607.

Barnett, M. A., Vitaglione, G. D., Harper, K. K. G., Quackenbush, S. W., Steadman, L. A., & Valdez, B. S. (1997). Late adolescents' experiences with and attitudes toward video games. *Journal of Applied Social Psychology, 27*(15), 1316–1334.

Blanchard, D. C., Graczyk, B., & Blanchard, R. J. (1986). Differential reactions of men and women to realism, physical damage, and emotionality in violent films. *Aggressive Behavior, 12*, 45–55.

Bryant, J., Carveth, R. A., & Brown, D. (1981). Television viewing and anxiety: An experimental examination. *Journal of Communication, 31*, 106–119.

Bushman, B. J., & Cantor, J. (2003). Media ratings for violence and sex: Implications for policymakers and parents. *American Psychologist, 58*, 130–141.

Cantor, J. (1998). *"Mommy, I'm scared": How TV and movies frighten children and what we can do to protect them.* San Diego, CA: Harcourt Brace.

Cantor, J. (2001). The media and children's fears, anxieties, and perceptions of danger. In D. G. Singer & J. L. Singer (Eds.), *Handbook of children and the media* (pp. 207—221). Thousand Oaks, CA: Sage.

Cantor, J., & Harrison, K. (1996). *Ratings and advisories for television programming.* Report for the National Television Violence Study. Los Angeles: Mediascope.

Cantor, J., & Nathanson, A. I. (1997). Predictors of children's interest in violent television programs. *Journal of Broadcasting & Electronic Media, 41*, 155–168.

Christenson, P. (1992). The effects of parental advisory labels on adolescent music preferences. *Journal of Communication, 42*, 106–113.

Cohen, J., & Weimann, G. (2000). Cultivation revisited: Some genres have some effects on some viewers. *Communication Reports, 13*, 99–105.

Collins-Standley, T., Gan, S., Yu, H. J., & Zillmann, D. (1995). *Choice of romantic, violent, and scary fairy-tale books by preschool girls and boys.* Unpublished manuscript.

Comstock, G., & Scharrer, E. (1999). *Television: What's on, who's watching, and what it means.* San Diego, CA: Academic Press.

Diener, E., & DeFour, D. (1978). Does television violence enhance program popularity? *Journal of Personality and Social Psychology, 36*, 333–341.

Drabman, R. S. & Thomas, M. H. (1974a). Does media violence increase children's toleration of real-life aggression? *Developmental Psychology, 10*, 418–421.

Drabman, R. S., & Thomas, M. H. (1974b). Exposure to filmed violence and children's toleration of real-life aggression. *Personality and Social Psychology Bulletin, 1*, 198–199.

Funk, J. B. (1993). Reevaluating the impact of video games. *Clinical Pediatrics, 32*, 86–90.

Funk, J. B., Baldacci, H. B., Pasold, T., & Baumgardner, J. (2004). Violence exposure in real-life, video games, television, movies, and the Internet. Is there desensitization? *Journal of Adolescence, 27*, 23–39.

Gentile, D. A., & Walsh, D. A. (1999). *MediaQuotient™: National survey of family media habits, knowledge, and attitudes.* Minneapolis, MN: National Institute on Media and the Family.

Gerbner, G., Gross, L., Morgan, M., & Signorielli, N. (1980). The "mainstreaming" of America: Violence profile no. 11. *Journal of Communication, 30,* 10–29.

Gerbner, G., Gross, L., Signorielli, N., Morgan, M., & Jackson-Beeck, M. (1979). The demonstration of power: Violence profile no. 10. *Journal of Communication, 29,* 177–196.

Gerbner, G., Morgan, M., & Signorielli, N. (1994). *Television violence profile no. 16.* Unpublished manuscript, Annenberg School of Communication, University of Pennsylvania, Philadelphia.

Goldstein, J. H. (1986). *Aggression and crimes of violence* (2nd edition). New York: Oxford University Press.

Hamilton, J. T. (1998). *Channeling violence.* Princeton, NJ: Princeton University Press.

Harrison, K., & Cantor, J. (1999). Tales from the screen: Enduring fright reactions to scary media. *Media Psychology, 1,* 97–116.

Hearold, S. (1986.) A synthesis of 1,045 effects of television on social behavior. In G. C. Comstock (Ed.), *Public communication and behavior: Vol. 1* (pp. 65–133). New York: Academic Press.

Hoekstra, S. J., Harris, R .J., & Helmick, A. L. (1999). Autobiographical memories about the experience of seeing frightening movies in childhood. *Media Psychology, 1,* 117–140.

Hoffner, C. A., & Levine, K. J. (2005). Enjoyment of mediated fright and violence: A meta-analysis. *Media Psychology, 7,* 207–237.

Hogben, M. (1998). Factors moderating the effect of television viewing on aggressive behavior. *Communication Research, 25,* 220–247.

Huesmann, L. R., Moise-Titus, J., Podolski, C. L., & Eron, L. D. (2003). Longitudinal relations between children's exposure to TV violence and their aggressive and violent behavior in young adulthood: 1977–1992. *Developmental Psychology, 39*(2), 201–222.

Johnson, B. R. (1980). General occurrence of stressful reactions to commercial motion pictures and elements in films subjectively described as stressors. *Psychological Reports, 47,* 775–786.

Knapp, H. E. (2002). *Desensitization aftereffects of playing violent video games.* Unpublished doctoral dissertation. University of California, Los Angeles. Accessed through *Dissertation Abstracts International* Section A: Humanities and Social Sciences, vol. 63 (5-A).

Lyle, J., & Hoffman, H. R. (1972). Children's use of television and other media. In E. A. Rubinstein, G. A. Comstock, & J. P. Murray (Eds.), *Television and social behavior* (vol. 4, pp. 129–256). Washington, D.C.: U.S. Government Printing Office.

Molitor, F., & Hirsch, K. W. (1994). Children's toleration of real-life aggression after exposure to media violence: A replication of the Drabman and Thomas studies. *Child Study Journal, 24,* 191–208.

Owens, J., Maxim, R., McGuinn, M., Nobile, C., Msall, M., & Alario, A. (1999). Television-viewing habits and sleep disturbance in school children. *Pediatrics, 104,* 552.

Paik, H., & Comstock, G. (1994). The effects of television violence on antisocial behavior: A meta-analysis. *Communication Research, 21,* 516–546.

Parents Television Council. (2002). *TV bloodbath: Violence on prime time broadcast TV.* Retrieved April 15, 2004, from www.parentstv.org/PTC/publications/reports/stateindustryviolence/main.asp.

Potter, W. J. (1999). *On media violence.* Thousand Oaks, CA: Sage.

Scharrer, E. (2004). Virtual violence: Gender and aggression in video game advertisements. *Mass Communication & Society, 7,* 393–412.

Sherry, J. (2001). The effects of violent video games on aggression: A meta analysis. *Human Communication Research, 27*(3), 409–431.

Signorielli, N. (2003). Prime-time violence, 1993–2001: Has the picture really changed? *Journal of Broadcasting & Electronic Media, 47*, 36–58.

Singer, M. I., Slovak, K., Frierson, T., & York, P. (1998). Viewing preferences, symptoms of psychological trauma, and violent behaviors among children who watch television. *Journal of the American Academy of Child and Adolescent Psychiatry, 37*, 1041–1048.

Smith, S. L., Lachlan, K., & Tamborini, R. (2003). Popular video games: Quantifying the presentation of violence and its context. *Journal of Broadcasting & Electronic Media, 47*, 58–76.

Smith, S. L., Wilson, B. J., Kunkel, D., Linz, D., Potter, W. J., Colvin, C. M., & Donnerstein, E. (1998). *National television violence study (vol. 3)*. Santa Barbara: Center for Communication and Social Policy, University of California.

Stipp, H. (1995, May). *Children's viewing of news, reality-shows, and other programming.* Paper presented at the annual meeting of the International Communication Association, Albuquerque, NM.

Thomas, M. H. (1982). Physiological arousal, exposure to a relatively lengthy aggressive film, and aggressive behavior. *Journal of Research in Personality, 16*, 72–81.

Thomas, M. H., & Drabman, R. S. (1975). Toleration of real aggression as a function of exposure to televised violence and age of subject. *Merrill-Palmer Quarterly, 21*, 227–232.

Thomas, M. H., Horton, R. W., Lippincott, E. C., & Drabman, R. S. (1977). Desensitization to portrayals of real-life aggression as a function of exposure to television violence. *Journal of Personality and Social Psychology, 35*(6), 450–458.

Thompson, K. M., & Haninger, K. (2001). Violence in E-rated video games. *JAMA, 286*, 591–598, 920.

Twitchell, J. B. (1989). *Preposterous violence.* New York: Oxford University Press.

U.S. Department of Health and Human Services. (2001). *Youth violence: A report of the Surgeon General.* Rockville, MD: U.S. Department of Health and Human Services, Centers for Disease Control and Prevention, National Center for Injury Prevention and Control; Substance Abuse and Mental Health Services Administration, Center for Mental Health Services; and National Institutes of Health, National Institute of Mental Health.

Wilson, B. J., Hoffner, C., & Cantor, J. (1987). Children's perceptions of the effectiveness of techniques to reduce fear from mass media. *Journal of Applied Developmental Psychology, 8*, 39–52.

Wilson, B. J., Kunkel, D., Potter, W. J., Donnerstein, E., Smith, S. L., Blumenthal, E., & Berry, M. (1997). *National television violence study (vol. 2)*. Santa Barbara: Center for Communication and Social Policy, University of California.

Wilson, B. J., Kunkel, D., Potter, W. J., Donnerstein, E., Smith, S. L., Blumenthal, E., & Gray, T. E. (1996). *National television violence study: Executive summary, 1994–1995.* Studio City, CA: Mediascope.

Wilson, B. J., Martins, N., & Marske, A. L. (2005). Children's and parents' fright reactions to kidnapping stories in the news. *Communication Monographs, 72*, 46–70.

Wilson, B. J., & Weiss, A. J. (1991). The effects of two reality explanations on children's reactions to a frightening movie scene. *Communication Monographs, 58*, 307–326.

Wober, M. (1988). The extent to which viewers watch violence-containing programs. *Current Psychology: Research and Reviews, 7*, 43–57.

Wood, W., Wong, F., & Chachere, J. (1991). Effects of media violence on viewers' aggression in unconstrained social interaction. *Psychological Bulletin, 109*, 371–383.

Woodard, E., & Gridina, N. (2000). *Media in the home 2000*. Philadelphia, PA: Annenberg Public Policy Center.

Yokota, F., & Thompson, K. M. (2000). Violence in G-rated animated films. *JAMA, 283*, 2716–2720.

Zillmann, D. (1980). Anatomy of suspense. In P. H. Tannenbaum (Ed.), *The entertainment functions of television* (pp. 133–163). Hillsdale, NJ: Lawrence Erlbaum.

CHAPTER NINE

Historically, How Have Researchers Studied the Effects of Media Violence on Youth?

JOHN P. MURRAY

In the conclusion to chapter 8 of this book, Erica Scharrer asserts that, "Yes, media violence is a cause for concern." She bases her assertion on the research evidence presented in that chapter relative to a variety of media, including television and video games. Given that the topic of the effects of media violence on youth has dominated not only the research agenda, but also public discourse and government involvement over the past fifty years, there are additional questions to be answered in a book such as this. The goal of this chapter is to take a historical look at how the research related specifically to television violence has been conducted and in what directions it is moving. It is not intended to duplicate the findings reported in chapter 8, but rather to complement them by taking a more historical and methodological focus. In answering the question posed by the chapter title, we can benefit from examining fifty years of research on television. For example, in our review of research over the past fifty years, Norma Pecora, Ellen Wartella, and I catalogued almost two thousand studies (1,945, to be precise) conducted on various aspects of television's impact, with about six hundred of these studies related directly to the violence issue (Pecora et al., 2006). Clearly, there is a lot of ground to cover.

Television broadcasting in the United States began in the early 1940s, with full development following the Second World War. The violent face of television has been presented to audiences from the first broadcasts of this medium. Although extensive broadcast schedules did not begin until the late 1940s, and violence was not as graphic as it would become in later years, the first public concerns about violence were evident in the 1950s. The early congressional hearings (United States Congress, 1952, 1955) set the stage for expressions of public concern that echoed throughout the twentieth century and into the twenty-first (United States Congress, 2003, 2006).

Over the Years

The extent of concern—social, political, and scientific—is demonstrated by the fact that over the past half century, about a thousand reports have been published on the issue of TV violence (Murray, 1980; Pecora et al., 2006). Of course, only a small percentage of these thousands of pages represent original studies or research reports, but nonetheless there is an extensive body of research on the impact of TV violence. The research history is best described in terms of the nature of the methodological approaches used: correlational, experimental (laboratory and field), and cross-lagged panel studies. Each of these methodologies will be discussed within a historical context, concluding with even newer directions for future research on the relationship between youth and media violence. But first we must understand the role played by the U.S. government over the years in setting the agenda both for the social science research and public discourse.

Setting the Agenda

As was noted previously, concern about the influence of TV violence began as early as the start of this new medium. The first congressional hearings were held in the early 1950s (United States Congress, 1952, 1955). At these early hearings, developmental psychologist Eleanor Maccoby (1954) and sociologist Paul Lazarsfeld (1955) presented testimony that relied upon some early studies of violence in films, such as the 1930s report *Boys, Movies and City Streets* (Cressey & Thrasher, 1933), to outline a necessary program of research on the issue of TV violence and its effects on children.

As the 1960s progressed, concern in the United States about violence in the streets and the assassinations of President John F. Kennedy, Dr. Martin Luther King, Jr., and Robert Kennedy stimulated continuing interest in media violence. In response, several major government commissions and scientific and professional review committees were established to summarize the research evidence and public policy issues regarding the role of television violence in salving or savaging young viewers.

Across four decades, five principal U.S. commissions and review panels—National Commission on the Causes and Prevention of Violence (Baker & Ball, 1969); Surgeon General's Scientific Advisory Committee on Television and Social Behavior (1972; Murray, 1973); National Institute of Mental Health (1982) Television and Behavior Project; Group for the Advancement of Psychiatry (1982) Child and Television Drama Review; and the American Psychological Association Task Force on Television and Society (Huston et al., 1992)—have been central to setting the agenda for research and public discussion.

In 1982 the National Institute of Mental Health (NIMH) published a ten-year follow-up to the 1972 Surgeon General's study. The two-volume report (National Institute of Mental Health, 1982; Pearl et al., 1982), collectively titled *Television and Behavior: Ten Years of Scientific Progress and Implications for the Eighties*, provided a reminder of the breadth and depth of knowledge that had accumulated on the issue of TV violence. In this regard, the NIMH staff and consultants concluded:

> After 10 more years of research, the consensus among most of the research community is that violence on television does lead to aggressive behavior by children and teenagers who watch the programs. This conclusion is based on laboratory experiments and on field studies. Not all children become aggressive, of course, but the correlations between violence and aggression are positive. In magnitude, television violence is as strongly correlated with aggressive behavior as any other behavioral variable that has been measured. (National Institute of Mental Health, 1982, p. 10)

In 1986 the American Psychological Association (APA) empanelled a Task Force on Television and Society to review the research and professional concerns about the impact of television on children and adults. The nine psychologists assigned to this committee undertook reviews of relevant research, conducted interviews with television industry and public policy professionals, and discussed concerns with representatives of government regulatory agencies and public interest organizations. The final report, entitled *Big World, Small Screen: The Role of Television in American Society*, included the following observation about television violence:

> American television has been violent for many years. Over the past 20 years, the rate of violence on prime time evening television has remained at about 5 to 6 incidents per hour, whereas the rate on children's Saturday morning programs is typically 20 to 25 acts per hour. There is clear evidence that television violence can cause aggressive behavior and can cultivate values favoring the use of aggression to resolve conflicts. (Huston et al., 1992, p. 136)

Clearly, both the federal government and the medical establishment had identified media violence as a problem worthy of extensive inquiry. It's not surprising that the social science researchers took up the topic as well.

Early Correlational (Survey) Studies

The early studies of television's influence began almost simultaneously in England, the United States, and Canada in the mid-1950s. They were designed to take advantage of the regulated introduction of the new medium in order to examine its impact in those early years. Later studies—in the 1970s—would revisit these issues and this research strategy when television was being introduced into isolated communities in Australia (Murray & Kippax, 1977, 1978, 1979) and Canada (Williams, 1986; MacBeth, 1996).

In England, a group of researchers at the London School of Economics and Political

Science, under the direction of Hilde Himmelweit, began the first study of children's television viewing patterns while TV was still relatively new. (At the time, there were only 3 million TV sets installed in the 15 million households in England.) Although proposed by the Audience Research Department of the British Broadcasting Corporation (BBC), the study was conducted by independent researchers. Begun in 1955, the study was published in a 1958 report, *Television and the Child: An Empirical Study of the Effect of Television on the Young* (Himmelweit et al., 1958). The American and Canadian study was conducted by Wilbur Schramm and his colleagues at Stanford University. Begun in 1957, the study was published in a 1961 report, *Television in the Lives of Our Children* (Schramm et al., 1961).

These studies, both correlational in that they compared television viewers and non-viewers in a real-world setting (as opposed to manipulating viewing in a laboratory), provided very important benchmarks for understanding the broad and general effects of television on children. For example, Himmelweit and her colleagues (1958, pp. 17–18) found "a number of instances where viewers and controls differed in their outlook; differences which did not exist before television came on the scene. There was a small but consistent influence of television on the way children thought generally about jobs, job values, success, and social surroundings." With regard to aggression, these correlational studies did not support an association. Himmelweit and her colleagues "did not find that the viewers were any more aggressive or maladjusted than the controls," and concluded that "television is unlikely to cause aggressive behaviour, although it could precipitate it in those few children who are emotionally disturbed. On the other hand, there was little support for the view that programmes of violence are beneficial; we found that they aroused aggression as often as they discharged it" (p. 20).

The conclusions of Schramm and his colleagues have become something of a mantra, and go a long way toward also summarizing (or foreshadowing) the findings of fifty years of research: "For *some* children under *some* conditions *some* television is harmful. For *other* children under the same conditions, or for the same children under *other* conditions, it may be beneficial. For *most* children under *most* conditions, *most* television is probably neither particularly harmful nor particularly beneficial" (Schramm et al., 1961, p. 1, italics in original). Yet they also concluded that those Canadian and American children studied who had high exposure to television and low exposure to print media were more aggressive than those with the reverse pattern. Thus, the early correlational studies identified some areas of concern about television violence and set the stage for more focused investigations.

Correlation Studies Come of Age

The demonstration of a relationship between viewing and aggressive behavior in daily life circumstances is a logical precursor to studies of the causal role that TV violence may play in promoting aggressive behavior. The correlational studies that followed the Himmelweit et al. (1958) and Schramm et al. (1961) studies mentioned earlier, including those conducted for the Surgeon General's research program (McLeod et al., 1972a, 1972b; Dominick & Greenberg, 1972; Robinson & Bachman, 1972), found consistent patterns of significant correlations between the number of hours of television viewed (or the frequency of viewing violent programs) and various measures of aggressive attitudes or behavior. Also, another study, conducted by Charles Atkin, Bradley Greenberg, Felipe Korzenny, and Steven McDermott (1979), found that heavy TV-violence viewers were more likely to choose physical and verbal aggressive responses to solve hypothetical interpersonal conflict situations (that is, 45 percent of the heavy violence viewers chose physical/verbal aggressive responses versus 21 percent of the low violence viewers). Similarly, a further study of this type (Walker & Morley, 1991) found that adolescents who reported enjoying TV violence were more likely to hold attitudes and values favorable to behaving aggressively in conflict situations.

In another correlational approach, a large database, the Cultural Indicators Project, has been used to explore the relationship between television portrayals and the viewer's fearful conception of the world. (See chapter 10 for a thorough discussion of this research project in general, and chapter 8 for more information on its application to the study of media violence.)

Correlational Panel Studies

While correlational studies can show us that there is a relationship between viewing media violence and behavior and/or beliefs, they do not address the issue of cause and effect. While authors might interpret correlational data to provide evidence of cause and effect, they can't say for sure in which direction the relationship goes. For example, might naturally aggressive children or teens be more drawn to violent media? And yet, there are some special-case correlational studies in which "intimations of causation" can be derived from the fact that these studies were conducted over several time periods. Three of these special surveys and "panel" studies (so named because the same panel of respondents are studied at various points in time) have been highly influential—a retrospective survey of viewing and current behavior, funded by CBS (Belson, 1978), a panel study, funded by NBC (Milavsky et al., 1982), and another panel study, funded by the Surgeon General's Committee and NIMH (Lefkowitz et al., 1972; Huesmann & Eron, 1986; Huesmann et al., 1984).

The CBS study (Belson, 1978) was conducted in England with 1,565 youths who were a representative sample of thirteen- to seventeen-year-old males living in London. This retrospective survey looked at the history of viewing violent programs that had been broadcast over twelve years in England and related that to the behavior of the boys during the previous six months. The boys were interviewed concerning the extent of their exposure to a selection of violent television programs (broadcast during the period 1959 through 1971 and rated by members of the BBC viewing panel for level of violence) as well as each boy's level of violent behavior as determined by his report of how often he had been involved in any of fifty-three categories of violence over the previous six months. The degree of seriousness of the acts reported by the boys ranged from only slightly violent aggravation, such as taunting, to more serious and very violent behavior such as: "I tried to force a girl to have sexual intercourse with me"; "I bashed a boy's head against a wall"; "I burned a boy on the chest with a cigarette while my mates held him down"; and "I threatened to kill my father." Approximately 50 percent of the 1,565 boys were not involved in any violent acts during the six-month period. However, of those who were involved in violence, 188 (12 percent) were involved in ten or more acts during the six-month period. When William Belson compared the behavior of boys who had higher exposure to televised violence to that of those who had lower exposure (and had been matched on a wide variety of possible contributing factors), he found that the high-violence viewers were more involved in serious interpersonal violence.

The NBC study (Milavsky et al., 1982) was conducted over a three-year period from May 1970 to December 1973 in two cities, Fort Worth and Minneapolis. Interviews were conducted with samples of second- to sixth-grade boys and girls and a special sample of teenage boys. In the elementary-school sample, the information on television viewing and measures of aggression was collected in six time periods over the three years. The aggression measure consisted of peer ratings of aggressive behavior based on the work of Leonard Eron and his colleagues (Eron et al., 1971). In the teenage sample there were five waves of interviews over the three years and the aggression measures were self-reported rather than peer-reported aggression. In summarizing the results of this study, the authors concluded, "On the basis of the analyses we carried out to test for such a causal connection there is no evidence that television exposure has a consistently significant effect on subsequent aggressive behavior in the sample of [elementary-school] boys" (Milavsky et al., 1982, p. 482). Similar null findings were reported for the elementary-school girls and the teenage boys. However, re-analyses of these data by David Kenny (1984) and Thomas Cook and his associates (Cook et al., 1983) have concluded that there are small but clear causal effects in the NBC data, and that these effects become stronger when analyzed over longer time periods through successive waves of interviews.

Finally, one of the longest panel studies, over twenty years, is the work of Eron and his colleagues (Eron, 1963, 1982; Huesmann & Eron, 1986; Huesmann et al., 1984; Lefkowitz et al., 1972). In the initial studies, conducted for the Surgeon General's investigation of TV violence (Lefkowitz et al., 1972), the researchers were able to document the long-term effects of violence viewing by studying children over a ten-year period from age eight to age eighteen. At these two time periods, the youngsters were interviewed about their program preferences and information was collected from peer ratings of aggressive behavior. The violence levels of their preferred TV programs and other media and measures of aggression across these two time periods suggested the possibility that early television violence viewing was one factor in producing later aggressive behavior. In particular, the findings for 211 boys followed in this longitudinal study demonstrated that TV violence at age eight was significantly related to aggression at age eight, and the eight-year-olds' violent TV preferences were significantly related to aggression at age eighteen, but TV violence preferences at age eighteen were not related to aggressive behavior at the earlier time period, age eight. When other possible variables, such as parenting practices and discipline style, were controlled it was still clear that early media violence could be part of the cause of later aggressive behavior. Furthermore, in a follow-up study, when these young men were age thirty (Huesmann et al., 1984), the authors found a significant correlation between TV violence levels at age eight and serious interpersonal criminal behavior (for example, assault, murder, child abuse, spouse abuse, rape) at age thirty. (Refer back to chapter 8 for additional discussion of this research.)

Thus, it seems clear that a correlation between television violence and aggression can be established from diverse studies. And some special cases of longitudinal correlational studies (described as cross-lagged/panel studies) can lead to intimations of causation. However, the issue of causation is best assessed in experimental designs that allow for random assignment of subjects to various treatment conditions or, in the case of field studies, take advantage of naturally occurring variations in television viewing experiences.

Early Experimental Studies

The earliest experimental studies on the effects of media violence on young people emerged in the 1960s, and have proven so influential (and even controversial) that they are still cited today. These initial experiments were conducted by Albert Bandura, at Stanford University, who studied preschool-age children, and Leonard Berkowitz, at the University of Wisconsin, who worked with college-age youth. In both instances, the studies were experimental in design, which meant that subjects were randomly assigned to various viewing experiences, enabling the researchers to apply the results of this manipulated viewing to address the issue of causal relationships between viewing and behavior. The early Bandura studies, such as *Transmission of Aggression through Imitation of Aggressive Models* (Bandura et al., 1961) and *Imitation of Film-Mediated Aggressive Models* (Bandura et al., 1963), were set within a social-learning paradigm and were designed to identify the processes governing the ways that children learn by observing and imitating the behavior of others. In this context, therefore, the studies used stimulus films (videotape was not generally available) back-projected on a simulated television screen. Immediately following the viewing period, the behavior of the children was observed and recorded in a playroom setting. Despite the structured nature of these studies, Bandura's research was central to the debate about the influence of media violence.

Moreover, the work of Berkowitz and his colleagues, such as *Effects of Film Violence on Inhibitions against Subsequent Aggression* (Berkowitz & Rawlings, 1963) and *Film Violence and the Cue Properties of Available Targets* (Berkowitz & Geen, 1966), studied the simulated aggressive behavior of youth and young adults following the viewing of segments of violent films, such as a Kirk Douglas boxing film, *The Champion*. The demonstration of increased willingness to use aggression against others following viewing further fueled the debate about the influence of media violence.

Experimental Studies Come of Age

While the studies of Bandura (for example, Bandura et al., 1961, 1963) and Berkowitz (for example, Berkowitz & Rawlings, 1963) set the stage, later experimental studies have employed both the structured, laboratory-based settings as well as more naturalistic settings in schools and communities. One of the earlier studies in this genre (Liebert & Baron, 1972) assessed the effects of viewing segments of a violent television program, *The Untouchables*, on the aggressive behavior of five- to nine-year-old boys and girls. In this study, the children viewed either *The Untouchables* or a neutral, but active, track race. Following viewing, the child was placed in a playroom setting in which he or she could help or hurt another child who was ostensibly playing a game in another room. The subject could help the other child by pressing a button that would make the game easier to play and allow the other child to win more points. Similarly, the child could hurt the other child by pressing a button that would make the game very difficult to play and hence lose points. The results indicated that youngsters who had viewed the violent program manifested a greater willingness to hurt the other child than youngsters who had watched the neutral program. Moreover, an elaboration of this study by Paul Ekman and colleagues (Ekman et al., 1972) included the recording of the facial expressions of these children while they were watching the television violence. In this instance, the children whose facial expressions indicated interest or pleasure while watching TV violence were more willing to hurt the other child than the youngsters whose facial expressions indicated disinterest or displeasure while watching TV violence. Thus, this set of studies identified some potential moderating variables in the violence-viewing/aggressive-behavior equation.

Other early experiments by researchers using physiological measures of arousal (for example, GSR—galvanic skin response, a measure of sweating on the palms of the hand—and heart rate and respiration changes) while watching violent cartoons (Osborn & Endsley, 1971; Cline et al., 1973) found that children were emotionally responsive even to cartoon violence. So too, other studies (Ellis & Sekyra, 1972; Hapkiewitz & Roden, 1971; Lovaas, 1961; Mussen & Rutherford, 1961; Ross, 1972) found that exposure to even one violent cartoon led to increased aggression in the structured playroom settings. Furthermore, studies by Ronald Drabman and his colleagues (Drabman & Thomas, 1974; Thomas et al., 1977) showed that children who viewed violent television programs became desensitized to violence and were more willing to tolerate aggressive behavior in others. Moreover, later studies with emotionally disturbed children (Gadow & Sprafkin, 1993; Grimes et al., 1997) found that these youngsters may have been more vulnerable to the influence of TV violence. For example, Tom Grimes and colleagues (1997) found that eight- to twelve-year-olds who were diagnosed as having either attention-deficit-hyperactivity disorder, oppositional defiant disorder, or conduct disorder manifested less emotional concern for victims and were more willing to accept violence as justified than a matched group of children who did not have these disorders.

All of the studies described above were conducted in fairly structured laboratory or playroom settings where the display of aggression or emotional arousal or desensitization were relatively contiguous to the viewing of TV violence. Questions remain about what might happen in more naturalistic settings or field studies of violence viewing and aggressive behavior. One early study that assessed these issues was the work of Aletha (Stein) Huston and Lynette (Friedrich) Cofer (Friedrich & Stein, 1973; Stein & Friedrich, 1972), in which they assessed the impact of viewing aggressive versus prosocial television programs on the behavior of preschoolers in their normal child-care settings.

In this study, the preschoolers were assigned to view a diet of either *Batman* and *Superman* cartoons, or *Mister Rogers' Neighborhood,* or neutral programming that contained neither aggressive nor prosocial material (special travel stories for preschoolers). The diet consisted of twelve half-hour episodes that were viewed one half hour per day, three days per week, for four weeks. The researchers observed the children in the classroom and on the playground for three weeks prior to the start of the viewing period, to establish a baseline for the amount of aggression or prosocial behavior, and continued to observe the children during the four weeks of viewing and for an additional two weeks.

The results were that children who were initially more aggressive and had viewed the diet of *Batman* and *Superman* cartoons were more active in the classroom and on the playground, played more roughly with toys, and got into more aggressive encounters. Conversely, youngsters from lower-income families who had viewed the *Mister Rogers'* diet increased their prosocial helping behavior. One suggestion from this early field study is that viewing aggressive program content can lead to changes in aggressive behavior, while the opposite is also true for prosocial programming. Moreover, these changes were demonstrated in a relatively short viewing period (twelve half hours) and in the context of other viewing that took place outside of the classroom setting.

Other field studies have used restricted populations such as boys in detention centers or secure residential settings. In one such study, conducted for NBC, Seymour Feshbach and Robert Singer (1971) presented preadolescent and adolescent males in a security facility with a diet of aggressive or nonaggressive television programs over a six-week period and measured their daily aggressive behavior. They found that the youngsters who watched the nonaggressive programs were more aggressive than the other group. However, this study was criticized on methodological grounds relating to the selection of subjects and the assignment of viewing conditions (Liebert et al., 1972), and a subsequent replication (Wells, 1973) failed to duplicate the findings. Moreover, a later study conducted by Berkowitz and his colleagues (Parke et al., 1977), using aggressive or nonaggressive films presented to adolescent males living in minimum-security institutions, did demonstrate increases in both verbal and physical interpersonal aggression among the teens viewing the aggressive diet.

Another approach to field studies involved the assessment of the effects of naturally occurring differences in the television exposure available to children in communities with or without television or communities with differing television content. In one set of studies (Murray & Kippax, 1977, 1978) the researchers were able to study the introduction of television in a rural community in Australia, in contrast to two similar communities that had differing experiences with television. In a second set of studies (Williams, 1986;

MacBeth, 1996) the research team studied the introduction of television in a rural Canadian community, in contrast to two similar communities with differing television experience. In general, the results of both the Australian and the Canadian studies converge in showing that the introduction of television had a major influence on restructuring the social lives of children in these rural communities. In this regard, both studies found that television displaced other media use and involvement in various social activities—a finding not dissimilar to the earlier studies of children in England (Himmelweit et al., 1958) or the United States and Canada (Schramm et al., 1961). However, with regard to the effects of TV violence, these newer field studies provide stronger evidence of negative influence, in differing but complementary ways. My colleague Susan Kippax and I (Murray, 1980) found changes in perceptions of the seriousness and prevalence of crime among children in the town exposed to higher levels of television violence, while Leslie Joy and her colleagues (Joy et al., 1986) found increases in aggression among children following the introduction of television in the town.

Future Directions in Media Violence Research

Research conducted over the past fifty years leads to the conclusion that televised violence does affect viewers' attitudes, values, and behavior (Hearold, 1986; Murray, 1994; Paik & Comstock, 1994). As pointed out in chapter 8, there seem to be three main classes of effects—aggression, desensitization, and fear/mean-world syndrome. Although the body of research on the effects of viewing television violence is extensive and fairly coherent in demonstrating systematic patterns of influence, we know surprisingly little about the processes involved in the production of these effects. Although we know that viewing televised violence can lead to increases in aggressive behavior or fearfulness and changed attitudes and values about the role of violence in society, it would be helpful to know more about how these changes occur in viewers.

To set the context for continuing research—within the broad framework of a social learning paradigm—we know that changes in behavior and thoughts can result from observing models in the world around us, be they parents, peers, or other role models, such as those provided by mass media. The processes involved in "modeling" or imitation and vicarious learning of overt behavior were addressed in social-learning theories in the 1960s (Bandura, 1962, 1965, 1969; Berkowitz, 1962, 1965), but we need to expand our understanding of the neurological processes that might govern the translation of the observed models into thoughts and actions.

As a start in this new direction, both Bandura (1994) and Berkowitz (1984) have provided some theoretical foundations for the translation of communication "events" into thoughts and actions. Bandura's "social-cognitive" approach and Berkowitz's outline of a "cognitive-neoassociation" analysis posit a role for emotional arousal as an affective tag that may facilitate lasting influences. As Bandura (1994, p. 75) notes, "People are easily aroused by the emotional expressions of others. Vicarious arousal operates mainly through an intervening self-arousal process. . . . That is, seeing others react emotionally to instigating conditions activates emotion-arousing thoughts and imagery in observers." With regard to aggression, we know that viewing television violence can be emotionally arousing (for example, Cline et al., 1973; Osborn & Endsley, 1971; Zillman, 1971, 1982), but we lack direct measures of cortical (brain) arousal or activation patterns in relation to violence viewing. Indeed, a National Research Council (1993) report from the Panel on the Understanding and Control of Violent Behavior concluded,

> All human behavior, including aggression and violence, is the outcome of complex processes in the brain. Violent behaviors may result from relatively permanent conditions or from temporary states. . . . Biological research on aggressive and violent behavior has given particular attention to the following in recent years: . . . (2) functioning of steroid hormones such as testosterone and glucocorticoids, especially their action on steroid receptors in the brain; . . . (6) neurophysiological (i.e., brain wave) abnormalities, particularly in the temporal lobe of the brain; (7) brain dysfunctions that interfere with language processing or cognition. (pp. 115–116)

Thus, one suggestion for further research on the impact of media violence is to assess some of the neurological correlates of viewing televised violence. In particular, the use of videotaped violent scenes can serve as the ideal stimulus for assessing activation patterns in response to violence. These neurobiological studies hold the key to understanding the ways in which children might respond to seeing violence in entertainment, and this might also be the key to thinking about the desensitization to violence, or what some might describe as a "drugging" effect on the developing child.

To assess this possibility, my colleagues and I have embarked on an initial study of children's brain activations while the youngsters view violent and nonviolent video program material. We reasoned that there may be similarities between the ways humans respond to the threats of physical violence in the real world and the neurobiological response to so-called entertainment violence. We began our study with some notions and expectations drawn from previous research suggesting that we might find the "threat recognition" system—involving the limbic system and right hemisphere of the brain—as an area that will be activated while viewing video violence. The development of hypotheses about violence viewing and brain activation, however, needs to start with research on physiological arousal (for example, Osborn & Endsley, 1971; Zillmann, 1982; Zillmann & Bryant, 1994) and link this to cortical arousal (Ekman & Davidson, 1993, 1994; Ekman et al., 1990; Davidson et al., 1990; Davidson & Tomarken, 1989).

In our pilot study (Murray, 2001; Murray et al., 2002), we found that both violent and nonviolent viewing activated regions implicated in aspects of visual and auditory processing. In contrast, however, viewing TV violence appears to activate brain areas involved in arousal/attention, detection of threat, episodic memory encoding and retrieval, and motor programming.

Our continuing research at Harvard Medical School, Children's Hospital, Boston, is designed to address these questions about violence viewing in a more robust study that employs a larger and more differentiated sample of children who have had differing experiences with violence (for example, children who are identified as high or low in aggressive tendencies and children who have been victims of abuse). We will continue to use the methods and procedures that were demonstrated to be effective in the pilot study—we will conjoin measures of physiological arousal (for example, GSR, heart rate) with neuroimaging techniques (for example, functional magnetic resonance imaging—fMRI) to track the emotional and neurological processes involved in viewing televised violence. We anticipate finding clear differences in the three groups of children, with the victims of violence (that is, the abused youngsters) being most responsive to viewing media violence and the aggressive youngsters being the least responsive to the entertainment violence. In this case, the heightened neurological response to seeing violence by victims or abused youngsters indicates an arousal or activation of fear, based on prior experience with real-world violence. Reduced arousal to the video violence by the aggressive youngsters indicates the desensitization effect that results from extensive violence viewing and acting out the violence witnessed in the entertainment world of film, television, and video-game violence.

So, what reasonable conclusions can be drawn from the data found in these and the hundreds of studies of media violence and children that have been conducted over the past half century? As the esteemed philosopher Plato (1991, p. 72) asked in 434 B.C., "And shall we just carelessly allow children to hear any casual tales which may be devised by casual persons, and to receive into their minds ideas for the most part the very opposite of those which we should wish them to have when they are grown up?" While this may sound like a very "paternalistic" comment on the part of a "very old man" almost 2,500 years ago, it is a cautionary note about the fact that a society should be very concerned about the ways in which its citizens choose to amuse themselves. We run the risk of amusing ourselves to death.

EXERCISES

1   Come up with a definition of media violence. Does your definition include only actual physical violence or does it include threats of violence? Does it include emotional/psychological violence? Verbal violence? What kind of physical violence does it include? Intentional only? Accidental? Humorous/slapstick? Do the consequences for the perpetrator factor into your definition? Once you've arrived at your definition of media violence apply it to your own viewing of television over the course of the next week. Specifically, how often do you see violence, as you define it, in the programs you watch? Provide specific examples.

2   Take the definition of violence you created in the previous exercise and apply it to study violence in children's television. Watch several hours of children's cartoons in order to determine how often you see violence, as you define it, in these cartoons. Provide specific examples.

3   Select one of the studies identified in each of the following sections of this chapter: "Correlational Studies Come of Age," "Correlational Panel Studies," and "Experimental Studies Come of Age." After reading these three studies, compare and contrast each

in terms of how they define violence/aggression, methodology employed, and overall findings. Which study do you find most compelling and why?

4   If your school library has the Frontline video *Does TV Kill?* (McLeod, 1995), watch it your- self or ask your instructor to show it in class. This video contains scenes/reports from many of the studies discussed in this chapter. How compelling is the evidence offered in the video?

REFERENCES

Atkin, C. K., Greenberg, B. S., Korzenny, F., & McDermott, S. (1979). Selective exposure to televised vio- lence. *Journal of Broadcasting, 23*(1), 5–13.

Baker, R. K., & Ball, S. J. (1969). *Mass media and violence: A staff report to the National Commission on the Causes and Prevention of Violence.* Washington, D.C.: United States Government Printing Office.

Bandura, A. (1962). Social learning through imitation. In M. R. Jones (Ed.). *Nebraska symposium on moti- vation* (pp. 211–269). Lincoln: University of Nebraska Press.

Bandura, A. (1965). Vicarious processes: A case of no-trial learning. In L. Berkowitz (Ed.), *Advances in exper- imental social psychology* (vol. 2, pp. 1–55). New York: Academic Press.

Bandura, A. (1969). Social-learning theory of identificatory processes. In D. A. Goslin (Ed.), *Handbook of socialization theory and research.* Chicago: Rand-McNally.

Bandura, A. (1994). Social cognitive theory of mass communication. In J. Bryant & D. Zillmann (Eds.), *Media effects: Advances in theory and research* (pp. 61–90). Hillsdale, NJ: Lawrence Erlbaum.

Bandura, A., Ross, D., & Ross, S. H. (1961). Transmission of aggression through imitation of aggressive mod- els. *Journal of Abnormal and Social Psychology, 63*(3), 575–582.

Bandura, A., Ross, D., & Ross, S. H. (1963). Imitation of film-mediated aggressive models. *Journal of Abnormal and Social Psychology, 66*(1), 3–11.

Belson, W. (1978). *Television violence and the adolescent boy.* Farnborough: Saxon House, Teakfield Limited.

Berkowitz, L. (1962). *Aggression: A social psychological analysis.* New York: McGraw-Hill.

Berkowitz, L. (1965). Some aspects of observed aggression. *Journal of Personality and Social Psychology, 2,* 359–365.

Berkowitz, L. (1984). Some effects of thoughts on anti- and prosocial influences of media events: A cognitive-neoassociation analysis. *Psychological Bulletin, 95,* 110–427.

Berkowitz, L., & Geen, R. G. (1966). Film violence and the cue properties of available targets. *Journal of Personality and Social Psychology, 3*(5), 525–530.

Berkowitz, L., & Rawlings, E. (1963). Effects of film violence on inhibitions against subsequent aggression. *Journal of Abnormal and Social Psychology, 66*(5), 405–412.

Cline, V. B., Croft, R. G., & Courrier, S. (1973). Desensitization of children to television violence. *Journal of Personality and Social Psychology, 27,* 360–365.

Cook, T. D., Kendzierski, D. A., & Thomas, S. A. (1983). The implicit assumptions of television research: An analysis of the 1982 NIMH report on "Television and Behavior." *Public Opinion Quarterly, 47*(2), 161–201.

Cressey, P. G., & Thrasher, F. M. (1933). *Boys, movies, and city streets.* New York: Macmillan.

Davidson, R. J., Ekman, P., Saron, C., Senulis, J, & Friesen, W. V. (1990). Emotional expression and brain physiology I: Approach/withdrawal and cerebral asymmetry. *Journal of Personality and Social Psychology, 58*, 330–341.

Davidson, R. J., & Tomarken, A. J. (1989). Laterality and emotion: An electrophysiological approach. In F. Boller & J. Grafman (Eds.), *Handbook of neuropsychology* (pp. 419–441). Amsterdam: Elsevier.

Dominick, J. R., & Greenberg, B. S. (1972). Attitudes toward violence: The interaction of television exposure, family attitudes, and social class. In G. A. Comstock & E. A. Rubinstein (Eds.), *Television and social behavior, vol. 3: Television and adolescent aggressiveness* (pp. 314–335). Washington, D.C.: United States Government Printing Office.

Drabman, R. S., & Thomas, M. H. (1974). Does media violence increase children's toleration of real-life aggression? *Developmental Psychology, 10*, 418–421.

Ekman, P., & Davidson, R. J. (1993). Voluntary smiling changes regional brain activity. *Psychological Science, 4*(5), 342–345.

Ekman, P., & Davidson, R. J. (1994). *The nature of emotion: Fundamental questions*. New York: Oxford University Press.

Ekman, P., Davidson, R. J., & Friesen, W. V. (1990). The Duchenne smile: Emotional expression and brain physiology II. *Journal of Personality and Social Psychology, 58*, 342–353.

Ekman, P., Liebert, R. M., Friesen, W., Harrison, R., Zlatchin, C., Malmstrom, E. V., & Baron, R.A. (1972). Facial expressions of emotion as predictors of subsequent aggression. In G. A. Comstock, E. A. Rubinstein, & J. P. Murray (Eds.), *Television and social behavior, vol. 5: Television's effects: Further explorations* (pp. 22–58). Washington, D.C.: United States Government Printing Office.

Ellis, G. T., & Sekyra, F. (1972). The effect of aggressive cartoons on behavior of first grade children. *Journal of Psychology, 81*, 37–43.

Eron, L. (1963). Relationship of TV viewing habits and aggressive behavior in children. *Journal of Abnormal and Social Psychology, 67*, 193–196.

Eron, L. (1982). Parent child interaction, television violence and aggression of children. *American Psychologist, 27*, 197–211.

Eron, L. D., Walder, L. O., & Lefkowitz, M. M. (1971). *Learning of aggression in children*. Boston: Little, Brown.

Feshbach, S., & Singer, R. D. (1971). *Television and aggression: An experimental field study*. San Francisco: Jossey-Bass.

Friedrich, L. K., & Stein, A. H. (1973). Aggressive and prosocial television programs and the natural behavior of preschool children. *Monographs of the Society for Research in Child Development* 38(4), serial no. 151.

Gadow, K. D., & Sprafkin, J. (1993). Television violence and children with emotional and behavioral disorders. *Journal of Emotional and Behavioral Disorders, 1*(1), 54–63.

Grimes, T., Vernberg, E., & Cathers, T. (1997). Emotionally disturbed children's reactions to violent media segments. *Journal of Health Communication, 2*(3), 157–168.

Group for the Advancement of Psychiatry. (1982). *The child and television drama: The psychosocial impact of cumulative viewing*. New York: Mental Health Materials Center.

Hapkiewitz, W. G., & Roden, A. H. (1971). The effect of aggressive cartoons on children's interpersonal play. *Child Development, 42*, 1583–1585.

Hearold, S. (1986). A synthesis of 1,043 effects of television on social behavior. In G. Comstock (Ed.), *Public communication and behavior, vol. 1* (pp. 65–133). New York: Academic Press.

Himmelweit, H. T., Oppenheim, A. N., & Vince, P. (1958). *Television and the child: An empirical study of the effects of television on the young*. London: Oxford University Press.

Huesmann, L. R. & Eron, L. D. (Eds.). (1986). *Television and the aggressive child: A cross-national comparison*. Hillsdale, NJ: Lawrence Erlbaum.

Huesmann, L. R., Eron, L. D., Lefkowitz, M. M., & Walder, L. O. (1984). Stability of aggression over time and generations. *Developmental Psychology, 20*, 1120–1134.

Huston, A.C., Donnerstein, E., Fairchild, H., Feshbach, N. D., Katz, P. A., Murray, J. P., Rubinstein, E. A., Wilcox, B., & Zuckerman, D. (1992). *Big world, small screen: The role of television in American society*. Lincoln: University of Nebraska Press.

Joy, L. A., Kimball, M., & Zabrack, M. L. (1986). Television exposure and children's aggressive behavior. In T. M. Williams (Ed.), *The impact of television: A natural experiment involving three towns* (pp. 303–360). New York: Academic Press.

Kenny, D. A. (1984). The NBC study and television violence. *Journal of Communication, 34*(1), 176–182.

Lazarsfeld, P. F. (1955). Why is so little known about the effects of television and what can be done? *Public Opinion Quarterly, 19*, 243–251.

Lefkowitz, M., Eron, L., Walder, L., & Huesmann, L. R. (1972). Television violence and child aggression: A follow up study. In G. A. Comstock & E. A. Rubinstein (Eds.), *Television and social behavior, vol. 3: Television and adolescent aggressiveness*. Washington, D.C.: United States Government Printing Office.

Liebert, R. M. & Baron, R. A. (1972). Short term effects of television aggression on children's aggressive behavior. In G. A. Comstock, E. A. Rubinstein, & J. P. Murray (Eds.), *Television and social behavior, vol. 2: Television and social learning*. Washington, D.C.: United States Government Printing Office.

Liebert, R. M., Sobol, M. D., & Davidson, E. S. (1972). Catharsis of aggression among institutionalized boys: Fact or artifact? In G. A. Comstock, E. A. Rubinstein, & J. P. Murray (Eds.), *Television and social behavior, vol. 5: Television's effects: Further explorations*. Washington, D.C.: United States Government Printing Office.

Lovaas, O. I. (1961). Effect of exposure to symbolic aggression on aggressive behavior. *Child Development, 32*, 37–44.

MacBeth, T. M. (1996). *Tuning in to young viewers: Social science perspectives on television*. Thousand Oaks, CA: Sage.

Maccoby, E. E. (1954). Why do children watch television? *Public Opinion Quarterly, 18*, 239–244.

McLeod, J. M., Atkin, C. K., & Chaffee, S. H. (1972a). Adolescents, parents, and television use: Adolescent self-report measures from Maryland and Wisconsin samples. In G. A. Comstock & E. A. Rubinstein (Eds.), *Television and social behavior, vol. 3: Television and adolescent aggressiveness* (pp. 173–239). Washington, D.C.: United States Government Printing Office.

McLeod, J. M., Atkin, C. K., & Chaffee, S. H. (1972b). Adolescents, parents, and television use: Self-report and other measures from the Wisconsin sample. In G. A. Comstock & E. A. Rubinstein (Eds.), *Television and social behavior, vol. 3: Television and adolescent aggressiveness*. Washington, D.C.: United States Government Printing Office.

McLeod, M. (Producer). (1995, January 10). *Does TV kill?* [Television Broadcast]. In D. Fanning (Executive Producer), *Frontline*. Alexandria, VA: Public Broadcasting Service.

Milavsky, J. R., Kessler, R. C., Stipp, H. H., & Rubens, W. S. (1982). *Television and aggression: A panel study*. New York: Academic Press.

Murray, J. P. (1973). Television and violence: Implications of the Surgeon General's research program.

American Psychologist, 28(6), 472–478.

Murray, J. P. (1980). *Television and youth: 25 years of research and controversy.* Boys Town, NE: Boys Town Center for the Study of Youth Development.

Murray, J. P. (1994). The impact of televised violence. *Hofstra Law Review, 22*(4), 809–825.

Murray, J. P. (2001). TV violence and brainmapping in children. *Psychiatric Times, 17*(10), 70–71.

Murray, J. P., & Kippax, S. (1977). Television diffusion and social behavior in three communities: A field experiment. *Australian Journal of Psychology, 29*(1), 31–43.

Murray, J. P., & Kippax, S. (1978). Children's social behavior in three towns with differing television experience. *Journal of Communication, 28*(1), 19–29.

Murray, J. P., & Kippax, S. (1979). From the early window to the late night show: International trends in the study of television's impact on children and adults. In L. Berkowitz (Ed.), *Advances in experimental social psychology, vol. 12* (pp. 253–320). New York: Academic Press.

Murray, J. P., Liotti, M., Ingmundson, P., Mayberg, H. S., Pu, Y., Zamarripa, F., Liu, Y., Woldorff, M., Gao, J-H., & Fox, P. T. (2002). Children's brain activations while viewing televised violence revealed by fMRI. *Media Psychology, 8*(1), 25–37.

Mussen, P., & Rutherford, E. (1961). Effects of aggressive cartoons on children's aggressive play. *Journal of Abnormal and Social Psychology, 62*(2), 461–464.

National Institute of Mental Health. (1982). *Television and behavior: Ten years of scientific progress and implications for the eighties, vol. 1: Summary report.* Washington, D.C.: United States Government Printing Office.

National Research Council. (1993). *Understanding and preventing violence.* Washington, D.C.: National Academy Press.

Osborn, D. K., & Endsley, R. C. (1971). Emotional reactions of young children to TV violence. *Child Development, 42*(1), 321–331.

Paik, H., & Comstock, G. (1994). The effects of television violence on antisocial behavior: A meta-analysis. *Communication Research, 21*(4), 516–546.

Parke, R. D., Berkowitz, L., Leyens, J. P., West, S. & Sebastian, R. J. (1977). Some effects of violent and nonviolent movies on the behavior of juvenile delinquents. In L. Berkowitz (Ed.), *Advances in Experimental Psychology, vol. 10* (pp. 135–172). New York: Academic Press.

Pearl, D., Bouthilet, L., & Lazar, J. (Eds.). (1982). *Television and behavior: Ten years of scientific progress and implications for the eighties, vol. 2: Technical reviews.* Washington, D.C.: United States Government Printing Office.

Pecora, N., Murray, J. P., & Wartella, E. (2006). *Children and television: 50 years of research.* Mahwah, NJ: Lawrence Erlbaum.

Plato. (1991). *The republic, book II* (Benjamin Jowett, Trans.). New York: Vintage. (Original work published in 432 B.C.).

Robinson, J. P., & Bachman, J .G. (1972). Television viewing habits and aggression. In G. A. Comstock & E. A. Rubinstein (Eds.), *Television and social behavior, vol. 3: Television and adolescent aggressiveness* (pp. 372–383). Washington, D.C.: United States Government Printing Office.

Ross, L. B. (1972). *The effect of aggressive cartoons on the group play of children.* Unpublished doctoral dissertation, Miami University.

Schramm, W., Lyle, J., & Parker, E. B. (1961). *Television in the lives of our children.* Palo Alto, CA: Stanford University Press.

Stein, A. H., & Friedrich, L. K. (1972). Television content and young children's behavior. In J. P. Murray, E. A. Rubinstein, & G. A. Comstock (Eds.), *Television and social behavior, vol. 2: Television and social learning*. Washington, D.C.: United States Government Printing Office.

Surgeon General's Scientific Advisory Committee on Television and Social Behavior. (1972). *Television and growing up: The impact of televised violence*. Washington, D.C.: United States Government Printing Office.

Thomas, M. H., Horton, R. W., Lippincott, E. C., & Drabman, R. S. (1977). Desensitization to portrayals of real life aggression as a function of television violence. *Journal of Personality and Social Psychology, 35*(6), 450–458.

United States Congress, House Committee on Interstate and Foreign Commerce. (1952). *Investigation of Radio and Television Programs, Hearings and Report, 82nd Congress, 2nd session, June 3–December 5, 1952*. Washington, D.C.: United States Government Printing Office.

United States Congress, Senate Committee of the Judiciary, Subcommittee to Investigate Juvenile Delinquency. (1955). *Juvenile Delinquency (Television Programs), Hearings, 83rd Congress, 2nd session, June 5–October 20, 1954*. Washington, D.C.: United States Government Printing Office.

United States Congress, United States Senate. (2003). Senate Commerce Committee, Subcommittee on Science, Technology and Space, Hearing, April 10, 2003, *Neurobiological Research and the Impact of Media*. Washington, D.C.

United States Congress, United States Senate (2006). Senate Commerce Committee, Subcommittee on Science Technology and Space, Hearing, 29 March 2006, *Video Game Violence and Youth Aggression*, Washington, D.C.

Walker, K. B., & Morley, D. D. (1991). Attitudes and parental factors as intervening variables in the television violence-aggression relation. *Communication Research, 8*(2), 41–47.

Wells, W. D. (1973). *Television and aggression: Replication of an experimental field study*. Unpublished manuscript, Graduate School of Business, University of Chicago.

Williams, T. M. (Ed.). (1986). *The impact of television: A natural experiment in three communities*. New York: Academic Press.

Wilson, B. J., Colvin, C. M., & Smith, S. L. (2002). Engaging in violence on American television: A comparison of child, teen, and adult perpetrators. *Journal of Communication, 52*(1), 36–61.

Zillmann, D. (1971). Excitation transfer in communication-mediated aggressive behavior. *Journal of Experimental Social Psychology, 7*, 419–434.

Zillmann, D. (1982). Television viewing and arousal. In D. Pearl, L. Bouthilet, & J. Lazar (Eds.), *Television and behavior: Ten years of scientific progress and implications for the eighties, vol. 2: Technical reviews*. Washington, D.C.: United States Government Printing Office.

Zillmann, D., & Bryant, J. (1994). Entertainment as media effect. In J. Bryant & D. Zillmann (Eds.), *Media effects: Advances in theory and research*. Hillsdale, NJ: Lawrence Erlbaum.

CHAPTER TEN

What Do Young People Learn about the World from Watching Television?

MICHAEL MORGAN

To ask the apparently simple question posed in the title above is to open up a vast array of complex issues. As the chapters in this book vividly demonstrate, there are many ways to think about the role of television and other media in the lives of young people. Television can potentially affect young people's behaviors regarding violence and aggression as well as sex; it can affect what they buy, how they want to dress and act, how they define their identities (and see others), and how they come to understand their place in the world. It can affect what they eat and what they read—even how much they sleep. It can offer them (for good or ill) ways of resolving their own personal problems as well as the larger society's. It can open them up to rich new ways of envisioning the world or numb them with mindless, unimaginative formulaic fare that discourages broader intellectual exploration. It can provide a common coin of exchange to facilitate family or peer interaction or set the stage for isolation or conflict. The list of possible impacts goes on and on.

These sorts of concerns about the effects of television on children and adolescents (especially the more negative ones) have been around since the very earliest days of the medium. Over the past fifty years, each new generation of parents, social critics, teachers, and politicians has sounded the same alarms about what television means for adolescents in terms of violence, sex, commercialism, stereotypes, school performance, moral values, and much more. Many of the same fears had been expressed about earlier media such as films and comic books (and earlier, even novels), and they have only been amplified by more recent developments such as video games and the Internet. (See chapter 3 for a discussion of such moral panics.)

Television, however, is different from other media (both new and old). In particular, it has been and continues to be the most common, pervasive, and massively consumed source of *stories*. As such, it has revolutionized the way children and adolescents are socialized, in the United States and around the globe. One particular way of looking at the storytelling role of television—and to answer the question posed in the title of this chapter—is through the lens of *cultivation analysis*, an approach to studying media effects originally developed by George Gerbner (see Gerbner, 1969; Gerbner et al., 2002; Morgan, 2002).

Cultivation analysis explores the implications of growing up and living with television, in terms of the extent to which people's beliefs and assumptions about the "real world" are shaped by long-term, heavy exposure to the stories that television presents. It is part of a broad-based research project called Cultural Indicators that began in 1969. The bibliography of studies relating to the Cultural Indicators Project currently includes over three hundred scholarly publications and is continuing to grow. It is a well-established and influential approach to studying television's effects, although it has also generated a great deal of controversy, over both theoretical and methodological issues (see Shanahan & Morgan, 1999).

Cultural Indicators

The Cultural Indicators research paradigm is based on the assumption that understanding the role and impacts of the media in society requires a holistic view that takes into account the institutions that produce media messages, the messages themselves, and the audiences who consume those messages. Accordingly, the approach involves a three-pronged research strategy. The first, called "institutional process analysis," is designed to shed light on the policies that shape the production of the massive flow of media messages, and the pressures and constraints that affect how decisions are made in media industries. The investigation pinpoints the operation of various power roles and functions within media industries, and provides a basis for comparing media structures across countries or political-economic systems.

Second, "message system analysis" is the systematic examination of annual samples of network television drama, in order to reliably delineate selected features and trends in the world that television presents to its viewers. These analyses began in 1967 and continue today, now incorporating cable programming and additional genres. The accumulated database contains detailed information on well over 3,500 programs and over 50,000 characters.

The goal of message system analysis is to describe "the world" as it is constructed on television. What are the dominant and most consistent patterns of the television world?

How many males and females live in that world, what is the distribution of characters by age, race, ethnicity, class, and occupation, among other things—and how do those patterns fit with or diverge from those of the "real world"? How much violence is there in the television world, and how is it represented—who commits violence and who is shown as a victim? How does television represent the family, science, religion, politics, sexuality, the world of work, childhood, old age, business, health, education, the environment, and other issues? These are the questions asked by message system analysis. The goal is not to describe any particular program or what any individual viewer might see but rather to illuminate the aggregate, overall patterns of casting, actions, stereotypes, representations, images, and narrative structures that emerge across all programs and that dominate the constructed world of television. (See, for example, Nancy Signorielli's research as described in chapter 11 of this book.)

The findings of message system analysis provide the basis for cultivation analysis, the third part of the inquiry, and the main focus of this chapter. In cultivation analysis, we examine the responses given to questions about social reality as they vary according to amount of exposure to the world of television. We want to determine whether those who spend more time watching television are more likely to perceive social reality in ways that reflect the potential lessons of the television world than are those who watch less television but are otherwise comparable (in terms of important demographic characteristics) to the heavy viewers.

Cultivation theory applies broadly to adults as well as to children and adolescents; it is not concerned exclusively with younger people. Nevertheless, adolescents are of special interest and they are frequently the focus of cultivation research. About one third of the nearly six thousand findings examined in a comprehensive review of cultivation studies (Shanahan & Morgan, 1999) refer to adolescents, and there are indications that adolescents are at least somewhat more influenced by television than are adults and older people. Young people are an especially important focus for cultivation research because they are in evolving and formative stages, undergoing dramatic transformations in their understandings of society and themselves, highly susceptible to external influences, and likely to have fewer real-world experiences to bring to bear in their interpretations of what they see on television.

Even with the growth of video games and the Internet, most children and adolescents spend a good bit of time watching television just about every day. Of course, "television" programs may now come to us in many forms—not just from over-the-air broadcast stations and cable networks, but also what we see via a VCR, TiVo, DVD, video on demand, or even a cell phone or an iPod. But the precise type of delivery system does not change the images, the stories, or their lessons; these technological developments mainly increase amount of exposure to television and allow viewers to watch programs whenever they want and wherever they are.

Storytelling

The most general hypothesis of cultivation analysis is that those who spend more time "living" in the world of television are more likely to see the "real world" in terms of the images, values, portrayals, and ideologies that emerge through the lens of television. The concept of "storytelling" is thus central to the theory of cultivation. Gerbner (1967) contends that the basic difference between human beings and other species is that we live in a world created by the stories we tell. All living organisms exchange energy with their environments, and many creatures exchange information and change their behavior as a result of learning. But only humans *communicate* by the manipulation of complex symbol systems. Humans therefore uniquely live in a world experienced and constructed largely through many forms and modes of storytelling. We have never personally or directly experienced great portions of what we know, or think we know; we "know" about many things based on the stories we are told.

Television has transformed the fundamentally human and cultural process of storytelling into a centralized, standardized, market-driven, advertiser-sponsored system. In earlier times, the stories of a culture were told face-to-face by members of a community, parents, teachers, or the clergy. Today television tells most of the stories to most of the people, most of the time. Therefore, as Gerbner points out, the cultural process of storytelling is now in the hands of global commercial interests who have little to tell but something to sell, and who in effect operate outside the reach of democratic decision-making.

Gerbner argues that, given its marketing and commercial imperatives, television tells three different kinds of stories. There are stories about how things *work*, in which the invisible dynamics of human life are illuminated. These stories are called "fiction," and they build a fantasy that informs the story we call reality. There are also stories about how things *are*; today, we mostly call these "news," and they tend to confirm the visions, rules, priorities, and goals of a particular society. And finally, there are stories of value and choice, of what to *do*. These have been called sermons, or instruction, or law; today they are called "commercials." Together, all three kinds of stories, organically related, constitute mediated culture; they are expressed and enacted through mythology, religion, legends, education, art, science, laws, fairy tales, and politics. What makes our age distinct is that all of these, increasingly, are packaged and disseminated by television, and that children today grow up in a world where the third kind of story pays for the other two.

Television has thus become our nation's (and increasingly the world's) most common and constant learning environment. The world of television shows and tells us about life—people, places, striving, power, fate, and family life. It presents the good and bad, the happy and sad, the powerful and the weak, and lets us know who or what is successful or a failure.

Television is only one of the many agencies and institutions that explain the world to us and our children. Television, however, is special because its socially constructed version of reality bombards all classes, groups, and ages with highly consistent and repetitive perspectives. More important, these images are presented primarily in the form of entertainment, whether in sitcoms, drama, action-adventures, TV movies, reality shows, or even news and information programs (and the lines between entertainment and information formats continue to erode).

Children are born into households in which television is virtually a member of the family. The parents of young people today—and increasingly, their grandparents as well—have themselves never lived without television. Young people spend more time watching television than they spend in school. Children enter kindergarten, their first formal exposure to the official public sphere, as already-experienced viewers, with thousands of viewing hours under their belts.

Unlike most other approaches to media effects, cultivation analysis is not concerned with the "impact" of any particular television program, genre, or episode. It is not concerned with formal aesthetic categories, style, artistic quality or creative originality, issues of high culture versus low culture, or specific, selective "readings" or interpretations of media messages. Rather, cultivation researchers approach television as a coherent system of messages, made up of aggregate and repetitive patterns of images and representations. This does not deny that any individual program, type of program, or channel (for example, family programs, soap operas, sports networks, cooking channels, news channels, violent films, and so on) might have some specific "effects" of some kind or another; the point is simply that cultivation analysis emphasizes the consequences of long-term exposure to the entire *system* of messages, in the aggregate.

Therefore, from the point of view of the cultivation of relatively stable and common images, what counts is the total pattern of programming to which total communities are regularly exposed over long periods of time. The pattern of settings, casting, social typing, actions, and related outcomes cuts across most program types and viewing modes and defines the world of television—a world in which many viewers live so much of their lives that they cannot avoid absorbing or dealing with its recurrent patterns, even as series and fads come and go. Even with hundreds of channels and viewing options available, the more people watch the less selective they can be.

Images of Violence

There are many critical discrepancies between "the world" and the "world as portrayed on television." Findings from message system analysis are used to formulate questions about the potential "lessons" viewing may hold for people's conceptions of social reality. Using questionnaires and other standard techniques of survey research, questions are posed to samples of adults, adolescents, or children. The questions have to do with people's beliefs about the world, their attitudes, assumptions, and orientations. Respondents are not asked for their opinions about television, or about any specific messages or programs. They are only asked about how much time they spend watching television (usually, on an "average day"). The sample is then divided into relatively "light," "medium," and "heavy" viewers, based on the distribution in the sample, with one third placed in each group.

The analysis then compares the responses of light, medium, and heavy viewers to the general belief questions, to see what difference (if any) television viewing makes to people's conceptions of the world. In other words, the goal of cultivation analysis is to see if heavier and lighter viewers have different beliefs about the world, and if the beliefs of heavy viewers are closer to the way things are presented on television. The analysis starts with the comparison of simple patterns of differences across light, medium, and heavy viewing groups, and controls for a wide variety of important background and demographic variables (such as age, sex, race, social class, and so on) are implemented, followed by more complex statistical tests.

For example, consider how likely people on television are to encounter violence compared to the rest of us. Over three decades of message system analyses have shown that half or more of television characters are involved each week in some kind of violent action. With minor variations across studies, television presents an average of five or six acts of violence per hour (Signorielli, 2003; Wilson et al., 1997). Although police and FBI statistics have clear limitations, they indicate that in any one year well under 1 percent of people in the United States are victims of criminal violence. According to the Bureau of Justice Statistics, in 2004 there was one rape or sexual assault, and two assaults with injury, per 1,000 persons age twelve or older, and there were about six murder victims per 100,000 persons in 2003 (U.S. Department of Justice, n.d.). Violence is therefore immensely more common on television than it is in the "real world" of the contemporary United States.

For decades, the most common concern about television violence in most public debate has been whether or not it contributes to aggressive behavior. The usual fear is that young people who are exposed to violence on television will imitate it and behave in a violent manner. Although there is much research evidence that suggests that viewing television violence can indeed increase the likelihood of aggressive behavior, it is clear that that is not the most widespread and common consequence of television violence for most people most of the time. Typical viewers see thousands of acts of violence a year on television—heavy viewers may see hundreds a week—and the vast majority of people who watch several hours of television each day do not respond by imitating what they see. But that does not mean that most people are not affected. Instead, it means that for most people the effects are more subtle. (For complete explanations of the research on media violence, refer to chapters 8 and 9.)

Cultivation theory suggests that heavy exposure to television violence will contribute to people's beliefs about the amount of violence in the real world. The core hypothesis of cultivation analysis is that the more time people spend watching television, the more likely they are to report conceptions of social reality that reflect television's most consistent portrayals. Accordingly, respondents (both adolescents and adults) are asked such questions as "In a given week, what percent of all people are involved in violence—is it closer to one in ten or closer to one in a hundred?" Neither of these answers is "correct," but the first one (one in ten) is more like television and is hence referred to as the "TV answer." Cultivation analysis shows that heavy viewers are more likely to give the "TV answer"—that is, to overestimate the amount of violence in society, to believe the world is more dangerous than it is, and to hold numerous inaccurate beliefs about crime and law enforcement (Gerbner et al., 1980, 1979).

All of us, not just young people, learn many such "facts" from watching television. Moreover, cultivation is a continuous process and not a one-time learning event, as regular viewing serves to refresh our images and remind us of many cultural lessons. In this way, cultivation involves the symbolic transformation of such "facts" into more general beliefs, values, and assumptions.

One example of this is what we have called the "mean-world syndrome." Long-term exposure to television, in which frequent violence is virtually inescapable, tends to cultivate the belief that we live in a relatively mean and dangerous world. Compared to those who watch less television, heavy viewers are more likely to think that most people "cannot be trusted," that most people are "just looking out for themselves," and that "you can't be too careful in dealing with people."

The Social Lessons of Violence

At a broader level, Gerbner and his colleagues (1979, 1980) argue that television violence should be seen as a scenario depicting social relationships that reflects the power hierarchy of society and reproduces the social order. Cultivation theory casts television violence as a dramatic demonstration of power that communicates much about social norms and relationships, about winners and losers, about the risks of life and the price for transgression of society's rules. Symbolic violence vividly shows who can get away with what against whom. It tells us who the aggressors are and who the victims are. From a systemic perspective of social control, these are important "lessons" for young people to learn.

Symbolic violence is a way for those *with* power to teach lessons *about* power: how to get it, how to have it, when it can be lost, when it can be used, and who can do so. And symbolic violence teaches these lessons in a fashion that most people see as innocuously entertaining. Again, one function of fictional stories is to make visible and clear that which in the real world is often hidden, blurred, or opaque. Violence is one convenient technique by which this done, as it is a simple and cheap way for a system to demonstrate the rules of its game.

If some people "learn" to be violent from watching television, then might not others learn to be *victims?* After all, there are more victims than aggressors in the television world, both roles are there to be learned by viewers. Apprehension, mistrust, and fear of victimization may be more widespread and general (and subtle) impacts of television violence than occasional acts of imitative aggression. In this way, the fear that may be cultivated by symbolic violence may be an even more effective (and entertaining) mechanism of social control than actual violence.

One may object that society is dangerous and violent, so why should television hide the realities of violence from its audience? Yet, in important ways, that is exactly what television does; the leading causes of real-world injuries, highway and industrial accidents, are difficult to find in the symbolic world. Television violence has little to do with real-world violence but much to do with real-world power.

Gerbner and Larry Gross (1976) also argue that a heightened and widespread sense of fear, danger, and apprehension can bolster demands for greater security; this in turn can mean greater legitimacy of the authority that can promise to meet those demands, creating conditions highly conducive to repression and undermining support for civil liberties. It can also mean greater acceptance of the use of violence as an appropriate means to solve disputes—whether interpersonal or international.

This suggests that television has significant ideological consequences for adolescents (Morgan & Shanahan, 1995). Indeed, James Shanahan (1998) found strong evidence that television cultivates authoritarian attitudes among adolescents. Heavy viewers were more likely to give the authoritarian response to such statements as "There should be clear limits on what people are allowed to say in public," "The government should do what it thinks is right, even if it's not what the majority wants," and "In making family decisions, parents ought to take the opinions of children into account." Authoritarianism generally tends to diminish as adolescents grow older, but this is less likely to happen among heavy viewers; the implication is that heavy television viewing retards adolescents' political development. Importantly, these patterns are independent of abstract/cognitive abilities.

Beyond Violence

Although early cultivation studies focused on the nature and functions of television violence, subsequent research has looked at images and beliefs television cultivates in terms of gender, minority and age-role stereotypes, health, science, the family, sexuality, occupations, political orientations, religion, the environment, and numerous other topics, and many of these have also been examined in a variety of cross-cultural comparative contexts.

Numerous studies have examined assumptions relating to traditional gender roles among young people. Heavy-viewing children and adolescents replicate the role expectations seen on television when asked about appropriate chores for boys and girls (Signorielli & Lears, 1992). Television can also strengthen the consistency between adolescents' gender-based attitudes about chores and their actual behavior in the family (Morgan, 1987).

Television's contributions to the endorsement and maintenance of traditional gender roles has been observed over time in longitudinal data, and in diverse cultural contexts (Morgan, 1982, 1990), through the cultivation of such notions as "women are happiest at home raising children" and "men are born with more ambition than women." Nancy Rothschild (1984) found that children who watch more television were more likely to stereotype both gender-related activities (for example, cooking, playing sports) and gender-related qualities (for example, warmth, independence) along traditional gender-role lines.

Reflecting the glamorization of work on television, Signorielli (1993) found that heavy-viewing adolescents were more likely to want a high-status, prestigious job that would be respected, that would give them a chance to earn a lot of money, and that would provide good chances for advancement. At the same time, adolescent heavy viewers also wanted their jobs to be relatively easy with long vacations and time to do other things. Interestingly, although adolescent girls who watch a lot of television are more likely to believe that "women in general" are happiest staying at home and not working, this does limit their own personal aspirations for the high-status careers they see on television (Gross & Morgan, 1985).

Signorielli (1991) found that television viewing cultivates profamily sentiments as well as conceptions that reflect what is an ambivalent presentation of marriage on television. Adolescents who watch more television are more likely to say they want to get married, to stay married to the same person for life, and to have children. Heavy-viewing high school students are more likely to disagree that having a close intimate relationship with only one partner is too restrictive for the average person. Nevertheless, a positive relationship was found between viewing and expressing the opinion that one sees so few good or happy marriages that one could question marriage as a way of life.

The rise of talk shows (especially sensationalistic "trash" talk shows) and their popularity among adolescents led to numerous studies of the cultivation-related impacts of these shows for adolescents in the late 1990s and early 2000s. Since these studies were exploring the impacts of this specific type of show, it is not surprising that they situated themselves squarely in the midst of debates over whether cultivation is genre-specific. As a genre, they are stylistically distinct (the shows of Jerry Springer and Ricki Lake do not seem to have much in common with sitcoms, for example), and they certainly do seem to emphasize a recurrent set of messages about "bizarre" social behavior. Thus, although cultivation tries to focus attention on the overall, aggregate system of messages, it is understandable that researchers would be interested in exploring what images of reality are "cultivated" among adolescents who watch a lot of these talk shows.

Stacy Davis and Marie-Louise Mares (1998) studied 292 adolescents in suburban and rural North Carolina and found that amount of talk show viewing was associated with adolescents' overestimation of the frequency of "deviant" behaviors frequently discussed on talk shows (for example, running away from home, premarital sex, teen pregnancy, bringing guns to school). On the other hand, they found no evidence that heavy viewers of talk shows were more likely to be desensitized to the suffering of others, or that heavy talk show viewers were more likely to trivialize social problems. Patrick Rössler & Hans-Bernd Brosius (2001) looked at the role of talk shows in cultivating worldviews among 165 German adolescents, in a prolonged-exposure experiment. Those who were more exposed to talk shows overestimated the percentage of gays and lesbians, transsexuals, and people with tattoos or piercings, and also expressed less restrictive attitudes toward these groups.

International Comparisons

Cultivation research has been done with adolescents in many other countries besides the United States. These studies are especially interesting because the sociocultural conditions in which young people grow up differ so much from country to country, as do institutional media structures and the types of television programs that are available (Morgan, 1990). Moreover, many countries broadcast a great many programs that were made in the United States, which allows researchers to explore the impacts of American programs in differing cultural contexts around the world.

For example, Suzanne Pingree and Robert Hawkins (1981) found that exposure to U.S. programs (especially crime and adventure) was significantly related to Australian students' scores on "Mean World" and "Violence in Society" measures concerning Australia, but not the United States. Viewing Australian programs was unrelated to these conceptions, but those who watched more U.S. programs were more likely to see Australia as dangerous and mean. Gabriel Weimann (1984) found that heavy-viewing Israeli students had an idealized, "rosier" image of the standard of living in the United States.

Cultivation analyses about adolescents' conceptions of violence, sex roles, political orientations, "traditional" values, social stereotypes, materialism, and other topics (often with a focus on the relative roles of various genres) have been carried out in places as diverse as Argentina (Morgan & Shanahan, 1995), Greece (Zaharopoulos, 2003), Hong Kong (Cheung & Chan, 1996), Iceland (Kolbeins, 2004), India (Varma, 2000), Israel (Cohen & Weimann, 2000), Korea (Kang, 1992; Kapoor et al., 1994), Portugal (Monteiro, 1999), Sweden (Hedinsson & Windahl, 1984; Reimer & Rosengren, 1990), and Trinidad (Phekoo et al., 1996), among others.

These studies show the complex ways in which the viewing of local or imported programming can interact with distinct cultural contexts, along with differing political and institutional structures. Morgan and Shanahan (1992) argue that adolescents will be most vulnerable to cultivation when they live in countries dominated by commercially supported television systems that feature many U.S. programs. On the other hand, cultivation is less pronounced when television is controlled by the state and offers fewer U.S. imports (partly because television viewing is lighter in such countries). The global trend of the past decade toward privatized, advertiser-sponsored, multichannel television systems suggests that cultivation will be playing an increasingly larger role internationally.

Conclusion

Cultivation analysis shows us how narrative operates in culture. Humans uniquely live in a world experienced and constructed through storytelling, in its many modes and forms. All of us learn about the world from cultural stories, but their impacts are especially noteworthy among children and adolescents, for whom they offer a pervasive source of facts, images, and social lessons about what they are supposed to take for granted.

The process of cultivation is subtle and far from uniform or automatic. Adolescents' personal and family interactions make a difference, for example. Depending on their precise nature, parental co-viewing patterns and orientations toward television can either increase (Gross & Morgan, 1985) or decrease (Rothschild & Morgan, 1987) cultivation among adolescents. Also, children who are more integrated into cohesive peer or family groups are more resistant to cultivation (Rothschild, 1984).

Cultivation theory helps us not lose sight of the larger cultural and ideological implications of television. In terms of violence, for example, more is at stake than the question of what is "good" for children versus the alleged First Amendment "rights" of powerful corporations. That is, television violence cannot be separated from the medium's representations of gender, race, ethnicity, age, sexuality, and class, as well as how it portrays the world of work, the "good life," the family, people in other countries, and much more.

Cultivation researchers claim that television's messages of power, dominance, and victimization cultivate relatively restrictive and intolerant views regarding personal morality and freedoms, women's roles, and minority rights. Rather than stimulating aggression, heavy exposure to television violence cultivates insecurity, mistrust, and alienation, and a willingness to accept potentially repressive measures in the name of security, all of which strengthen and help maintain the prevailing hierarchy of social power. Children and adolescents are especially vulnerable to such messages.

DISCUSSION QUESTIONS

1   Think about how much violence there is in society. Now think about what came to mind when you thought about that. On what did you base your ideas?

    Most of us have vivid images about places such as courtrooms, police stations, and hospitals—but how do we know about them? From where do we get these images? How many other things can you think of that you "know" about that you haven't experienced directly?

2   How do the assumptions and methods of cultivation analysis differ from other ways of studying media effects?

3   What are some of the long-term social consequences of media violence on young people?

4   What may happen when our own experiences about something are different from what we see on television?

EXERCISES

1   Discuss television's portrayals of certain occupations with people who work in those jobs in real life. For example, ask doctors or lawyers to describe the way they are represented on television.

2   Although cultivation analysis needs to be done with large groups of people, you could conduct a mini-survey, asking people various questions. Are crime levels in America increasing, decreasing, or staying the same? How dangerous is it to walk alone in a city at night? How much can other people be trusted? See if their answers vary in terms of how much television they watch.

3 Cultivation analysis argues that overall amount of viewing is more important than what particular shows people watch, and that many important messages that are relevant to cultivation cut across all kinds of programs. Choose some major dimensions of content (for example, the portrayal of violence, or gender, or class) and see how similar or different they are in different types of programs.

4 Compile a list of as many occupations held by your parents, relatives, neighbors, and others you know well. Compare that to a list of occupations shown on television on a given night. How similar or different are they, and what might account for the differences?

5 Select three or four dramatic television programs you regularly watch. Count the number and types of violent acts depicted in the program. Make note of who commits each act of violence (by gender, age, race, and so on) and who is the victim. Is the violence rewarded or punished? What are its physical consequences? What might people learn from watching these portrayals?

REFERENCES

Cheung, C.-K., & Chan, C. F. (1996). Television viewing and mean world value in Hong Kong's adolescents. *Social Behavior & Personality, 24*, 351–366.

Cohen, J., & Weimann, G. (2000). Cultivation revisited: Some genres have some effects on some viewers. *Communication Reports, 13*, 99–114.

Davis, S., & Mares, M.-L. (1998). Effects of talk show viewing on adolescents. *Journal of Communication, 48*(3), 69–86.

Gerbner, G. (1967). Mass media and human communication theory. In F. E. X. Dance (Ed.), *Human communication theory: Original essays* (pp. 40–60). New York: Holt, Rinehart & Winston.

Gerbner, G. (1969). Toward "cultural indicators": The analysis of mass mediated message systems. *AV Communication Review, 17*, 137–148.

Gerbner, G., & Gross, L. (1976). Living with television: The violence profile. *Journal of Communication, 26*(2), 173–199.

Gerbner, G., Gross, L., Morgan, M., & Signorielli, N. (1980). The "mainstreaming" of America: Violence profile no. 11. *Journal of Communication, 30*(3), 10–29.

Gerbner, G., Gross, L., Morgan, M., Signorielli, N., & Shanahan, J. (2002). Growing up with television: Cultivation processes. In J. Bryant & D. Zillman (Eds.), *Media effects: Advances in theory and research* (pp. 43–67). Hillsdale, NJ: Lawrence Erlbaum.

Gerbner, G., Gross, L., Signorielli, N. Morgan, M., & Jackson-Beeck, M. (1979). The demonstration of power: Violence profile no. 10. *Journal of Communication, 29*(3), 177–196.

Gross, L., & Morgan, M. (1985). Television and enculturation. In J. R. Dominick & J. E. Fletcher (Eds.), *Broadcasting research methods* (pp. 221–234). Boston: Allyn & Bacon.

Hedinsson, E., & Windahl, S. (1984). Cultivation analysis: A Swedish illustration. In G. Melischek, K. E. Rosengren, & J. Stappers (Eds.), *Cultural indicators: An international symposium* (pp. 389–406). Vienna: Verlag der Osterreichischen Akademie der Wissenschaften.

Kang, J. G. (1992). Television and enculturation among Korean adolescents: Cultivation analysis. *Intercultural Communication Studies, 2*, 1–22.

Kapoor, S., Kang, J. G., Kim, W. Y., & Kim, K. (1994). Televised violence and viewers' perceptions of social reality: The Korean case. *Communication Research Reports, 11*, 189–200.

Kolbeins, G. H. (2004). The non-finding of the cultivation effect in Iceland. *Nordicom Review, 25*, 309–314.

Monteiro, M. B. (1999). Meios de comunicação social e construção da realidade social: Crescer com a violência televisiva em Portugal. *Psicologia: Revista da Associação Portuguesa Psicologia, 12*, 321–339.

Morgan, M. (1982). Television and adolescents' sex-role stereotypes: A longitudinal study. *Journal of Personality and Social Psychology, 43*(5), 947–955.

Morgan, M. (1987). Television, sex-role attitudes, and sex role behavior. *Journal of Early Adolescence, 7*(3), 269–282.

Morgan, M. (1990). International cultivation analysis. In N. Signorielli & M. Morgan (Eds.), *Cultivation analysis: New directions in media effects research* (pp. 225–248). Newbury Park, CA: Sage.

Morgan, M. (Ed.). (2002). *Against the mainstream: Selected writings of George Gerbner.* New York: Peter Lang.

Morgan, M., & Shanahan, J. (1992). Comparative cultivation analysis: Television and adolescents in Argentina and Taiwan. In F. Korzenny & S. Ting-Toomey (Eds.), *Mass media effects across cultures: International and intercultural communication annual* (pp. 173–197). Newbury Park, CA: Sage.

Morgan, M., & Shanahan, J. (1995). *Democracy tango: Television, adolescents, and authoritarian tensions in Argentina.* Cresskill, NJ: Hampton.

Phekoo, C. A., Driscoll, P. D., & Salwen, M. B. (1996). U.S. television viewing in Trinidad: Cultural consequences on adolescents. *Gazette: International Journal for Communication Studies, 57*, 97–110.

Pingree, S., & Hawkins, R. P. (1981). U.S. programs on Australian television: The cultivation effect. *Journal of Communication, 31*(1), 97–105.

Reimer, B., & Rosengren, K. E. (1990). Cultivated viewers and readers: A life-style perspective. In N. Signorielli & M. Morgan (Eds.), *Cultivation analysis: New directions in media effects research* (pp. 181–206). Newbury Park, CA: Sage.

Rössler, P., & Brosius, H.-B. (2001). Do talk shows cultivate adolescents' views of the world? A prolonged-exposure experiment. *Journal of Communication, 51*(1), 143–164.

Rothschild, N. (1984). Small group affiliation as a mediating factor in the cultivation process. In G. Melischek, K. E. Rosengren, & J. Stappers (Eds.), *Cultural indicators: An international symposium* (pp. 377–387). Vienna: Verlag der Osterreichischen Akademie der Wissenschaften.

Rothschild, N., & Morgan, M. (1987). Cohesion and control: Relationships with parents as mediators of television. *Journal of Early Adolescence, 7*, 299–314.

Shanahan, J. (1998). Television and authoritarianism: Exploring the concept of mainstreaming. *Political Communication, 15*, 483–495.

Shanahan, J., & Morgan, M. (1999). *Television and its viewers: Cultivation theory and research.* London: Cambridge University Press.

Signorielli, N. (1991). Adolescents and ambivalence towards marriage: A cultivation analysis. *Youth & Society, 23*(1), 121–149.

Signorielli, N. (1993). Television and adolescents' perceptions about work. *Youth & Society, 24*(3), 314–341.

Signorielli, N. (2003). Prime-time violence, 1993–2001: Has the picture really changed? *Journal of Broadcasting & Electronic Media, 47*, 36–57.

Signorielli, N. & Lears, M. (1992). Children, television and conceptions about chores: Attitudes and behaviors. *Sex Roles, 27*, 157–170.

U.S. Department of Justice, Bureau of Justice Statistics. (n.d.). Criminal victimization. Retrieved January 11, 2006, from http://www.ojp.usdoj.gov/bjs/cvictgen.htm.

Varma, A. (2000). Impact of watching international television programs on adolescents in India: A research note. *Journal of Comparative Family Studies, 31*, 117–26.

Weimann, G. (1984). Images of life in America: The impact of American TV in Israel. *International Journal of Intercultural Relations*, 8(2), 185–197.

Wilson, B. J., Kunkel, D., Linz, D., Potter, J., Donnerstein, E., Smith, S. L., Blumenthal, E., & Gray, T. (1997). Violence in television programming overall: University of California, Santa Barbara study. In M. Seawall (Ed.), *National television violence study, vol. 1* (pp. 3–184). Thousand Oaks, CA: Sage.

Zaharopoulos, T. (2003). Perceived foreign influence and television viewing in Greece. In Elasmar, M. G. (Ed)., *The impact of international television: A paradigm shift* (pp. 39–54). Mahwah, N.J.: Lawrence Erlbaum.

CHAPTER ELEVEN

How Are Children and Adolescents Portrayed on Prime-Time Television?

NANCY SIGNORIELLI

The Centrality of Television

Television continues to be a central and pervasive mass medium in the American culture. It plays a distinctive and historically unprecedented role as our nation's most common, constant, and vivid learning environment. Americans spend much of their time in the world of television, whether watching broadcast programming, cable, time-shifting programs, or a theatrical movie on their DVD or VCR. In the average home, the set is turned on for about seven hours each day and the average person watches more than three hours a day (Vivian, 2005). Children, the older generation, and minorities typically watch the most television. In today's multimedia environment children between the ages of eight and eighteen spend, on average, six and a half hours a day with different media (Rideout et al., 2005). This includes time spent with the computer and video games as well as watching about three hours of television each day with an additional hour watching DVDs or videotapes. Even today's college students, with the proliferation of cable systems on most college campuses, watch a considerable amount of television. Consequently, at the beginning of the twenty-first century, very few escape exposure to television's vivid and recurrent patterns of images, information, and values.

Television is a lucrative business. The business of television is selling, which is usually transparent to most viewers. Television sells most of the products to most of the people most of the time by attracting audiences for its commercials. Most people think that television is free or relatively inexpensive because we do not "pay" for television each time we turn on the set, nor do we have to obtain a license to view it. Moreover, the charges we pay for cable (without premium channels such as HBO) are relatively inexpensive. But television is not free, and our basic cable fees are reasonable because we "pay" for television in the form of the higher prices we pay for most of the products we buy (to cover the cost of advertising). Consequently, we pay for television when we wash our hair or brush our teeth. Children and adolescents, in particular, are often unaware of this important function and approach viewing relatively naively.

Television is the nation's and the world's primary storyteller—it tells most of the stories to most of the people, most of the time. We find stories in dramas, action adventures, situation comedies, reality programs, the news, and even in commercials. (See chapter 10 for a thorough discussion of how the role of television as storyteller is at the heart of cultivation theory and is applied to studying its effects on young people.) Today, children are born into homes in which, for the first time in human history, a centralized commercial institution, rather than parents, church, or school, tells most of the stories. The world of television shows and tells us about life—people, places, striving, power, and fate. It shows and tells us how things work and what to do about them. It presents the good and bad, the happy and sad, the successes and failures, and tells us who's on the top and who's on the bottom. The characters in television programs do not live or die but are created or destroyed to tell the story. This storytelling function of television is extremely important because these stories teach viewers about the intricacies of the world and its peoples and provide a wealth of images, all of which become part of the cycles of socialization and resocialization through which we move during our lifetimes.

The Life Cycle

Aging is a process that starts with birth and continues throughout life. Lifestyles associated with different stages of the life cycle are roles learned in a culture. Images of childhood and adolescence cultivate conceptions of how children and adolescents act and behave. Children, in particular, learn about these roles as well as begin to develop expectations of what their teen and adult years will be like based on what they see on television. Television, with its abundance of characters in all phases of the life cycle, thus provides an almost inescapable set of messages about aging and that unique period of childhood and adolescence.

Roles, such as those related to age, are created in direct relation to their usefulness on television. The most numerous—and hence most useful—roles involve jobs, adventure, sex, power, and other opportunities and chances in life. Like most resources, these values are distributed according to status and power. Dominant social groups tend to be overrepresented and overendowed, not only absolutely but even in relation to their actual percentages in the real population. Minorities are defined by having less than their proportionate share of values and resources, meaning less usefulness, fewer opportunities, and fewer but more stereotyped roles. Underrepresentation signifies restricted scope of action, stereotyped roles, diminished life chances, and underevaluation ranging from relative neglect to symbolic annihilation.

This does not imply that faithful proportional representation of reality is necessarily fair or just. Artistic and dramatic functions require selection, amplification, and invention, all of which may deviate from what the census reports or independent experience reflects. Reality provides a standard by which the nature and extent of deviations can be measured. The important question is not so much whether deviations exist, but rather what kinds of deviations occur and with what consequences for thinking, action, and policy.

Nowhere is this more apparent than in the presentation of children and adolescents on television. There are relatively few studies on this topic in the large body of research focusing on the content of television programming (see, for example, Signorielli, 1985, for examples of studies from the 1970s and early 1980s). Existing research shows that children have been consistently underrepresented in all prime-time programs (Signorielli, 1983; Greenberg, 1982) and are most often seen in situation comedies (Heintz-Knowles, 2000; Jordan, 1995) and in Saturday-morning and weekday-afternoon cartoons. In prime time, children (especially young boys) tend to be one of the groups most likely to be victimized (Gerbner et al., 1980). As Richard Peck (1982, p. 63) has aptly noted, in prime time "The young are either played for laughs, kept subordinate to adult roles, or cast as victims—three states they are anxious to avoid in their own lives."

This chapter describes some of the messages and stories about children and childhood that television tells its audiences. It will focus upon some of the existing studies about the image of children and adolescents on television, particularly images in prime-time programs. It will begin with a description of how often children and adolescents appear, focusing on gender representations. This is followed by a description of how often children and adolescents are involved in violence on television. Finally, the last portion of the chapter will discuss, in greater detail, how adolescents are seen on television. Woven throughout this chapter are the findings of two studies I conducted—one on 1980s television (Signorielli, 1987) and one reflecting my ongoing research that examines major and supporting characters in five week-long samples of prime-time network programming broadcast between fall 2000 and fall 2005.[1] Both studies analyze the portrayal of children and adolescents in prime-time television and provide compelling points of comparison of how things have changed (or rather, *not* changed) over the decades.

Age Distributions

Previously I found that children under ten years of age were very underrepresented on 1980s television (Signorielli, 1987). This group made up 15 percent of the U.S. population in the mid-1980s but less than 1 percent of the characters in prime-time network dramatic programs (when most children and adults watch television) and only 3.6 percent of the characters in children's weekend-daytime (mostly cartoon) programs. These figures were similar for boys, girls, Whites, and African Americans. Recently collected data show that these distributions have not changed in the past twenty years. According to the United States Census of 2000,[2] children under the age of ten still make up 14 percent of the U.S. population (15 percent for boys and 14 percent for girls). Similarly, children under the age of ten continue to make up 1 percent of the characters in network prime-time programs. White children under ten make up 14 percent of the U.S. population but less than 1 percent of the characters in prime time; African-American children under ten make up 17 percent of the U.S. population and 1.5 percent of the characters in prime time.

In the mid-1980s, I also found that adolescents (between the ages of ten and nineteen) made up 15 percent of the U.S. population divided equally between those aged ten to fourteen (early adolescents) and those aged fifteen to nineteen (late adolescents) (Signorielli, 1987). This group, particularly the older adolescents, appeared more frequently on television because they have more dramatic and romantic potential. Nevertheless, in prime-time programs early-adolescent girls, boys, African Americans, and Whites were underrepresented (about 3 percent of the characters). In the cartoon, weekend-daytime programs, on the other hand, girls, boys, and Whites were more equally represented (about 9 percent of the characters). Interestingly, African-American early adolescents were overrepresented by a factor of four (35 percent of the African-American characters). The late-adolescent group appeared more frequently in prime-time, showing greater parity with the U.S. population in the mid-1980s. Moreover, older adolescents were overrepresented in the weekend-daytime (largely cartoon) programs in this sample. Yet, overall, in prime time only one in ten characters was a child or adolescent.

Data from the 2000 census show that population parameters have not changed much from the mid-1980s. Adolescents still make up about 14 percent of the population, again evenly divided between those in the early and later adolescent years. There are also few differences in the age distribution of characters in the more recent sample of prime-time programs. Early adolescents again made up less than 3 percent of the characters while about 10 percent were judged to be aged fifteen to nineteen. Interestingly, older adolescent girls appeared more frequently than older adolescent boys—13 percent of the females were aged fifteen to nineteen compared to 7 percent of the males. The data for African Americans and Whites were similar for both the younger and older adolescent groups.

Another consistent finding of studies of the characters in prime-time programs has been that men outnumber women. The earliest content analyses (see Signorielli, 1985) found three men for each woman in prime time, and four males for each female in children's cartoon or weekend-daytime programs. There has been some improvement in these distributions during the past twenty years. My colleague and I, for example, found that the major and supporting characters in prime-time network programs were 60 percent male and 40 percent female (Signorielli & Bacue, 1999). Similarly, prime-time network programs broadcast between 2000 and 2005 had a 60/40 percent male/female distribution. These distributions change, however, by age. Characters under fifteen years old tend to have a somewhat more equal male-female split, while characters between fifteen and nineteen favor females, with a 45 percent male to 55 percent female split. Interestingly, male characters dominate in middle and old age with a 75 percent male to 25 percent female split. Race also makes a difference, particularly at the younger ages. African-American males under the age of fifteen outnumber African-American females by four to one. Yet, in the fifteen-to-nineteen and twenty-to-twenty-four age groups, there are proportionally more African-American females than African-American males.

Gender representations also differ according to program genres. Situation comedies tend to have more equal male-female distributions, while action adventure programs tend to have more men than women. Amy Jordan (1995), in an analysis of children seventeen and younger in family-based situation comedies aired in 1990, found that 42 percent of these children were boys and 58 percent were girls. Moreover, eight out of ten of these children were White and the rest were African American—there were no children of any other minority group. The prime-time world also tends to be somewhat segregated, with a large proportion of African Americans in programs with other African Americans and Whites in programs with other Whites (Signorielli et al., 2004). Jordan's (1995) analysis of family-oriented situation comedies also found that there were very few programs in which African-American and White children interacted with each other.

Character Roles and Family Life

I found that children and adolescents in mid-1980s TV were portrayed as "good" or "successful" rather than "bad" or "unsuccessful." Moreover, most younger characters were seen in "light" or "comic" as opposed to "serious" roles (Signorielli, 1987). The programs from the 2000s were similar—children and adolescents were in "light" or "comic" roles and usually portrayed "good" characters.

I also found that children and adolescents were traditionally cast in situation comedies or serious dramas rather than action adventure programs, trends that continued in the more recent samples of programs (Signorielli, 1987). Similarly, I found that family life was more important for children and adolescents than older characters in prime-time programs (Signorielli, 1987). Interestingly, the analysis of weekend-daytime (cartoon) programs broadcast between 1969 and 1985 found that family life was relatively unimportant in programs created primarily for children.

Jordan (1995) also found that in family-oriented situation comedies children were more likely to interact with other adults than with other children and that these interactions were more likely to be positive and harmonious than child-to-child interactions were. Most of these child-adult interactions involved bantering or talking, with the adult (parent) telling the child what to do. Child-to-child interactions, on the other hand, typically revolved around fighting or skirmishes. Similarly, Mary Strom Larson (1989), in an analysis of three family-oriented situation comedies, found that even though sibling interactions were more likely to be positive than negative, they were also somewhat conflictual, with the younger sister–older brother interactions particularly hostile and the older sister–younger brother interactions more supportive. Larson thus concludes that some family-oriented situation comedies "do not present a view of siblings as primarily loyal, positive, or supportive" (p. 312). Interestingly, while programs rated as acceptable for children and adolescents include off-color language, children are not the target of such language and do not typically use profanities (Kaye & Sapolsky, 2004).

Katharine Heintz-Knowles (1995), in a study conducted for Children Now, found that children (from birth to eighteen) in entertainment television (network broadcast, PBS, cable, and syndicated programs seen in early morning, afternoons, prime-time, and Saturday mornings) were not motivated by school-related issues but rather by peer relationships, sports and hobbies, family, and romance. They tended to lead simple lives and rarely had to grapple with tough or important issues such as racism, substance abuse, or safety. In addition, this analysis found children engaged in both pro- and antisocial behaviors. The prosocial behaviors, including cooperation and affection, were effective behaviors, particularly for the girls. Although the antisocial behaviors were less effective overall, some types of antisocial behaviors, such as physical aggression and deceitfulness, were seen as effective ways for the children, particularly boys, to satisfy their goals and often did not have negative ramifications.

The Social Role of Violence

Violence is a complex social scenario that demonstrates who is powerful and who is weak on television. It shows who can get away with what against whom and, in turn, who should submit to whom. Violence shows us who matters and who doesn't as well as who wins and who loses (Gerbner et al., 2002). In previous research, I found that half of the major characters in prime-time programs were involved in violence, while almost three quarters of the characters in children's weekend-daytime (cartoon) programs either hurt or killed others or were hurt or killed themselves (Signorielli,1987). In both prime-time and weekend-daytime programs more men than women, and more adults than children, were involved in violence. In addition, children and adolescents, particularly the females, were more likely to be victimized than the older characters.

Of course, on television, where stories often, if not always, deal with "good" and "evil" and the triumph of "good" over "evil," violence is shown as provoked and punished and victimization is deserved or avenged (Signorielli, 1987). There was relatively little killing involving children and younger adolescents. Overall, young boys were the most underrepresented, the most racially diverse but most badly battered group. While young girls were also underrepresented, as they matured through adolescence they became more numerous but much more vulnerable.

Although many of the patterns of the representation of violence on television have not

changed during the last thirty years, the percentages of characters in leading and supporting roles who are involved in violence have diminished (Signorielli, 2003). Yet today the
patterns of involvement are similar to those found in 1970s and '80s. Children under ten
are still more likely to be hurt and not hurt others and there is little, if any, killing involving these groups. The pattern is similar for those in early adolescence (aged ten to fourteen), but changes for characters in the later adolescent years. In this case characters were
equally likely to hurt others and not be hurt as to be hurt but not hurt others. Again, the
boys under ten are the group most likely to be battered—almost one in three were hurt,
but did not hurt others. While boys in early adolescence are considerably more likely to
be hurt but not hurt others, in the later adolescent years they are equally likely to hurt others but not get hurt themselves or to be hurt but not hurt other characters. Although the
girls are less likely overall to be involved in violence, there are similar patterns of involvement, with those in the early-adolescent years more likely to hurt others than be hurt
themselves.

Another view on the image of children on television in relation to violence comes from
data collected as part of the National Television Violence Study (NTVS), which compared
child and adolescent perpetrators with adult perpetrators of violence (Wilson et al., 2002).
This study focused on violence in a composite week of randomly sampled programs from
twenty-three cable and broadcast channels seen from 6:00 A.M. to 11:00 P.M. during the
1995–96 television season (N=3,235). Few children or adolescents were seen as perpetrators of violence—roughly one child every four hours and one teen every two and a half hours.
Most of these perpetrators were males and many possessed qualities that would make
them appear as good role models. Children typically targeted other children, and teen perpetrators were most likely to target other teens. In short, perpetrators were most likely to
target victims who were close to them in age. Last, violence of a lethal nature was only
engaged in by one third of the perpetrators who were teens or children. Overall, the
NTVS found few children and teens cast as perpetrators and/or targets of violence.

Adolescents on Television

There are several studies looking at how youth are presented on television. Heintz-Knowles
(2000) found that young people (thirteen to twenty-one) in prime-time entertainment programs were evenly split by gender and were mostly White. Minority young people were most
often African American; Latinos and other minority young people appeared very infrequently. Young characters often portrayed roles in which they were seen coping with
problems about romance, friendships, and popularity as well as family issues. Moreover, they
solved their problems without help from adults. Similarly, Axel Aubrun and Joseph Grady
(2000, p. 8) found that teens on television are often presented as "super-individuals"—
"models of what American adults wish they themselves could be." Adolescents are also more
likely to be portrayed as autonomous rather than in mentoring relationships between
adolescents and adults. Moreover, parents, if seen, are often presented as foolish or incom-

petent (Heintz-Knowles, 2000).

Two studies examined the portrayal of teens, primarily teen girls, in programs cited as the favorites of teenage girls in the United States. These findings provide an interesting picture of the messages teenage girls get about their cohort in their favorite programs, although they do not generalize to all of television because they examine only a small subset of prime-time programs.

The National Commission on Working Women (n.d.) examined over two hundred episodes of nineteen prime-time entertainment programs that featured adolescent girls broadcast in the late 1980s or early 1990s. Most of the characters in these programs presented "outmoded and damaging stereotypes of teenage girls" (p. 2). The analysis showed that girls' looks were much more important than their brain power, and often the more intelligent girls were characterized as misfits. The plots of these programs centered on grooming, dating, and shopping. These programs rarely showed the main characters talking with teachers, parents, or even their friends about academics, career goals, or what they would like to achieve in the future.

Consistent with my analyses (Signorielli, 1987), this study of teen programming found that teenage girls appeared more frequently than teenage boys—there were thirty-two regularly appearing female characters compared to twenty-four regularly appearing male characters. All of these girls were in school and all of those shown as high school students planned to attend college.

I also looked at those programs favored and regularly viewed by adolescent girls between the ages of twelve and seventeen (Signorielli, 1997). The analysis found that children made up only 1 percent of the characters, while 16 percent of the females in these programs were adolescent girls and 11 percent of the males were adolescent boys. Young adults also made up a sizable portion of the characters in these programs—41 percent of the women and 50 percent of the men. African Americans were a sizable portion of the characters in these programs as well—19 percent of the women and 20 percent of the men. These proportions indicate an overrepresentation of African-American characters compared to the U.S. Census (see Signorielli et al., 2004, for a discussion of African Americans in recent prime-time programs). Similarly, this study found that women were underrepresented in these prime-time programs.

The characters in the programs favored by adolescent girls presented rather mixed messages. Many of the female characters were positive role models of independent women who could solve their own (and others') problems. Yet these same programs contained many stereotypical messages about relationships, careers, and appearance, particularly for the young women. For example, four out of ten of the men were seen "on the job" compared to only one in four of the women, Similarly, four out of ten of the women, compared to about one in three of the men, talked about romantic relationships, and one in four of the women, compared to less than one in five of the men, were seen "dating." The females in these programs also were more likely than the men to participate in activities best described as stereotypically female—grooming or preening, doing dishes, cooking, shopping. Moreover, a substantial portion of the women, almost half, were see as "thin" or "very thin," and the physical appearance of more than a quarter of the women was acknowledged by other characters. Male characters were also seen in gender-stereotyped behaviors. For example, men were more likely to use brawn and physical force than women; however, they were portrayed with "average" bodies and practically none had other characters talk about or acknowledge what he looked like.

Finally, Heintz-Knowles (2000) found that adolescents rarely were shown using drugs or alcohol. Similarly, I found that children under ten and those in the early-adolescent years were rarely shown smoking or drinking but that these behaviors were more apparent in the older adolescent group of characters (Signorielli, 1987). In addition, while drug use did not appear very frequently on television, the older adolescent characters were the most likely to be portrayed as either using or experimenting with drugs.

Conclusion

Overall, prime time presents a very limited and static image of children and adolescents that has not changed much in the past thirty years. This portrayal, in essence, does little to enhance self-esteem or to show that childhood is a good time in life. Rather, it presents very stereotypical images that do not serve as adequate role models for today's children and adolescents. Young children are underrepresented and symbolically annihilated, while adolescents, particularly adolescent girls, appear more frequently but in roles that focus more on romance and adult-type relationship-related behaviors. Children, while presented as "cute" and "good," are also found in very limiting roles that serve primarily to enhance the adult characters rather than show that childhood is a good time of life. Finally, children, especially young boys, are often seen as victims of violence, and in the teen years seen drinking and smoking. The overall image is one that devalues children, teenagers, and childhood. Once again, we can only hope that writers and producers will work to provide children with programming with relevant role models who can be emulated to help young viewers mature into adulthood.

EXERCISE

1   Conduct a small content analysis of the portrayal of children and adolescents on prime time and in cartoons. Begin by selecting (1) a prime-time program that you believe is geared especially for children and early adolescents and (2) two cartoon programs, one targeted primarily to boys (with mostly male characters, such as the *Teenage Mutant Ninja Turtles: Fast Forward*) and one targeted primarily to girls (mostly female characters, such as *Winx Club*) Record two to three episodes of each of these programs and then identify:

   ■   the major or leading characters; and
   ■   the minor characters with speaking roles.

Note the following demographic and substantive data for each of these characters:

   ■   sex, race, age, marital status, occupation, socioeconomic status;

- role (comic or serious); type (good/bad; protagonist/antagonist; hero/villain);
- substance use and/or abuse (smoking, drinking, using illicit or over-the-counter drugs);
- violence committed and/or victimization; and
- body type/clothing (conservative, trampy, sexy).

Write a short paper about the demography of these characters in each of these programs and be prepared to discuss what you found in class. Two class periods could be devoted to these discussions, one for the prime-time programs and one for the cartoon programs.

NOTES

1   A full description of the methods used to generate these data may be found in Signorielli, 2004. Corresponding data are not available for children's weekend-daytime (cartoon) programs.

2   U.S. Census Bureau, Census 2000 Summary File 1, available at www.census.gov.

REFERENCES

Aubrun, A., & Grady, J. (2000). Aliens in the living room: How TV shapes our understanding of "teens." A report prepared for the W. T. Grant Foundation and the Frameworks Institute.

Gerbner, G., Gross, L., Morgan, M., Signorielli, N., & Shanahan, J. (2002). Growing up with television: The cultivation perspective. In J. Bryant & D. Zillmann (Eds.), *Media effects: Advances in theory and research* (pp. 43–68). Hillsdale, NJ: Lawrence Erlbaum.

Gerbner, G., Gross, L., Signorielli, N., & Morgan, M. (1980). Aging with television: Images on television drama and conceptions of social reality. *Journal of Communication, 30*(1), 37–47.

Greenberg, B. S. (1982). Television and role socialization: An overview. In D. Pearl, L. Bouthilet, & J. Lazar (Eds.), *Television and social behavior: Ten years of scientific progress and implications for the eighties* (pp. 179–190). Rockville, MD: National Institute of Mental Health.

Heintz-Knowles, K. (2000). *Images of youth: A content analysis of adolescents in prime-time entertainment programming.* Washington, D.C.: W. T. Grant Foundation and the Frameworks Institute.

Heintz-Knowles, K. (1995). *The reflection on the screen: Television's image of children.* Los Angeles, CA: Children Now.

Jordan, A. (1995). The portrayal of children on prime-time situation comedies. *Journal of Popular Culture, 29*(3), 139–147.

Kaye, B. K., & Sapolsky, B. S. (2004). Watch your mouth: An analysis of profanity uttered by children on prime-time television. *Mass Communication and Society, 7*(4), 429–452.

Larson, M. S. (1989). Interaction between siblings in primetime television families. *Journal of Broadcasting & Electronic Media, 33*(3), 305–315.

National Commission on Working Women. (n.d.). Growing up in prime time: An analysis of adolescent girls on television. Washington, D.C.: NCWW.

Peck, R. (1982). Teenage stereotypes. In M. Schwarz (Ed.), *TV and teens: Experts look at the issues* (pp. 62–65). Reading, MA: Addison-Wesley.

Rideout, V., Roberts, D. F., & Foehr, V. G. (2005). Generation M: Media in the lives of 8–18 year olds. Report of the Kaiser Family Foundation.

Signorielli, N. (1983). The demography of the television world. In O. H. Gandy, Jr., P. Espinosa, & J. A. Ordover (Eds.), *Proceedings from the tenth annual Telecommunications Policy Research Conference* (pp. 53–76). Norwood, NJ: Ablex.

Signorielli, N. (1985). *Role portrayal and stereotyping on television: An annotated bibliography of studies relating to women, minorities, aging, sexual behavior, health, and handicaps*. Westport, CT: Greenwood.

Signorielli, N. (1987). Children and adolescents on television: A consistent pattern of devaluation. *Journal of Early Adolescence, 7*(3), 255–268.

Signorielli, N. (1997). A content analysis: Reflections of girls in the media. Menlow Park, CA: Kaiser Family Foundation.

Signorielli, N. (2003). Prime-time violence, 1993–2001: Has the picture really changed? *Journal of Broadcasting & Electronic Media, 47*(1), 36–57.

Signorielli, N. (2004). Aging on television: Messages relating to gender, race, and occupation in prime time. *Journal of Broadcasting & Electronic Media, 48*(2), 279–301.

Signorielli, N., & Bacue, A. (1999). Recognition and respect: A content analysis of prime-time television characters across three decades. *Sex Roles, 40*(7/8), 527–544.

Signorielli, N., Horry, A., & Carlton, K. (2004). Minorities in prime time: Is there parity? Paper presented at the annual conference of the National Communication Association, Chicago.

Vivian, J. (2005). *The mass media of communication*. Boston, MA: Allyn & Bacon.

Wilson, B. J., Colvin, C. M., & Smith, S. L. (2002). Engaging in violence on American television: A comparison of child, teen, and adult perpetrators. *Journal of Communication, 52*(1), 36–61.

CHAPTER TWELVE

Learning while Viewing

Urban Myth or Dream Come True?

DEBORAH L. LINEBARGER & DEBORAH K. WAINWRIGHT

Television is an often-maligned and underused resource available in over 98 percent of U.S. homes (U.S. Census Bureau, 2006). Most children watch about four hours per day (Nielsen Media Research, 2005). Talking heads bemoan the ills of the medium, citing its insidious pervasiveness as the reason our children are hyperactive and lagging behind international peers. Criticisms leveled at television include that it promotes intellectual passivity (Singer & Singer, 1983), undermines intellectual curiosity (Healy, 1999), and rots our children's brains (Gentzkow & Shapiro, 2006; Westphal, 2006). Research investigating these claims suggests a more nuanced view whereby content rather than television as a whole determines the kinds of effects children generally experience.[1] When age-appropriate, carefully constructed educational television is used, it becomes a powerful and effective tool, promoting prosocial behavior (Friedrich & Stein, 1973; Hearold, 1986); less sex-role stereotyped beliefs (Davidson et al. 1979); general academic and intellectual skills (Anderson et al., 2001; Wright et al., 2001; Crawley et al., 1999); specific cognitive skills such as reading behavior and achievement (Anderson et al., 2001; Linebarger, 2001; Linebarger et al., 2004); vocabulary and communication skills (Linebarger & Walker, 2005; Rice et al., 1990; Rice & Woodsmall, 1988); math and problem-solving skills (Hall et al., 1990); and civic engagement and social studies knowledge (Calvert & Tart, 1993; Calvert, 2001).

In 1961 Newton Minnow called television a vast wasteland, stating that "when television is bad, nothing is worse. I invite you to sit down in front of your television set when your station goes on the air and stay there without a book, magazine, newspaper, profit-and-loss sheet or rating book to distract you—and keep your eyes glued to that set until the station signs off. I can assure you that you will observe a vast wasteland." In a later book Marshall McLuhan argued that the medium of television was inherently problematic: "The medium is the message" because it is the "medium that shapes and controls the scale and form of human association and action" (McLuhan, 1964, p. 9). However, other research underscores the idiosyncratic nature of television's influence. Just as with learning from books, computers, electronic toys, peers, parents, and general everyday experience, children will learn from television. What children learn depends upon what they view; that is, the content of the messages attended to and processed determine the type of influence that content has (Anderson et al., 2001; Wright et al., 2001). Since the introduction of television and content specifically for children in the 1950s, researchers, policymakers, and the general public have been arguing about or working to determines how children are affected by it (Alexander, 2006). In 1952 the House Interstate and Foreign Commerce Subcommittee was convened to address the problems of television and violence. Despite the enormous body of literature demonstrating a clear and causal effect between televised violence and aggression in children (for example, Huesmann et al., 2003), this issue continues to be debated and often overshadows the more positive benefits of educational programs. (For a thorough discussion of the effects of media violence, see chapters 8 and 9.)

Television is not a monolithic entity. The content of programming found on television is as varied as the diversity of books in a library. Therefore, it is crucial to account for this diversity when considering the potential effects it can have on children. To learn from viewing, children must be able to relate the lessons offered on screen to their own lives and be able to transfer what they have learned to personal future situations (Bransford et al., 1999). To this end, content is the key, and this content is mediated by a host of stimulus-specific and viewer-specific characteristics (Fisch, 2004). When viewing violent messages, children learn that it is acceptable to use violence as a means to solve conflict (Huesmann et al., 2003); when viewing sexually explicit messages, adolescents are more likely to initiate sexual intercourse earlier and believe that casual sex is acceptable than their peers who did not view these same messages (Brown & Newcomer, 1991; Bryant & Rockwell, 1994); when viewing messages supporting creative thinking, children engage in more imaginative play and demonstrate more divergent thinking (Anderson et al., 2001; Friedrich-Cofer et al., 1979; Singer & Singer, 1990); when viewing prosocial messages, children learn to be more altruistic (Mares, 1996); when viewing messages designed to teach young children to read, young children improve their oral language knowledge, phonological awareness, and fluency skills (Linebarger, 2001; Linebarger et al., 2004). In 2001 researchers also established the long-term influence of television. Daniel Anderson and his colleagues (2001) found that early (that is, at age five) viewing of educational content was related to a number of educationally important outcomes during adolescence, including higher grades, more leisure book reading, greater academic self-concept, and more out-of-school creative activities, even when gender, parent education, and birth order were controlled. Ultimately, children learn what they view. If what they view is educational, age-appropriate, and carefully constructed, children can learn educationally important material leading to potentially immediate and lifelong positive consequences. Anderson and his colleagues are correct when they argue that "the medium is NOT the message, the message is the message" (Anderson et al., 2001, p. 134).

What Is Educational Television?

While it is often said that all television is educational, only a small portion of what we see on screen has been designed with that intent. Defining what comprises educational programming has been difficult, especially within a regulatory framework. In the 1970s, with pressure from parent and other advocacy groups, the Federal Communications Commission (FCC) issued guidelines asking broadcasters to voluntarily make a "meaningful effort" to provide a "reasonable amount" of educational programming for children (Jordan, 1996), with a warning that stricter measures would be taken if the broadcasters did not comply. Given that not much changed between 1974 and 1978, the FCC proposed new regulations to increase both the quantity (that is, five hours of educational programming for preschoolers and two and a half hours of educational programming for school-aged children) and quality of programming (that is, programs should address "history, science, literature, the environment, drama, music, fine arts, human relations, other cultures and languages, and basic skills such as reading and math") (Jordan, 1996, p. 8). In 1980 Ronald Reagan appointed Mark Fowler as FCC chairperson. Pressure from the networks, and the more powerful producers and programmers in the field, convinced Fowler that regulation would limit the programs being offered to home viewers, and that attempts to regulate might be in contravention of their First Amendment rights. In the end, Fowler's decision to deregulate did little to improve the quantity or quality of children's programming and probably contributed greatly to the rise of programming driven by product profit. (See chapter 2 for a complete review of the history of media regulation and deregulation.)

Advocacy groups continued to pressure lawmakers to intervene and eventually were instrumental in creating and enacting the Children's Television Act (CTA) of 1990. Unlike FCC guidelines, the CTA originated in Congress and required that broadcasters meet the educational and informational needs of children as a requirement for license renewal. Educational and information television was defined as content that would "further the positive development of the child in any respect, including the child's cognitive/intellectual or emotional/social needs" (Jordan, 1996, p. 8). Unfortunately, the CTA left much wiggle room for interpretation, and this wiggle room resulted in several problems, including the identification of programs such as *Mighty Morphin Power Rangers*, *American's Funniest Home Videos*, *X-Men*, *The Jetsons*, and *Yogi Bear* as educational (Kunkel & Canepa, 1994). As a result of careful scrutiny of the broadcasters' license renewal applications (Kunkel & Canepa, 1994) and on-air content of so-called educational shows (Jordan, 1996), revisions to the CTA were completed and implemented in the 1997–98 viewing season (FCC, 1996). These new FCC processing guidelines are informally known as the Three-Hour Rule. This rule specified that broadcasters must air at least three hours a week of "core" programming in order to qualify for expedited license renewal. The programs must be at least thirty minutes in length, air between 7:00 A.M. and 10:00 P.M., and be specifically designed to meet the educational needs of a child audience. Broadcasters were required to identify these "core" programs as educational in multiple locations: on the air (using visible icons), in documents filed with the FCC, and in station files that were publicly available. Finally, programs could be considered educational if they "contributed to children's healthy development by addressing their cognitive/intellectual or social/emotional needs" (Jordan, 2000, p. 5).

Table 1: Educational Strength Scale

Item	Description
Lesson clarity	The presence of a message that is clearly and explicitly laid out so that it can be easily comprehended by the target audience
Lesson integration	The consistent conveyance of the lesson or the culmination of the program in a lesson so that it is integral to the program as a whole
Lesson involvement	Presentation of the lesson in a way that is engaging and appropriately challenging for the child audience, including the incorporation of: (a) children or childlike characters in significant roles, (b) age-appropriate production technique, and (c) age-appropriate lessons

Source: (Jordan and Woodard, 1997)

One of the more difficult aspects of the CTA has been defining what content constitutes educational and informational programming. The CTA provides only broad-strokes guidelines, and the FCC does not engage in judgments about quality. Fortunately, Amy Jordan and her colleagues (Jordan et al., 2001; Jordan & Woodard, 1997) have provided much clearer guidelines in this regard. In their analysis of the state of children's programming, they provide a definition of educational strength that is easy to operationalize (that is, a definition that is objectively and reliably measured), applicable to a variety of programs, sensitive to different educational approaches, and able to capture the positive features while highlighting the absence of negative content. Components coded included target age, primary lesson, episode lesson, educational strength, violence, and gender and ethnic diversity. Educational strength was evaluated in four ways: lesson clarity, lesson integration, lesson involvement, and lesson applicability. (See table 1 for detailed definitions of the code). By developing a code that included both positive and negative components, Jordan and her colleagues (Jordan et al., 2001; Jordan & Woodard, 1997) were able to reduce the likelihood that programs such as *Mighty Morphin Power Rangers* and *X-Men* (that is, programs that attempt to include some prosocial content but that steep that content in violent behavior and situations) would be included or, more importantly, counted as educational and informational programs in a license renewal application. Finally, because scholars and industry members were concerned that this objective index might miss more nuanced elements of shows that could enhance program quality, Jordan and her colleagues (2001, p. 92) included a simple but subjective measure of quality: coders rated programs as "minimally educational" (that is, does not contain a discernible lesson or have education as a significant purpose), "moderately educational" (that is, containing educational content but suffering from problems that might interfere with children's learning of the lessons), or "highly educational" (that is, engaging, challenging, and relevant to the target age group with no significant problems in the conveyance of the lesson).

The Science of Learning

Creating television programming that will support the cognitive and social development of viewers requires an understanding of how children learn, and also an awareness of how these elements might be accounted for and integrated into the noninteractive format of broadcast television. The process of acquiring new information from any medium (for example, television, computers, print) is a complex one involving attention to and comprehension of these stimuli and then the transfer of this understanding to novel problems or situations one encounters in real life (Fisch, 2004). Facilitating this learning process involves helping children (1) learn with understanding, (2) construct new knowledge from existing knowledge, (3) take control of their own learning, and, ultimately, (4) develop competence in a particular domain (Bransford et al., 2000).

Learning with Understanding

Children begin to make sense of the world from birth. Over time and with experience, children will create an understanding of how the world works. This understanding will have a profound effect on the way in which new concepts or information are integrated. Piaget referred to this process as assimilation, or the practice of taking new information and relating that information to existing knowledge (Flavell et al., 2002). Children's early preconceptions are fairly stable and resistant to change, but change is essential if knowledge is to be extended. One way to facilitate change is to expose children in a repetitive manner to the new information using varied formats and contexts (Fisch, 2004). This repeated exposure helps to ensure that newly formed knowledge structures will be supported and maintained. As we will discuss below, repetition is a learning tool that is easily incorporated into a television program's content.

Constructing New Knowledge from Existing Knowledge

Prior knowledge, skills, beliefs, and concepts influence what information, experiences, or actions children notice, how this new knowledge is subsequently organized, and how children then make sense of it. In turn, noticing, organizing, and interpreting will influence remembering, reasoning, and problem solving as well as the acquisition of new knowledge. Tied to the notion above that learning is best accomplished with understanding as the goal, learning a set of facts disconnected from a larger conceptual understanding prohibits children from developing a deep understanding or from transferring this knowledge to future situations. Instead, organizing information into an existing knowledge structure by helping children make connections, identify patterns, and conceptualize an organizing framework can facilitate their ability to successfully apply this knowledge to new situations or problems.

Taking Control of One's Learning

Successful learners are considered active learners. Active learners are aware that they are learning. They know their learning strengths and weaknesses and are able to identify the demands of the task at hand, monitor their understanding of the content, and make reflections on their performance. They are constantly making adjustments that will support their comprehension during the learning process. Active learning is referred to as metacognition, or an awareness of how one thinks. As children get older, they can be taught ways to improve their metacognitive abilities, including making predictions, identifying failures to comprehend, activating appropriate background knowledge, planning ways to remember important content, and monitoring one's ability to comprehend (Bransford et al., 2000). Successful educational television programs will stimulate these same metacognitive skills.

Developing Competence

Each of the steps involved in learning described above helps children to develop competence in a particular domain as they move from novice to expert. Children need to acquire a body of factual knowledge, understand the place this factual knowledge holds in a larger context, and then organize this knowledge into concepts, categories, patterns, relationships, and discrepancies so that it might be easily retrieved and applied in future. To aid the development of competence and become an expert, children must be able to relate the knowledge to new information, represent new problems successfully, make inferences beyond the facts available, and draw conclusions based on these identified relationships (Bransford et al., 2000). Finally, expert learners must be active learners—able to monitor and regulate their own learning and make changes in their learning to accommodate changes in the task at hand. The more a child knows about a particular domain, the easier it becomes for that child to learn new information (Bransford et al., 2000).

Learning to View

For an educational television program to successfully teach, it is necessary to remember that two important players are involved in the experience—the production team who creates the educational content and the at-home viewer. While producers of educational programming must keep in mind each of the four elements of learning mentioned above, before children can learn from the content of a television show they first have to learn how to view.

Just as children who are beginning to read spend enormous amounts of time learning the correspondence between printed letters and word recognition before they can read for content, novice television viewers must learn some rules about the forms of a medium before they can become efficient processors of its messages (Huston & Wright, 1983). These "forms" or "formal features" of television may be invisible to experienced viewers; they include the sound and picture editing techniques; camera tilts, pans, and zooms; the music, sound effects, and pacing of the show. These features provide structure and give meaning to the sensory images contained in the programs (Calvert et al., 1982; Campbell et al., 1987). They are used to denote key moments and critical content—content to which attention should be paid. They are the means by which information is conveyed, and thus they influence how that information is processed (Neuman, 1995). It is the manner in which these features are employed that helps children make sense of the content being offered. Particularly important events are indicated by sound effects, changes in music, and rapid cuts; reflection is identified by long zooms, singing, and moderate levels of physical activity; and valuable plot and character development is offered through dialogue and peculiar voices. As children become adept at using television's symbol system, the same kinds of higher-order cognitive skills used effectively in other media will then be used for deeper processing of televised information (Neuman, 1995; Salomon, 1979).

While a child develops an understanding of the ways that television works, she or he is also actively working to understand the content. Once this understanding is formed, learning can proceed more efficiently. Of course, learning substantive information while viewing requires more than simply staring at the screen. This is where the program's design comes into the equation. A successful educational television program will capture a child's attention, engage her or him cognitively, and maintain that attention throughout the lesson—no easy feat.

Capture the Viewer's Attention

A quick scan of any television show, educational or otherwise, tells us that entertaining details may be the soul of this medium. After all, in order for children to be motivated to watch a television program over the bounty of other activities available as ways to pass their time, the program simply must appeal to them. Much research has examined what elements of television capture the attention of child viewers, suggesting that a program must maintain a fine balance between the informational and noninformational content. The noninformational or entertaining elements of a television program, the formal features of the medium discussed above (Huston & Wright, 1983), seem to be the impetus for capturing the child's attention. In particular, the formal features that appeal to children include women's voices, wacky characters, bright-colored graphics, and fun sound effects (Anderson & Lorch, 1983; Huston & Wright, 1989). Still, it is a child's comprehension of the informational content of a program that will maintain attention to the screen. Furthermore, it is the manner in which the entertaining elements are merged with the educational content that seems to determine the message received by the viewer (Fisch, 2004).

Children as Active Learners

Anderson and his colleagues (Anderson & Lorch, 1983; Anderson, Lorch, Field, & Sander, 1981) proposed an active theory of attention to television in which the comprehensibility of the program's content drives a child's attention to that program. In a series of studies, Anderson and his colleagues identified a set of principles describing the relationship between attention and comprehension such that comprehension determines subsequent attention to on-screen stimuli. They formulated these principles by examining children's attention to and understanding of clips of *Sesame Street*. In some of the studies, they varied the levels of comprehensibility by showing a typical program, randomly ordered segments, segments in which the English narration/dialogue was replaced with a Greek-language equivalent, and segments in which the English narration/dialogue was dubbed in backward. In other studies, they analyzed attention to and comprehension of a single episode of *Sesame Street*. To test whether children are active viewers, they divided children into two groups. Some children were placed in a room with both the television program and alternate activities available (for example, toys and coloring books), while other children had access only to the television program (Lorch, Anderson, & Levin, 1979). There were dramatic differences in visual attention (that is, eyes-on-screen): children in the TV program–only group attended 87 percent of the time, while children in the TV program and alternate activities group attended 44 percent of the time. Although those in the TV/alternate-activity group attended just under half as long as the other group, there were no differences in comprehension levels. Anderson and his colleagues speculated that children were strategic in their visual attention to the programs, relying on auditory cues to direct attention back to the program. Conversely, increasing visual attention did not result in greater levels of comprehension. In a moment-to-moment analysis of attention while children viewed one of fifteen episodes of *Sesame Street*, they found that children attended more to those segments in which the dialogue and the visuals matched compared with segments where there were no visuals to match the dialogue or when dialogue was absent (Anderson et al., 1981). Finally, they manipulated the comprehensibility of the content while maintaining the same formal features structures using the language and editing manipulations described above to determine if children relied on the formal features as a cue for content. They found that decreasing the level of comprehensibility resulted in lower levels of visual attention. The most comprehensible clips, structured the same as the on-air program, garnered the greatest percentage of attention, while those in which the language track was spoken in Greek or dubbed in backward received the least attention. Clips ordered randomly (with no changes in the narration/dialogue) were modestly attended. However, Toni Campbell, John Wright, and Aletha Huston (1987) also manipulated content comprehensibility and formal features, finding that children paid more attention to program content that they perceived was designed for them no matter how difficult the content might be (Campbell et al., 1987). But, in this study, the formal features contrasted child-typical features with adult-typical features. Anderson's study used formal features typically found in children's programming and then varied the difficulty of the content. The formal features distinctions were much sharper in the study conducted by Campbell and colleagues (1987), suggesting that children's interpretations of formal features may vary along a continuum from child-only to adult-only and that children will make attempts to understand content that they perceive is for them even when that content is particularly difficult.

All of these studies underscore the active nature of television viewing as well as the direction of the relationship between comprehensibility and attention—from comprehension to attention. A television show that weaves its educational content within a program designed with the child viewer in mind (that is, by using the child-focused production elements) will be most successful at motivating children to watch and sustaining their interest throughout.

Content That Supports Learning

There has always been some discomfort with the idea of wrapping important lessons in an entertaining package (Garner, 1992; Healy, 1999). The concern has been that the fun might overwhelm the lesson. After much investigation, researchers have determined certain strategies that, when used appropriately in programming and content decisions, make the programming more effective as instruction. These strategies include a "doubling up" of the lesson's key points, familiarity of the characters and format, direct interaction between on-screen characters and the viewer at home, and repetition of the lesson.

Doubling up the Lesson

Researchers who have investigated the impact that entertaining content has on learning have found that interesting but irrelevant information can significantly thwart lesson comprehension (Renninger et al., 1992). Amusing but extraneous details, if not handled properly, can distract the learner's attention, leaving fewer cognitive resources for processing the important content. Overwhelming the main idea with fun but nonessential information is called "the seductive detail effect" (Garner, 1992, p. 53). However, when learning objectives are provided prior to students reading a passage, their recall of the main ideas was increased whether or not seductive details were present (Harp & Mayer, 1998).

By making the learning objectives explicit and the exciting formal features supportive to the lesson, educational television programs are more likely to be successful teachers.

Many researchers have sought to understand this possible interaction between the visual and auditory elements of television (Linebarger, 2001; Rolandelli et al., 1991; Walma van der Molen & van der Voort, 1997). Their aim has been to determine if the audio competes with the visuals, rendering learning less complete than when information is presented visually or aurally only. These studies found that when the audio portion of a television program is accompanied by supportive visual images the viewer more easily assimilates the information being presented. Rather than competing for cognitive resources, the doubling up of information maximizes the information-processing abilities of the learner (Gunter et al., 2000; Mayer, 1997). Christine Ricci and Carole Beal (2002), in their study of the influence of interactive media on lesson recall, found similar results. The children in their study who were exposed to lessons verbally, but were given no visual support, recalled less of the content than those who saw an audiovisual presentation. Their research supports the suggestion that it is a combination of auditory information and supportive visual information that enables better recall of a lesson. Perhaps this is a key to the use of entertaining elements in educational television. As long as audio and video are not competing against one another, as long as the visual information and auditory information are supporting each other, the lesson will get through. There are several ways this doubling up can be handled without making the content trite or dull.

If, for example, the entertaining elements are colorful graphics offering text that supports the verbal lesson (Linebarger, 2001) or songs that are accompanied by supportive visuals (Calvert, 2001), then the learning may be enhanced by their inclusion. I found that children who watched videotaped clips accompanied by on-screen captions were more likely to recognize target words and transfer those words to text not related to the video, more so than children who watched without captions, even several days after viewing (Linebarger, 2001). Sandra Calvert (2001) was interested in whether and how children learn through song. It is not uncommon, in children's educational programming, to see attempts at teaching through tunes. In her research, Calvert examined the impact of televised songs on children's recall of educational content. She found that, when accompanied by animated pictures supporting the lyrics, both children and adults showed increases in verbatim memory more often than when they heard songs with no such visual accompaniment. However, her results suggest that while mastery of certain types of tasks are improved by televised songs, true learning or deep processing of the educational content is better enhanced when the factual information is spoken and not sung. Therefore, programs that offer educational content in song are well advised to provide this same content in spoken word at another time in order to ensure that the lesson is learned.

Familiarity

If we think about the programs that stop our channel surfing, we choose them because they are familiar to us in some way. Perhaps the program's music or images are recognizable?

Perhaps something cues us that the program is similar to one we have enjoyed in the past? In their research on mental effort when viewing, Barbara Bordeaux and Garrett Lange (1991) found that having an idea regarding what we are about to watch or experience makes us more comfortable and more interested in attending. If we are familiar with a program's format and know what to expect for the duration of the show, we relax into the watching. This familiarity or preexisting schema for a particular program provides the child viewer with expectations pertaining to what events might occur during the show—how the characters will behave, and what the motives are behind their actions (Bordeaux & Lange, 1991; Fisch & Truglio, 2001). In *Sesame Street*, for example, familiarity means knowing the show will offer Muppets who discover things; grown-ups who explain things; and songs, letters, and numbers. Similarly, animation signals to children that a program may be of interest to them. This preexisting schema may cause some parents grief in the case of the numerous adult-focused animated programs that have been added to the broadcast schedule over the past few years! Nevertheless, in the case of educational programming, familiarity with a television show's purpose and characters will reduce the demands of processing the entertaining content and result in a more efficient processing of the lesson (Fisch, 2000, 2004). Therefore, a television program with a standard set of characters, or a regular episodic process, will draw on existing knowledge and facilitate learning more readily. Furthermore, it seems reasonable to expect that children may attend more to, and learn more from, models who are like them or familiar to them (Van Evra, 1998). Shalom Fisch (2000, 2004) found that a program that offers a diverse set of characters who represent the viewer ethnically and developmentally, and that puts these characters into situations reflecting a viewer's real life, can similarly enhance the child's learning from viewing.

Direct Interaction with the Viewer

One obvious difference between children's programming and other television productions is that, on children's shows, characters often speak directly to the viewer at home by asking questions, giving supportive comments, or letting the viewer in on a joke. Research on interactive media and distance education has investigated this on-screen character to home viewer interaction to determine if it is having any instructional effect (Kawachi, 2003; Ricci & Beal, 2002). While television may not be the archetype of interactive media, the research of Ricci and Beal (2002) and Kawachi (2003) provides insight into how children may be learning from on-screen characters on television. When on-screen characters speak directly to the home viewer, they are offering a face-to-face experience similar to that of a teacher who has a one-on-one interaction with a learner in a classroom. Kawachi (2003) found that this face-to-face interaction by an online tutor who gave explicit examples of relevance to the at-home learner increased that learner's intrinsic motivation for academic and vocational tasks.

Still, there is more to computer-based learning than simple direct interaction with the instructor. In some cases the learner at home can guide her or his own way through the lesson by using her or his mouse and clicking on different aspects of a program. Ricci and Beal (2002) hypothesized that the learner's control over the lesson may be influencing the impact on her or his learning more so than the instructor alone. Since a television viewer has no control over the direction or speed at which information is offered, it is important to note that Ricci and Beal (2002) found no indication that actual physical interaction (the ability to click on particular elements on screen and control the direction of the lesson) enhanced recall of the main ideas of the lesson. Learners retained the same amount of information whether they were simply viewing the lesson or in control of it. The direct speaking of the on-screen instructor to the learner at home, therefore, seems to be enough to pass on vital information.

Repetition

Repetition is perhaps the most elementary of all learning strategies and, as mentioned earlier, it is essential for permanent long-term memory of learning material (Cornford, 2002; Weinstein & Mayer, 1991). Children often repeat the names of things as they discover them in order to remember them. Similarly, adults do this at cocktail parties and business meetings when trying to remember someone's name. Successful learning of new information always appears to involve repetition. From repetition we can move on to elaboration, which involves building on what we already know, relating things we learn to that which we already understand, or summarizing what we have discovered in order to make it a more manageable size. As we discussed earlier, these learning strategies lead to deeper processing and longer-term learning (Bransford et al., 2000).

In children's educational programming, repetition or multiple contexts for portraying the same information may be a producer's most valuable tool. Mabel Rice and Linda Woodsmall (1988) found that repetitions, along with a clear presentation of the educational information, are critical in children's ability to learn words from television. When children see something they already know or understand, they approach the repeated exposure to it with less discomfort, and their motivation for attempting the learning task increases. In fact, repetition is one of the most powerful tools employed by the successful preschool program *Blue's Clues* (Anderson et al., 2000). *Blue's Clues* repeats the same episode on five consecutive days. Anderson and his colleagues (Anderson et al., 2000) found that repeated exposure to the program allowed for viewers' increased comprehension. However, they also determined that a substantial amount of the content has been learned after viewing the episode just one time.

Repetition also is a key element in enabling a child to transfer learning from one situation to another. Fisch (2001) suggests that presenting the same educational material in several different forms and in different contexts throughout the length of a television program might help children transfer what they have learned to new but similar situations (see also Salomon & Perkins, 1989). Anderson and his colleagues (2000) found that multiple viewing of the same episode of *Blue's Clues* significantly increased transfer. Children in their study who watched an episode five times were more likely to use the strategies they observed during the *Blue's Clues* episode when they were presented with new problems than were children who had not seen the episode multiple times.

Conclusion

Research indicates that television programs designed to be educational can be powerful tools for teaching children. They not only are able to prepare children for school but they also enhance their achievement in later grades (Anderson et al., 2001; Wright et al., 2001). Still, designing a program that educates while it entertains requires awareness that attention to the television screen and comprehension of the material being offered are inextricably intertwined (Anderson & Lorch, 1983).

The elements of educational programming that must be carefully considered in order to ensure that a program can enhance a child's learning while viewing include both the noninformational formal features of the medium that are particularly appealing to children and the informational elements of content that enhance the comprehension of the child viewer. Programs with bright colors, lively music, child voices, and wacky characters are likely to appeal to young children (Anderson & Lorch, 1983; Huston & Wright, 1989). Shows that include characters representative of the child at home, who model desired behaviors (Wright & Huston, 1984) and speak directly to the camera with enthusiasm (Kawachi, 2003; Ricci & Beal, 2002), will keep children watching and expand their curiosity. Nevertheless, it is a fine balance of ensuring that the entertaining elements do not overwhelm the educational lesson (Fisch, 2004; Garner, 1992). When combined, in educationally effective ways, these features can provide a quality learning opportunity for young viewers.

Television is not the problem many argue it is (for example, Healy, 1999; Winn, 1977), and vilifying it is not useful. Instead, we should be more proactive in protecting children from harmful content, helping producers create educationally appropriate content, and then conducting studies to determine whether that content is educational and engaging. It's time that the medium and the message work hand in hand.

DISCUSSION QUESTIONS & EXERCISES

1   Run your own mini–content analysis of a children's educational television program to determine if and what children might learn while they view. To do this, record one episode and watch it carefully, segment by segment, keeping track of the following elements:

- How many children are seen on screen?
- Are characters of a variety of cultural backgrounds?
- Are both males and females represented? Is it an even mix?
- What about voiceovers—are they male, female, or one of the program's characters?

- Is there one main lesson or are there many lessons in this episode?
- Are lessons repeated in different ways throughout the episode?
- Does the lesson support cognitive (for example, numbers, letters, words, shapes, science concepts) or prosocial (for example, be kind, share, cooperate, help others, don't lie) skills?

2   We often hear it said that "children are little sponges," but in order for them to soak up the informational content of a television program they have to be engaged in "active viewing." What types of on-screen elements are necessary to capture and maintain a young child's attention? Are these being used in the program you viewed?

3   To you, science is the most important of all academic school activities, but you've noticed that elementary-school children, especially the older ones, seem more interested in surfing the net and listening to music than discovering the ways of the natural world. You've decided that the best way to get these kids excited about science is to create a television program. What does this program look like?

4   Many talking heads argue that television is inherently bad—the medium is the message. Many academics and educational television producers argue that content matters most. What do you think? Describe both and argue for one of the following perspectives: form matters, content matters, both matter. If you choose the third perspective (both matter), describe the relative contributions of each.

NOTES

*   The authors are indebted to Amy Jordan and Jessica Taylor-Piotrowski for comments on previous drafts.

1   Even further complicating this issue are the cumulative effects associated with television use. For instance, in the debate regarding children's viewing habits and obesity, the underlying concerns involve both content (for example, commercials featuring sugary or unhealthy products or programming supporting the use of junk foods) and time (for example, more time spent with viewing is associated with greater rates of obesity).

REFERENCES

Alexander, A. (2006). Children and television. Retrieved February 2, 2006, from http://www.museum.tv/archives/etv/C/htmlC/childrenand/childrenand.htm.

Anderson, D. R., Bryant, J., Wilder, A., Santomero, A., Williams, M., & Crawley, A. M. (2000). Researching Blue's Clues: Viewing behavior and impact. Media Psychology, 2, 179–194.

Anderson, D. R., Huston, A. C., Schmitt, K. L., Linebarger, D. L., & Wright, J. C. (2001). Early childhood television viewing and adolescent behavior: The recontact study. Monographs of the Society for Research in Child Development, 66: serial no. 264.

Anderson, D. R., & Lorch, E. P. (1983). Looking at television: Action or reaction? In J. Bryant & D. R. Anderson (Eds.), Children's understanding of television: Research on attention and comprehension (pp.

1–34). New York: Academic Press.

Anderson, D. R., Lorch, E. P., Field, D. E., & Sanders, J. (1981). The effects of TV program comprehensibility on preschool children's visual attention to television. *Child Development, 52*, 151–157.

Bordeaux, B. R., & Lange, G. (1991). Children's reported investment of mental effort when viewing television. *Communication Research, 18*, 617–631.

Bransford, J., Brown, A., & Cocking, R. (2000). *How people learn: Brain, mind, experience, and school.* Washington, D.C.: National Academy of Science.

Brown, J., & Newcomer, S. (1991). Television viewing and adolescents' sexual behavior. *Journal of Homosexuality, 21*(1/2), 77–91.

Bryant, J., & Rockwell, S. C. (1994). Effects of massive exposure to sexually oriented prime-time television on adolescents' moral judgment. In D. Zillmann, J. Bryant, & A. C. Huston (Eds.), *Media, children, and the family* (pp. 183–195). Hillsdale, NJ: Lawrence Erlbaum.

Calvert, S. L. (2001). Impact of televised songs on children's and young adults' memory of educational content. *Media Psychology, 3*, 325–342.

Calvert, S. L., Huston, A. C., Watkins, B. A., & Wright, J. C. (1982). The relation between selective attention to television forms and children's comprehension of content. *Child Development, 53*, 601–610.

Calvert, S. L., & Tart, M. (1993). Song versus verbal forms for very-long-term, long-term, and short-term verbatim recall. *Journal of Applied Developmental Psychology, 14*, 245–260.

Campbell, T. A., Wright, J. C., & Huston, A. C. (1987). Form cues and content difficulty as determinants of children's cognitive processing of televised educational messages. *Journal of Experimental Child Psychology, 43*, 311–327.

Cornford, I. R. (2002). Learning-to-learn strategies as a basis for effective lifelong learning. *International Journal of Lifelong Education, 21*, 337–368.

Crawley, A. M., Anderson, D. R., Wilder, A., Williams, M. & Santomero, A. (1999). Effects of repeated exposures to a single episode of the television program *Blue's Clues* on the viewing behaviors and comprehension of preschool children. *Journal of Educational Psychology, 91*, 630–637.

Davidson E. S., Yasuna A., & Tower, A. (1979). The effects of television cartoons on sex-role stereotyping in young girls. *Child Development, 50*, 597–600.

Federal Communications Commission. (1996). *Policies and rules concerning children's television programming: Revision of programming policies for television broadcast stations.* (MM Docket No. 93–48). Washington, D.C.: U.S. Government Printing Office.

Fisch, S. M. (2000). A capacity model of children's comprehension of educational content on television. *Media Psychology, 2*, 63–91.

Fisch, S. M. (2001). Transfer of learning from educational television: When and why does it occur? Paper presented at the biennial meeting of the Society for Research in Child Development, Minneapolis, MN.

Fisch, S. M. (2004). *Children's learning from educational television: Sesame Street and beyond.* Mahwah, NJ: Lawrence Erlbaum.

Fisch, S. M., & Truglio, R. T. (2001). *"G" is for growing: Thirty years of research on children and Sesame Street.* Mahwah, NJ: Lawrence Erlbaum.

Flavell, J. H., Miller, P. H., & Miller, S. A. (2002). *Cognitive development* (4th ed.). Upper Saddle River, NJ:

Prentice-Hall.

Friedrich-Cofer, L. K., Huston-Stein, A., Kipnis, D. M., Susman, E. J., & Clewett, A. S. (1979). Environmental enhancement of prosocial television content: Effects on interpersonal behavior, imaginative play, and self-regulation in a natural setting. *Developmental Psychology, 15,* 637–646.

Friedrich, L. K., & Stein, A. H. (1973). Aggressive and prosocial television programs and the natural behavior of preschool children. *Monographs of the Society for Research in Child Development, 38* (4, whole no. 151).

Garner, R. (1992). Learning from school texts. *Educational Psychologist, 27,* 5–63.

Gentzkow, M., & Shapiro, J. M. (2006, January). *Does television rot your brain? New evidence from the Coleman study* (National Bureau of Economic Research Working Paper No. 12021). Retrieved February 20, 2006, from http://www.nber.org/papers/w12021.

Gunter, B., Furnham, A., & Griffiths, S. (2000). Children's memory for news: A comparison of three presentation media. *Media Psychology, 2,* 93–118.

Hall, E. R., Esty, E. T., & Fisch, S. M. (1990). Television and children's problem-solving behavior: A synopsis of an evaluation of the effects of *Square One TV. Journal of Mathematical Behavior, 9,* 161–174.

Harp, S. F., & Mayer, R. E., (1998). How seductive details do their damage: A theory of cognitive interest in science learning. *Journal of Educational Psychology, 3,* 414–434.

Healy, J. M. (1999). *Endangered minds: Why our children don't think.* New York: Simon and Schuster.

Hearold, S. (1986). A synthesis of 1,043 effects of television on social behavior. In G. Comstock (Ed.), *Public communication and behavior, vol. 1* (pp. 65–133). New York: Academic Press.

Huesmann, L. R., Moise, J., Podolski, C. P., & Eron, L. D. (2003). Longitudinal relations between childhood exposure to media violence and adult aggression and violence, 1977–1992. *Developmental Psychology, 39*(2), 201–221.

Huston, A. C., & Wright, J. C. (1983). Children's processing of television: The informative functions of formal features. In J. Bryant & D. R. Anderson (Eds.), *Children's understanding of television: Research on attention and comprehension* (pp. 37–68). New York: Academic Press.

Huston, A. C., & Wright, J. C. (1989). The forms of television and the child viewer. *Public communication and behavior, vol. 2.* New York: Academic Press.

Jordan, A. B. (1996). *The state of children's television: An examination of quantity, quality, and industry beliefs* [Report No. 2]. Philadelphia: University of Pennsylvania, Annenberg Public Policy Center.

Jordan, A. B. (2000). *Is the three-hour rule living up to its potential? An analysis of educational television for children in the 1999/2000 broadcast season* [Report No. 34]. Philadelphia: University of Pennsylvania, Annenberg Public Policy Center.

Jordan, A. B., Schmitt, K. L., & Woodard, E. (2001). Developmental implications of commercial broadcasters' educational offerings. *Journal of Applied Developmental Psychology, 22,* 87–101.

Jordan, A. B., & Woodard, E. (1997). *The state of children's television report: Programming for children over broadcast and cable television* [Report No. 14]. Philadelphia: University of Pennsylvania, Annenberg Public Policy Center.

Kawachi, P. (2003). Initiating intrinsic motivation in online education: Review of the current state of the art. *Interactive Learning Environments, 11,* 59–81.

Kunkel, D., & Canepa, J. (1994) Broadcasters' license renewal claims regarding children's educational programming. *Journal of Broadcasting and Electronic Media, 38,* 397–416.

Linebarger, D. L. (2001). Learning to read from television: The effects of using captions and narration. *Journal of Educational Psychology, 93,* 288–298.

Linebarger, D. L., Kosanic, A., Greenwood, C. R., & Doku, N. S. (2004). Effects of viewing the television program *Between the Lions* on the emergent literacy skills of young children. *Journal of Educational Psychology, 96*(2), 297–308.

Linebarger, D. L., & Walker, D. (2005). Infants' and toddlers' television viewing and relations to language outcomes. *American Behavioral Scientist, 46,* 624–645.

Lorch, E. P., Anderson, D. R., & Levin, S. (1979). The relationship of visual attention to children's comprehension of television. *Child Development, 50,* 722–727.

Mares, M. (1996). *Positive effects of television on social behavior: A meta-analysis* [Report No. 3]. Philadelphia: University of Pennsylvania, Annenberg Public Policy Center.

Mayer, R. E. (1997). Multimedia learning: Are we asking the right questions? *Educational Psychologist, 32,* 1–19.

McLuhan, M. (1964) *Understanding media: The extensions of man.* New York: McGraw-Hill.

Mielke, K. (1994). *Sesame Street* and children in poverty. *Media Studies Journal, 8,* 125–134.

Minnow, N. (1961). *Television and the public interest: Speech to the National Association of Broadcasters* (May 9). Retrieved February 2, 2006, from http://www.americanrhetoric.com/speeches/newtonminow.htm.

Neuman, S. (1995). *Literacy in the television age: The myth of the TV effect* (2nd ed.). Norwood, NJ: Ablex.

Nielsen Media Research. (2005). *2005 report on television.* New York: Nielsen Media Research.

Renninger, K. A., Hidi, S., & Krapp, A. (1992). *The role of interest in learning and development.* Hillsdale, NJ: Lawrence Erlbaum.

Ricci, C. M., & Beal, C. R. (2002). The effect of interactive media on children's story memory. *Journal of Educational Psychology, 94,* 138–144.

Rice, M. L., Huston, A. C., Truglio, R., & Wright, J. (1990). Words from *Sesame Street:* Learning vocabulary while viewing. *Developmental Psychology, 26,* 421–428.

Rice, M. L., & Woodsmall, L. (1988). Lessons from television: Children's word learning when viewing. *Child Development, 59,* 420–429.

Rolandelli, D. R., Wright, J. C., Huston, A. C., & Eakins, D. (1991). Children's auditory and visual processing of narrated and non-narrated television programming. *Journal of Experimental Child Psychology, 51,* 90–122.

Salomon, G. (1979). Media and symbol systems as related to cognition and learning. *Journal of Educational Psychology, 71,* 131–148.

Salomon, G., & Perkins, D. N. (1989). The rocky road to transfer: Rethinking mechanisms of a neglected phenomenon. *Educational Psychologist, 24,* 113–142.

Singer, D., & Singer, J. (1990). *The house of make-believe: Play and the developing imagination.* Cambridge, MA: Harvard University Press.

Singer, J. L., & Singer, D. G. (1983). Implications of childhood television viewing for cognition, imagination, and emotion. In J. Bryant & D. R. Anderson (Eds.), *Children's understanding of television* (pp. 265–295). New York: Academic Press.

U.S. Census Bureau. (2006). Table 1117: Utilization of selected media, 1980 to 2003 [electronic version]. *Statistical abstract of the United States: 2006.* Washington, D.C.: Government Printing Office.

Van Evra, J. (1998). *Television and child development.* Mahwah, NJ: Lawrence Erlbaum.

Walma van der Molen, J. H., & van der Voort, T. H. A. (1997). Children's recall of television and print news: A media comparison study. *Journal of Educational Psychology, 89,* 82–91.

Weinstein, C. E., & Mayer, R. F. (1991). Cognitive learning strategies and college teaching. *New Directions for Teaching and Learning, 45,* 15–26.

Westphal, K. (2006). Trash your TV for a happier, healthier life! Retrieved February 2, 2006, from http://www.trashyourtv.com/index.php.

Winn, M. (1977). *The plug-in drug: Television, children, and the family.* New York: Viking.

Wright, J. C., & Huston, A. C. (1984). The potentials of television for young viewers. In J. P. Murray & G. Salomon (Eds.), *The future of children's television* (pp. 65–80). Boys Town, NE: Father Flanagan's Boys Home.

Wright, J. C., Huston, A. C., Murphy, K. C., St. Peters, M., Pinon, M., Scantlin, R., & Kotler, J. (2001). The relations of early television viewing to school readiness and vocabulary of children from low-income families: The early window project. *Child Development, 72,* 1347–1366.

CHAPTER THIRTEEN

What Are Media Literacy Effects?

W. JAMES POTTER & SAHARA BYRNE

In order to answer the question posed in the title, we need to address four component questions. First, how is a media literacy effect different from other effects of the media? Second, how do media literacy effects come about? Third, how can people increase the media literacy effects in their own lives? And fourth, what media literacy–enhancing techniques have researchers found to work best?

How Is a Media Literacy Effect Different from Other Media Effects?

Media literacy is not one effect; instead it refers to many effects (Potter, 2004). Moreover, media literacy effects are distinct from all other kinds of media effects, especially the ones described in most of the other chapters in this section of the book. There are three characteristics that make media literacy effects different from other kinds of media effects. First, media literacy effects are positive, not negative in the sense that most media effects are considered to be harmful to the audience. Second, media literacy effects are proactive, not reactive, in that they represent a conscious attempt to create a positive effect. And third, media literacy effects are broad. Let's examine each of these three characteristics in more detail.

Media Literacy Effects Are Positive

Almost all of the media effects literature is concerned with negative effects. For example, cultivation research (see chapter 10) is designed to show that audiences are constantly presented with distorted messages in the media, and that the application of these distortions to their real lives results in false expectations that cannot be met in their careers, interpersonal relationships, economic situation, and so on. In another example, gender-role socialization research documents the manner by which the media provide stereotypical gender roles that are neither realistic nor helpful as role models for real-life decisions. In addition, violence research (see chapters 8 and 9) offers extensive examples of how exposure to aggression in the media leads to many different kinds of effects, all negative.

Media literacy effects, in contrast, focus on the positive. They do this in two ways. First, media literacy focuses attention on the many positive things that can result from media exposure, such as becoming better informed about our world, increasing happiness through listening to music or watching comedies, and strengthening beliefs that are valuable to us, such as beliefs about family, religion, and the political system. Second, media literacy research tries to identify techniques that audience members can use to increase the occurrence of the positive effects and reduce the occurrence of negative effects.

Media Literacy Effects Are Proactive

Most media effects are regarded as nonintentional. By this we mean that the senders of the messages did not plan for the effects to happen, and neither did the receivers of the messages. For example, when producers create action adventure movies with a great deal of violence, they do not intend to make audiences behave in a violent manner or to desensitize them to the suffering of victims of violence, or for their movies to have any other negative effect. These producers simply want to entertain audiences and make money. When producers of situation comedies use gender-stereotyped, verbally aggressive characters, they simply want to entertain audiences and make them laugh at the foibles of some characters and at the wit of other characters. They do not intend to teach audiences gender stereotypes, nor do they intend that audiences become verbally aggressive. Furthermore, audiences of all these messages do not watch them so they can experience negative effects. Yet negative effects do occur.

In contrast to most media effects, media literacy effects are intentional. Either audience members intend to experience a positive effect—and they control their exposures in order to achieve those intended effects—or producers create messages, such as educational programming and public service announcements, for the purpose of generating positive effects on their audiences. Thus media literacy effects require a higher degree of consciousness to consider intentions and to make those intentional effects happen.

Media Literacy Effects Are Extremely Broad

Media literacy effects are broad in the sense that they are not limited to one type of content, one type of audience member (for example, children), what happens during the exposure to a particular media message, or only behaviors or attitudes. For example, media literacy treatments can help people avoid negative effects when they are exposed to violence in the media. But media literacy treatments can help with much more than just violent messages. They can help people get more out of any entertainment-type message while avoiding negative effects. They can help people get more out of advertising while helping them avoid being manipulated by those commercial messages. They can help people increase their appreciation of credible information in news messages and at the same time decrease their exploitation by superficial, biased news treatments of complex events.

Although media literacy is most often considered in terms of children, its effects can be of great value to adolescents, adults, and especially the elderly. Of course, children are vulnerable to negative effects of the media and it is important to help them become more media literate so they can avoid harmful effects. But aging past childhood does not guarantee that people will automatically make good decisions about using the media and make useful interpretations of those messages. By the time people reach retirement age, they have experienced more than six decades of media conditioning—conditioning that serves to narrow their range of media use as well as the way they interpret media messages. Media literacy can help these people expand the range of their media exposure into new media and a wider variety of messages.

Most research on media effects focuses on what happens during exposure to a particular media message or shortly after that exposure. Media literacy effects, of course, can show up during exposures or immediately afterward, but most media literacy effects take a longer period of time to manifest themselves.

Media effects researchers are fond of examining how media influence audience members' behaviors and attitudes. With media literacy, the focus is broadened to include cognitions, beliefs, emotions, and even a person's physiology. Cognitive effects include how a person thinks as well as the acquisition of knowledge—a very important positive effect for students. Beliefs refer to those things audience members think are true about the world. For example, many people have come to believe the world is a mean and violent place after watching many movies and TV shows that depict horrible crimes. Media messages trigger all kinds of emotional reactions, some positive and some negative. As for physiology, the media can present messages that cause audience members' hearts to beat faster, their pupils to dilate, their breathing to become shallow, and other changes to their bodies.

In summary, media literacy is concerned with positive effects as well as negative ones. It encourages a proactive stance in which people can control the effects process to deliver the more positive effects while avoiding the more negative ones. It takes a broad view of media influences to include the effects of all kinds of messages on all kinds of people, both immediately during exposure and in the long term, and in the areas of thinking, believing, feeling, behaving, and bodily functions.

How Do Media Literacy Effects Come About?

In order to understand how we can achieve media literacy effects rather than the typically negative effects from the mass media, we need to understand the contrast between the default model of information processing and the media literacy model (Potter, 2004).

Under the default model of information processing, the media exert a great deal of power over how audience members are attracted to messages and the meanings they get from those exposures. The media exert this power in a process that begins by constraining choice of messages (Shoemaker & Reese, 1996). Only certain types of products and services are advertised, while others are ignored (Leiss et al., 1988). Only certain types of events are covered in the news, while other important events are ignored (Ettema & Whitney, 1994; Jensen, 1997). This media-dominated process continues as the media work to attract certain kinds of audience members to each of their messages (Webster & Phalen, 1997). Once audience members are exposed to media messages, they are conditioned for repeated exposures until their choices are habitual. The media are very sophisticated in using various techniques to attract audiences, hold their attention, and condition their behavior. This sophistication helps the media become extremely successful in meeting their financial goals. However, this process rarely, if ever, delivers the best set of positive effects for individual audience members.

Audience members, however, have an alternative to following the default model. This alternative is a media literacy model, in which audience members are shown how to access a wider range of media messages, how to make better exposure choices, and how to construct their own meanings from the messages they choose for their exposures. In order to do these things well, they need good sets of knowledge structures and information-processing skills (Potter, 2005b). Specifically, they need to develop five types of knowledge structures (about media effects, media content, media industries, the real world, and self) and seven skills (analysis, evaluation, induction, deduction, grouping, synthesis, and abstracting). When people have well-developed knowledge structures and information-processing skills, they can be much more powerful in taking control over their media exposure experiences and use those experiences to achieve their own goals rather than letting the media use their exposure experiences to achieve their business goals. However, most people are willing to stay in the default model of information processing because it is easier. There is a trade-off between effort and control. When people are not willing to expend much effort to develop their skills or knowledge structures, they are likely to stay in the default model during media exposures and turn over control of meaning construction to the media.

How Can People Increase the Media Literacy Effects in Their Own Lives?

People can increase their media literacy and thus take more control over their exposure patterns and be more active in constructing meaning for themselves rather than allowing the media to construct meaning for them. In order to be successful at this task, they need to work in the areas of context, tools, and desire.

Context: Elaborating Knowledge Structures

Knowledge structures provide context for decisions about media exposures and what to get out of those exposures. The more context people have, the more choice they are aware of and the more information they have to make good choices. Context resides in a person's set of knowledge structures. In the section above, we mentioned that five knowledge structures are important for people to avoid the default model and use the media literacy model during exposure to media messages. In this section, we will detail what those five knowledge structures are and why they are important to media literacy.

Media effects. When people have a broad understanding about what media effects can occur and the influences that bring about these effects, they have the context to be able to know when the probability that a negative effect will occur is high. This knowledge puts them in a position to do things to avoid the negative effects before they happen. Also, an elaborate knowledge of media effects gives people the context for making good decisions about which effects are positive and therefore desirable for them to achieve.

Media content. Having knowledge about patterns of media content gives people the context to make better decisions about which messages to seek and which to avoid in order to achieve their goals. It also helps people understand more about what messages underlie media content and are not obvious on the surface. For example, most people do not realize that most of the characters in television programs are males (between two thirds and three quarters). This leads people to believe that males are more important and more prevalent than females. Also, people of color—especially Latino/as and Native Americans—often are absent or underrepresented in media portrayals. This leads people to believe that these groups are much smaller in number than they are in real life, and therefore that they are not important.

Media industries. People need a well-developed knowledge structure about the media industries so they can appreciate how people in those industries make decisions about creating certain kinds of content and ignoring other kinds. The media are businesses, so there is a strong economic basis for almost all the decisions that are made about content.

Real world. People need a broad understanding of the real world because without accurate knowledge about what occurs in all sorts of facets of the real world, audience members cannot compare the media-world messages with real-world patterns and thereby realize how subtly unrealistic the media world is. If people cannot make this comparison and therefore come to believe that the media-world patterns apply to the real world, they will be repeatedly disappointed when their expectations are not realized.

Self. People need a good knowledge of themselves; that is, they need an accurate understanding of their own strengths, emotions, and desires. Often, people will want things because the media have conditioned them to want those things, but those things may be things that cannot make them happy and may even harm them.

Tools: Strengthening Meaning Construction Skills

In order to build strong context through knowledge structures, people also need well-developed information-processing skills. People need to be stronger in their analysis of media messages and break those messages down into component parts to understand more fully the elements to which they are constantly being exposed. People need to evaluate the worth of those message components in terms of their own goals and desires. People need to be strong in applying the skill of induction and look for patterns across media messages. People also need to be strong in applying the skill of deduction to use general principles that they learn about the media in order to make better sense out of individual examples. The skill of grouping is also important so that people can organize their options and thus make choices more efficiently. The skill of synthesis is valuable in sorting through all the messages and claims from the media and assembling the most valuable of those to construct opinions that are informed and logical. And finally, people need to develop the skill of abstracting so as to be able to focus on the most important elements in any media message. For more detail on these skills and how to develop them, see *Becoming a Strategic Thinker* (Potter, 2005a).

Desire: Strengthening Personal Locus

Knowing that knowledge structures and skills are important to increasing media literacy is not enough. People need to become committed to developing these knowledge structures and skills. They need the desire. This desire rests in a personal locus that motivates people to increase their effort and hence gain more control over their media exposures and interpreting meaning from those exposures. If a person's locus is weak, there is not much motivation to improve one's self and that person is likely to remain in the default model of processing information, where the media will exert a powerful influence over conditioning exposure habits.

The personal locus is in constant flux. People who ignore their personal locus allow it to grow weaker over time. Knowledge structures deteriorate as old information goes out of date and is not replaced with good new information. Skills deteriorate without practice. In contrast, people who are constantly building stronger knowledge structures and exercising their skills are increasingly likely to experience many positive effects from the media.

What Media Literacy–Enhancing Techniques Have Been Found to Work by Researchers?

There are many questions to ask when designing a media literacy lesson. Who should deliver a media literacy lesson? Who should receive the lesson? Should the lesson focus on teaching facts about the media, or should the lesson involve students in designing messages so they can develop insights into the aesthetic challenges inherent in creating media messages? What is the outcome we can expect from the lesson; that is, how can we tell if the lesson was successful? This section of the chapter will focus on research findings that can help answer these questions.

From a research point of view, media literacy lessons have been named "interventions." Researchers design interventions with different features, then run an experiment to test which interventions (and hence which features) lead to the greatest gains in media literacy. These interventions generally have four components: the agent, target, the treatment, and the outcome. The agent is the person or vehicle delivering the lessons. The target of the intervention is the person who is receiving the media literacy lesson or intervention. The treatment is the content and design of the intervention. And the outcome is some aspect of the target that should change as a result of the intervention.

The Agent

In experiments, the agent is typically the researcher, the teacher, or the parent. The most common of these is when the researcher takes on a teacher or parentlike role (Huesmann et al., 1983; Nathanson, 2004). There also are examples of when the agent is a classroom teacher who is trained by the researcher to deliver a specific intervention (Abelman & Courtright, 1983). Parents are sometimes studied as agents (Valkenburg et al., 1999). Typically, when parents are the agents in a media literacy study they are not trained by the researcher; instead, the parents' typical behaviors are observed as they view television with their children.

Most intervention studies do not evaluate the relative effectiveness of different types of agents. Most do not, for example, compare the effect of an intervention given by an existing teacher with the same intervention given by another type of agent, such as an outside researcher. One of the few studies that looked at varying the agent embedded an intervention containing adult commentary within a television program and compared the results to that of an adult standing in the room giving the exact same commentary (Corder-Bolz, 1980). The study found that the embedded procedure was similar in effectiveness when compared to live mediators. Another consideration is that the opportunity for the children to interact with an agent is lost with this type of intervention. Clearly, there is ample opportunity to research the effectiveness of various agents in media literacy interventions.

The Target

The most common participants used for media literacy intervention studies are children. Researchers develop various curricula depending on the age and developmental stage of the target. Children in the preoperational stage of processing information (Piaget, 1953), such as kindergarten through second-graders, tend to respond positively to evaluative mediation, which highlights the undesirability of certain aspects of a media stimulus or attributes of the characters within it. (See chapter 4 for a discussion of developmental psychology's application to studies of youth and media.) Amy Nathanson (2004) found that both younger children (five to seven years) and heavy-viewing older children (ten to twelve) processed and remembered evaluative content (they were able to be critical of the use of violence) more easily than they did facts about TV production. In fact, younger children exposed to a factual mediation reported more aggressive attitudes than children with no mediation at all!

Unfortunately, there is very little media literacy research devoted to adults at all, which is unfortunate considering that it is adults who are expected to teach the initial concepts of media literacy. There is certainly room in the research landscape to determine whether certain media literacy skills will be more beneficial to people if these concepts are introduced in a specific age window.

Intervention Treatment

We do know a few things about what kind of content should be included in a media literacy intervention aimed to reduce negative effects. One of the most consistent findings is that providing facts about the media, or media production, has been shown to be less effective than evaluative content. Evaluative content in a media literacy intervention refers to critical judgments or praising of media content or the behavior of media characters. As a direct test of factual versus evaluative mediation, Nathanson (2004) assigned children to three conditions: factual mediation, evaluative mediation, and no mediation. The children heard the various mediations during edited pauses while watching a violent live-action children's television show. The children in the factual mediation condition were given information about how the fighting, actors, and camera moves were fake and that the producers of the show used tricks to make the actions look real. In the evaluative condition, the children were told that the characters were not "cool" and that they probably didn't have any friends. The children in the no-mediation condition were simply told that the commercials had been edited out and to wait a minute for the show to come back on. The children in the evaluative-mediation condition were less accepting of the characters and program overall. They were also less involved with the aggressive characters and perceived the violent behavior as less justified.

Interventions that increase emotional involvement with characters also tend to promote desired results. For example, Amy Nathanson and Joanne Cantor (2000) asked children to consider the feelings of a victim before viewing a violent cartoon and found that the children in this group reported liking the perpetrator less and thought he was meaner than the children in the control group.

Similarly, an intervention that makes a direct attempt to motivate children not to encode, store, retrieve, and employ aggressive behaviors in the first place has been shown to be more effective than simply telling children information about media effects. For example, an intervention that requires participants to be active in the process of learning, such as writing or making a videotape, might encourage children to more deeply process and store the content of the intervention (Huesmann et al., 1983).

The Outcome

One of the most important components of media literacy interventions is being clear about what attribute of the target you are looking to change. The most common outcome that researchers have measured is the ability of people to recall facts learned during an intervention (Abelman & Courtright, 1983; Corder-Bolz, 1980; Dorr et al., 1980; Huesmann et al., 1983; Rapaczynski et al., 1982; Singer et al., 1980; Valkenburg et al., 1998; Voojis & van der Voort, 1993). Generally, the researchers are interested in factual knowledge about production techniques and camera tricks (Rapaczynski et al., 1982), content of the intervention (Valkenburg et al., 1998), and industry motives (Dorr et al., 1980). The awareness that the media are not accurately depicting reality is also a concern (Huesmann et al., 1983; Voojis & van der Voort, 1993). In addition, researchers have measured the ability of media literacy interventions to increase awareness of the availability of certain types of programs, such as those with pro-social content (Abelman & Courtright, 1983).

Researchers also have looked at how intervention can change attitudes and emotions. For example, Nathanson and Cantor (2000) found that mediation could decrease liking of a violent program and the characters performing the violence, reduce fictional involvement with a perpetrator, and decrease willingness to perceive violence as justified. Research has confirmed the ability of interventions to produce at least a temporary change in evaluations of a program (Nathanson, 2004; Nathanson & Cantor, 2000; Valkenburg et al., 1998) and viewer evaluations of violent characters (Nathanson, 2004; Nathanson & Cantor, 2000; Voojis & van der Voort, 1993). Researchers also have attempted to find evidence that intervention can decrease feelings that the world is a mean and scary place (Robinson et al., 2001). The ability of an intervention to change emotional attachment to media has been measured as well. For example, Singer and colleagues (1980) asked participants if they would miss television if it disappeared from their lives.

A few studies have looked at the change in behavioral measures as a result of intervention. Change in aggressive behavior, for example, has been reported in the form of peer nominations (Huesmann et al., 1983), parental reports (Robinson et al., 2001), playground observation (Robinson et al., 2001), and self-reported approval of, or willingness to use, aggressive behavior (Corder-Bolz, 1980; Nathanson, 2004; Voojis & van der Voort, 1993).

Another behavior that media literacy interventions have attempted to change is television-viewing habits in general. Thomas Robinson and colleagues (2001) attempted a six-month classroom intervention to reduce TV viewing and measured whether or not watching less TV made children less aggressive.

Only a few studies have provided longitudinal measurements capable of evidencing a long-term effect. For example, two years after the completion of their intervention, Marcel Voojis and Tom van der Voort (1993) found that their experimental group still had more factual knowledge and reduction in their perceived reality of the way things are portrayed on television. Three months after their intervention, L. Rowell Huesmann and colleagues (1983) also found a reduction in peer-rated aggression.

While the studies above provide promising evidence for the ability of interventions to reduce some of the negative effects of the media, it should be noted that a "boomerang" or backfire effect also has been found (Cantor & Wilson, 2003). Several studies have shown that certain types of interventions, such as those that do not encourage deeper learning and/or are focused on reducing the effect of sexual violence in the media, run the risk of *increasing* the negative effects of the media stimulus (Byrne, 2005; Doolittle, 1980; Mattern & Lindholm, 2001; Nathanson, 2004; Wilson et al., 1992; Winkel & DeKleuver, 1997).

Conclusion

Most of the research on media literacy interventions relies on an immediate postintervention measure. Although establishing an immediate effect is certainly important, when we are attempting to change the way humans process media messages, our result will be more accurate if we can confirm that the effect is lasting over time. Additional research also is needed to explore the boomerang pattern evidenced in media literacy research. In the meantime, practitioners, scholars, and researchers should take care when designing interventions aiming to reduce any negative effect of the media.

DISCUSSION QUESTIONS

1 Why are some people more media literate than others?

2 What can you do in your own life to increase the media literacy effects on you?

3 What can you do to help others increase the media literacy effects on them?

EXERCISES

1   According to the chapter, one way to become more media literate is to have a well-developed knowledge structure about the media industries. Using the example of a popular, youth-oriented television network such as MTV, Nickelodeon, or the Disney Channel, research the ownership and corporate structure. What other media outlets does your network's corporate owner also own? What might the significance of this be?

2   According to the chapter, another way to become media literate is to understand patterns occurring in media content such as patterns of character portrayals and/or casting. Watch the five current top-selling movies on DVD and construct a demographic breakdown of the primary and secondary characters. (A current ranking of DVD sales is easily available online.) In other words, classify each character by such demographic characteristics as gender, race, age range, social class, and so on. How many primary characters fit each of your categories? How many secondary? What is the significance of this?

REFERENCES

Abelman, R., & Courtright, J. (1983). Television literacy: Amplifying the cognitive level effects of television's prosocial fare through curriculum intervention. *Journal of Research and Development in Education, 17*, 46–57.

Byrne, S. (2005, May). Effective and lasting media literacy interventions. Paper presented at the annual meeting of the International Communication Association, New York.

Cantor, J., & Wilson, B. J. (2003). Media and violence: Intervention strategies for reducing aggression. *Media Psychology, 5*, 563–403.

Corder-Bolz, C. R. (1980). Mediation: The role of significant others. *Journal of Communication, 30*, 106–118.

Doolittle, J. C. (1980). Immunizing children against possible antisocial effects of viewing television violence: A curricular intervention. *Perceptual and Motor Skills, 51*, 498.

Dorr, A., Graves, S. B., & Phelps, E. (1980). Television literacy for young children. *Journal of Communication, 30*(3), 71–83.

Ettema, J. S., & Whitney, D. C. (Eds.). (1994). *Audiencemaking: How the media create the audience.* Thousand Oaks, CA: Sage.

Huesmann, L. R., Eron, L. D., Klein. R., Brice, P., & Fischer, P. (1983). Mitigating the imitation of aggressive behaviors by changing children's attitudes about media violence. *Journal of Personality and Social Psychology, 44*, 899–910.

Jensen, C. (1997). *Twenty years of censored news.* New York: Seven Stories.

Leiss, W., Kline, S, & Jhally, S. (1988). *Social communication in advertising: Persons, products, and images of well-being.* Ontario: Nelson Canada.

Mattern, K. I., & Lindholm, B. (2001). Effect of maternal commentary in reducing aggressive impact of televised violence on preschool children. *Journal of Genetic Psychology, 146*, 133–134.

Nathanson, A. I. (2004). Factual and evaluative approaches to modifying children's responses to television. *Journal of Communication, 54*, 321–336.

Nathanson, A. I., & Cantor, J. (2000). Reducing the aggression-promoting effect of violent cartoons by increasing children's fictional involvement with the victim: A study of active mediation. *Journal of Broadcasting & Electronic Media, 44*, 125–142.

Piaget, J. (1953). *The origin of intelligence in the child.* London: Routledge.

Potter, W. J. (2004). *Theory of media literacy: A cognitive approach.* Thousand Oaks, CA: Sage.

Potter, W. J. . (2005a). *Becoming a strategic thinker: Developing skills for success.* Upper Saddle River, NJ: Pearson Prentice Hall.

Potter, W. J. (2005b). *Media literacy* (3rd ed.). Thousand Oaks, CA: Sage.

Rapaczynski, W., Singer, D. G., & Singer, J. L. (1982). Teaching television: A curriculum for young children. *Journal of Communication, 32*, 46–54.

Robinson T. N., Wilde M. L., Navaracruz, L. C., Haydel, K. F., & Varady, A. (2001). Effects of reducing children's television and video game use on aggressive behavior: A randomized controlled trial. *Archives of Pediatrics and Adolescent Medicine, 155*, 17–23.

Singer, D. G., Zuckerman, D. M, & Singer, J. L. (1980). Helping elementary school children learn about TV. *Journal of Communication, 30*, 84–93.

Shoemaker, P. J., & Reese, S. D. (1996). *Mediating the message: Theories of influences on mass media content* (2nd ed.). White Plains, NY: Longman.

Valkenburg, P. M., Krcmar, M., & de Roos, S. (1998). The impact of a cultural children's program and adult mediation on children's knowledge of and attitudes toward an opera. *Journal of Broadcasting & Electronic Media, 42*, 315–396.

Valkenburg, P. M., Krcmar, M., Peeters, A. L., & Marseille, N. M. (1999). Developing a scale to assess three styles of television mediation: "Instructive mediation," "restrictive mediation," and "social coviewing." *Journal of Broadcasting & Electronic Media, 43*, 52–66.

Voojis, M. W., & van der Voort, T. H. A. (1993) Learning about television violence: The impact of a critical viewing curriculum on children's attitudinal judgments of crime series. *Journal of Research and Development in Education, 26*, 133–142.

Webster, J. G., & Phalen, P. F. (1997). *Mass audience: Rediscovering the dominant model.* Mahwah, NJ: Lawrence Erlbaum.

Wilson, B. J., Linz, D., Donnerstein, E., & Stipp, H. (1992). The impact of social issue television programming on attitudes toward rape. *Human Communication Research, 19*, 179–208.

Winkel, F. W., & DeKleuver, E. (1997). Communication aimed at changing cognitions about sexual intimidation: Comparing the impact of perpetrator-focused versus a victim-focused persuasive strategy. *Journal of Interpersonal Violence, 12*, 513–529.

The "Kids"

Youth, Culture, and Media

CHAPTER FOURTEEN

What Are Teenagers up to Online?

SUSANNAH R. STERN & TAYLOR J. WILLIS

Contemporary American teenagers have been intermittently labeled as "compulsive self chroniclers" (Nussbaum, 2004), "little angels raising hell online" (Pardington, 2005), and, in aggregate, as the "constant contact generation" (Clark, 2005). Although these characterizations tend to promote the often misguided image of neurotic teenagers glued desperately to their computer screens, many adults agree that the most distinguishing trait of young people today is their connectedness to the Internet. Indeed, the majority of teenagers in the United States today have used the Internet since they were children. What is the experience of growing up online like?

This chapter will discuss how much and in what ways teenagers use the Internet, as well as describe what we know about how they may be affected by their Internet use. Throughout our discussion, we will pay particular attention to adolescence as a distinct life stage during which Internet use can have particular appeal and utility.

Who's Online . . . and Who Isn't?

Teenagers comprise one of the fastest-growing segments of the online population. Currently, 87 percent of American teens use the Internet, compared to only 66 percent of adults. Internet use starts early; most teens have logged on by the seventh grade, and the frequency with which they use the Internet tends to increase with age throughout adolescence. Half of teen Internet users say they go online at least once every day. Among the many possible places to access the Internet, home is the place where most online teens say they go online most often. Many young people also go online from school, libraries, or community centers (Lenhart et al., 2005).

Girls and boys go online at relatively equal rates (DeBell & Chapman, 2001), and a 2005 Gallup poll reported that 28 percent of teens have a computer with Internet access in their own bedrooms (Kaplan, 2005). Although teens spend more time watching the television than using the Internet, the Internet ties for first place when teens are asked which medium they would pick as their first choice. Most studies show that the Internet hasn't replaced other media use, but rather that it complements many other teen tasks, including watching television, doing homework, listening to music, and talking on the phone (Rideout et al., 2005).

Despite the regularity with which most teens go online these days, there are still marked differences in Internet access across race and class. In fact, 13 percent of American teenagers still do not use the Internet. These unwired teens are more likely than wired teens to come from families with low incomes and are significantly more likely to be African American (Lenhart et al., 2005).

Not surprisingly, inequities are larger for Internet use in the home than they are for access in public and school sites (Hellenga, 2002). White youths, those whose parents have more education, and those whose families earn a higher income are significantly more likely to have Internet access at home and to use the Internet on a typical day (Rideout et al., 2005). The ability to access the Internet at home is important for a number of reasons, not least of which is that home access can consistently ensure more time for a teen to spend online.

Ironically, as more and more teens go online, the negative ramifications for those who are not online grow exponentially. Unwired teens miss out on opportunities to play with the Internet in ways that foster familiarity and comfort with the technology. They also fail to benefit from the array of resources that might assist them in their educational and employment pursuits. More immediately, lack of Internet access often leads some young people to feel left out or isolated, since the Internet has come to play a key role in social interactions and event planning among young people (Skinner et al., 2003). Although the rest of this chapter will focus on what we know about wired teens, we feel it is important to forefront the digital divide among teenagers from the outset. Omitting from the conversation any discussion about the 13 percent of American teens who do not use the Internet renders the inequity invisible, and thus less likely to be addressed. At a time when an overwhelming majority of educators believe that students with home Internet access enjoy an educational advantage (Rosato, 2002) and most parents consider the Internet "essential" to their teen's future success (Lenhart, Simon & Graziano, 2001), greater attention to unwired teens is clearly warranted.

What Are Teens Doing Online?

Although discussions about teen Internet use often focus on how much teens use "the Internet" and how "it" affects them, it is remiss to suggest that the Internet is only one thing, or that it is used in one way by all teens. Rather, the range of activities in which young people engage online is extensive and diverse. We organize these activities into three main categories: communication, information seeking, and content creation.

Communication

Similar to other new technologies over the years, the Internet was initially heralded as a tool that young people would avail themselves of to gain valuable, employable skills. The Internet, it was predicted, would help to restructure adolescence into a period of disciplined information seeking, increased world awareness, and greater productivity. Despite debates over whether such premonitions have come to fruition, the current reality is that teenagers primarily use the Internet for social reasons. Although adults often rue this "unproductive" use of precious online time, it's important to remember that managing social relationships and playing around with self-expression styles, as teens figure out who they are, is as developmentally functional as it is fun.

Indeed, after decades of comparatively low-tech phone calls and note-passing, the Internet has quickly become one of the main ways that American teenagers correspond with one another. Although more teens (89 percent) have used email than any other online communication application, instant messaging (IM) has quickly replaced email as the most frequently used communication tool among online teens. IM allows users to correspond in real time with multiple people at once and to monitor whether their friends are logged on. An overwhelming three fourths of online teens use IM, and half of them use IM every single day (Lenhart et al., 2005).

Why is instant messaging so much more popular with teens than other forms of mediated communication? My conversations with teenagers and review of relevant literature point to several reasons, including that it is relatively easy to use, it's inexpensive, it allows for multitasking, and it's efficient—in the sense that teens can correspond with multiple people at the same time. IM is also casual; formal spelling and grammar are unnecessary and, consequently, some young people feel less constrained in their communication style and content. IM also appears to enhance many teens' network of relationships. Because IMing is so easy, teens find themselves talking more to friends and peers than they would otherwise have time to in and out of school. Communication can also be less awkward online; on IM, there are no gaping silences or nervous giggles, and when either communication partner has had enough of the conversation, they can simply stop IMing or sign off quickly. These possibilities help teens to feel more in control of their social interactions, a welcome feeling during adolescence, when building and managing social relationships is a key developmental task.

Shayla Thiel's (2005) qualitative interviews with girls also revealed that IM provides girls with what they perceive to be a free or safe space in which they could experiment with using different language styles (for example, word choice, tone), allowing them to break norms that they can find restrictive in other settings, such as school. Moreover, girls in Thiel's study described the ways in which IM can elevate users' social status by allowing them to control their self-presentation. For instance, engaging in numerous, simultaneous online conversations on IM conveys to others that a girl is popular and well liked. Experimenting with sexuality and relationships is another preoccupation common during adolescence, and IM allows for new ways to play out sexuality and test social norms in a safe space (Thiel, 2005).

Information Seeking

Having grown up with access to the vast network of entertainment, educational, and informational sites that comprise the World Wide Web, most teens report that the Web has content to fulfill nearly every want or need. Its rapid search capabilities, twenty-four-hour availability, and the fact that users can browse anonymously from any wired location often make the Web the first place that young people turn for a broad array of information, ranging from entertainment and shopping to academic and health-related topics (see, for example, Hempel, 2005; Lenhart et al., 2005; Rideout et al., 2005; Weiss, 2003).

Keeping abreast of popular culture is a common teenage preoccupation, and the Web has made this task easier than ever. In fact, the second most common activity teens engage in online (after sending and reading email) is visiting Web sites about movies, TV shows, music groups, or sports events (Lenhart et al., 2005). Staying informed about bands, popular programs, new films, and other cultural phenomena helps many teens feel connected to particular subcultures within the teen community. Web access is especially valuable to youth who lack the discretionary income to buy the magazines and media products that feature and report on their interests. Game playing on the Internet is also widely popular, as is downloading music (Lenhart & Madden, 2005). General sites that promote interactivity—such as sites with trivia, games, fantasy sports leagues, and quiz generators—are also well liked by online teens.

Many teens also have begun to use the Web as a resource for shopping. Online, teens have greater access to products to support their diverse interests than they typically do in their nearby geographic communities. The downside for adolescents is that most e-shopping requires credit cards, which teens are less likely to have. Nonetheless, as of 2005, 43 percent of online teens had made purchases online (Lenhart et al., 2005). More frequently, teens use the Internet to "window shop" before making offline purchases (Pastore, 2001).

Teenagers are using the Web for academic and career purposes as well. For example, 94 percent of online teens use the Internet for school-related research (U.S. Department of

Education, 2004), including researching for projects and papers and using online tutoring sites for difficult subjects. The Web is also a major resource for future planning, including researching potential colleges and universities and searching for jobs. And, despite adults' constant lamentations that teens today are politically apathetic and disinterested in current events, teenagers are just as likely as adults to get news and political information online. In fact, three fourths of online teens report using the Web to read the news, and more than half say they seek political information online (Lenhart et al., 2005).

Another reason teens consult the Web is for information on a variety of health issues. Online health information is valuable because it can help adolescents determine if certain conditions are normal or if they warrant treatment from a doctor or other professional. Also, it allows teens to research their situation or symptoms online before doctor visits so that they can ask more focused questions, and afterwards, learn more about things like prescriptions and the course of their condition. In certain cases, access to emergency phone numbers and information about emergency contraception can be vital too (Borzekowski & Rickert, 2001). Because the Web can be navigated anonymously, the Internet may be particularly useful to teens who view discussions with doctors, parents, and peers with apprehension. The Web is a useful alternative because teens can navigate in private while still receiving current information (Suzuki & Calzo, 2004). Nearly a third of teen Internet users go online for information about health, dieting, or fitness, and about a fifth of online teens look for information online about a health topic that's "hard to talk about," such as drug use, sexual health, or depression (Lenhart et al., 2005).

Not all of teens' health information queries online are directed toward information sites, nor are they explicitly geared toward finding out facts about bodies and illnesses. Rather, it is also common for young people to use the Web to learn more about and engage in conversations about sexual norms, attitudes, and experiences. For example, Ashley Grisso and David Weiss (2005) examined the ways in which girls use gURL.com to explore issues of sexuality. They found that girls not only asked questions about basic sexual details (for example, "What is premarital sex?"), but that they also used the site to explore and begin to define themselves as sexual beings. Similarly, Stern found that girls used their personal Web home pages to explore sexual identity via their poetry, biographies, and essays, providing the opportunity for other teen visitors to gain a better sense of the diverse range of sexual expression and experiences that young people engage in (2002a).

Creating Content

One of the most unique opportunities the Internet provides teens is the ability to publish their own creative works to a potentially large audience online. The appeal of sharing original art and ideas online cannot be underestimated for teenagers, in particular, who historically have had few avenues for making their thoughts and creations visible to a general public. Because the search for a coherent identity constitutes one of the major tasks of adolescence, it has been argued that the Internet can actually help facilitate healthy self-reflection, identity experimentation, and self-disclosure (Stern, 2002b). Accordingly, it should come as little surprise that more and more young people engage in online content creation every day. In fact, according to a 2005 study, some 57 percent of online teens—more than half of *all* teenagers in the United States—create content for the Internet. This includes creating a blog, working on a Web page, publishing artwork, photos, stories, or videos online, or remixing content found online into a new creation (Lenhart & Madden, 2005).

Blogs have received the bulk of recent attention from the scholarly community and popular press, as the number of teens who create and read them steadily climbs. Blogs—or Web logs—are essentially online journals in which people document their lives, thoughts, philosophies, and anxieties for the rest of the online community to read. The rates of blog authorship and readership among teens far surpasses those for adults; in fact, one fifth of online youths (ages twelve to seventeen) have created their own online journal or blog, and more than a third of all online teens say they read others' blogs. Teen girls ages fifteen to seventeen are the most likely of all to blog; fully one fourth of online girls in this age group keep a blog, compared to 15 percent of boys in this age group (Lenhart & Madden, 2005).

Personal home pages are another popular way that teens create content for the Internet. Personal home pages are Web sites authored by young people that include anything from text and images to sounds and links. More than a fifth of online teens in 2005 reported keeping their own personal home page (Lenhart & Madden, 2005). Stern qualitatively analyzed teen girls' home pages to conclude that

> when given a virtual space to express themselves . . . girls tell stories that are very personal, intimate, and immediate. They construct an online identity based on a narrative about who they are and who they wish to become. Their narrative highlights their emotional and relational lives, rather than their connection to a greater societal (political, economical, etc.) context. They tell stories of self, of developing personalities, of loneliness and depression, of disappointment with reality, but also of hopefulness about love and their futures. (2002b, p. 224)

In a follow-up study comparing and contrasting teen boys' and girls' home pages, Stern (2004) found that the variety of topics and components exhibited suggested that home pages both simulated and supplemented traditional (offline) forums for self-disclosure (such as diaries and face-to-face conversations). Much like other personal spaces such as school lockers or bedrooms, the home pages allowed their authors to signal who they were and how they wished others to view them, but with the additional benefit of a potentially large audience. Although intimate topics were mentioned less frequently than authors' general interests, the fact that some adolescents shared such personal thoughts and experiences was deemed notable, since their very existence suggested that home pages were serving as an auspicious location for some young people to engage in self-clarification and self-expression. Stern also concluded that the greater frequency with which general interests were discussed (compared to intimate topics) also reflected disclosure patterns in offline (for example, face-to-face) communication. For example, some gendered communication patterns appeared to translate from the offline setting to the online setting, in that girls were more likely to disclose personal information, feelings, and concerns on home pages than were boys.

Although the popular press has tended to dwell on the potential negative ramifications of teens' online self-publications (for example, inappropriately airing one's "dirty laundry"), some scholars have examined the positive ramifications as well. Sharon R. Mazzarella (2005), for example, notes how girls' cultural production on the Internet allows them to participate in fan culture, to create a sense of community, and to construct spaces in which they can feel safe. Mazzarella (2005, p. 157) concludes, "Girls are willing to exert their control as cultural producers to create the kind of atmosphere/environment they want and need."

On another positive note, teens who create home pages and blogs can receive feedback from their site visitors, which helps them feel less isolated and more "normal." As Emily Nussbaum (2004) puts it, "So much high-school pain comes from the sense of being alone with one's stupid, self-destructive impulses. With so many teenagers baring their vulnerabilities, there is the potential for breaking down isolation." The ability of teens to continually refashion themselves in their online publications is particularly compelling, since home pages and blogs can be updated as often as desired and because they may be produced anonymously. Especially during adolescence, when saying certain things, wearing certain clothes, and engaging in certain behaviors can have severe ramifications, blogs and home pages can enable teens to feel freer to express their ideas, to address taboo or unsavory topics, and to experiment with different self-presentation styles. Most psychologists concur that speaking up is significant for teens' healthy development, but finding safe spaces to engage in self-expression has traditionally been difficult. The Internet appears to provide a promising new location.

Why Do People Worry about Teen Internet Use, and Is There Any Evidence That These Concerns Are Warranted?

On the Internet, teens have more autonomy to do, say, and go where they wish than they have had historically. Of course, this type of freedom is precisely what concerns many adults. Indeed, despite the fact that most adults agree that the Internet is vital to young people's lives, fears about what the Internet is doing to young people—and what young people are doing with the Internet—are rampant. Kate Hellenga (2002, p. 209) poignantly articulated the paradox:

> Internet optimists focus on the increased social connections made possible by online communication, while Internet pessimists attend more to the ways that online activity will dehumanize us, damaging or diminishing existing, offline social connections. Thus we are warned of the dangers of computer-mediated connections: the decrease in social skills and intimacy, the potential for misinformation and exploitation, and the possibilities of "internet addiction." . . . From this perspective, adolescents who spend too much time online run the risks of losing their friends, their mental health, or their social skills, being made prey to all manners of exploitation and falsehood, or even becoming online addicts or delinquents.

At this point in time, there is not enough research on the effects of various types of Internet use among teenagers to corroborate any speculation about the "promise and perils" of the Internet. Nevertheless, the research community has begun to preliminarily address an array of the most common concerns. We offer a brief summary of this work here.

Access to "Inappropriate" Content

One of the oldest concerns raised in connection with teen Internet use is the easy access the Web provides teens to what many adults consider inappropriate content. Among the most criticized Web sites are those featuring eating disorders, bomb making, hate groups, gambling, alcohol, smoking, and, most of all, pornography. Adults worry that teens who intentionally seek information of these sorts will easily find an abundance of visual and textual content that can be unhealthy or even dangerous. Unintentional experiences with such content is troubling because young people can be caught off guard at ages and times when they may be ill-equipped to understand or handle what they have seen.

Most of the research focusing on inappropriate content has centered on pornography, and there is no shortage of studies investigating youth porn viewing, in particular. One study found that a fifth of adolescents reported that they had visited a pornographic site for more than three minutes (Stahl & Fritz, 2002), and another found that a quarter of adolescents have been exposed to unwanted sexual material while surfing the Web or through email (Finkelhor et al., 2001). Although most adult sites warn visitors about their explicit content and make attempts to restrict underage users from entering, it can be difficult or even impossible to verify users' ages. In fact, 15 percent of all online teens and 25 percent of older male online teens have lied about their age to access a Web site—often a pornographic site (Lenhart, Rainie & Lewis, 2001). Nearly all (95 percent) teens who access porn online are male, and most are over fourteen years of age, when sexual curiosity is developmentally appropriate. Researchers who analyzed the Youth Internet Safety Survey concluded that concerns about large numbers of healthy, well-adjusted young children being exposed to online pornography are overstated (Ybarra & Mitchell, 2005).

The implications of youths' exposure to online sexual content are unclear. Some adults speculate that accessing porn online will lead to sex addiction, distortions about sexual norms, and moral deterioration. One way many parents handle the situation is by monitoring their teens' Internet use. For instance, three fourths of families oblige teens to go online from a "public" area of their home (such as a living room or den), where family members can observe each others' Internet use (Lenhart et al., 2005). Research suggests, however, that this does not decrease amounts of exposure to sexual content (Mitchell et al., 2003). The most effective method to date is blocking or filtering programs like Net Nanny and those provided by AOL and Microsoft, which filter lists of sites and language to protect users. More than half of parents with online teens say they use Internet filters (Lenhart, 2005). Such devices have limitations, however. Kimberly Mitchell and colleagues (2003) found that they failed to block 25 percent of objectionable sites, and blocked 21 percent of nonobjectionable ones.

Online Predators

Another frequently voiced concern regarding teen Internet use is the possibility that unsuspecting teens will be lured into dangerous relationships or sexual interactions with online predators. Computer-mediated communication occurs on digital screens, where non-verbal cues are absent, potential consequences seem distant, and correspondence can take place pseudonymously. These features can facilitate interesting new relationships and conversations among young people, but may also lead to potentially risky situations. Although the popular press is notorious for highlighting sensational but rare instances in which online teens are stalked by predators (Edwards, 2005), concerns are not altogether unwarranted. After all, an eighth of young people have received unwanted sexual advances online (Stahl & Fritz, 2002). Fortunately, chat rooms, the most common site of sexual solicitations, are becoming less and less popular as they are traded for IM, a more controllable medium with built-in blocking features in which teen users are well versed. Notably, however, troubled youths are more likely to visit chat rooms and are thought to be more vulnerable to unwanted online sexual solicitations than other young people (Beebee et al., 2004).

Many teens have communicated with strangers online. A 2002 study found that three fourths of seventh- through tenth-graders had communicated with a stranger through email or chat (Stahl & Fritz, 2002), and more recently, the national Youth Internet Safety Survey concluded that 55 percent of youths used chat rooms, IM, or email to communicate with strangers (Wolak et al., 2002). In and of itself, of course, communicating with strangers is not problematic, nor does it appear to be teens' primary online goal. In fact, most teens simply aren't interested in developing relationships with strangers online (Gross et al., 2002) and they rarely sustain online relationships that don't coexist in the offline world. Moreover, most teens who communicate with people they don't know online have been introduced to the "stranger" by friends or family, and only an eighth of these relationships turn into a close relationship. Moreover, the large majority of close online relationships that grow out of online correspondences includes offline contact by mail or telephone after the initial online encounter, and parents are typically kept informed of the relationship (Wolak et al., 2002).

Nevertheless, young people do appear remarkably lax about relinquishing personal information in chat rooms, IM, blogs, Web pages, and social networking spaces, such as Myspace.com. Although it may come as little surprise that four fifths of parents of online teens say that teens aren't careful enough when giving out information about themselves online, a surprising four fifths of online *teens* agree (Lenhart, 2005). Corroborating such perceptions, Christianne Stahl and Nancy Fritz (2002) found that 25 percent of the teens they studied divulged information online regarding their name, address, school, or phone number. Educating teens about Internet safety seems to be the wisest course of action for parents and teachers who hope to encourage teens to make smart and careful decisions online.

Social Interaction

How does Internet use impact teens' social lives? The short answer is: we don't know yet. However, Sean Seepersad (2004) summarizes the two main perspectives that dominate the research literature: (1) the Internet increases social isolation and (2) the Internet enables relationship development. The logic of the first perspective is that the more time people spend on the Internet, the less time they have to engage in "real" interactions that are inherently more valuable and substantive than online interactions. The logic of the second perspective is that the Internet can help users expand their network of friends and enhance their existing relationships through frequent and engaging online interactions. Effects studies focusing on teenagers, in particular, provide a mix of loosely related findings, offering only mild support for either of these perspectives. For example, Christopher Sanders and his colleagues (2000) found moderate evidence that high Internet use among teens was related to weaker social ties. Specifically, low Internet users reported significantly better relationships with their mothers and friends than did high Internet users. On the other hand, a different set of researchers found that the time teens spent online was not related to loneliness, social anxiety, or teens' subjective sense of their own well-being (Gross, 2004; Gross et al., 2002). Lonelier or socially anxious adolescents in school communicated more with strangers online than did other students, who more commonly communicated with friends (Gross et al., 2002). Louis Leung (2002) studied college students to find that the lonelier the student, the more dishonest, more negative, and less revealing their online self-disclosures were in chat rooms. Yifeng Hu and colleagues (2004) also studied college students' IM use, noting a positive association between frequency of IM use and social intimacy.

Although studies such as these help to shed light on the ways the Internet appears to be functioning in teens' lives, they offer only limited information since most of the studies reported here and elsewhere are based on small, nonrepresentative samples and typically describe survey research, which can only demonstrate correlations between Internet uses and effects, but cannot prove that the Internet actually causes any of the studied effects. Thus, despite the frequently voiced concerns about how teens' relationships with their friends and families are impacted by their Internet use, the only thing we can safely conclude at this time is that the Internet likely affects different teens in different ways depending on what they are doing, why they're doing it, and for how long. Such a conclusion offers little comfort, but is most reasonable at this time given the paucity of longitudinal inquiry into this topic.

Amid the growing attention paid to the Internet's impact on teens, it is worth mentioning that teens themselves overwhelmingly report that the Internet has positively impacted their social lives. Two thirds of online youth say that "teens' use of the Internet does little or nothing to detract from the time teens spend together" (Lenhart, Rainie, & Lewis, 2001). And despite adults' worries that the Internet has displaced real-life interactions among young people, teens report spending more time physically with their friends doing social things outside of school than they report interacting with friends through technology (Lenhart et al., 2005). Moreover, when given the choice, teens unquestionably enjoy face time with their friends in real physical spaces (Albero-Andres, 2004), and they prefer the land-line telephone as their next most preferable way to communicate with friends (Lenhart et al., 2005).

Conclusion

In short, it is clear from this review of adolescent Internet use that although the popularity of the Internet among teens is high and growing, we still have much to learn. Most teens use the Internet frequently for a variety of tasks ranging from correspondence to self-expression. Their online pursuits and interactions appear in many ways to be developmentally appropriate and functional. Some of the key areas that are ripe for exploration include the consequences of the growing digital divide among teens, the utility of online communication and content creation for online teens, and, finally, the effects different uses of the Internet may have on different types of teens. Listening to what teens have to say about their experiences on the Internet is likely the best place to start as we hope to learn more about what it means to grow up online.

DISCUSSION QUESTIONS

1   How common is Internet use among American teens? What advantages do "wired" teens have? What are the disadvantages for teens without access? What, if anything, do you think can be done about this digital divide?

2   Which of the issues discussed in this chapter do you think adults are most concerned about when they think about teen Internet use? Were there any issues you can think of that weren't mentioned in the chapter? What are they? Which, if any, of the concerns raised in this chapter do you think are warranted? Explain.

3   Based on your personal (and possibly recent) experience as an online teen, what would you add to this chapter about teen Internet use? Is your online experience represented well in this chapter? What else should be included for people to have a comprehensive understanding of what it's like to grow up online?

EXERCISE

1   Take a look at your own use of the Internet. Specifically:

■   Take a moment to jot down how much you think you use the Internet on an average day.

■   Next, create an Internet Log by dividing up a blank sheet of paper into fifteen-minute increments over a twenty-four-hour period of time.

■   Then, pick a day during which you will document all of your Internet use. Remind yourself throughout the day to jot down when you are online, as well as all the things you're doing online during that fifteen-minute time period (for example, IMing, school work, surfing the Web). Be diligent; if you need to, set your watch alarm to beep every hour (during the hours you are awake) to remind you to record your Internet use in your log.

- Finally, after your twenty-four-hour period is complete, compare your time estimate with the actual time you spent online. Was your estimate close to the actual amount of time you spent online? Why or why not, in your opinion?

- Based on your evaluation of your twenty-four-hour Internet Log, what role(s) does the Internet seem to serve for you? Do you think this is similar to the role it plays for middle- and high-school-aged kids? Why or why not?

REFERENCES

Albero-Andres, M. (2004). The Internet and adolescents: The present and future of the information society. In J. Goldstein, D. Buckingham, and G. Brougere (Eds.), *Toys, games, and media* (pp. 109–129). Mahwah, NJ: Lawrence Erlbaum.

Beebee, T., Asche, S., Harrison, P., & Quinlan, K. (2004). Heightened vulnerability and increased risk-taking among adolescent chat room users: Results from a statewide school survey. *Journal of Adolescent Health, 35*,116–123.

Borzekowski, D. L. G., & Rickert, V. I. (2001). Adolescent cybersurfing for health information: A new resource that crosses barriers. *Archives of Pediatrics & Adolescent Medicine, 155*(7), 813–817.

Clark, L. S. (2005). The constant contact generation: Exploring teen friendship networks online. In S. R. Mazzarella (Ed.), *Girl wide web: Girls, the Internet, and the negotiation of identity* (pp. 141–160). New York: Peter Lang.

DeBell, M., & Chapman, C. (2001). Computer and Internet use by children and adolescents in 2001. *Education Statistics Quarterly, 5*(4). Retrieved January 5, 2006, from http://nces.ed.gov/programs/quarterly/vol_5/5_4/2_1.asp#tab_a.

Edwards, L. Y. (2005). Victims, villains, and vixens: Teen girls and Internet crime. In S. R. Mazzarella (Ed.), *Girl wide web: Girls, the Internet, and the negotiation of identity* (pp. 13–30). New York: Peter Lang.

Finkelhor, D., Mitchell, K., & Wolak, J. (2001). *Highlights of the Youth Internet Safety Survey.* Washington, D.C.: Office of Juvenile Justice and Delinquency Prevention.

Grisso, A., & Weiss, D. (2005). What are gURLS talking about? Adolescent girls' construction of sexual identity on gURL.com. In S. R. Mazzarella (Ed.), *Girl wide web: Girls, the Internet, and the negotiation of identity* (pp. 31–50). New York: Peter Lang.

Gross, E. (2004). Adolescent Internet use: What we expect, what teens report. *Applied Developmental Psychology, 25,* 633–649.

Gross, E. F., Juvonen, J., & Gable, S. (2002). Internet use and well-being in adolescence. *Journal of Social Issues, 58,* 75–90.

Hellenga, K. (2002). Social space, the final frontier: Adolescents on the Internet. In J. T. Mortimer and R. W. Larson (Eds.), *The changing adolescent experience* (pp. 208–249). Cambridge: Cambridge University Press.

Hempel, J. (2005, December 12). The Myspace generation. *BusinessWeek Online.* Retrieved December 20, 2005, from www.businessweek.com/print/magazine/content/05_50/b3963001.htm.

Hu, Y., Wood, J. F., Smith, V., & Westbrook, N. (2004). Friendships through IM: Examining the relationship between instant messaging and intimacy. *Journal of Computer Mediated Communication, 10*(1), article 6. Retrieved December 10, 2005, from http://jcmc.indiana.edu/v0110/issue1/hu.html.

Kaplan, D. (2005). Go log on to your room, Johnny: Kids' rooms prove multimedia paradise. *Online Media Daily*. Retrieved January 14, 2006, from http://publications.mediapost.com/index.cfm?fuseaction=Articles.san&s-27497&Nid=12287&p=240323.

Lenhart, A. (2005). *Protecting teens online*. Washington, D.C.: Pew Internet and American Life Project.

Lenhart, A., & Madden, M. (2005). *Teen content creators and consumers*. Washington, D.C.: Pew Internet and American Life Project.

Lenhart, A., Madden, M., & Hitlin, P. (2005). *Teens and technology*. Washington, D.C.: Pew Internet and American Life Project.

Lenhart, A., Rainie, L., & Lewis, O. (2001). *Teenage life online: The rise of the instant-message generation and the Internet's impact on friendships and family relationships*. Washington, D.C.: Pew Internet and American Life Project.

Lenhart, A., Simon, M., & Graziano, M. (2001). *The Internet and education: Findings of the Pew Internet and American Life Project*. Washington, D.C.: Pew Internet and American Life Project.

Leung, L. (2002). Loneliness, self-disclosure, and ICQ ("I Seek You") Use. *Cyberpsychology & Behavior, 5*(3), 241–251).

Mazzarella, S. R. (2005). Claiming a space: The cultural economy of teen girl fandom on the web. In S. R. Mazzarella (Ed.), *Girl wide web: Girls, the Internet, and the negotiation of identity* (pp. 141–160). New York: Peter Lang.

Mitchell, K. J., Finkelhor, D., & Wolak, J. (2003). The exposure of youth to unwanted sexual material on the Internet, a national survey of risk, impact, and prevention. *Youth & Society, 34*(3), 330–358.

Nussbaum, E. (2004, January 11). My so-called blog. *New York Times Magazine*, p. 33.

Pardington, S. (2005, November 27). Is your little angel raising hell online? *Sunday Oregonian*, p. A1.

Pastore, M. (2001). Web influences offline purchases, especially among teens. Retrieved November 1, 2005, from http://www.clickz.com/stats/sectors/retailing/article.php/804141

Rideout, V., Roberts, D., & Foehr, U. (2005). *Generation M: Media in the lives of 8–18 year-olds*. Menlo Park, CA: Kaiser Family Foundation.

Rosato, D. (2002, November 18). Bringing free wireless access to the people. *USA Today*, p. E5.

Sanders, C., Field, T., Diego, M., & Kaplan, M. (2000). The relationship of Internet use to depression and social isolation among adolescents. *Adolescence, 35*(138), 237–242.

Seepersad, S. (2004). Coping with loneliness: Adolescent online and offline behavior. *Cyberpsychology & Behavior, 7*, 35–39.

Skinner, H., Biscope, S., & Poland, B. (2003). Quality of Internet access: Barrier behind Internet use statistics. *Social Science & Medicine, 57*, 875–880.

Stahl, C., & Fritz, N. (2002). Internet safety: Adolescents' self-report. *Journal of Adolescent Health, 31*, 7–10.

Stern, S. (2002a). Sexual selves on the World Wide Web: Adolescent girls' homepages as sites for sexual self-expression. In J. Brown, J. Steele, & K. Walsh-Childers (Eds.), *Sexual teens/sexual media: Investigating media's influence on adolescent sexuality* (pp. 265–286). Mahwah, NJ: Lawrence Erlbaum.

Stern, S. (2002b). Virtually speaking: Girls' self-disclosure on the WWW. *Women's Studies in Communication, 25*, 223–253.

Stern, S. (2004). Expressions of identity online: Prominent features and gender differences in adolescents' WWW home pages. *Journal of Broadcasting & Electronic Media, 48*(2), 218–243.

Suzuki, L. K., & Calzo, J. P. (2004). The search for peer advice in cyberspace: An examination of online teen bulletin boards about health and sexuality. *Journal of Applied Developmental Psychology, 25*(6), 685–698.

Thiel, S. M. (2005). "IM Me": Identity construction and gender negotiation in the world of adolescent girls and instant messaging. In S. R. Mazzarella (Ed.), *Girl wide web: Girls, the Internet, and the negotiation of identity* (pp. 179–201). New York: Peter Lang.

U.S. Department of Education. (2004). Toward a new golden age in American education: How the Internet, the law and today's students are revolutionizing expectations. Retrieved January 1, 2006, from http://www.ed.gov/about/offices/list/os/technology/plan/2004/plan_pg7.html.

Weiss, D. (2003). Going online: Youth and the Internet. *Focus on Social Issues.* Retrieved August 20, 2003, from http://www.family.org/cforum/fosi/p_friendly.cfm?articleurl=/cforum/fosi/pornography.

Wolak, J., Mitchell, K., & Finkelhor, D. (2002). Close online relationships in a national sample of adolescents. *Adolescence, 37*(147), 441–456.

Ybarra, M., & Mitchell, K. (2005). Exposure to Internet pornography among children and adolescents: A national survey. *CyberPsychology & Behavior, 8*(5), 473–486

CHAPTER FIFTEEN

How Do Kids' Self-Identities Relate to Media Experiences in Everyday Life?

JOELLEN FISHERKELLER

That is what television is saying now. It's not emphasizing family, it's not empha-
sizing growth. You know, "money-money-money, you got to get yours, you got to
look like this, you gotta get this." And I know, um, a lot of adolescents who are going
through such terrible times, trying to conform to what they see in music videos,
to what they see in ads, to what the media says is cool. The media have become
so bold, like they will literally say: "this is cool, this is not; go with this, don't go
with that." And it's a marketing ploy.

—Chris

In the quotation above, Chris, a twenty-one-year-old African-American male whom I interviewed in New York, sums up some of the challenges kids face growing up in a world saturated with multiple media messages and images that are, as he says, all part of "a marketing
ploy" (Fisherkeller, 2002, p. 146). Many adolescents, and younger children, too, do look
to the media to see what is "cool," how to look, and what to get, or as Chris says, what to
"go with." For all of us, there is no escaping consumer culture and all of the commercial

media systems that promote and maintain it, locally as well as globally. Chris seems to acknowledge this when he states that "a lot of adolescents" are "going through such terrible times, trying to conform" to media definitions of cool.

However, kids' relationships to media are not so straightforward. Chris's critical comments about television and the "marketing ploys" of media have developed out of his experiences with his family members, neighborhoods, schools, peers, jobs, as well as his experiences with multiple forms of commercial media over the years. As cultural and constructivist approaches to the study of audiences suggest overall (Buckingham, 2000; Hall, 1992), kids are not influenced directly by media any more than adults are. According to these approaches, kids are diverse social agents who are situated dynamically in particular places and times, and these realities shape how kids make sense of the media they encounter every day. That is, kids are unique individuals who have powerful relationships with many different real people in their lives, and who locate themselves historically and regionally; these relationships and locations have a bearing on how kids access, use, understand, and interpret media. At the same time, kids' relationships with real people, their historical and regional locations, and their media experiences together contribute to the development of their self-identities, which in turn contribute to how kids engage with media (Buckingham, 2000; Fisherkeller, 2002; Steele & Brown, 1995).

These processes are woven together, much like fibers in a tapestry, but, unlike a tapestry, these processes never result in a final product. Kids relating to others, being in specific places and times, experiencing media, and developing their self-identities are ongoing, intertwined processes. My longitudinal, in-depth research with Chris, and with other diverse youth in the United States, shows how, over time, kids adjust to new experiences with people, changes in social and material contexts, a plethora of emergent media and new technologies, and, consequently, their own sense of themselves (Fisherkeller, 2002). In addition, these case studies show how certain themes relevant to individual self-identities can remain constant as kids negotiate new experiences, whether mediated or actual.

Thus the answer to the question "How do kids' self-identities relate to media experiences in everyday life?" is complex, nuanced, highly variable, and constantly in need of revision and research. In this chapter, I trace some of the threads of what is known about kids, their self-identities, and their media experiences, always mindful that this tapestry is a work in progress. In what follows, I begin by defining key concepts of the chapter and by further laying bare the theoretical assumptions that underpin my perspective as well as guide my selection of research studies. Then I present some key studies that focus on kids and their engagements with different media in specific social contexts, and the complex negotiations of self-identities that are at play in these cases. I have clustered the review to focus initially on kids' engagements with media and negotiations of self-identities that take place in conceptually immediate, more local contexts of their everyday lives, which are home, neighborhood and region, school, and being with friends and peers. Then I move to consider their experiences of more conceptually distant contexts of media systems and globalized networks. Finally, I offer some suggestions for future research and activities for reader reflection.

Approaching Kids, Self-Identities, and Media in Context

What makes a kid a kid, and who says? The term *kid* is generally applied to those individuals who are not yet considered grown-ups, and therefore not given adult responsibilities and privileges. However, different cultures vary on when kids are considered capable of taking on various grown-up responsibilities, and historically there have been debates within cultures on the relative nature of childhood (Buckingham, 2000). For example, currently in the United States, when young people turn eighteen years old, legally they are no longer considered dependent on and controlled by their parents or guardians. At eighteen, young people in the United States are allowed to vote, to get married, and work without parental or caregiver permission. But in many other countries, younger kids might be allowed, and perhaps even encouraged, to engage in these kinds of activities. Also, in the pre- and early-industrial periods of the Western world, very young children participated in the political economy as agricultural and factory laborers and as domestic servants. (See chapter 3 for a historical discussion of the evolution of the cultural definition of childhood in the United States during the twentieth century.) Today, there are many regions in the world where this is still the case.

How kids are marked off as not grown up, and the criteria used to categorize different age groups (such as, toddlers, middle-schoolers, adolescents) are cultural processes that are part of defining age-related and other self-identities. Age is one criterion used for the social construction of kids' self-identities, but age identity is not just a matter of numbers. Labels such as "toddler," "middle-schooler," "adolescent," and "Generation Y" have been created by different adult groups such as health professionals, educators, policymakers, and marketers, who all have different vested interests in defining who belongs in these different categories. For example, psychologists and physicians categorize kids who are going through puberty using the term *adolescent*, a label associated with specific norms of biological, social, and mental development in the Western world. Commercial marketers target "teenagers" as a distinct and desirable audience, since many teens are more capable of making purchases on their own, compared to young children whose parents make most purchasing decisions for them.

Adult groups' labeling of kids as adolescents, teenagers, and so on gives shape to kids' experiences of everyday reality as well as their formation of self-identities. How adults shape kids' everyday experience via group categories is most clearly seen in the systems of schooling that structure kids' daily lives—physically, socially, and academically. Schooling structures and the practices they support have a powerful influence on how kids' activities are regulated, monitored, researched, and understood (or not). Likewise, families, nation-states, religions, and other systems—such as the media—shape kids' experiences and activities.

But kids' self-identities are not just a matter of adult groups categorizing kids and structuring their daily lives. In this chapter, self-identities are understood to be a dynamic interplay among individuals and different social and cultural groups, a matter of self- and other identification using categories (and labels) of age, as well as gender, sexuality, ethnicity/race, class, region, nation, and a host of others. Individual selves identifying with categories defined by others, and others identifying individuals as members of social or cultural categories, are dialectic processes that are continually negotiated (Eisenhart, 1995; Hall, 1992). Also, all selves are multiply identified, as any one individual is situated in many social and cultural categories at any given point and has relationships with many different kinds of others that change over time. For example, Marina, a girl I interviewed originally when she was twelve, was all at once a daughter, a sister, a niece, a Latina, a Dominican immigrant, an intelligent middle school student, a dedicated friend, a New Yorker, a basketball player, an energetic dancer, a fan of Madonna, and an outspoken and proud member of a working-class family. Later, as a young adult, some of these identities moved into the background or were redefined, while some new identities were claimed by her, such as feminist (Fisherkeller, 2002). All in all, self-identities are not simplistic or static entities.

These dialectic and multiple self-identity processes are intricately bound up in how kids experience media. Depending on their circumstances, kids every day might encounter an array of different media, such as broadcast and satellite/cable TV, radio, at-home rental and theater-based movies, popular and educationally intended books, comics, magazines, posters, ads, newspapers, computer software, online environments, console and handheld video games, and, increasingly, some convergences of these media packaged together for cell-phone and mobile technology uses. All of these media are variably encountered and used in a variety of local contexts, such as home, school, neighborhood, and shopping and recreation centers. In all of these contexts, kids' sense of themselves along with their relationships to others plays a part in how kids make sense of media (Buckingham, 2000; Fisherkeller, 2002). Furthermore, kids encounter different media in different regional, national, and global contexts, which also have a bearing on how they make sense of their media experiences.

How do studies account for all of the complexity and dynamics of kids' self-identities and their experiences with media in everyday life? Cultural studies and constructivist approaches use a variety of fieldwork and interpretive methods to describe and understand kids' actual experiences, and kids' own sensibilities about their everyday lives. Interviews, participant observations, focus group discussions, analyses of media materials that kids say they encounter on a regular basis, and other methods associated with cultural anthropology and qualitative fieldwork are typical means of gathering information that is accurate, systematic, and grounded in kids' actual lives and perspectives. In addition, cultural studies approaches are critically aware of the economic, political, and other institutional forces that structure kids' everyday lives as well as give shape to the media contents and forms that kids encounter. What, then, do actual studies tell us about kids' self-identities and their everyday experiences with media?

Kids Making Sense of Themselves
and Media in Local Contexts

How do kids use and interpret media they encounter every day, and how does this relate to their self-identities? One group of researchers answered this question investigating what they call "adolescent room culture" (Steele & Brown, 1995, p. 553). These researchers regard bedrooms as a place where adolescents engage in identity work (McRobbie, 1994; Willis, 1990) and investigate their future possibilities through media. Jane Brown and her colleagues asked a diverse array of adolescents in the southeastern United States to describe and explain the media in their bedroom spaces, which contained an array of popular media, including music players and recordings, radio, TV and video players/recorders, magazines, books, posters, bumper stickers, and some computer and video games. Many rooms also displayed media and artifacts associated with younger kids, such as stuffed animals and toys, as well as personally created items such as drawings, photographs, and collages. What particular kinds of media were present, and how they were used by these teens, varied overall, although some trends of gender were noted. For example, more often boys were engaging with sports media and sports-related artifacts. However, the reasons that teens provided for engaging with different kinds of media in their rooms not only reflected their different individual tastes, beliefs, attitudes, and life circumstances, but also seemed to project the kind of selves they wanted others to see. Out of this research, Brown and her colleagues developed a "media practice model" that centers on how individual identities are active, consciously or not, in selecting, interacting with, and applying media toward their ongoing identity work (Steele & Brown, 1995, p. 556).

Other researchers have focused on how home environments and family dynamics play a role in how kids use and interpret media, and how kids construct a sense of themselves as members of home cultures (which include the material, social, and symbolic aspects of home). What media are actually available to kids at home is pertinent here, because material access to all media, especially newer media, is related to the socioeconomics of the home, and all kids construct a sense of self that is in part grounded by these circumstances. Also, how kids and other household members negotiate time with and interpretations of various media at home can literally and symbolically indicate kids' relative status as a child or a sibling, as well as indicate family styles, or family values, that kids can acquire (Bryce & Leichter, 1983; Buckingham, 1993; Lull, 1990). (See chapter 16 for an examination of the role of media in families.) For example, what kinds of media are located in common or more personalized areas of the home can suggest families' differential valuing of communal or individualized interactions around multiple media, as well as indicate who is in control of the media at hand, and thus how particular home-based identities have more or less power. That is, in homes where the computer is located in a common space or a parent's space, children, especially younger ones, are more likely to be restricted in how much time they can play games or be online, as well as monitored in terms of what kinds of materials they should or should not encounter in cyberspace (Clark, 2005; Holloway & Valentine,

2003; Sefton-Green, 1998). Likewise, how different families actually talk about different media contributes to how kids use and evaluate media, and then how kids position themselves as a kind of media user at home. Many kids seek to set themselves apart from their parents (and other adults) by engaging with media that kids view as theirs (Buckingham, 2000; Dyson, 1997; Finders, 1997). However, many kids also strongly identify with their home culture through their media uses and interpretations. For example, I argue that home cultures provide individual adolescents with "guiding motivations" (Fisherkeller, 2002, p. 105) that drive their social interactions and also their visions for the future, both of which give shape to how kids might identify with particular media personas. Chris, quoted at the beginning of this chapter, talked at length when he was thirteen and then again when twenty-one years old about how Bill Cosby's 1980's TV sitcom featuring the fictional Huxtable family presented Chris and his fellow adolescent viewers with positively influential messages about "maturity, responsibility, and growth" (Fisherkeller, 2002, p. 145)— messages that Chris also received at home, where his father in particular was telling him to "walk straight up" and "do the right things" (Fisherkeller, 2002, p. 73).

Some kids use different media as a means of claiming a more mature identity, as defined by their home, local community, school, and peer cultures. Margaret Finders (1997) found that some young adolescent girls in a midwestern United States school were using their reading of popular teen girl magazines—which represent femininity, stereotypically, as knowing how to dress, wear makeup, and be involved in romantic relationships via the consumption of commodities (Mazzarella, 2002; McRobbie, 1991)—to learn about growing into womanhood and to define the borders of their friendship group. However, not all home and peer cultures support girls' use of such magazines and their commercial representations of femininity. Other girls in Finders's (1997) study were referring to other media sources and were more reliant on their own mothers for information on growing up, though these girls were then perceived as less grown up by the girls who read the teen magazines.

In an urban neighborhood in Britain, Marie Gillespie (1995) found that South Asian immigrant youth and their families regarded being able to understand and talk knowledgeably about news media as a marker of adult identity. News media they encountered, both local and global, provided information about regional, national, and international affairs and policies, many of which pertained to these young people's everyday lives. As these youth talked about relevant news media, they made sense of their identities as immigrants, as members of specific ethnic/racial and religious groups, as well as members of particular families and peer groups, where issues of gender, class, and sexuality were relevant (see also Clark, 2003; Durham, 2002). As immigrants, these youth wanted to belong in British society, but their parents did not want them to forget their home country and traditions. They were also part of an identifiable ethnic/racial group in a nation dominated by White people, as well as members of religious groups considered marginal to mainstream British traditions. Youth who could talk competently and critically among family members and peers about news media events and issues relevant to these aspects of their identities and everyday life were considered to be mature.

Gillespie (1995) also found that South Asian immigrant youth were talking about popular British soap operas and commercial advertisements and products to connect themselves with various peer and neighborhood groups. Many studies show how kids identify themselves as members of friendship and peer cultures through media (Buckingham, 1993, 1996, 2000; Hebdige, 1988; Willis, 1990), as well as position themselves in fan cultures that cluster around specific media genres, particular programs, characters, or celebrities (Jenkins, 1992; Lewis, 1990). But friendship, peer, and fan-based connections are always situated in specific places and times, and involve negotiations of kids' other identities as well. For example, Ann Haas Dyson (1997, 2003) studied young children learning to read and write in West Coast United States urban school contexts. Her in-depth investigations showed how kids use popular media such as TV shows, music and ad jingles, sports, movies, and popular figures in all these media to communicate with classroom peers, who often share similar home cultures, neighborhoods, and also appreciate the same popular media. However, in these classroom contexts, popular media are typically regarded as "unofficial texts" because they are not sanctioned by educators or recognized through standards for achievement (see also Buckingham, 1994). What Dyson noticed in her research is that, by communicating and connecting with their peers using unofficial, popular media, young children were also making sense of "official" print media endorsed by the schools, and so developing their identities as print-literate students. In this process, they were developing their own unique styles of expression, often blending popular, unofficial media with the official school media.

Newer media such as computer and video games, email, Web sites, chat rooms, text messaging, blogs, and cell phones provide kids who have access to such technologies with additional means of negotiating identities and expressing themselves, and with digital spaces for communicating and connecting with friends, peers, and fellow fans (Clark, 1998, 2005; Gregson, 2005; Grisso & Weiss, 2005; Holloway & Valentine, 2003; Mazzarella, 2005; McMillin, 2005; Murray, 1999; Scodari, 2005; Stern, 2002; Thiel, 2005; Turkle, 1984, 1995). Yet any media that are produced and distributed via global systems and networks, including relatively older media such as television, provide kids with a means of negotiating identities that transcend their local cultures, even while local cultures still ground how they make sense of themselves in global media contexts.

Kids Making Sense of Themselves and Media in Global Contexts

In my in-depth and longitudinal studies of adolescents in New York (Fisherkeller, 2002), I found that different individuals identified with specific TV personas and program situations. These identifications were in part a matter of these kids seeing certain similarities among their own situated self-identities, their local lives, and those represented by TV personas and programs. These identification processes involve kids in interpreting how well the narratives of television (or other media) are representing the world of social relations that kids know every day through their local lives. When interpreting media at the narrative level, kids must compare the media content to what they know in real life, as well as judge how well the form, or aesthetics, of media are presenting the content as realistic, relying on what they know about the codes and conventions of different media forms and genres. David Buckingham (1993), Máire Messenger Davies (1997), and Robert Hodge and David Tripp (1986) have shown how kids as young as six are knowledgeable about media in these ways, due to their daily encounters with media, as well as their talking with others such as family and friends (and sometimes teachers) about the relative realism and meanings of media contents and forms.

But kids today are also identifying with and interpreting media beyond the narrative; they are identifying with and interpreting media as commercial and global systems in the world. For example, the adolescents in my study (Fisherkeller, 2002) were aware of how television operates as an industry, as a business in the United States. Recall how Chris, in the quotation that opened this chapter, regarded media targeting of adolescents as a "marketing ploy." He and others in this study recognized the logic of programming schedules and ratings systems, and they certainly knew the function of advertisements. They also noticed how TV programs have formulaic elements, a consequence of a system that regards programs and even people as interchangeable commodities to be bought and sold to advertisers (Gandy, 1990). These kids were also aware that the real people who are part of the TV industries make money, sometimes a great deal, and that some of these people, as celebrities and spokespeople, have power in the world, in real life.

Regarding TV (and other media such as movies, music, video games, and Web sites) as industrial systems of product creation, and viewing the real people who participate in these systems as actually successful and powerful in the world, allows for self-identity negotiations beyond the level of media narratives, and conceptually outside of local cultures. When kids make sense of media at system levels, they position themselves as current, or potential, participants in this system. Kids can identify themselves as particular kinds of media consumers who might have certain advantages and disadvantages within this system. In addition, kids might identify themselves as media producers in this system, now or in the future. However, issues of access, education, and opportunity will confine many kids to identifying with and interpreting media systems mostly as consumers (Buckingham, 2000; Goodman, 2003).

Kids who have access to online media of all kinds have distinct advantages as participants in media systems, as consumers and as producers. Kids themselves understand that going online is a means of connecting to a global context, which encourages a kind of global identity. Divya McMillin (2005) conducted research with urban teens in a central Indian city where the presence and use of information technologies (IT) have been steadily on the rise for over a decade. India's national and regional policies and rhetoric, which have fostered growth in IT, regard computer usage and Internet (as well as cell-phone) connectivity as symbols of modernity and global competitiveness. McMillin's surveys, interviews, and participant observations of teens at school and in cyber cafés show how using computers and going online allowed these teens to transcend the restrictions of their local lives, especially those restrictions experienced by girls. While boys in India spend most of their time outside of school in public spaces away from home, girls are usually confined to the private, domestic sphere due to cultural norms about gender. By using computers and going online at school or at home, teen girls could see themselves as participants in a virtual public space. At the same time, when girls and boys use IT in India they are negotiating a sense of themselves that is situated within national discourses about being modern, as well as global discourses about economic, social, and political power in the world.

Discourses about information technologies and being modern and powerful in the world are not exclusive to India, of course. Sarah Holloway and Gill Valentine (2003) found that kids (and their parents) in nonurban regions of Britain viewed going online as a means of transcending the limits of their local geographical and social spaces. When navigating the Web to find out about products and services not available in their immediate region, these kids saw themselves as informed and fortunate consumers in a global market. When conducting research online to gather information for school assignments and written reports, they thought of themselves as competent, tech-savvy students with better chances for future success in the workplace. And when emailing youth in distant lands to discuss issues and problems of everyday life, they imagined themselves as world-wise citizens of a networked planet.

Kids anywhere in the world who use online spaces to create and circulate their own texts, sounds, and visuals are further advantaged in the global context, because they can develop their self-identities as producers of multiple media. Indeed, whenever kids themselves produce media of any kind they are able to participate more fully in powerful systems that today require people to be multiply literate—meaning they can access, use, understand, and produce all media, including print, audio-visual, and digital forms (Alvermann, 2004; Buckingham, 2003; New London Group, 1996; Tyner, 1998). However, while kids who are multiply literate are at an advantage locally and globally, there are limits to their power. Kids who can access, use, understand, and produce all media do not necessarily challenge problematic aspects of media systems or address the inequities and constraints of their own local cultures. On a daily basis, most kids engage with mainstream commercial media because these media are ubiquitous. The quality, nature, and purposes of mainstream commercial media are constrained by the bottom-line values of corporate capitalist culture, which often conflict with the ideals of democracy and humanity (Gerbner et al., 1994; McChesney, 2004). When engaging with mainstream media, even as producers, kids tend to represent the dominant formats, styles, and even stereotypes of media, thus perpetuating, albeit unwittingly, the constraining values of corporate capitalist culture (Goodman, 2003). Thus the personal and cultural integrity of kids' self-identities can be compromised, as consumers and producers, as their participation in global media systems might mean adapting—however locally defined or personally meaningful—to limiting formulas of the market. In addition, while some teen girls in India might be able to expand their local horizons by using information technologies (McMillin, 2005), their use of these media does not appear to change familial and social expectations about who is supposed to stay home and tend to the domestic workplace and who is allowed to roam safely in public places—issues of gender equity and opportunity not exclusive to India.

Furthermore, as McMillin (2005) and Lynn Schofield Clark (2005) suggest, youth who engage with media in accordance with the norms of corporate capitalist culture might be more easily exploited as workers. Specifically, Clark (2005) discusses her research with teens in the midwestern United States, who felt compelled to be in "constant contact" with their peers, families, and online informational sources via instant text messaging, cell phones, email, chat rooms, and various Web-based media. Clark speculates that the constant contact these teens achieve and enjoy via these multiple media could be preparing them to meet the demands of contemporary workplaces, which require similar kinds of multitasking skills. While teens might enjoy being masters of multitasking in leisure contexts, in the workplace constant contact via multiple media might not be fun, and could even feel oppressive.

How do kids all over the world encounter media narratives, systems, and expectations, and also make sense of these media in relation to their self-identities in local and global contexts? Many more grounded investigations are needed to further understand how kids in different local regions, cultures, and situations are coming to terms with media narratives, systems, and global networks. Comparative and longitudinal examinations of how kids make sense of themselves, and how media narratives and systems play a role in their self-identity development, are needed as well. At the same time, educators, media makers, policymakers, concerned adults, and kids themselves need to work together to provide all kids with access to and education about participating in local and global contexts in a critical, practical, and creative manner, so that kids can see themselves as powerful members of the world, as well as effective change agents where necessary.

EXERCISES

1   Do a tour of your current personal space. What media do you use in this space? How do these media reflect and express different aspects of who you are at this point in time? Which are most important to you, in terms of your current sense of yourself and your sense of yourself in the future?

2   Write a media autobiography, describing your own meaningful experiences with media at different ages (for example, ages four to seven, ages eight to thirteen, ages fourteen to eighteen). How did your media use change over the years? How do you think these media helped you to do "identity work" at these different ages? What role did your home, school, peer, and other cultures play in your media uses and identity work?

3   Interview adults in your parents' and grandparents' age groups, and ask them about what media were available to them when (and where) they were children and adolescents. What memories do they have about media in those times and places? What were their favorite media experiences? How might their media experiences have been related to their self-identities in those times and places?

REFERENCES

Alvermann, D. (2004). Preface. In D. Alvermann (Ed.), *Adolescents and literacies in a digital world.* (pp. vii–xii) New York: Peter Lang.

Bryce, J., & Leichter, H. J. (1983). The family and television. *Journal of Family Issues, 4*(2), 309–328.

Buckingham, D. (1993). *Children talking television: The making of television literacy.* London: Falmer.

Buckingham, D. (1994). *Cultural studies goes to school.* London: Taylor and Francis.

Buckingham, D. (1996). *Moving images: Understanding children's emotional responses to television.* Manchester: Manchester University Press.

Buckingham, D. (2000). *After the death of childhood: growing up in the age of electronic media.* Cambridge: Polity.

Buckingham, D. (2003). *Media education: literacy, learning and contemporary culture.* Cambridge: Polity.

Clark, L. S. (1998). Dating on the net: Teens and the rise of "pure" relationships. In S. Jones (Ed.), *Cybersociety 2.0: Revisiting computer mediated communication and community* (pp. 159–183). Thousand Oaks, CA: Sage.

Clark, L. S. (2003). *Angels to aliens: Teenagers, the media, and the supernatural.* New York: Oxford University Press.

Clark, L. S. (2005). The constant contact generation: Exploring teen friendship networks online. In S. R. Mazzarella (Ed.), *Girl wide web: Girls, the Internet, and the negotiation of identity* (pp. 203–222). New York: Peter Lang.

Davies, M. M. (1997). *Fake, fact and fantasy: Children's interpretations of television reality.* Mahwah, NJ: Lawrence Erlbaum.

Durham, M. G. (2002). Out of the Indian diaspora: Mass media, myths of femininity, and the negotiation of adolescence between two cultures. In S. R. Mazzarella & N. O. Pecora (Eds.), *Growing up girls: Popular culture and the construction of identity* (pp. 193–208). New York: Peter Lang.

Dyson, A. H. (1997). *Writing superheroes: The social and ideological dynamics of child writing.* New York: Teachers College Press.

Dyson, A. H. (2003). *The brothers and sisters learn to write: Popular literacies in childhood and school cultures.* New York: Teachers College Press.

Eisenhart, M. (1995). The fax, the jazz player, and the self-story teller: How do people organize culture? *Anthropology and Education Quarterly, 26*(1), 3–26.

Finders, M. (1997) *Just girls: Hidden literacies and life in junior high.* New York: Teachers College Press.

Fisherkeller, J. (2002). *Growing up with television: Everyday learning among young adolescents.* Philadelphia: Temple University Press.

Gandy, O. (1990). Tracking the audience. In J. Downing (Ed), *Questioning the media: A critical introduction* (pp. 166–179). Newbury Park, CA: Sage.

Gerbner, G., Gross, L., Morgan, M., & Signorielli, N. (1994). Growing up with television: The cultivation perspective. In J. Bryant & D. Zillman, (Eds.), *Media effects: Advances in theory and research* (pp. 17–42). Hillsdale, NJ: Lawrence Erlbaum.

Gillespie, M. (1995). *Television, ethnicity and cultural change.* London: Routledge.

Goodman, S. (2003). *Teaching youth media: A critical guide to literacy, video production, and social change.* New York: Teachers College Press.

Gregson, K. S. (2005). "What if the lead character looks like me?" Girl fans of Shoujo anime and their Web sites. In S. R. Mazzarella (Ed.), *Girl wide web: Girls, the Internet, and the negotiation of identity* (pp. 121–140) New York: Peter Lang.

Grisso, A. D., & Weiss, D. (2005). What are gURLS talking about? Adolescent girls' construction of sexual identity on gURL.com. In S. R. Mazzarella (Ed.), *Girl wide web: Girls, the Internet, and the negotiation of identity* (pp. 31–50) New York: Peter Lang.

Hall, S. (1992). The question of cultural identity. In S. Hall, D. Held, & T. McGrew (Eds.), *Modernity and its futures* (pp. 273–326). Cambridge: Polity.

Hebdige, D. (1988). *Subculture: The meaning of style.* London: Routledge.

Hodge, R., & Tripp, D. (1986). *Children and television: A semiotic approach.* Stanford, CA: Stanford University Press.

Holloway, S. L., & Valentine, G. (2003) *Cyberkids.* London: Routledge.

Jenkins, H. (1992). *Textual poachers: Television fans and participatory cultures.* New York: Routledge.

Lewis, L. (1990). *Gender politics and MTV: Voicing the difference.* Philadelphia, PA: Temple University Press.

Lull, J. (1990). *Inside family viewing: Ethnographic research on television's audiences.* London: Comedia/Routledge.

Mazzarella, S. R. (2002). The "Superbowl of all dates": Teenage girl magazines and the commodification of the perfect prom. In S. R. Mazzarella & N. O. Pecora (Eds.), *Growing up girls: Popular culture and the construction of identity* (pp. 97–112). New York: Peter Lang.

Mazzarella, S. R. (2005) Claiming a space: The cultural economy of teen girl fandom on the web. In S. R. Mazzarella (Ed.), *Girl wide web: Girls, the Internet, and the negotiation of identity* (pp. 141–160). New York: Peter Lang.

McChesney, R. (2004). *The problem of the media: U.S. communications politics in the 21st century.* New York: Monthly Review Press.

McMillin, D. C. (2005). Teen crossings: Emerging cyberpublics in India. In S. R. Mazzarella (Ed.), *Girl wide web: Girls, the Internet, and the negotiation of identity* (pp. 161–178). New York: Peter Lang.

McRobbie, A. (1991). *Feminism and youth culture: From Jackie to Just Seventeen.* Boston: Unwin Hyman.

McRobbie, A. (1994). *Postmodernism and popular culture.* London: Routledge.

Murray, S. (1999). Saving our so-called lives: Girl fandom, adolescent subjectivity and *My So-Called Life.* In M. Kinder (Ed.), *Kids' media culture* (pp. 221–235). Durham, NC: Duke University Press.

New London Group. (1996). A pedagogy of multiliteracies: Designing social futures. *Harvard Educational Review, 66*(1), 60–92.

Scodari, C. (2005). You're sixteen, you're dutiful, you're online: "Fangirls" and the negotiation of age and/or gender subjectivities in TV newsgroups. In S. R. Mazzarella (Ed.), *Girl wide web: Girls, the Internet, and the negotiation of identity* (pp. 105–120) New York: Peter Lang.

Sefton-Green, J. (1998). Digital visions: Children's "creative" uses of multimedia technologies. In J. Sefton-Green (Ed.), *Digital diversions: Youth culture in the age of multimedia* (pp. 62–83). London: UCL Press/Taylor and Francis.

Stern, S. (2002). Sexual selves on the World Wide Web: Adolescent girls' home pages as sites for sexual self expression. In J. D. Brown, J. R. Steele, & K. Walsh-Childers (Eds.), *Sexual teens, sexual media: Investigating media influence on adolescent sexuality* (pp. 265–285). Mahwah, NJ: Lawrence Erlbaum.

Steele, J. R., & Brown, J. D. (1995). Adolescent room culture: Studying media in the context of everyday life. *Journal of Youth and Adolescence, 24*(5), 551–576.

Thiel, S. M. (2005). "IM me": Identity construction and gender negotiation in the world of adolescent girls and instant messaging. In S. R. Mazzarella (Ed.), *Girl wide web: Girls, the Internet, and the negotiation of identity* (pp. 179–202). New York: Peter Lang.

Turkle, S. (1984). *The second self: Computers and the human spirit.* New York: Touchstone/Simon and Schuster.

Turkle, S. (1995). *Life on the screen: Identity in the age of the Internet.* New York: Simon and Schuster.

Tyner, K. (1998). *Literacy in a digital world: Teaching and learning in the age of information.* Mahwah, NJ: Lawrence Erlbaum.

Willis, P. (1990). *Common culture: Symbolic work at play in the everyday cultures of the young.* Boulder, CO: Westview.

CHAPTER SIXTEEN

Just Part of the Family?

Exploring the Connections between Family Life and Media Use[1]

CHRISTINE M. BACHEN

More and more American families are plugged into an ever-expanding array of communication technologies (Rideout et al., 2003; Roberts et al., 2005). The newer communication technologies, including computers, the Internet, cellular phones, beepers, personal organizers, portable MP3 players (including iPods), and digital video recorders (DVRs), join with the more traditional media technologies such as radio, television, and videocassette recorders (VCRs) to connect family members to one another and to the outside world. They offer entertainment, information, and the extension of the classroom or workplace to family members, individually and collectively. The changes brought about by these communication technologies in how families experience domestic life are profound. No longer a sanctuary where the family was relatively shielded from intrusions from the outside world, the home is now a communication hub, infused with messages of diverse and increasingly global origins (Gumpert & Drucker, 1998).

The study of family life and communication technologies requires attention to changing family structures and to expanding and evolving technologies. For the purposes of this chapter, a "family" is defined as a group of intimates including children who generate a sense of home and group identity, complete with strong ties of loyalty and emotion, and an experience of a history and a future (Fitzpatrick & Wambolt, 1990). This definition encompasses not only nuclear families, but also groups where all members may not share the same residence. Communication technologies are not simply on the sidelines of family life; rather, family members and technologies in households are interconnected as elements of the same system. The introduction or change of any element—human or technological—may result in a reorganization of roles, relationships, and functions (Kayany & Yelsma, 2000).

Availability of Communication Technologies in American Homes

Just how connected are American families to communication media? Recent statistics show that American households with children are "media saturated" (Roberts et al., 2005, p. 10), even more so than those households without children (Woodard & Gridina, 2000). According to a study of a nationally representative sample of more than two thousand households with children eight to eighteen years of age, television, VCRs, radio, and CDs or tapes are in nearly every American home (99 percent, 97 percent, 97 percent, and 98 percent, respectively), while cable or satellite TV is found in 82 percent of U.S. households (Roberts et al., 2005). Home computers are present in 86 percent of households, 74 percent have Internet access, 83 percent have video games, and 60 percent of homes have instant messaging systems. Just over one third of homes have DVRs.

Moreover, most American families own multiple instances of many media (Roberts et al., 2005). Nearly three quarters of families with eight- to eighteen-year-olds own three or more TVs, just over half have three or more VCRs, nearly two thirds have three or more radios or CD/tape players, and 57 percent have two or more video-game consoles. For half or more of these families, these media are found in children's bedrooms, giving them exclusive and often-unsupervised access. Additionally, many children in the eight-to-eighteen age group have their own portable media devices: 61 percent have portable CD or tape players, just over half (55 percent) have handheld video games, 39 percent have cell phones, and 18 percent have MP3 players. Even younger children show some of these same trends. As another national study revealed, televisions are present in the bedrooms of one third of families with children under the age of seven (Rideout et al., 2003).

Despite the fact that media are largely ubiquitous across American households, it is important to understand why some families are more likely to have access to certain communications technologies than others. The most critical differentiating factors are socioeconomic status as reflected in household income and parental education, race and ethnicity, and children's age (Roberts et al., 2005).

Media that require ongoing monthly payments like cable or satellite TV or Internet service prove out of reach for many families with limited means, and it is questionable whether these media will achieve the kind of universal penetration as broadcast media (unless municipalities step in to ensure equal access). Parental education, a factor that is related to household income, is part of the picture, but it also signifies differences in orientation toward certain media (Roberts et al., 2005). Families in which parents have high school educations are more likely to place televisions in children's bedrooms compared to college-educated parents, an action that reflects their greater (and less critical) acceptance of television generally as a medium.

Media access is also associated with a family's race and ethnicity. African-American and Hispanic youths are less likely to have a computer, Internet connections or instant messaging capabilities in their home than White youths (Roberts et al., 2005). Income likely explains part of this difference, but beliefs about the fit between media and other family values are important as well. Some Hispanic families who do not own home computers or maintain Internet connections refrain because of expressed concerns that computers and Internet access could compromise some important family values by exposing children to pornographic Internet sites or by isolating members of the family (see Becht et al., 1999).

The ages of children in the family also play a role in the media environment. In families with children over ten, there is greater access to cable or satellite TV, computers, and the Internet (Roberts et al., 2005). For older children, too, access to these media is more likely to move into a private sphere—their bedroom.

Media Use as a Central Activity

Not only are media present in the home, but much of the activity in the home involves their use. It is estimated that Americans overall use media during 59 percent of their waking hours, or an average of nine hours per day (see Biagi, 2001). This is fairly similar to the results from the research conducted with families with children eight to eighteen years old, where total media *exposure* amounted to about eight and a half hours per day (Roberts et al., 2005). In this study, researchers were able to factor in the proportion of time young people spent using more than one medium simultaneously, and with this adjustment total media *use* dropped to six hours and twenty-one minutes. Younger children (under seven years old) spend less time with media—just over three and a half hours (Rideout et al., 2003).

In families with children aged eight to eighteen, young people's television, video, or DVD viewing occupies about four and a half hours per day (Roberts et al., 2005), compared to about one and three quarters hours in families with children under age seven (Rideout et al., 2003). Radio, CD, tape, or MP3 listening is the second most popular activity, claiming two hours of time for both eight- to eighteen-year-olds and one hour for the younger set. Recreational computer use follows, with eight- to eighteen-year-olds spending about one and three quarters hours on the computer, while the under-seven group is on for an average of ten minutes. Reading (nonhomework-based) accounts for about forty-three minutes for the eight- to eighteen-year-olds and thirty-nine minutes for the under-seven-year-olds. Finally, older children spend on average just over one half hour with video games daily, compared to five minutes given to this activity by younger children.

These averages help us see what media are typically prioritized across American families, but they also mask the notable variations in media use according to children's spe-

cific age, gender, ethnicity, and, more central to our focus here, the influences on usage resulting from the way in which parents structure the media environment in the home (Rideout
et al., 2003; Roberts et al., 2005). Indeed, in families where television is a constant or nearly
constant presence, turned on even when no one is watching, children are likely to begin
watching earlier in their lives, watch daily, watch longer, and read less (Rideout et al., 2003).
This pattern of heavier viewing and less reading holds even when children are older
(Roberts et al., 2005). The decision about where to place media in the home can have consequences on consumption patterns as well. Having a television, video-game console, or
computer in one's bedroom leads children and adolescents to consume more of these
media. In fact, personal possession of any of these media is associated with an additional
two hours per day in average media exposure for youth aged eight to eighteen (Roberts et
al., 2005).

Rules about Media Use

Parents mediate children's media use in a variety of ways, including the establishment of
rules. One approach is through "restrictive mediation," a practice in which parents make
rules about amount or time of viewing allowed, define forbidden content, and use media
as part of a reward or punishment system (Valkenburg, 1999).

Rules about content take precedence in most homes with children under seven, with
90 percent of parents claiming to have content rules about TV, 87 percent about video-game
content, and 79 percent about computer content (Rideout et al., 2003). Time restrictions
are slightly less common: 69 percent of parents limit time with TV, 76 percent with video
games, and 61 percent with computers. Children whose parents have rules about the
amount of TV they can view do indeed watch on average half an hour *less* than other children. While degree of enforcement of rules varies across families, children in homes where
parents say the rules are always reinforced tend to read or be read to more and spend more
time outdoors.

As children age, fewer families articulate specific rules about content or the quantity
of television that can be viewed (Schmidt, 2000; Roberts et al., 2005). Still, the presence
of rules impacts media use. For the 46 percent of eight- to eighteen-year-olds who acknowledge any type of family rules about TV, research finds that their overall media exposure is
nearly two hours less than the no-rules group—even though the amount of television exposure only accounts for forty minutes of the difference (Roberts et al., 2005). The presence
of TV rules is associated with a lesser use of all individual media studied, with the exception of print material, where there is an increase in use. Rules about video-game content
or time spent playing are reported in only 24 percent of homes, while such rules exist in
35 percent of homes in regards to computer use. Based on ethnographic research, Elaine
Lally (2002) observes that parents' regulation of the computer tends to be grounded in their
more general attitudes and control of children's activities. Some rules may evolve as parents' familiarity and comfort with the medium grows and as children's commitment to it

increases as well. The Digital Future Report (2004) has documented a 13 percent increase in parents who deny access to the Internet as a punishment tool since 2000, with 45.1 percent of parents now admitting that they have done this.

Explicit rules may give way to implicit understandings about what kind of content is acceptable or not, or when media use is permissible, or for how long, especially as children get older (Lally, 2002; Schmidt, 2000; Roberts et al., 2005). Furthermore, children join parents as active players in the regulatory process (Buckingham, 1996). Consistent with the notion that families constitute dynamic systems in which each member can influence others, children will question, challenge, or subvert rules, or bring new types of media content or experiences into the home, and parents respond or adjust guidelines accordingly. As David Buckingham (1996, p. 257) writes about TV, "television viewing is merely part of the broader struggle for power and control between parents and children." The nature of this struggle can change as families mature and as the family composition shifts. For example, rules that apply to first-born children often become more flexible with subsequent children (Buckingham, 1996).

Communication Technologies and Patterns of Social Interaction

The introduction of radio and television demonstrated the potential for communication technology to become an electronic hearth, the focal point in a centralized living space around which people gather (Gumpert & Drucker, 1998). But even as these media drew people together with a common purpose, they entered into the dynamics of family life in terms of organizing the family in time and space, and thus affecting social interaction.

The process by which media are integrated into the rhythm of a family's daily life is shaped by family members' beliefs about time (Jordan, 2002). Results from Amy Jordan's (2002) work show that more affluent families socialize their children to see time as a "scarce" resource that should not be "wasted" through excessive television viewing, while families from less affluent homes tend to emphasize restrictions around content rather than amount of time spent viewing.

Some families emphasize a more "monochromic" approach (segmenting activities, focus, promptness), while others are more "polychromic," characterized by multiple and simultaneous tasking (Jordan, 2002, p. 146). These orientations toward time have been linked to cultural background (Hall, 1959 as cited in Jordan, 2002) and socioeconomic status. Perhaps related to experiences in different occupations where managing and scheduling time is more or less internally controlled, more affluent families tend to see time as a precious resource not to be wasted with excessive use of television. This can translate into more strict rules about amount of time allowed for TV (Jordan, 2002). This sense of the appropriateness of different uses of time can also result in self-regulation. Too much use—especially of certain media like TV or computer games—can be associated with guilt or regret, and then family members make an adjustment. Besides the setting up of daily routines, Lally

(2002) reminds us that the temporal patterning of family life is also influenced by life-cycle changes associated with children's and parents' ages and career development. A new medium in the house (for example, a computer), however, can lead to the restructuring of routines (Lally, 2002). Not only do family beliefs or norms affect media use, but, as André Caron (2000) observes, when new technologies are adopted in a household they begin a process of domestication, wherein the technologies and their uses are constantly being redefined and reconstructed, as well as possibly redefining those who use them.

As families acquire more media, the decision about *where* to locate those media has consequences (Buckingham, 1996), even beyond the changes in amount of children's viewing as noted earlier. For example, the placement of a television set in a child's bedroom may facilitate the goal of family harmony by eliminating conflicts over programming selections, but also may remove the child from the mainstream of family life and give the child one less opportunity to practice conflict-resolution skills. Parents concerned about children's access to adult-oriented Web sites on the computer may put the computer in a common area of the house so they can keep a watchful eye over their children's use. These parents may thus be more likely to be drawn into conversations about a school assignment as a result.

Social consequences may result from the move toward "personalization" or "individualization" of communication technologies in the home (Gumpert & Drucker, 1998; Wartella & Jennings, 2001), where each person is using their own medium (or media) on their own. One outcome of personalization may be greater social distance between children and adults or males and females, as people from each group listen to their own music device, talk on their own telephones, watch their own programs, play their own video games, and, in wealthier families, use their own computers (Gumpert & Drucker, 1998). This may reduce both the amount and the quality of experiences families share in common and limit the exchange of information and perspectives.

With the increasing portability of communication technologies, family members have additional opportunities to pursue their media preferences outside the home as well. Even car rides allow family members to pursue separate audio or video entertainment, with headphones ensuring that one's differing taste does not inconvenience the others—one more example of personalization. In the case of teenagers, somewhat ironically, the cellular phone or beeper is an important tool for deepening contact with their peer group, but the freedom it offers in building friendships becomes less attractive when parents insist on using these devices for monitoring their child's whereabouts (Hafner, 2000).

Another trend that can affect social interaction within the family is the growing tendency for individuals to use more than one medium at once. While there is little research on this, as family members each pursue his or her own unique combination of media (for example, watching television while checking email; listening to an iPod while reading a magazine), it will be important to examine how this type of media multitasking shapes the social dynamics in the home.

Given these developments toward more personalized and multiple media use, is the notion of the "electronic hearth," where families gather to experience a media event in common, still meaningful, or simply out of date? We can begin to answer this question by asking just how much time young people are using media in companionship with family, where they are engaged with the same content.

It is estimated that young people aged eight to eighteen spend on average two hours and seventeen minutes per day "hanging out" with parents (Roberts et al., 2005). Watching television together appears to be a fairly common activity in families. Despite the increasing opportunities to watch alone, 61 percent of young people's television viewing tends to be with someone else "most" or "some" of the time. Siblings are the most common viewing partners (57 percent), followed by mothers (41 percent) and, finally, fathers (27 percent). Nearly two thirds of families (63 percent) watch television during family mealtimes. Fewer young people on a daily basis use computers with their parents. Only 17 percent use the computer with mothers and 8 percent with fathers, while 27 percent use computers with siblings.

Parents of younger children are fairly likely to be near them when television is being used (Rideout et al., 2003). Over two thirds (69 percent) of parents with children under seven reported that they were in the room either all or most of the time while their child was viewing television. It is also common for parents to use television as a way to keep their children entertained when they have something important to get done (45 percent say they have done so), so one should not assume that even when parents are in the room while children are viewing, they are necessarily coviewing with them. In fact, one study that used media-use diaries suggests that only 19 percent of two- to seven-year-olds' viewing is with their parents; for eight- to eighteen-year-olds, it drops to 5 percent (Roberts et al., 1999). In a study of mothers and third- to ninth-grade children, Kelly Schmidt (2000) found a similar decline, further noting that while third-grade children wish their mothers would watch more with them, mothers were more mixed. Some saw it as a good way to spend time with their children, but others were less enthusiastic about watching TV together, preferring to check on children periodically or do something else while the TV is on. Sixth- and ninth-grade children, on the other hand, perceived some conflicts while watching with parents, such as embarrassment over content or annoyance at the lessons parents might teach, but mothers saw TV as a useful way to establish a connection with their children or to check on what they're watching.

If parents are not consuming media with their children to any great extent, it is unlikely that they will have many interactions about media. Some research finds that actual conversation time between parents and children about programs is fairly limited (Austin, 1993). Alison Alexander (2001), however, points to interview and observational data showing that parents (and siblings) do make interpretive comments concerning television realism. Mothers also were found to provide evaluations of characters' behaviors and advertising (Schmidt, 2000). While parents may not be engaged in frequent conversation about media with children, what they do say can have an effect. Alexander (2001, p. 27) observes that "coviewing does not equal interaction, and it is interaction with children that most clearly influences their interpretation of the [television] medium."

Can we say that media use has displaced face-to-face contact within the family? This concern was evident in the popular discourse about television, and has now motivated considerable research and a debate on the effects of home computing. While there was some evidence that television reduced the amount of time conversing in the home when the medium was newly introduced (Kestnbaum et al., 2002), research findings on the question of whether online media use has displaced the amount of time spent in domestic conversation has been somewhat mixed, but is leaning toward a conclusion that there are not negative social outcomes from Internet use (Bargh & McKenna, 2004). Some research has found a relationship between use of the Internet and displacement of face-to-face communication with family (Kayany & Yelsma, 2000; Nie & Hillygus, 2002), but other research has not found reductions in the time family members spend communicating due to Internet use (Kraut et al., 2002; Digital Future Report, 2004). The vast majority (87.6 percent) of Internet users say that since being connected to the Internet at home, they spend the same amount of time with their family face-to-face (Digital Future Report, 2004). Interestingly, more than 40 percent say that the use of the Internet has increased or greatly increased contact with family and friends. Time spent online is often devoted to mediated forms of interpersonal communication with family or friends through email or instant messaging (Papadakis, 2003). (For a complete discussion of young people's use of the Internet, refer to chapter 14.)

Still, there are some misgivings on the part of young people and their parents about the impact of Internet use on the quantity and quality of their family time (Allen & Rainie, 2002). In one study, 61 percent of teens felt that the Internet was not helping their relationships with their families, and nearly two thirds (64 percent) were concerned that it took away time they would otherwise spend with their families (Allen & Rainie, 2002). Further, parents were even more wary about its impact, with 79 percent claiming that the Internet had not helped at all or only a little bit in the time they spend with their children. Interestingly, the longer parents were online, the more they found positive impacts associated with the planning of family activities or caring for their children's health, but their overall assessment of how the Internet affected the time spent with children did not improve as much. Common disputes within families over how much time teens spend online, the content of Web sites visited, and the kind of personal information given out on the Web may discount other perceived positive interactions afforded by the Internet for both parents and children, even though other types of relationships such as with more distant family or friends might be enhanced (Allen & Rainie, 2002).

Reinforcing and Changing Family Roles

Because communication technologies are so integrated into family life, they can be used to reinforce certain roles assumed by members of the family or as vehicles to alter family roles. Traditional gender roles have guided the dynamics of media use in some homes. In two-parent families, more mothers than fathers take on establishing rules about television as an extension of their greater role in determining what's appropriate and "healthy" in children's upbringing (Jordan, 2002). On the other hand, males typically control the remote control and thus play a more dominant role in choosing programming for the family during the times they are home (Morley, 1986; Seiter, 1999), and sometimes "undo" mothers' guidelines (Jordan, 2002). Males more typically make decisions about computer purchases (Jordan, 2002) and assume the expert role in computer technologies, with females more often asking for help (English-Lueck, 1998).

In addition to the role of parent, many mothers and fathers are assuming a second role as "worker," within the family sphere, as discussed more in the following section. Communications technology in the home is allowing many American workers to be "on call" even on sick days or during vacations, in addition to evenings—a time previously claimed for putting on the hat of parent, spouse, or housemate. This "privileging" of the worker role may undermine the sense of commitment perceived by others in the family.

The "manager" is another emerging role within the family enhanced by communication technologies. As noted by one analyst, "families increasingly view themselves as management problems to be solved, just as they would be at work, with technology" (English-Lueck, 1998). Pagers, cell phones, answering machines, and electronic organizers are the tools by which schedules are coordinated and responsibilities are divided as families negotiate a seemingly endless array of work, school, recreational, and domestic activities (English-Lueck, 1998).

Yet, as technology has been used to reinforce certain roles, it has also been used to challenge or subvert others (English-Lueck, 1998). A young person's use of music—through highly portable devices—can help that person fashion an identity separate from and sometimes in opposition to the family (Christenson & Roberts, 1998). A mother rebels against being available any time, anywhere to her children via her cell phone (Wise, 2000). She sees merit in her children having to turn to others, or look to themselves, when facing some situations in order to learn important life skills. An older mother finds her role as the family center challenged by her children, who communicate directly with each other rather than going through her (English-Lueck, 1998).

Interestingly, communication technologies enable a reversal of the role of the parent as expert and the child as learner in some homes with young people present (Lally, 2002). One study of families who were newly equipped with a home computer and Internet connection found that the teenager often became the most involved user—the family guru (Kiesler et al., 1999). Moreover, the teenage guru served as the bridge to the outside world, when additional technical assistance was sought, developing a further role for the teenager as representative of the family.

Finally, technologies such as email and the cellular phone are playing an increasingly important part in connecting extended family members (even across national borders), thus enhancing the various family roles—grandparent, parent, or sibling (Rainie et al., 2000). Lee Rainie and colleagues (2000) found that women were particularly likely to use email for furthering family contact. As families relocate or change in configuration, email is likely to play an important role in maintaining relational ties (Jaffe & Aidman, 1997).

The Blending of Home Life and Work Life

Communication technologies such as the computer, fax, cellular phone, voice-mail systems, and pagers are eroding the boundary between work and home (Gumpert & Drucker, 1998). A national survey conducted in 2005 found that 45.1 million American workers, out of an estimated 134.5 million, spent a portion of their working hours working at home during the previous month (Telework Advisory Group, 2005). Census data from 2001 estimates that 15 percent of employed persons worked from home at least once a week (U.S. Census Bureau, 2003). Even those not part of a formal teleworking relationship often use computers at home for job-related work—according to one study, more than one third of employees (35 percent) sometimes used a computer for work purposes at home (Bond et al., 2002).

The blending of workplace into the living space has important implications for the meaning of family life, the use of domestic space, and the kind of interactions that take place in the home. Teleworking implies a work arrangement in which hours that would be spent in the workplace are now spent working at home. On the positive side, teleworking is seen as a major social benefit of communication technologies by enabling individuals to stay home and work (National Science Foundation, 2002). Its benefits include flexible work hours, lower household costs, less stress from family-work conflicts, and reduced commuting times. Yet, for many teleworkers, the experience brings about a new host of problems: difficulties in managing roles and relationships within the family, a sense of loss as the home no longer serves as a kind of sanctuary, and social isolation from other important reference groups (National Science Foundation, 2002; Papadakis, 2003).

Researchers in California's Silicon Valley note that some individuals who work significant hours at home are also putting in a full schedule at work (English-Lueck, 1998). A study of home life in "infomated" households, or homes containing at least five information devices, including some combination of VCRs, CDs, laser discs, fax machines, answering machines, voice-mail services, computers, and cellular phones, found that these households revolve around work. Working at home may begin with one set of expectations that the boundaries between work and home life will be clearly maintained, and that a balance between working and pursuing other goals is achievable. But the following comment from one of the interviewees in Jan English-Lueck's (1998) study reveals the kind of slippery slope many workers experience as work begins to come home:

> At the time, there was a lot of hard copy paper at my job. I thought it would be real convenient to have a fax modem . . . I also hoped the computer would save me time, and get me ahead at work. I mean, I don't work at home because it is so great. I would rather do other things, but I saw, or hoped, that working at home would allow me to get even more done and give me an advantage at work. And then I thought that if I need an occasional afternoon off, it would be okay because I would be ahead. Of course, that was naïve. Everybody works at home and now it is a standard. Working at home doesn't let me get ahead; it stops me from falling behind.

Furthermore, the "infomated" household study found that the work that comes home requires the uninterrupted attention that a work-saturated business environment can no longer provide. This, then, places a demand on the home to provide a setting where few interruptions take place, a difficult task indeed in a multimember household. Tensions between family members and longer waking hours (for example, if some of the work is delayed until children's bedtimes) may result.

Conclusion: Challenges and Promises for the Networked Family

Communication technologies constitute an integral part of the dynamic quality of family life. They function as an easy conduit to a vast and, at times, disturbing outside world. As a result, family life may be enriched, but due to the amount and variety of information that comes into the home, value systems may be tested continuously and may sometimes be threatened. The personalization of communication technology devices allows family members to enhance their personal interests and growth, but may limit opportunities for shared experiences within the family group. Additionally, the new forms of interactive technologies dramatically reduce the barriers of time and space as family members interact with each other, with others, or with their work sites. Here, too, the consequences may be mixed. The advantages of greater flexibility in one's schedule and increased opportunities to be in contact with others are countered by greater demands by others and more accountability, perhaps to the point where privacy is threatened and other roles are diminished.

We also should remember that not all families or individuals are equally connected to a number of the communication technologies that are becoming more important socially and economically. Understanding the nature and consequences of this so-called digital divide will be important as we look at families' experiences in the future.

Research has only begun to delve into the ways that communication technologies—especially the newer forms—are integrated into family life. More work of an ethnographic nature is needed, where close observations are made of families of differing cultural, economic, and social backgrounds. The insights that will result from this type of research will allow families to make the best use of the technologies as they plan their living spaces and manage their personal, family, and work lives.

DISCUSSION QUESTIONS

1 How does the perspective of the family as a "system" shape the research questions we ask about media use in the family?

2 How can media use be shaped by a family's orientation toward time?

3 How does placement of media in the home affect media use? How can the placement of media in the home, in turn, affect social relations among family members?

4 Thinking about your current use of media, in what ways do you feel it is shaped by experiences with media growing up (for example, parents' attitudes or rules about media use)?

5   What roles can emerge within the family with respect to media use? How can these change over time?

EXERCISE

1   Examine some Web sites created for parents about media use. What themes are emphasized the most? What image of the media is reflected in the Web sites? What are the primary concerns about media use? What recommendations are offered?

NOTE

1   Adapted with permission of the publisher from C. Bachen. (2001). The family in the networked society. *STS Nexus* 1(1): 22–27. Available at http://www.scu.edu/sts/nexus/winter2001/BachenArticle.cfm.

REFERENCES

Alexander, A. (2001). The meaning of television in the American family. In J. Bryant & J. A. Bryant (Eds.), *Television and the American family* (3rd ed., pp. 273–288). Mahwah, NJ: Lawrence Erlbaum.

Allen, K., & Rainie, L. (2002). *Parents online*. Pew Internet and American Life Project. Retrieved March 8, 2006, from http://www.pewinternet.org/PPF/r/75/report_display.asp.

Austin, E. (1993). Exploring the effects of active parental mediation of television content. *Journal of Broadcasting & Electronic Media, 37*, 147–158.

Bargh, J. A., & McKenna, K. Y. A. (2004). The Internet and social life. *Annual Review of Psychology, 5*, 573–90.

Becht, D., Taglang, K., & Wilhelm, A. (1999, August). The digital divide and the U.S. Hispanic population. *Digital Beat, 1*, 13. Retrieved March 8, 2006, from http://www.benton.org/publibrary/digitalbeat/db080699.html.

Biagi, S. (2001). *Media/impact*. Belmont, CA: Wadsworth/Thomson Learning.

Bond, J. T., Thomspon, C., Galinsky, E., & Prottas, D. (2002). *Highlights of the national study of the changing workforce*. New York: Families and Work Institute.

Buckingham, D. (1996). *Moving images: Understanding children's emotional responses to television*. Manchester: Manchester University Press.

Caron, A. H. (2000, November). New communication technologies in the home: A qualitative study on the introduction, appropriation and uses of media in the family. Paper presented at the meeting of the International Forum of Researchers, Young People and the Media. Sydney, Australia.

Christenson, P., & Roberts, D. F. (1998). *It's not only rock and roll: Popular music in the lives of adolescents*. Cresskill, NJ: Hampton.

Digital Future Report. (2004). *Surveying the digital future: Year four*. Los Angeles: University of Southern California. Retrieved February 12, 2006, from http://www.digitalcenter.org/pages/site_content.asp?intGlobalId=20.

English-Lueck, J. (1998, June). *Technology and social change: The effects on family and community*. Paper presented at the COSSA Congressional Seminar. Retrieved December 28, 2005, from http://www2.sjsu.edu/depts/anthropology/svcp/SVCPcosa.html.

Fitzpatrick, M. A., & Wambolt, F. S. (1990). Where is all said and done? Toward an integration of intra-personal and inter-personal models of marital and family communication. *Communication Research*, *17*, 421–430.

Gumpert, G., & Drucker, S. J. (1998). The mediated home in the global village. *Communication Research*, *254*, 422–439.

Hafner, K. (2000, March 16). Hi, Mom. Hi, Dad. At the beep, leave a message: Teenagers connected by cell phones and pagers find ways to stay out of touch. *New York Times*, p. D1.

Hall, E. (1959). *The silent language*. Greenwich, CT: Fawcett.

Jaffe, M. J., & Aidman, A. (1997). Families, geographical separation, and the Internet. In A. S. Robertson (Ed.), *The proceedings of the Families, Technology, and Education Conference October 30–November 1*. Champaign, IL: ERIC Clearinghouse on Elementary and Early Childhood Education.

Jordan, A. B. (2002). A family systems approach to examining the role of the Internet in the home. In S. L. Calvert, A. B. Jordan, & R. R. Cocking (Eds.), *Children in the digital age: Influences of electronic media on development* (pp. 231–247). Westport, CT: Praeger.

Kayany, J., & Yelsma, P. (2000). Displacement effects of online media in the socio-technical contexts of households. *Journal of Broadcasting & Electronic Media*, *44*, 215–229.

Kestnbaum, M., Robinson, J. P., Neustadtl, A., & Alvarez, A. (2002). Information technology and social time displacement. *IT & Society*, *1*, 21–37.

Kiesler, S., Lundmark, V., Zdaniuk, B., Kraut, R., Scherlis, W., & Mukhopadhyay, T. (1999). *Troubles with the Internet: The dynamics of help at home*. Retrieved January 28, 2006, from http://homenet.hcii.cs.cmu.edu/progress/helpdesk.html.

Kraut, R., Kiesler, S., Boneva, B., Cummings, J., Helgeson, V., & Crawford, A. (2002). Internet paradox revisited. *Journal of Social Issues*, *58*(1),49–74.

Lally, E. (2002). *At home with computers*. Oxford: Berg.

Morley, D. (1986). *Family television: Cultural power and domestic leisure*. London: Comedia.

National Science Foundation, Division of Science Resources Statistics. (2002). *Science and engineering indicators, 2002*, Arlington, VA (NSB 02–01). Retrieved January 15, 2006, from http://www.nsf.gov/statistics/seind02/.

Nie, N. H., & Hillygus, D. S. (2002). The impact of Internet use on sociability: Time-diary findings. *IT & Society*, *1*, 1–20. Retrieved January 29, 2005, from http://www.stanford.edu/group/siqss/itandsociety/v01i01.html.

Papadakis, M. (2003). Data on family and the Internet: What do we know and how do we know it? In J. Turow & A. L. Kavanaugh (Eds.), *The wired homestead: An MIT Press sourcebook on the Internet and the family* (pp. 121–140). Cambridge, MA: MIT Press

Rainie, L., Fox, S., Horrigan, J., & Lenhart, A. (2000). *Tracking online life: How women use the Internet to cultivate relationships with family and friends*. Washington, D.C.: Pew Internet and American Life Project. Retrieved February 18, 2006, from http://www.pewinternet.org/PPF/r/11/report_display.asp.

Rideout, V. J., Vandewater, E. A., & Wartella, E. A. (2003). *Zero to six: Electronic media in the lives of infants, toddlers and preschoolers*. Kaiser Family Foundation Report.

Roberts, D. F., Foehr, U. G., & Rideout, R. J. (2005). *Generation M: Media in the lives of 8–18 year-olds*. Kaiser Family Foundation Report.

Roberts, D.F., Foehr, U. G., Rideout, V. J., & Brodie, M. (1999). *Kids & media @ the new millennium*. Kaiser Family Foundation Report.

Schmidt, K. L. (2000). *Public policy, family rules and children's media use in the home*. The Annenberg Public Policy Center of the University of Pennsylvania. Retrieved January 25, 2005, from www.annenbergpublicpolicycenter.org/05_media_developing_child/childrensprogramming/ppfr.pdf.

Seiter, E. (1999). *Television and new media audiences*. New York: Oxford University Press.

Telework Advisory Group for WorldatWork. (2005). Annual survey shows Americans are working from many different locations outside their employer's office. Press release. Retrieved January 30, 2006, from http://www.workingfromanywhere.org/news/pr100405.htm.

U.S. Census Bureau. (2003). Statistical Abstract of the United States, 2003. National data book, section 12: Labor force, employment, and earnings: Table no. 605: Persons doing job-related work at home, 2001. Washington, D.C.: U.S. Census Bureau.

Valkenburg, P. M., Kremar, M., Peeters, A. L., & Marseille, N. M. (1999). Developing a scale to assess three styles of television mediation: "Instructive mediation," "restrictive mediation," and "social coviewing." *Journal of Broadcasting & Electronic Media, 43*, 52–66.

Wartella, E., & Jennings, N. (2001). New members of the family: The digital revolution in the home. *Journal of Family Communication, 1*(1), 59–69.

Wise, N. (2000, August 7). Parents shouldn't be on call all the time. *Newsweek*, pp. 6, 15.

Woodard, IV, E. H., & Gridina, N. (2000). *Media in the home, 2000: Survey series 7*. Annenberg Public Policy Center of the University of Pennsylvania. Retrieved December 28, 2005, from http://www.annenbergpublicpolicycenter.org/05_media_developing_child/mediasurvey/mediasurvey.htm.

CHAPTER SEVENTEEN

How Are Girls' Studies Scholars (and Girls Themselves) Shaking up the Way We Think about Girls and Media?

SHARON R. MAZZARELLA

Before answering the question posed by this chapter's title, I must first answer another question: Why is there a chapter on girls' studies in this book, but not a corresponding chapter on boys' studies? Quite simply, at least in relationship to the discipline of communication, there has been no cohesive, well-developed field of boys' studies.[1] On the other hand, there is a long history of studies of girls, media, and culture, although not all of it, as I will explain in this chapter, can accurately be called "girls' studies." In order to address the topic at hand, this chapter begins by clarifying the differences between studies of girls and "girls' studies." It then situates the evolution of girls' studies within a broader shift in academic theories of youth in general and girls in particular. Finally, it identifies the dominant trends and findings in girls' studies scholarship, at least as they relate to the media and popular culture.

What Is Girls' Studies? Girls' Studies versus Studies of Girls

As mentioned in the previous paragraph, within the discipline of communication there has been a long history of studying girls, media, and other cultural artifacts. However, for years the focus of such studies was on girls as consumers of media and other products (Kearney, 2006) and/or as passive victims of mediated portrayals of femininity. Specifically, researchers centered their studies on those kinds of media products targeted directly and specifically to girls—teen magazines and teen romance novels, for example (see Christian-Smith, 1988, 1990; Peirce, 1990, 1993; to name just a couple). Such studies included content analyses documenting "sexist and otherwise problematic representations of adolescent girls" in the media (Durham, 1999, p. 211)—a trend that continues to some extent today. At the same time, it was common to define girls as potential victims of this content, a definition resulting in audience studies (surveys and experiments) examining how girls were negatively affected by such content, particularly teen magazines, advertising, and fashion models (see Durkin & Paxton, 2002; Levine et al., 1994; Martin & Gentry, 1997; Martin & Kennedy, 1993; Turner et al., 1997; Vaughan & Fouts, 2003; to name just a few).

This tendency of many in the academy to label girls as victims of mass culture found a parallel in U.S. public discourse as well, a predisposition that was evident throughout the twentieth century (Kearney, 2006) and particularly during the 1990s. At that time several influential and high-profile studies of girls were published (for example, American Association of University Women, 1991; Brumberg, 1997; Orenstein, 1994; Pipher, 1994; Sadker & Sadker, 1994) addressing such issues as girls' declining self-esteem, negative body image, and poor school performance. Simultaneously, U.S. newspapers were constructing girls as a "generation in crisis" (Mazzarella & Pecora, 2007) and in need of adult intervention. Indeed, girls' studies scholar Mary Celeste Kearney (2006, p. 109) warns of the dangers of such constructions of girls as needing to be saved by adults—specifically that they "unwittingly construct girls as disempowered in the present."

Shauna Pomerantz, Dawn Currie, and Deidre Kelly (2004, p. 548) have pointed out that the focus of the academic and public discourse dealing with girls as consumers and/or as victims, such as those that dominated the 1990s, were rooted in "psychological discourse." What was missing, until very recently, however, were studies of girls as able to resist questionable messages as well as girls as active producers of their own messages (Kearney, 2006)—scholarship grounded more in cultural studies and feminist theory. (Interestingly, much of the work in girls' studies has been grounded in third-wave feminism.[2]) This recent trend has been dubbed "girls' studies" (as opposed to simply studies of girls)—a field Gayle Wald (1998, p. 587) has defined as "a sub-genre of recent academic feminist scholarship that constructs girlhood as a separate, exceptional, and/or pivotal phase in female identity formation." No one can deny that girls have achieved a new visibility both in the press and in the academy (Mazzarella & Pecora, 2007). As Catherine Driscoll (2002, back cover) argues, this visibility has been related to "the evolution and expansion of theories about feminine adolescence in fields such as psychoanalysis, sociology, anthropology, history, and politics." Clearly, as with all youth, there has been a cyclical relationship between academic, clinical, and public discourses about girls.

"Youth" Does Not Always Equal Boys

On one level, that was a good thing, since until the latter half of the twentieth century academic and clinical studies of females were virtually absent (Brown & Gilligan, 1992; de Beauvoir, 1949; Gilligan, 1982). Much of what we know (or thought we knew) about youth as a generation has come from male scholars studying male children and adolescents. As feminist scholar Carol Gilligan reminds us, those theories guiding the public and media discourse on youth development throughout much of the twentieth century (for example, Erikson, 1963; Kohlberg, 1981; Piaget, 1965) told us nothing about girls as a distinct group. Gilligan's own work has gone a long way toward showing us the unique ways female youth develop as well as the ways in which girls and women communicate and reason (see, for example, Brown & Gilligan, 1992; Gilligan, 2004; Gilligan et al., 1990; Gilligan et al., 1991; Gilligan et al., 1988; Taylor et al., 1995), notably that girls and women speak in "a different voice" (Gilligan, 1982). Gilligan's work has proven to be highly influential in the way we as scholars study girls and girl culture, but she is not alone in her influence.

While Gilligan focused on the biases inherent in long-standing psychological theories of youth development, Angela McRobbie reminded us that these same biases and absences were extant in theories of youth culture, in particular youth subcultures (for example, Hebdige, 1979; Willis, 1977). Grounded in both feminist and cultural theories, McRobbie's own work on girls has expanded the dialogue about girls and girl culture (McRobbie, 1982, 1991, 1993, 2000, 2004; McRobbie & Garber, 1976; McRobbie & Nava, 1984) and, like Gilligan's, has had a profound influence on the development of girls' studies as a field. In fact, her book *Feminism and Youth Culture* (1991) has been described as "a landmark work for taking seriously the culture of girls" (Wald, 2004, p. 1145). The revised edition of this book (2000), in fact, evidences the scope and focus of McRobbie's work, including chapters on girls and subcultures (co-written in 1976 with Jenny Garber) as a direct response to the male bias of previous subculture studies, a chapter on sexuality and rock music (co-written with popular music scholar Simon Frith), and a concluding chapter on "new ways of being young women."

In addition to shifting the focus of youth studies away from solely boys, Gilligan's and McRobbie's contributions to the development of girls' studies have also been methodological, specifically advocating the need to listen to the voices of girls themselves rather than relying on adult academicians' interpretations of girl culture. Girls' studies scholars often rely on qualitative and cultural methods of studying girls, including focus groups, one-on-one interviews, and ethnographies. (See chapter 5 for a thorough explanation of these methods and their role in studying youth and media.) Such methods enable girls to speak for themselves. Indeed, as McRobbie (2000, p. 4) recollects, her goal has always been to understand how "young women saw themselves as women." I will have more to say about girls' studies' emphasis on girls as active agents in a later section.

Girls' Studies of Media and Popular Culture

Media Representations of Girls

While long ignored in the academic discourse on youth, girls had also been positioned as a less-than-desirable audience by all but the most female-centered media outlets (for example, teen and women's magazines) as media industries sought to reach a more lucrative male audience. Paralleling and contributing to the growing academic and public discourse about U.S. girls in the 1990s, however, girls proved to be a highly profitable audience for the media industries, a phenomenon attributed to the movie *Titanic*, whose financial success has been linked to repeat viewings by preadolescent and adolescent girls (Weinraub, 1998). But it was not just *Titanic* that benefited from a newly powerful young female audience. Girls helped ensure both the financial and cult success of such youth-oriented television programs as *Buffy the Vampire Slayer, Party of Five*, and *Dawson's Creek*, not to mention a new wave of pop music acts such as the Spice Girls and the Backstreet Boys (Weinraub, 1998). At the time of this writing, the glut of girl-centered cultural products continues and has influenced a new wave of scholars studying the relationship between girls and these artifacts from a girls' studies tradition.

The television program *Buffy the Vampire Slayer*, for example, has been the focus of countless articles, chapters, and entire books (for example, Buttsworth, 2002; Campbell & Campbell, 2001; Driver, 2007; Early, 2001; Heinecken, 2003; Owen, 1999; Ross, 2004; Rutkowski, 2002; Wilcox, 2005; Wilcox & Lavery, 2002), many focusing on the role of the teenaged Buffy Summers as "transgressive," a "disruptive woman warrior hero" (Early, 2001, p. 24), and as a "disruption of masculine warrior identity" (Buttsworth, 2002, p. 194). Similarly, a wave of animated powerful girl programs such as *The Powerpuff Girls, Sailor Moon*, and *My Life as a Teenage Robot* has received extensive academic attention (Banet-Weiser, 2004; Hains, 2004, in press; Newsom, 2004; Potts, 2001). The latest round of teen movies has not escaped academic study (Bain, 2003; Boyd, 2004; Driver, 2007; Jenkins, 2005), nor has the growing cadre of feminist popular music performers such as Gwen Stefani (Wald, 1998), Alanis Morissette (Schilt, 2003), Fiona Apple (Schilt, 2003), and, of course, the Spice Girls—the group typically credited with popularizing and commodifying the concept of "girl power"—(Brabazon & Evans, 1998; Dibben, 1999; Douglas, 1997; Driscoll, 1999; Gillis & Munford, 2004; Lemish, 2003; Railton, 2001; Riordan, 2001). Moving beyond knee-jerk reactions to controversial portrayals and/or messages, girls' studies scholars typically offer nuanced and theoretically grounded deconstructions of such cultural texts. For example, Catherine Driscoll (1999) offers a compelling and multifaceted deconstruction of the controversial Spice Girl phenomenon in her article "Girl Culture, Revenge and Global Capitalism: Cybergirls, Riot Grrls, Spice Girls." Comparing the Spice Girls with more "radical" female musicians such as various Riot Grrl groups, Driscoll concludes that, despite their controversial nature, the Spice Girls are important in that "they belong in the long history of relations between girl culture and feminism, and they produce both girls and feminism in ways that warrant further consideration" (p. 190).

This upsurge of academic studies of girls' cultural artifacts, while still grounded primarily in content analysis methodology, differs greatly from previous studies of cultural artifacts targeted to girls. First, they are not limited to studies of print media such as teen girl magazines, thereby acknowledging the range of media producing cultural artifacts representing and targeting girls. Second, they do not begin with an assumption that cultural messages are harmful to girls and that girls are the hapless victims of the culture industries. Indeed, it is this movement away from defining girls as victims that leads to the most compelling area of current girls' studies scholarship—studies that listen to the voices of girls themselves, whether it be related to their active resistance to and negotiation of the messages produced by mass culture or related to their own creation of cultural artifacts.

Activ(ist) Girls: Resisting and Producing Messages

Certainly the kind of studies identified in the previous section represent a starting point enabling us to understand the media and cultural environment surrounding girls. Following from Gilligan and McRobbie, many girls' studies scholars remind us of the need to incorporate the voices of girls themselves in the dialogue, in this case when discussing how girls actively negotiate and even resist cultural messages (for example, Duke, 2002; Durham, 1999). For example, a trio of chapters in my co-edited anthology on the relationship between popular culture and girls' construction of identity foreground "conversations" between feminist scholar mothers and their adolescent daughters (Mazzarella & Pecora, 1999). Specifically, in each, mother and daughter "discuss" the daughters' relationship to various cultural artifacts such as Barbie (Rakow & Rakow, 1999), the American Girl doll collection (Stumbar & Eisenstein, 1999), and girls' own roles as cultural producers (Valdivia & Bettivia, 1999). While I acknowledge that not all girls have academic feminists for mothers, taken as a whole, these conversations evidence the ways in which *some* girls actively negotiate, resist, and challenge cultural messages while still, at times, finding pleasure in such content.

Dawn Currie (1999) moved beyond academic content analyses of teen girl magazines—analyses in which adult scholars traditionally impose their own interpretations on the content targeted to young girls—by interviewing teen girls themselves about their negotiation and interpretation of this content. What emerges from her work is a portrait of "the complexity of not only meaning, but also of social life" (p. 308), highlighting the importance of researchers "moving beyond the immediacy of the text" (p. 309). Again, the key is in listening to the voices of girls, something Dafna Lemish (1998) did through focus groups with Israeli girls in order to understand their feelings about the Spice Girls. By listening to the voices of girls, Lemish, like Currie, documents the complexity in girls' relationships with popular cultural texts. She concluded that these girls "were active constructors of possible oppositional meaning [to the dominant messages of the Spice Girls]" (p. 164), but that "adoring the Spice Girls, so it seems, gives the female adolescent a voice while retaining the unresolved complexity of contradictions into which girls are socialized" (pp. 164–165), in particular in regard to cultural dictates related to the importance of physical appearance for females. Quite simply, girls' studies scholars acknowledge the complexity of girls' relationship to media and cultural practices.

While it is important to listen to the voices of girls as they tell us about their relationships to cultural artifacts that we, as adult scholars, would likely miss or misinterpret without their help, it is equally, if not more, important to listen to, to see, and to read their voices through the cultural products they themselves create. Technological innovations such as digital video/filmmaking and the Internet have enabled young people to produce their own media messages—a phenomenon that is particularly prevalent in girl culture. (See chapter 14 for a thorough discussion of young people's use of the Internet.) But even such low-tech pursuits as publishing a handmade zine that has been photocopied and handed out at a concert (Kearney, 2006) are important forms of cultural production for girls.

Nearly a decade ago, Mary Celeste Kearney (1998, p. 285) labeled the "emergence of girls as cultural producers" as "one of the most interesting transformations to have occurred in youth culture in the last two decades." While writing at a time when others both in the academy and the media were focusing on girls as victims of media content, Kearney advocated for seeing girls as active and capable of doing more than *consuming* media content. She reminded us, "If scholars involved in the field of Girls' Studies desire to keep current with the state of female youth and their cultural practices, we must expand the focus of our analyses to include not only texts produced for girls by the adult-run mainstream culture industries, but also those cultural artifacts created by girls" (Kearney, 1998, p. 286).

In response, the field of girls' studies has generated a plethora of studies documenting girls' active production of culture (both media and otherwise), including music (Driver, 2007; Harris, 2001; Jennings, 1999; LeBlanc, 1999; Wald, 1998), zines (Ferris, 2001; Harris, 2001, 2003), Web sites and blogs (Bortree, 2005; Driver, 2007; Gregson, 2005; Harris, 2001; Mazzarella, 2005; Stern, 1999, 2002a, 2002b, 2004), films (Kearney, 2003, 2006; Sweeney, 2005, forthcoming), and "sk8ter" culture (Kelly et al., 2005; Pomerantz et al., 2004), to name only a handful of examples. Kearney's own work has proven to be instrumental in this movement, as her most recent book, *Girls Make Media* (2006), attests. In this extensive work, she addresses the riot grrrl movement as well as girls as zine producers, filmmakers, and Web designers—phenomena she situates within a broad historical and theoretical context.

Kearney is not alone, as academic studies of girls as cultural producers are proliferating rapidly. Susan Driver (2007), for example, focuses on how queer girls use their role as producers of such artifacts as music and Web sites in the process of coming out as well as the development of both identity and community. Similarly, Kathleen Sweeney (2005, forthcoming) looks at organized filmmaking initiatives for girls, including Divas Direct/San Diego Girl Film Festival, Girls-Eye View, GirlsFilmSchool, Girls Incorporated: Girls Make the Message, and Reel Grrls—organizations that provide opportunities, safe spaces, and communities for girls to produce their own movies. (Kearney [2006] looks at such programs as well.) According to Sweeney (2005, p. 37), "women filmmakers, youth advocates, media artists, and self-proclaimed 'geek chicks' have moved beyond media critique and hand-wringing to proactive girls programming via digital filmmaking." Similarly, a recent review of Marnina Gonick's (2003) ethnographic study of an organized group of schoolgirls making a video described Gonick's book as a "postmodernist privileging of girls' voices, resistance and agency" (Jiwani, 2004, p. 14). Such a "privileging" can be said to define not only Gonick's book, but also girls' studies as a field.

Girls' studies scholars have not limited their research solely to media as a form of cultural production, and neither have girls. Two recently published studies by Dawn Currie and her colleagues have explored what they call "skater girlhood"—girls who engage in the sport of skateboarding, a pursuit dominated by male youth (Kelly et al., 2005; Pomerantz et al., 2004). From their interviews with these girls, it is clear that these girls are knowingly and purposely transgressing against traditional norms of feminine behavior, define themselves in opposition to the giggly, fashion-conscious girlfriends of the male skaters, and are actively appropriating spaces previously dominated by males. These girls, they argue, are engaging in their own style of feminism—a third-wave feminism that is dramatically different from the "collective social action and explicit political agenda" of second-wave feminism (Pomerantz et al., 2004, p. 554).

While culturally active girls can be found in such public spaces as skateboard parks, girls' studies scholar Anita Harris (2001, p. 132) calls also for "revisiting bedroom culture"— private spaces "as a site for girls' resistance." She shows how girls are "choosing, politicizing and re-invigorating the private" (p. 132) "marginal or underground" spaces (p. 133), and calls on girls' studies scholars to address these spaces "as sites where young women deliberate over their place in the world" (p. 133). Harris identifies zines, alternative music, and Web pages/e-zines as sites through which girls act on their social change and political agendas. Referring specifically to zines (a topic also covered extensively by Kearney [2006]), she documents how girls use such cultural productions to "create a community for young women within which they can participate in debates about the meaning of girlhood under late modernity" (p. 38). While girls are actively producing zines, music, films, and so on, the proliferation of and access to Internet technology (for many girls in many countries) have proven to have had the biggest influence on girls' ability to produce media messages.

As shown in chapter 14 of this book, U.S. youths' access to and use of the Internet has grown exponentially in recent years, a phenomenon affecting girls as well as boys. While at one time there may have been a gendered digital divide such that boys were more likely to use computer technology than were girls, that divide no longer exists. In fact, in many ways girls are more active Internet creators than are boys, especially when it comes to such things as blogs.

A study by the Pew Internet and American Life Project (Lenhart & Madden, 2005, p. ii) found that "older girls [aged fifteen to seventeen] lead the blogging activity among teens"; that 25 percent of U.S. fifteen- to seventeen-year-old girls who go online keep a blog while only 15 percent of boys in that age group do; and that "when it comes to sharing self-authored creative content, older girls stand out" (Lenhart & Madden, 2005, p. 3). Thirty-eight percent of U.S. girls aged fifteen to seventeen versus only 29 percent of U.S. boys in this age group create and share such self-authored content as photos, artwork, videos, and stories.[3]

Not surprisingly, as girls' use of the Internet has increased, so too has academic inquiry into this use. Susannah Stern has pointed out that most of these initial studies focused on Web sites created *for* girls or other Internet content *about* girls with little early scholarly inquiry into sites created *by* girls. Paralleling trends in girls' studies scholarship in generally, this tendency has changed, and Stern's own work (1999, 2002a, 2002b, 2004) has led the way. For example, by deconstructing personal home pages created by girls, Stern (1999, p. 23) shows how they use these "safe" spaces as forms of "constructed self-presentations." Based on her research, Stern (1999, p. 38) has concluded that "it is clear that adolescent girls are speaking on the web—speaking in ways and words that are infrequently heard. . . . [H]ome pages provide girls with greater opportunity to openly express thoughts, interests, and to create a public identity."

Including Stern, a range of girls' studies scholars have examined the Internet as a space fostering girls' self-expression, community building, and identity play. For example, scholars have investigated how the Web sites girls create function as forms of identity expression, self-disclosure, communication, and community building (Bortree, 2005; Mazzarella, 2005; Stern, 1999, 2002a, 2002b, 2004; Takayoshi et al., 1999). Others have documented how girls use organizational and commercial Web sites targeted to them to explore their identities in general (Merskin, 2005) and their sexual identities in particular (Grisso & Weiss, 2005). Still others have highlighted the role of instant messaging in girls' identity development and peer networking (Thiel, 2005; Stern, 2007).

In my study of how teenage girl fans of young actor Chad Michael Murray express this fandom through their fan Web sites, I document the manner in which girls use their technological expertise to actively create a community and celebrate their shared fandom (Mazzarella, 2005). While expressions of fandom by teen girls have often been stigmatized and/or trivialized by the adult culture, and therefore often remained hidden, I argue that the process of creating a Web site that can be accessed by millions of people enables girls to publicly proclaim their fandom—not to mention their technological skills.

Conclusion

In her call for girls' studies scholars to study girls as cultural producers, Kearney (2006) makes it clear that she is not dismissing the role consumerism plays in girls' lives. Rather, she is attempting to broaden our focus to include areas of scholarship and ways of defining girls' relationship with media that had been previously neglected. Specifically, such studies, she argues, enable us to redefine adolescent girls as active agents, acting on their world. As the culture, technology, and society evolve, so too must the questions we as academics ask and the methods we use to answer them. This is crucial not just for those of us working the field of girls' studies in particular, but for all of us studying youth and media in general. Indeed, I would echo Lemish's call in chapter 5 of this book that we as scholars should attempt to reach a "fuller and more comprehensible understanding of the role of media in children's lives."

DISCUSSION QUESTIONS

1 Early in the chapter, I point out that there has been a cyclical relationship between academic, clinical, and public discourse about girls. What do I mean by that and what might
   be the role of girls' studies scholars in contributing to that discourse?

2 Girls' studies scholars argue for the importance of listening to the voices of girls themselves. Why is this so important?

EXERCISES

1 Select and access one of the studies identified in the "Girls' Studies versus Studies of
   Girls" subsection of this chapter and another identified in the "Activ(ist) Girls: Resisting
   and Producing Messages" subsection. Compare and contrast them in terms of methodology, questions asked, and implied definition of *girls*.

2 Using an online database such as Communication and Mass Media Complete, conduct
   a search for refereed (scholarly) articles using the following two keywords: *girl* and *media*.
   Looking at the article titles and abstracts, answer the following questions: What topics are covered? What medium/media is/are being studied? What methods are the
   authors using? Which articles fit the definition of girls' studies?

NOTES

1 I would be remiss to ignore the work of Jackson Katz, particularly his video *Tough Guise*, produced
   for the Media Education Foundation (Jhally, 1999). Katz links such examples of real-life violent masculinity as the Columbine High School shootings to mediated portrayals of violent masculinity.
   However, one video does not a "field" make. While the interdisciplinary field of masculinity studies has a significant presence within media studies, such scholarship typically focuses on mediated
   portrayals of adult men. Yet, while studies of boys and boy culture are not prevalent in media studies, they are quite important in sociology and education (see, for example, Connolly, 2004;
   Garbarino, 2002; Gurian & Stevens, 2005; Martino & Pallotta-Chiarolli, 2003; to name just a few).

2 Begun in the early 1990s by young women born since the second wave of feminism of the 1960s and
   '70s, third-wave feminism typically transcends a focus solely on gender by addressing such issues as
   transnationalism, race, sexual orientation/identity, and postcolonialism. Specifically third-wavers
   have challenged both the second wave's narrow focus on the lives of White, middle-class women
   as well as the second wave's rejection of the word *girl*—a moniker proudly appropriated and celebrated by even adult third-wavers.

3 While there may no longer be a gendered digital divide, at least when talking about youth, as Stern
   and Willis accurately point out in chapter 14 of this book, some 13 percent of U.S. youth lack Internet
   access—a divide generally considered to be directly related to family income and race.

REFERENCES

American Association of University Women. (1991). *Shortchanging girls, shortchanging America: A nation-
    wide poll to assess self-esteem, educational experiences, interest in math and science, and career aspirations*

of girls and boys aged 9–15. Washington, D.C.: Author. ED 340–657.

Bain, A. L. (2003). White Western teenage girls and urban space: Challenging Hollywood's representations [electronic version]. *Gender, Place & Culture: A Journal of Feminist Geography, 10*(3), 197–213.

Banet-Weiser, S. (2004). Girls rule! Gender, feminism, and Nickelodeon [electronic version]. *Critical Studies in Media Communication, 21*(2), 119–139.

Bortree, D. S. (2005). Presentation of self on the Web: An ethnographic study of teenage girls' weblogs [electronic version]. *Education, Communication & Information, 5*(1), 25–39.

Boyd, J. (2004). Dance, culture, and popular film [electronic version]. *Feminist Media Studies, 4*(1), 67–83.

Brabazon, T., & Evans, A. (1998). I'll never be your woman: The Spice Girls and new flavours of feminism [electronic version]. *Social Alternatives, 17*(2), 39–42.

Brown, L. M., & Gilligan, C. (1992). *Meeting at the crossroads: Women's psychology and girls' development.* Cambridge, MA: Harvard University Press.

Brumberg, J. J. (1997). *The body project: An intimate history of American girls.* New York: Random House.

Buttsworth, S. (2002). "Bite me": Buffy and the penetration of the gendered warrior-hero [electronic version]. *Continuum: Journal of Media & Cultural Studies, 16*(2), 185–199.

Campbell, R., & Campbell, C. (2001). Demons, aliens, teens and television. *Television Quarterly, 31*(4), 56–64.

Christian-Smith, L. K. (1988) Romancing the girl: Adolescent romance novels and the construction of femininity. In L. G. Roman, L. K. Christian-Smith, & E. Ellsworth (Eds.), *Becoming feminine: The politics of popular culture* (pp. 76–101). London: Falmer.

Christian-Smith, L. K. (1990). *Becoming a woman through romance.* New York: Routledge.

Connolly, P. (2004). *Boys and schooling in the early years.* Oxford: RoutledgeFalmer.

Currie, D. (1999). *Girl talk: Adolescent magazines and their readers.* Toronto: University of Toronto Press.

de Beauvoir, S. (1949). *The other sex.* New York: Knopf.

Dibben, N. (1999). Representations of femininity in popular music. *Popular Music, 18*(3), 331–355.

Douglas, S. J. (1997, August 25). Girls 'n' Spice: All things nice? [electronic version]. *Nation*, pp. 21–24.

Driscoll, C. (1999). Girl culture, revenge and global capitalism: Cybergirls, riot grrls, Spice Girls [electronic version]. *Australian Feminist Studies, 14*(29), 173–193.

Driscoll, C. (2002). Girls: Feminine adolescence *in popular culture and cultural theory.* New York: Columbia University Press.

Driver, S. (2007). *Queer girls and popular culture: Reading, resisting, and creating media.* New York: Peter Lang.

Duke, L. (2002). Get real! Cultural relevance and resistance to the mediated feminine ideal [electronic version]. *Psychology & Marketing, 19*(2), 211–233.

Durham, M. G. (1999). Articulating adolescent girls' resistance to patriarchal discourse in popular media [electronic version]. *Women's Studies in Communication, 22*(2), 210–229.

Durkin, S. J., & Paxton, S. J. (2002). Predictors of vulnerability to reduced body image satisfaction and psychological wellbeing in response to exposure to idealized female media images in adolescent girls [electronic version]. *Journal of Psychosomatic Research, 53*(5), 995–1005.

Early, F. H. (2001). Staking her claim: Buffy the Vampire Slayer as transgressive woman warrior. *Journal of Popular Culture, 35*(3), 11–27.

Erikson, E. (1963). *Childhood and society*. New York: W. W. Norton.

Ferris, M. A. (2001). Resisting mainstream media: Girls and the act of making zines. *Canadian Woman Studies*, *20*(4), 51–55.

Garbarino, J. (2002). *Lost boys: Why our sons turn violent and how we can save them*. New York: Anchor.

Gilligan, C. (1982). *In a different voice: Psychological theory and women's development*. Cambridge, MA: Harvard University Press.

Gilligan, C. (2004). Recovering psyche. *Annual of Psychoanalysis*, *32*, 131–147.

Gilligan, C., Lyons, N., & Hanmer, T. (Eds.). (1990). *Making connections: The relational world of adolescent girls at the Emma Willard School*. Cambridge, MA: Harvard University Press.

Gilligan, C., Rogers, A. G., & Tolman, D. L. (Eds.). (1991). *Women, girls and psychotherapy: Reframing resistance*. New York: Harrington Park.

Gilligan, C., Ward, J. V., & Taylor, J. M. (Eds.). (1988). *Mapping the moral domain*. Cambridge, MA: Center for the Study of Gender, Education and Human Development.

Gillis, S., & Munford, R. (2004). Genealogies and generations: The politics and praxis of third wave feminism. *Women's History Review*, *13*(2), 165–182.

Gonick, M. (2003). *Between femininities: Ambivalence, identity and the education of girls*. Albany: State University of New York Press.

Gregson, K. S. (2005). "What if the lead character looks like me?" Girl fans of *Shoujo* anime and their Web sites. In S. R. Mazzarella (Ed.), *Girl wide web: Girls, the Internet, and the negotiation of identity* (pp. 121–140). New York: Peter Lang.

Grisso, A. D., & Weiss, D. (2005). What are gURLS talking about? Adolescent girls' construction of sexual identity on gURL.com. In S. R. Mazzarella (Ed.), *Girl wide web: Girls, the Internet, and the negotiation of identity* (pp. 31–49). New York: Peter Lang.

Gurian, M., & Stevens, K. (2005). *The minds of boys: Saving our sons from falling behind in school and life*. Hoboken, NJ: Jossey-Bass.

Hains, R. C. (2004). The problematics of reclaiming the girlish: *The Powerpuff Girls* and girl power. *Femspec*, *5*(2), 1–39.

Hains, R. C. (in press). Inventing the teenage girl: The construction of female identity in Nickelodeon's *My Life as a Teenage Robot*. *Popular Communication*, *5*(3).

Harris, A. (2001). Revisiting bedroom culture: New spaces for young women's politics [electronic version]. *Hecate*, *27*(1), 128–139.

Harris, A. (2003). gURL scenes and grrrl zines: The regulation and resistance of girls in late modernity. *Feminist Review*, *75*(1), 38–56.

Hebdige, D. (1979). *Subculture: The meaning of style*. London: Methuen.

Heinecken, D. (2003). *The warrior women of television: A feminist cultural analysis of the new female body in popular media*. New York: Peter Lang.

Jenkins, T. (2005). Potential lesbians at two o'clock: The heterosexualization of lesbianism in the recent teen film [electronic version]. *Journal of Popular Culture*, *38*(3), 491–504.

Jennings. C. (1999). Girls make music: Polyphony and identity in teenage rock bands. In S. R. Mazzarella & N. O. Pecora (Eds.), *Growing up girls: Popular culture and the construction of identity* (pp. 175–192). New York: Peter Lang.

Jhally, S. (Director and executive producer). (1999). *Tough guise* [video documentary]. Northampton, MA: Media Education Foundation.

Jiwani, Y. (2004). Review of the book *Between femininities: Ambivalence, identity and the education of girls*. *Resources for Feminist Research, 31*(1/2), 14–16.

Kearney, M. C. (1998). Producing girls. In S. A. Inness (Ed.), *Delinquents and debutantes: Twentieth-century American girls' cultures* (pp. 285–310). New York: NYU Press.

Kearney, M. C. (2003). Girls make movies. In K. Mallin & S. Pearce (Eds.), *Youth cultures: Texts, images, and identities* (pp. 17–34). Westport, CT: Praeger.

Kearney, M. C. (2006). *Girls make media*. New York: Routledge.

Kelly, D., Pomerantz, S., & Currie, D. (2005). Skater girlhood and emphasized femininity: "You can't land an ollie properly in heels" [electronic version]. *Gender and Education, 17*(3), 229–248.

Kohlberg, L. (1981). *Essays on moral development*. San Francisco: Harper and Row.

LeBlanc, L. (1999). *Pretty in punk: Girls' gender resistance in a boys' subculture*. New Brunswick, NJ: Rutgers University Press.

Lemish, D. (1998). "Spice Girls" talk: A case study in the development of gendered identity. In S. A. Inness (Ed.), *Millennium girls: Today's girls and their cultures* (pp. 145–167). New York: Rowman and Littlefield.

Lemish, D. (2003). Spice world: Constructing femininity the popular way [electronic version]. *Popular Music and Society, 26*(1), 17–29.

Lenhart, A., & Madden, M. (2005). *Teen content creators and consumers*. Washington, D.C.: Pew Internet & American Life Project. Retrieved January 23, 2006, from http://www.pewinternet.org/.

Levine, M. P., Smolak, L., & Hayden, H. (1994). The relation of sociocultural factors to eating attitudes and behaviors among middle school girls. *Journal of Early Adolescence, 14*, 471–490.

Martin, M. C., & Gentry, J. W. (1997). Stuck in the model trap: The effects of beautiful models in ads on female pre-adolescents and adolescents. *Journal of Advertising, 26*, 19–33.

Martin, M. C., & Kennedy, P. F. (1993). Advertising and social comparison: Consequences for female pread-olescents and adolescents. *Psychology and Marketing, 10*, 513–530.

Martino, W., & Pallotta-Chiarolli, M. (2003). *So what's a boy? Addressing issues of masculinity and schooling*. Berkshire: Open University Press.

Mazzarella, S. R. (2005). Claiming a space: The cultural economy of teen girl fandom on the web. In S. R. Mazzarella (Ed.), *Girl wide web: Girls, the Internet, and the negotiation of identity* (pp. 141–160). New York: Peter Lang.

Mazzarella, S. R., & Pecora, N. (1999). *Growing up girls: Popular culture and the construction of identity*. New York: Peter Lang.

Mazzarella, S. R., & Pecora, N. (2007). Girls in crisis: Newspaper coverage of adolescent girls. *Journal of Communication Inquiry, 31*(1), 6-27.

McRobbie, A. (1982). *Feminism for girls*. London: Routledge.

McRobbie, A. (1991). *Feminism and youth culture: From Jackie to Just Seventeen*. Boston: Unwin Hyman.

McRobbie, A. (1993). Shut up and dance: Youth culture and changing modes of femininity. *Cultural Studies, 7*(3), 406–426.

McRobbie, A. (2000). *Feminism and youth culture: From Jackie to Just Seventeen* (2nd ed.). London: Routledge.

McRobbie, A. (2004). Post-feminism and popular culture. *Feminist Media Studies*, 4(3), 255–264.

McRobbie, A., & Garber, J. (1976). Girls and subcultures. In S. Hall & T. Jefferson (Eds.), *Resistance through ritual*. London: Hutchinson.

McRobbie, A., & Nava, M. (1984). *Gender and generation*. London: Macmillan.

Merskin, D. (2005). Making an about-face: Jammer girls and the World Wide Web. In S. R. Mazzarella (Ed.), *Girl wide web: Girls, the Internet, and the negotiation of identity* (pp. 51–67). New York: Peter Lang.

Newsom, V. A. (2004). Young females as superheros: Super heroines in the animated *Sailor Moon*. *Femspec*, 5(2), 57–81.

Orenstein, P. (1994). *Schoolgirls: Young women, self-esteem, and the confidence gap*. New York: Doubleday.

Owen, S. A. (1999). Vampires, postmodernity, and postfeminism: *Buffy the Vampire Slayer*. *Journal of Popular Film and Television*, 27(2), 24–28.

Peirce, K. (1990). A feminist theoretical perspective on the socialization of teenage girls through *Seventeen* magazine. *Sex Roles*, 23, 491–500.

Peirce, K. (1993). Socialization of teenage girls through teen-magazine fiction: The making of a new woman or an old lady? *Sex Roles*, 29, 59–68.

Piaget, J. (1965). *The moral judgment of the child*. New York: Free Press.

Pipher, M. (1994). *Reviving Ophelia: Saving the selves of adolescent girls*. New York: Ballantine.

Pomerantz, S., Currie, D. H., & Kelly, D. M. (2004). Sk8er girls: Skateboarders, girlhood and feminism in motion [electronic version]. *Women's Studies International Forum*, 27, 547–557.

Potts, D. (2001). Channeling girl power: Positive female media images in *The Powerpuff Girls*. *Similie: Studies in Media and Information Literacy Education*, 1(4). Retrieved February 14, 2006, from http://www.utpjournals.com/jour.ihtml?lp=simile/issue4/potts1.html.

Railton, D. (2001). The gendered carnival of pop [electronic version]. *Popular Music*, 20(3), 321–331.

Rakow, L. F., & Rakow, C. S. (1999). Educating Barbie. In S. R. Mazzarella & N. O. Pecora (Eds.), *Growing up girls: Popular culture and the construction of identity* (pp. 11–20). New York: Peter Lang.

Riordan, E. (2001). Commodified agents and empowered girls: Consuming and producing feminism. *Journal of Communication Inquiry*, 25(3), 279–297.

Ross, S. (2004). Dangerous demons: Fan response to girls' power, girls' bodies, and girls' beauty in *Buffy the Vampire Slayer*. *Femspec*, 5(2), 82–100.

Rutkowski, A. (2002). Why chicks dig vampires: Sex blood, and Buffy. *Iris: A Journal about Women*, 45, 12–18.

Sadker, M., & Sadker, D. (1994). *Failing at fairness: How America's schools cheat girls*. New York: Charles Scribner's Sons.

Schilt, K. (2003). "A little too ironic": The appropriation and packaging of riot grrrl politics by mainstream female musicians. *Popular Music and Society*, 26(3), 5–16.

Stern, S. R. (1999). Adolescent girls' expression on Web home pages: Spirited, sombre and self-conscious sites. *Convergence: The Journal of Research into New Media Technologies*, 5(4), 22–41.

Stern, S. R. (2002a). Sexual selves on the World Wide Web: Adolescent girls' home pages as sites for sexual self-expression. In J. D. Brown, J. R. Steele, & K. Walsh-Childers (Eds.), *Sexual teens, sexual media: Investigating media's influence on adolescent sexuality* (pp. 265–285). Mahwah, NJ: Lawrence Erlbaum.

Stern, S. R. (2002b). Virtually speaking: Girls' self-disclosure on the WWW [electronic version]. *Women's Studies in Communication*, 25(2), 223–252.

Stern, S. R. (2004). Expressions of identity online: Prominent features and gender differences in adolescents' World Wide Web home pages. *Journal of Broadcasting & Electronic Media, 48*(2), 218–243.

Stern, S. T., (2007). *Instant identity: Girls and the culture of instant messaging.* New York: Peter Lang.

Stumbar, S. E., & Eisenstein, Z. (1999). Girlhood pastimes: "American Girls" and the rest of us. In S. R. Mazzarella & N. O. Pecora (Eds.), *Growing up girls: Popular culture and the construction of identity* (pp. 87–96). New York: Peter Lang.

Sweeney, K. (2005). Girls make movies: The emergence of woman-led filmmaking initiatives for teenage girls. *Afterimage, 33*(3), 37–42.

Sweeney, K. (2007). *Maiden USA: An icon comes of age.* New York: Peter Lang.

Takayoshi, P., Huot, E., & Huot, M. (1999). No boys allowed: The World Wide Web as clubhouse for girls. *Computers and Composition, 16,* 89–106.

Taylor, J. M., Gilligan, C., & Sullivan, A. M. (1995). *Between voice and silence: Women and girls, race and relationship.* Cambridge, MA: Harvard University Press.

Thiel, S. (2005). "IM me": Identity construction and gender negotiation in the world of adolescent girls and instant messaging. In S. R. Mazzarella (Ed.), *Girl wide web: Girls, the Internet, and the negotiation of identity* (pp. 179–201). New York: Peter Lang.

Turner, S. L., Hamilton, H., Jacobs, M., Angood, L. M., & Dwyer, D. H. (1997). The influence of fashion magazines on the body image satisfaction of college women: An exploratory analysis. *Adolescence, 32,* 603–614.

Valdivia, A. N., & Bettivia, R. S. (1999). A guided tour through one adolescent girl's culture. In S. R. Mazzarella & N. O. Pecora (Eds.), *Growing up girls: Popular culture and the construction of identity* (pp. 159–174). New York: Peter Lang.

Vaughan, K. K., & Fouts, G. T. (2003). Changes in television and magazine exposure and eating disorder symptomatology [electronic version]. *Sex Roles, 49*(7/8), 313–320.

Wald, G. (1998). Just a girl? Rock music, feminism, and the cultural construction of female youth [electronic version]. *Signs, 23*(3), 585–610.

Wald, G. (2004). Review of the book *Feminism and youth culture. Signs, 29,* 1144–1148.

Weinraub, B. (1998, February 23). Who's lining up at the box office? Lots and lots of girls [electronic version]. *New York Times,* p. E1.

Wilcox, R. (2005). *Why Buffy matters: The art of* Buffy the Vampire Slayer. New York: I. B. Tauris.

Wilcox, R., & Lavery, D. (Eds.). (2002). *Fighting the forces: What's at stake in* Buffy the Vampire Slayer. Lanham, MD: Rowman and Littlefield.

Willis, P. (1977). *Learning to labour.* Aldershot: Saxon House.

CHAPTER EIGHTEEN

Just How Commercialized Is Children's Culture?

MATTHEW P. MCALLISTER

Bratz are big! Beginning in 2001, Bratz became a cultural sensation, at least for a certain demographic in the United States and Europe. If you don't know Bratz, you were not an eight-year-old girl in the early 2000s. In their original form, they are dolls (marketed to ten-year-old "tween" girls and even younger) with stylish—some might say slutty—clothes, large anime-like eyes, Angelina Jolie–esque mega-lips, and the catchphrase "Girls with a Passion for Fashion!" How big are Bratz? They sold $2.5 billion in global merchandise in 2004, and their marketing success led the advertising trade press to declare about their "old-school" competition, "Barbie hits the skids" (Stanley, 2005).

Bratz are also controversial. Critics have attacked Bratz for being too sexual given their young target market and for even promoting alcohol consumption through their poolside or dance-club play sets, at least one of which came with champagne-style glasses (Linn, 2004; Schor, 2005); one anti-Bratz commentator asked, "What next? Beer for the dolls? A mirror, some fake cocaine?" (Beckham, 2005, p. 7).

But, above all, Bratz are commercialized. At first glance, this is pretty obvious: they are, after all, dolls that are sold and advertised. But they also are dolls with an unapologetic consumer orientation. Their "passion for fashion" is explicitly about consumption in a way that's even greater than the Queen of All Dolls, Barbie. Barbie was about collecting Barbies, and maybe *someday* having things like Barbie does (Cross, 1997; Kline, 1993; Rogers, 1999). Since the Bratz dolls are closer in age to the girls who play with them than Barbie, girls are not just encouraged to dress and accessorize the dolls, but they are encouraged to dress and accessorize *like* the dolls (more on this below). In addition to the dolls, the Bratz line also offers a huge range of product merchandise: in February 2006, Amazon.com listed 360 different Bratz items in the "Toy and Games" category alone. Besides the dolls, clothes for the dolls, and play sets, one can also buy Bratz bedding, shoes, sleeping bags, makeup kits, a digital camera, and an MP3 player (the last in the shape of a lipstick). Of course, ads for these products may be found throughout much of children's television.

Finally, though, and perhaps most central to this chapter, Bratz, beyond the toys and other products, are also a media brand. There are scores of Bratz books. There are Bratz DVDs, Bratz video games (customize their virtual outfits!), and a Bratz CD (featuring the music of the Bratz Rock Angelz). There's a *Bratz* magazine, which has many pictures of the dolls but also, like a weird-kiddie version of *Vogue*, offers kids specific clothing tips to copy the look of Bratz. There's a Saturday-morning Bratz TV show on the Fox broadcast network, co-produced by 4Kids Entertainment (a children's television production company) and MGA Entertainment, the Bratz company. And these media forms—media forms that are de facto ads for the toys—do not just encourage girls to buy Bratz dolls and merchandise. Nor do they just encourage kids to buy the look of Bratz for themselves. In the Bratz media stories, shopping and buying are celebrated. Bratz media bring, then, a commercial mentality—the ideology of advertising—to the programming. One Bratz book is entitled *Bratz: All Night Mall Party*. Another book aimed at an even younger demographic (four to eight years old) is *Lil' Bratz Lil' Shopping Adventures!*

Enough with Bratz (for now). Bratz may seem extreme, but they actually are fairly indicative of the current state of children's media and culture, in which the logic of licensing and selling is fundamental to the creation—and often the messages—of high-profile cultural texts for kids, cultural texts that are also surrounded by explicit product commercials and media promotions. So let's now answer the title question of this chapter: kids' culture in the United States is pretty darned commercialized. By "commercialized" I mean the involvement of advertising or product promotion in the creation or funding (direct or indirect) of media and cultural phenomena (see the discussion in Mosco, 1996). Of course, much of our culture—kids' and adults'—is commercialized: we see ads everywhere, and nearly all of our media are funded and influenced by advertising. But to say that children's culture is commercialized doesn't quite get at the extreme level of commercial involvement. Again like a lot of adult culture, kids' culture is really *hyper*commercialized (to use a term from McChesney, 1999). Advertising, marketing, and selling pervade nearly all elements of modern kids' culture. The claim that modern children's culture is commercialized (even when using the *hyper* prefix) is not in much dispute: just about everyone agrees on this. In dispute are the differences this may make, and the ways commercialism may harm or help (or both) kids and society generally.

This chapter will try to do several things. First, it will offer a brief history of commercialism in children's culture. Then, it will discuss some of the recent factors that seem to increase, or at least encourage in new ways, commercialism in modern kids' media. Finally, some of the relevant issues and debates of commercialization in modern kids' culture will be touched upon. Just to make things manageable, the discussion here will focus on the U.S. experience, arguably the most commercialized of all countries in terms of its media.

Historical Precedents

Historical reviews of children's culture argue that commercialization and licensing have been a part of this culture since virtually the beginnings of the modern industrialized age (see, for example, Cross, 2004; Kline, 1993). The Yellow Kid, one of the first regularly appearing characters in a U.S. newspaper comic strip, in the late 1800s, for example, spun off a large number of authorized and bootleg merchandise. This precedent led the way for even heavier commercial integration of later popular characters such as Buster Brown, originally a comic-strip character that later became so commercialized that its enduring legacy was as a children's shoe mascot (Cross, 2004; Gordon, 1998). Popular characters were licensed to different media. Superman appeared in comic books, newspaper comic strips, film serials, radio (and later television) programs, and even a novel. In the same vein, icons that were originally created for advertising could also be licensed as toys or other products, such as the Campbell Soup kids (Cross, 2004).

One trend that has developed is the gradual use of children's culture to sell products directly to children. Early industrialized toys and games tended to target parents as the market more than children themselves. There were exceptions to this, even in the early 1900s, however. Children's magazines were economically designed to sell to children early on; beginning in the 1930s and '40s, comic books and radio also produced content for kids that was advertising supported (Cross, 2004). Sometimes, of course, the advertising would bleed over into the content, such as a Superman comic-book story that featured a real tie-in licensed toy—the Krypto-Ray Gun—as a plot device (Gordon, 1998). Radio, as a sponsored medium in which advertisers often acted as program producers, would even more fundamentally blur the commercial into the program as a way to sell to kids. This is why Ralphie, in the 1983 movie *A Christmas Story*, experiences such a crushing loss of innocence when decoding a secret message from the radio program *Little Orphan Annie*, prompting him to exclaim, "'Be sure to drink your Ovaltine.' Ovaltine? A crummy commercial? Son of a bitch!"

These dynamics increased dramatically with the rise of broadcast television. When looking at the history of kids' TV programming, the level of commercialism has ebbed and flowed with both the regulatory environment of the time as well as industrial and technological trends. In the late 1940s and early 1950s, many early kids' television programs were "sustaining," meaning that they had no advertising or sponsor. However, even this noncommercial strategy had a commercial purpose: early television companies saw children's programming as a way to entice parents to buy television sets (Pecora, 1998). Such very early nonadvertised programming may also have been designed as a tactic to convince (or, perhaps, con) the FCC and other regulators into thinking that this new medium—a federally licensed medium—would be "responsible" to the public interest.

This promotional coyness did not last long, and as the sponsorship model grabbed hold of children's programming, viewers saw a level of commercial-program integration that was crude both in its explicitness and in its lack of coherent marketing strategy. Techniques such as "host selling"—where human or puppet hosts of programs would tout their sponsor's product—and "integrated commercials"—skits or other program segments featuring sponsors' products—were commonplace (Alexander et al., 1998; Samuel, 2001). Kids would soon get used to selling as part of the show, such as *Howdy Doody*'s Buffalo Bob Smith touting Wonder Bread (Samuel, 2001).

With the 1955 debut of *The Mickey Mouse Club* on ABC and the various toy merchandise that followed, the links between toys and children's programming strengthened. Companies such as Mattel used kids' shows to sell directly and year-round to children, and increased the number of licensed products based upon children's programming as well as visually oriented toys that looked good on television (Cross, 2004; Kline, 1993). Although the 1960s saw the single-sponsorship model gradually erode, the migration of children's network programming to Saturday morning was primarily in response to kids marketers' need to efficiently reach specialized niche audiences (Mittell, 2004). A potentially more activist stance by the Federal Communications Commission and Federal Trade Commission in the late 1960s and '70s helped somewhat to keep growing commercialism in check, but a movement toward free-market ideologies in the late 1970s—reinforced by the election of Ronald Reagan as president—ended any significant federal challenges (Cross, 2004). Beginning in the early 1980s, even modest industry self-regulation of children's TV programming was virtually eliminated (Johnson & Young, 2003; Kunkel, 2001). (See chapter 2 for a complete history of the regulation of children's media and chapter 7 for a discussion of the role and effects of advertising in children's media.)

The 1980s, then, saw a greater integration of toys and culture that influenced later legislation but also established models of strategic synergy that still exist today to perhaps an even greater extent (Pecora, 1998). Licensing activity in the film industry beginning in the late 1970s played a key role. The nature and success of *Star Wars* toys, according to historian Gary Cross, "helped to change the meaning of play" by offering not just Luke Skywalker and Darth Vader action figures, but practically everyone in that whole galaxy far, far away. The prolific *Star Wars* toy line promised near-complete duplication of characters and sets from the films such that "the child was invited to stage scenes from the movies, to play a god orchestrating a miniature world of high-tech adventure" (Cross, 2004, p. 158).

Other toy companies could not help notice the success of the Jedi. Some companies altered the formula by turning (1) from film to TV and (2) from a stance that was reactive to cultural trends to one that was profoundly proactive. Implementing what Thomas Engelhardt (1986) called "The Shortcake Strategy," toy companies would develop toy lines that were created to be turned into television programs. The toys, then, come first, the TV shows second. Such product lines—like Care Bears, Masters of the Universe, G.I. Joe (the post-Vietnam, Cobra-hating version) and of course Strawberry Shortcake—were comprised of multiple characters and emphasized the importance of teamwork, both illustrated by the plots of programs. The purpose of the TV show, then, was to promote the toys: they were "program-length commercials," the small-fry version of infomercials. Product commercials for the toys also aired during the programs, just in case kids didn't get the message. This era helped to legitimize the large amount of licensed-based programs we still see today, such as the video game–influenced *Sonic X* and the huge global phenomenon of the late 1990s, *Pokémon* (Tobin, 2004).

Another consequence was a regulatory backlash that, as explained in chapter 2, resulted in the Children's Television Act of 1990. This legislation implemented or reasserted rules and applied to both cable and broadcast television for children. The act placed several restrictions on commercialism, including a limit on the amount of time devoted to product commercials, the mandated use of "bumpers" or program separators, designed to separate programs from commercials, and the elimination of "program-length commercials." However, as a result of industry lobbying, the definition of this last concept is not nearly as restricted as it could be. Instead of being defined as TV shows based on toys (which would bump off shows like *Bratz*), the term is instead defined as "a program associated with a product in which commercials for that product are aired" (quoted in Kunkel, 2001). A show based on Bratz is okay, but no commercials for Bratz dolls during *Bratz* the show. Later in that decade and addressing the Internet, the Children's Online Privacy Protection Act of 1998 (COPPA) restricted Web sites both in terms of collecting information about users under thirteen and therefore sharing such information to third-party marketers without explicit, verifiable parental consent.

So things have to be better than they were in the 1950s, right? The Children's Television Act, after all, is a sweeping piece of regulation that applies to both ABC and Nickelodeon. We no longer see "host selling" on children's television as a consequence. Online data collection about kids is also regulated. But if things should be better, then why do critics say that the single biggest change in consumer culture since the 1990s—at any level—has been marketers' "imperative to target kids" (Schor, 2005, p. 12) or that we need to "protect our children from the onslaught of marketing and advertising" (Linn, 2004, cover)? Why do academics write that "[t]he explosive growth in the children's market over the last two decades is responsible for a sea-change in the media" (Preston & White, 2004, p. 126)? Why did consumer advocates in 2006 feel the need to file a $2 billion lawsuit against Viacom and Kellogg's for being too chummy and effective in their cross promotions (via such products as SpongeBob SquarePants Wild Bubble Berry Pop-Tarts), thereby perpetuating childhood obesity (Thompson, 2006)? It's because, despite legislation like the Children's Television Act or COPPA, the commercialization of children's culture has increased dramatically since the 1980s. The next section explains a few of the reasons why this is so.

The Modern Context of Kids' Commercialism

This section will focus on three elements that increase the pressure to blur differences between culture and commercial with children's media: (1) recent incentives to create "aggressive" advertising, (2) the growth of synergistic, mega-media corporations, and (3) the proliferation of new media (creating new marketing and media-selling venues).

Part of the reason we're seeing increased commercialization in children's culture is that, as noted at the beginning of this chapter, we are seeing this accelerated movement in all of culture, not just kids' (Andersen, 1995; Budd et al., 1999; Jacobson & Mazur, 1995; McAllister, 1996; McChesney, 1999). In the 1980s, we saw trends that have either frustrated or, conversely, delighted advertisers, with the result being more aggressive and, therefore, more intrusive promotional forms. Television technologies like the remote control and recording devices (VCRs and DVRs) have made it easier for television audiences to "escape" the traditional thirty-second spot advertisement. The growing amount of advertising in our society (often called "clutter") also reduces the effectiveness of traditional advertising techniques, as one ad might be lost in an avalanche of modern advertising. New media like the Internet and cable television threaten to reduce advertising revenue of traditional media like newspapers, magazines, and network television. These traditional media, then, might be willing to strike permissive deals with advertisers given their desperation to avoid becoming mediated dinosaurs.

The above factors have led to many intrusive promotional trends by advertisers, either because they feel they have to do these things to counter trends (DVRs, clutter), or they now are allowed to do these things (traditional media desperation for ad dollars). We have seen over the last twenty years, then, an increase in such promotional techniques as sponsorship (like the Tostitos Fiesta Bowl). Product placement is routine in both film and television these days, even "plot-enhancing" product placements like FedEx in *Castaway* or the iPod in an 2005 episode of NBC's *The Office*. Other techniques like "place-based advertising" in such locations as airports, medical facilities, and schools; and viral marketing—the use of manufactured word-of-mouth or chat-room conversations to promote products—would also be part of this promotional aggressiveness.

A trend that is strongly linked to this commercial push but also has its own promotional trajectory is the continued domination of corporate media synergy (Bagdikian, 2004; McChesney, 1999). With the growth of media entertainment conglomerates sparked by such factors as deregulation, digital convergence, and globalization, larger media corporations have grown larger in their search for "synergistic efficiencies." Synergy encourages media corporations to grow by acquiring different media outlets in which licensed products can be produced, distributed, and exhibited. From an entertainment point of view, then, a synergistically pure media conglomerate would own different subsidiaries dealing with books, comic books, film, recorded music, television, video games, and Web sites. Such corporations, then, are promotionally oriented, with one subsidiary, through shared licensing, promoting the other subsidiaries (and often the corporate brand as a whole). While *Star Wars* may have shown the economic value of prolific toy and licensing output, it was 1989's *Batman* that showed how one corporation (at that time Warner Communications) can move a character license effectively through different internally owned media outlets, creating one massive, multimedia "commodity inter-text" (Meehan, 1991).

Synergistic companies that are especially relevant to children's culture are News Corp. (Kinder, 1999), Disney (Budd & Kirsch, 2005; Wasko, 2001), Time Warner (Sandler, 2003), and Viacom (Hendershot, 2004). This ownership pattern can be seen with children's television, given that Viacom owns both Nickelodeon and CBS's Saturday-morning lineup, Disney owns the Disney Channel and ABC's Saturday-morning lineup, News Corp. controls Fox's Saturday children's programming, and Time Warner is the parent corporation for both the Cartoon Network and the Kids WB. A key implication of this is that these conglomerates are simultaneously among the largest advertisers of media products in the world, and, as owners of media supported by advertising, they are also among the largest receivers of advertising revenue in the world.

A third factor in the enhanced commercial/promotional ethos of kids' culture is the use of new media technologies. Obviously, the media landscape has changed dramatically since the 1980s with the creation and diffusion of digital media such as the Internet, video-game systems, DVDs (now a bigger revenue generator than films released in theaters), and mobile media like MP3 players and cell phones with downloadable media options. These have all significantly influenced how product manufacturers and media corporations operate. These new media serve multiple functions. They can be integrated into the larger corporate synergy, promoting other properties. They themselves can be sold, generating direct sales revenue. They can be used to carry product commercials, generating indirect advertising revenue. And all of them are key players in the commercialization of children's culture.

Given these factors, what are some of the ways that we see children's culture being commercialized in the modern age?

Categories of Kids' Commercialization

The Commercial Logic of Media Systems

Let's just start out with the basic one: unsurprisingly, sales are at the heart of children's culture. This is obvious to see when we're talking about "direct" sales—like kids buying, or influencing their parents to buy, DVDs, books, and CDs. But most children's media, in some way, is also supported by advertising sales. The history of broadcasting shows that commercial interests fundamentally shaped the development of radio and television (McChesney, 1993). When kids (or any audience members) watch TV, they are being sold to advertisers (Smythe, 1977). Child viewers are "hailed" as consumers by the system, not as children to be educated or publics to be engaged. Commercial interests, then, will do and say whatever is in their legal rights (and sometimes beyond such rights) to persuade kids to purchase or influence a purchase. Media companies are economically rewarded to support that commercial imperative; economically, programs are subordinate to the ads.

Given this, it is no surprise that commercials and programs look and sound alike, despite mandated separators, and often share similar kid-appealing themes of fun adventure, kid empowerment, and anti-adultism (McAllister & Giglio, 2005). Networks will often partner with product advertisers to give these advertisers more bang for their buck. For example, a cross-promotional commercial for the Green Slime flavor of Airheads candy aired repeatedly on Nickelodeon in 2003. *Green Slime* is a copyrighted phrase associated with the Nickelodeon brand, and the Nick logo was featured in the ad. The ads' narrator orders, "Log on to Airheads.nick.com to vote in the Airheads Green Slime flavor poll." The connection between advertiser and network is symbolized by the very Web address that combines the advertiser and the network name.

The Power of the Media Brand

As noted, children's media companies do not just carry other companies' advertising, they also have their own products to advertise and promote. In this case, media companies use children's culture to "brand" themselves. They sell their own products with messages and appeals that, like commercials, exploit kids' desires and need for autonomy (Preston & White, 2004; White & Preston, 2005; Sandler, 2003). This has several implications. First, many commercials for synergistic products (an ad for the DVD of Disney's *Bambi II*) will air on subsidiary networks (ABC and ABC Family, both owned by Disney). But it will also mean that promotions for shows with Disney in the title will air—including promos for shows on other owned channels—and these promotions will not be counted as advertisements under the Children's Television Act of 1990. So, for example, the television series based upon the movie *Lilo & Stitch* is officially titled *Disney's Lilo & Stitch*. In this way, program separators can also integrate Disney iconography, making these separators part of the branding strategy rather than truly separating the commercial from, well, anything noncommercial (McAllister & Giglio, 2005).

Programs themselves on Saturday morning are extremely commodified, of course. The ABC and Disney Channel program *That's So Raven* can be purchased as books, DVDs, CDs (with songs also heard on the Disney Radio Network), video games, calendars, a "cosmic cosmetic set," cologne spray, and various other merchandise—all for sale at various outlets, including the Disney Store.

New Integration, Old Policy

Although such legislation as the Children's Television Act and COPPA place some limits on some media, there are plenty of loopholes in the system, loopholes that are enacted by new technologies and new corporate trends. The branding of promos and separators are such loopholes. Similarly, while the FCC bans the narrowly defined "program-length commercials" on cable and broadcast TV, no such restriction exists on media like the Internet and DVDs. This works both for licenses that were originally media oriented, and licenses that were also originally toys or even advertising mascots.

Web sites often combine media characters, product advertisers, and shopping opportunities in ways that virtually eradicate these differences. Web sites like that of the Cartoon Network, for instance, have a "Shop" link (although there is a nonenforceable disclaimer that says "You must be at least 18 years old to make a purchase"). This link allows visitors to either "Shop by [Product] Category," or "Shop by Show," so one can search for, say, *Codename: Kids Next Door* toys. Similarly, branded Web sites for product advertisers such as Postopia.com (for Post foods) features games such as the Kool-Aid "Skip and See Riddle Show." If you click on the Kool-Aid Jammers icon, you can read about the latest Kool-Aid products. Ties with Time Warner characters are also found on this site, so that you see an ad for the latest DVD of the *Flintstones*.

And although there can legally be no commercials for Bratz products during the *Bratz* TV show, no such commercial restrictions exist for Bratz magazines or DVDs. On the *Bratz Rock Angelz* DVD, one can click on the "Bratz Rock Angelz Cross Sell Gallery" to see and read about other merchandise that's for sale. One can also watch the "Bratz Rock Angelz CD TV spot" (a commercial that is billed, then, as a "DVD extra").

Dangers and Dilemmas

Often, when I lecture about these issues to students, a question that may be asked is, "So what? Does it really hurt that kids are sold to, and that there's a blurring of the commercial with the culture?" It is true, as we'll see, that there is not complete agreement about this issue among scholars of society and culture. But many believe that these commercial characteristics are harmful, a position to which I am sympathetic.

The mix of the commercial and the cultural, adding in modern marketing research techniques, may make the construction of promotional messages especially manipulative and strategic, involving consistent messages that celebrate consumption in a variety of media. Some critics argue that heavy immersion in commercial/consumer culture can lead to the cultivation of commodity-influenced self-concepts that are fraught with potential social and economic division and insecurity, vulnerable to the commercial message, and therefore potentially harmful to well-being (Schor, 2004). The consistent "pro-kid, anti-adult" message found in children's media and commercials, coupled with the "nag factor" commercialism encourages, may add stress to the household (Schor, 2004). The drive for ever more efficient niche marketing may entice media creators and marketers to target ever-younger potential consumers, even those less than a year old (Linn, 2004). Products that are sold on television may even be physically harmful, such as foods high in sugar and fat (Harrison & Marske, 2005). Commercially based culture like Postopia.com and *The M&M's Counting Board Book* (recommended reading level: baby to preschool) again spreads such influence beyond the contained TV commercial. Another argument has to do with the potential effect of environmental waste on the planet that commodity culture encourages, especially when such values are inculcated at a young age (Jhally, 2000).

Some scholars dispute that a commodity-based children's culture is all bad, however. While recognizing the ideological dilemmas of commodity culture, Ellen Seiter (1993) argues that niche marketing can open up spaces for some groups such as young girls, who otherwise may be undervalued or to a large degree ignored in a predominantly patriarchal culture. Both Seiter and David Buckingham (2000) note the critical stance kids may bring to commercialism, and even the creative power of play with licensed-driven toys and the shared community that kids can construct with them. Maya Götz, Dafna Lemish, Amy Aidman, and Hyesung Moon (2005) conclude from their international, ethnographic study of children's play that commercially supported television viewing does not seem to significantly restrict children's imagination, although such results may have been more clear outside of the United States. Buckingham (2000) further argues that critics of toy-based media content do not understand historical trends that have always blurred the toy-media connection in the industrial age or the complexities of the market.

What to do about the dangers of commercialism in kids' culture is also complex and multidimensional. Critics such as Juliet Schor (2005) and Susan Linn (2004) suggest multifaceted approaches, including activist- and community-group alliances, media literacy programs, the support of alternative and children-created media, parental awareness and mediation, and increased lobbying for more assertive legislation for children's consumer rights and against excessive commercialism. Although it's likely that he would be in favor of many of these ideas, Buckingham (2000) warns against the "wag of the finger" approach to children and their culture, especially with media literacy programs. He argues that when adults bad-mouth to kids the commercial culture that kids take pleasure in, it reinforces the distance between kids and adults and becomes a self-defeating teaching tactic. In a "back-at-ya" response, though, Shirley Steinberg and Joe Kincheloe (2004, p. 10) argue that stances like Buckingham's are too dismissive of media literacy efforts that reveal manipulative techniques and that such stances even encourage a "pedagogy of nihilism" that justifies educational apathy about commercialism and underplays the gross power discrepancy between corporate marketers and children.

Going back to our opening example, there is no doubt that many girls are very much into Bratz and have an accompanying passion for fashion. For some of them this attraction may amount to very little in terms of their lives. Others may benefit from the themes of girl power and friendship that accompany the consumption orientation in Bratz and the larger commercial culture that targets them. But make no doubt that there is a targeting, fueled by an increasingly elaborate and well-funded targeting system.

The resources of the children's cultural industries—fed by and integrated with the children's commercial industries—are formidable and, I believe, quite destructive on the whole. Scholars have argued that anti-commercial critics often seem engaged in unreasonable and emotional "moral panics" that blind complexities (Götz and colleagues [2005] make such charges against anti-TV critics, for instance). When I see the incredible level of commercialism that drives all of culture—not just for kids—I will admit that, yes, I'm a little bit worried, even sometimes panicked, about generations of people whose life passion is for fashion.

DISCUSSION QUESTIONS

1   In what ways are children's media content and the product advertising adjacent to this content similar in sounds, language, visual style, and themes?

2   How do large corporations that specialize in children's media try to brand themselves to children? What themes and symbols do they use in this branding?

3   What are recent examples of "cross promotions" between media companies and product advertisers in children's media? What messages do these cross promotions send to kids about the connection of advertising and media content?

4   What are some of the most important negative consequences of the commercialization of children's culture? What are some positive consequences?

EXERCISES

1   Find a schedule of Saturday-morning television programs targeted at children. How many of the programs are based upon licensed properties? Be sure to list programs based upon established media characters as well as programs based upon toys or other children's products.

2   Watch an hour of children's television, noting especially what Web sites are advertised or promoted during this time. Visit these Web sites and document the ways that media brands and children's products are further promoted and sold in virtual space.

REFERENCES

Alexander, A., Benjamin, L. M., Hoerrner, K., & Roe, D. (1998). "We'll be back in a moment": A content analysis of advertisements in children's television in the 1950s. *Journal of Advertising, 27*(3), 1–9.

Andersen, R. (1995). *Consumer culture and TV programming*. Boulder, CO: Westview.

Bagdikian, B. (2004). *The new media monopoly* (7th ed.). Boston: Beacon.

Beckham, B. (2005, November 17). Childhood lost to pop culture. *Boston Globe*, p. 7.

Buckingham, D. (2000). *After the death of childhood: Growing up in the age of electronic media*. Cambridge: Polity.

Budd, M., Craig, S., & Steinman, C. (1999). *Consuming environments: Television and commercial culture*. New Brunswick, NJ: Rutgers University Press.

Budd, M., & Kirsch, M. H. (Eds.). (2005). *Rethinking Disney: Private control, public dimensions*. Middletown, CT: Wesleyan University Press.

Cross, G. (1997). *Kids' stuff: Toys and the changing world of American childhood*. Cambridge, MA: Harvard University Press.

Cross, G. (2004). *The cute and the cool: Wondrous innocence and modern American children's culture*. New York: Oxford University Press.

Engelhardt, T. (1986). The shortcake strategy. In T. Gitlin (Ed.), *Watching television* (pp. 68–110). New York: Pantheon.

Gordon, I. (1998). *Comic strips and consumer culture, 1890–1945*. Washington, D.C.: Smithsonian Institution Press.

Götz, M., Lemish, D., Aidman, A., & Moon, H. (2005). *Media and the make-believe worlds of children: When Harry Potter meets Pokémon in Disneyland*. Mahwah, NJ: Lawrence Erlbaum.

Harrison, K., & Marske, A. L. (2005). Nutritional content of foods advertised during television programs children watch most. *American Journal of Public Health, 95*(9), 1568–1574.

Hendershot, H. (Ed.). (2004). *Nickelodeon nation: The history, politics, and economics of America's only TV channel for kids*. New York: New York University Press.

Jacobson, N. F., & Mazur, L. A. (1995). *Marketing madness: A survival guide for a consumer society*. Boulder, CO: Westview.

Jhally, S. (2000). Advertising at the edge of the apocalypse. In R. Andersen & L. Strate (Eds.), *Critical studies in media commercialism* (pp. 27–39). Oxford: Oxford University Press.

Johnson, M. D., & Young, B. M. (2003). Advertising history of televisual media. In E. L. Palmer & B. M. Young (Eds.), *The faces of televisual media: Teaching, violence, selling to children* (2nd ed., pp. 265–285). Mahwah, NJ: Lawrence Erlbaum.

Kinder, M. (1999). Ranging with power on the Fox Kids Network: Or, where on earth is children's educational television? In M. Kinder (Ed.), *Kids' media culture* (pp. 177–203). Raleigh, NC: Duke University Press.

Kline, S. (1993). *Out of the garden: Toys and children's culture in the age of TV marketing*. London: Verso.

Kunkel, D. (2001). Children and television advertising. In D. G. Singer & J. L. Singer (Eds.), *Handbook of children and the media* (pp. 375–393). Thousand Oaks, CA: Sage.

Linn, S. (2004). *Consuming kids: Protecting our children from the onslaught of marketing and advertising*. New York: Anchor.

McAllister, M. P. (1996). *The commercialization of American culture: New advertising, control and democracy*. Thousand Oaks, CA: Sage.

McAllister, M. P., & Giglio, J. M. (2005). The commodity flow of U.S. children's television. *Critical Studies in Media Communication, 22*(1), 26–44.

McChesney, R. W. (1993) *Telecommunications, mass media, and democracy: The battle for the control of U.S. broadcasting, 1928–1935*. New York: Oxford University Press.

McChesney, R. W. (1999). *Rich media, poor democracy: Communication politics in dubious times*. Urbana: University of Illinois Press.

Meehan, E. (1991). "Holy commodity fetish, Batman!" The political economy of a commercial intertext. In R. E. Pearson & W. Uricchio (Eds.), *The many lives of the Batman: Critical approaches to a superhero and his media* (pp. 47–65). New York: Routledge.

Mittell, J. (2004). *Genre and television: From cop shows to cartoons in American culture*. New York: Routledge.

Mosco, V. (1996). *The political economy of communication*. Thousand Oaks, CA: Sage.

Pecora, N. (1998). *The business of children's entertainment*. New York: Guilford.

Preston, E., & White, C. L. (2004). Commodifying kids: Branded identities and the selling of adspace on kids' networks. *Communication Quarterly, 52*(2), 115–128.

Rogers, M. F. (1999). *Barbie culture*. Thousand Oaks, CA: Sage.

Samuel, L. R. (2001). *Brought to you by: Postwar television advertising and the American dream*. Austin: University of Texas Press.

Sandler, K. S. (2003). Synergy nirvana: Brand equity, television animation, and Cartoon Network. In C. A. Stabile & M. Harrison (Eds.), *Prime time animation: Television animation and American culture* (pp. 89–109). New York: Routledge.

Schor, J. B. (2004). *Born to buy.* New York: Scribner.

Seiter, E. (1993). *Sold separately: Children and parents in consumer culture.* New Brunswick, NJ: Rutgers University Press.

Smythe, D. W. (1977). Communications: Blindspot of Western Marxism. *Canadian Journal of Political and Social Theory, 1*(3), 1–27.

Stanley, T. L. (2005, October 31). Barbie hits the skids. *Advertising Age,* p. 1.

Steinberg, S. R., & Kincheloe, J. L. (2004). Introduction: Kinderculture, information saturation, and the socioeducational positioning of children. In S. R. Steinberg & J. L. Kincheloe (Eds.), *Kinderculture: The corporate construction of childhood* (2nd ed., pp. 1–47). Boulder, CO: Westview.

Thompson, S. (2006, January 26). Standing still, Kellogg gets hit with a lawsuit. *Advertising Age,* p. 1.

Tobin, J. (Ed.). (2004). *Pikachu's global adventure: The rise and fall of Pokémon* (pp. 3–11). Durham, NC: Duke University Press.

Wasko, J. (2001). *Understanding Disney: The manufacture of fantasy.* Boston: Polity.

White, C. L., & Preston, E. H. (2005). The spaces of children's programming. *Critical Studies in Media Communication, 22*(3), 239–255.

CHAPTER NINETEEN

When It Comes to Consumer Socialization, Are Children Victims, Empowered Consumers, or Consumers-in-Training?

STEPHEN KLINE

You can't control us in our homes with our parents. You know some day kids will RULE, RULE I tell you, and when it happens you will be banished.

—Ten-year-old male

In this book you already have read about the increasingly influential role that media have played in children's lives over the last fifty years—not only as key information and entertainment resources from which children learn about the social world in which they live (for example, in terms of class, gender, ethnicity, and so on), but also as a channel for advertising that addresses them as consumers growing up in a market economy. Most commentators agree that by age eight, contemporary children are interested in, and knowledgeable about, a wide variety of consumer goods. Today's children have and spend more money than previous generations; they are more knowledgeable about a wider range of brands and marketing; and they have more say in what their families consume (Dotson & Hyatt, 2005; McNeal, 1999). Yet as you also have seen, a recurring theme in this book has been the many ways that mediated childhood has become a site of ideological struggle between old orders and new orders in the modernizing world (Jenks, 1996). From moral panics about comics to video-game violence, the growing commodification of children's lives, coupled with the obesity crisis, has fomented a debate about whether young consumers are unduly pressured by marketing (Linn, 2004). Arguing that advertising pester-power results in conflicts in the family, many adults attribute direct-to-child marketing with making it harder for parents to socialize their children in a healthy manner (Schor, 2004). These concerns have recently resulted in renewed calls for banning food and soft drink advertising to children in both Europe (Cultures of Consumption, 2004) and the United States (Campaign, 2006). Yet the obesity panic has led other commentators to argue that children's growing interest in consumerism should be celebrated as an expression of their freedom to choose their own pleasures, identities, and lifestyles, liberated from their parents' moralizing control (Davies et al., 2000).

Children are interested in advertising and actively choose to watch ads, not only because TV is fun, but also because ads provide them with an important source of information about products they aspire to have, such as snacks, treats, cereals, movies, toys, and games. As Dan Cook explains, cultural studies researchers have questioned the myth of the vulnerable child, arguing that we must now theorize an empowered and savvy child consumer who is "an active, knowing being who makes her or his own meaning out of every morsel of culture" (Cook, 2005, p. 156). This image of the agentive, competent child consumer gets repeated by industry spokespersons when calls for banning advertising to children under age twelve arise, as they have repeatedly over the last forty years (Preston, 2004). In this chapter, I trace this growing controversy by putting our increased interest in children's consumer socialization in a historical context of changing perspectives on the role of parents, educators, peers, and the media. I argue for a definition of consumer socialization that acknowledges that this complex negotiation between generations involves children's "willing" acquisition and identification with the consumption attitudes and skills required of them in a market-intensive society. I then argue that the policy debates have placed excessive attention on the developmentalist issue of children's growing cognitive competence at the expense of the part played by familial, media, and peer social relations within which children acquire their power and identity as consumers. I go on to suggest that from birth children are consumers-in-training as parents participate both consciously and unconsciously in the formations of "taste" and "cultural capital" that children require in a consumer society. Although they are learning to manage their own consumption, they do not do so in contexts of their own making.

The Emerging Debates about Modern Childhood

Social reproduction requires that each society prepare its young by transmitting the common beliefs, roles, identities, and mores to succeeding generations. In most historical societies, rearing of the young took place primarily within the extended family, which was responsible for ensuring that appropriate customs, values, and competencies were communicated, internalized, and practiced by the next generation (Frones, 1995). Recognizing the limited ability of one generation to shape the actions and ideals of the next, Enlightenment thinkers like John Locke and Jean-Jacques Rousseau began a centuries-long debate about the appropriate methods of training future democratic citizens (Kline, 2006). Locke particularly emphasized the formal education of youth as both autonomous and self-regulating individuals, stating, "This I am sure, that if the foundation of it be not laid in the education and principling of the youth, all other endeavors will be in vain." His program for childrearing stressed the importance of parental guidance, discipline, and moral instruction throughout childhood. Locke also touched on children's nutrition, their active leisure, and even their toys, warning that providing them with too many playthings could make them "wanton and careless" (Locke, 1692, as reprinted in Halsall, 1998).

Tracing the evolving intrigue with children's maturational experiences, psycho-historian Lloyd DeMause (1974) noted how educators and psychologists during the nineteenth century fostered and professionalized the idea that character formation was the center of education. The modern curriculum was not solely conceived around literacy and morality taught in the schools, but included a civilizing mission associated with developing the child's understanding of social roles and his or her station in life. In the paintings of the eighteenth century, artists depict this broadening conception of character formation in scenes in which clothes, games, and domestic objects came to be part of the socialization agenda. So, too, the Duke of Wellington's quip that the battle of Waterloo was won on the playing fields of Eton indicated the growing recognition of the role that games and sports played in children's character formation. Developmental psychologists like Jean Piaget expanded this idea, recognizing that the stages of conceptual growth were propelled by children's active and playful exploration of the material world. (Refer to chapter 4 for an application of Piaget's theories to studies of youth and media.) Exploring and manipulating objects, children acted like little scientists, learning to master their world by testing and elaborating their conceptual schemas. During the early twentieth century educational theory thus began to value children's domestic play as a form of active learning, making educational toys the preferred modern tools for fostering mental development (Sutton-Smith, 1986). Believing children learn naturally by "reflecting on doing," early educational experiences became structured around playing with developmental toys, games, and household objects (play houses, shops) rather than rote memorization from books.

Of course, psychologists were not alone in their interest in children's encounters with material goods. Indeed, since the late nineteenth century, parenting advisors picked up on this idea and began recommending specialized products like toys, soap, and clothes as crucial aspects of children's proper upbringing. So, too, marketers increasingly began to depict the family's relationship to goods as an essential part of modern domesticity. As Cook (2004b) has shown, during the 1920s merchandisers began to redesign stores as places where goods for children—from toys to clothes—could be featured. In department store Christmas windows, specialty toy stores, and clothing shops, children were recognized as part of the consumer marketplace: they influenced their parents' purchasing behavior and were seen both as consumers-in-the-making and as purchasers in their own right (Cook, 2004b).

The interest in children's daily consumption was taken one step further by Sigmund Freud's argument that the psychopathologies and neuroses of adult life could be explained by the early emotional disturbances and fantasy life of the child. Freud's crucial insight was that identity formation begins at birth in the simple and intimate relationships of feeding and caring for the child. After all, the child is born programmed but helpless, requiring parental care and attention for many years. Thus, the child's earliest experiences are contingent on the relationship with the provisioning parent. The child, however, is not a tabula rasa. From birth, children can communicate their pleasure by crying or smiling benignly, and often sleep contentedly when they are satisfied. Parents must develop strategies for responding to these communications by either harkening to every cry for hunger or enforcing a schedule that integrates the child's consumption into the established patterns of family life. Freudian psychoanalyst Melanie Klein (1950) stressed these earliest interactions during the oral phase, when children's drive for nutrition at the breast lays the cornerstone of both their social relations and experiences of desire and pleasure. These theories became endlessly discussed in popular parenting guides so that the importance of early consumption experiences had an impact on twentieth-century public discourses about the healthy development of the child. With this discussion, the language of trauma, oral fixation, identity crisis, transitional objects, the Oedipus complex, and personality type also pervaded both academic discourses and popular culture, laying the foundation for our growing anxieties about the modern child's treacherous maturation as a socialized member of an affluent society. (See chapter 3 for a discussion of how such concerns have led to the proliferation of various moral panics about the relationship between youth and media since the early twentieth century.)

The makers of children's goods responded happily to these new ideas about the modern family, in which the provisioning of children's food, toys, storybooks, games, piggy banks, and leisure were becoming the signs of a loving middle-class family. In the 1950s, marketers of children's products, like baby foods, clothes, and toys, joined a growing chorus of health professionals proclaiming the importance of the twinned deities of love and permissive leisure in children's lives, thus banishing the idea that idleness and materialism were harmful. The family circle became a primary motif in advertising; it articulated the warm glow of domestic consumption as the counterpoint to the alienation associated with industrial production (Marchand, 1985). Gary Cross (2004) has shown how the toy industry played a crucial role in the circulation of new ideas about the modern family constellation, articulating clearly how parents could use objects to support the formation of the child's character. The responsibilities and practices of socializing the modern child became a central theme in many ads selling domestic goods, as families not only configured themselves around providing suitable consumer goods for their children, but also became responsible for passing on consumer knowledge and cultural capital. Advertisers used the mother-child trope to emphasize the mother's role in passing on consumer knowledge and skills. Not only does modern Suzy have her mother instructing her in the role of a discriminating homemaker, she has now acquired her own play kitchen where she can practice these skills.

Providing goods that help children become autonomous individuals was celebrated in the fatherly advice offered in Benjamin Spock's best-selling 1964 book, *Baby and Child Care*, which became the bible of postwar American childrearing. Spock advocated a less controlling approach to childrearing that he thought befitted a generation that could claim a windfall of affluence and comfort. Unrestricted leisure and free play were no longer perceived as the "devil's work," but were then seen as necessary conditions for promoting self-regulated consumption. Children's freedom to explore and assess the world for themselves was essential to their healthy maturation, as was parental love and support of their accomplishments. A "helping" strategy was widely discussed in health magazines, promoted in parenting manuals, and also expressed regularly in advertising directed at the fledgling baby boom parent, in which the child's struggles for autonomy and his or her perpetual needs for self-expression were celebrated from birth.

By granting children secure environments and supporting their formation of peer relations and cultural tastes, parents were encouraging children's development *according to their own needs and timing*. As the war economy was transformed into consumer culture, the Spock psychology of supportive parenting was woven into public discourses about leisure for the baby boom generation, yet it also intensified public anxieties about the failure of many parents to curb children's antisocial impulses, idleness, and moral laxity.

Out of the Closet: Consumer Socialization Discovered

Amid the concerns about a passive and spoiled generation, the debates about consumer socialization emerged slowly in the postwar period, paralleling social scientists' broadening awareness of the role that consumption acquired in an increasingly affluent society. A growing concern with materialism was presaged eloquently in Eric Fromm's (1947) attempts to apply Freudian psychoanalysis to the problems associated with the "market orientation" in postwar America. Fromm (1947, p. 66) refused to blame children for the changing patterns of socialization, arguing, "The character of the child develops in response to the character of the parents," whose "methods of child training are in turn determined by the social structure of their culture." Fromm takes pains to differentiate his own interest in consumption from that of Freud by asserting that "the fundamental basis of character is not about the organization of the libido," but instead about how, in the process of living, a person relates himself or herself to the world in two ways: "by acquiring and assimilating things" and "by relating to people (and himself) in a process of socialization." Therefore, consumer socialization must be understood as a historically situated social communication processes whereby individuals *learn to behave willingly* in accordance with the prevailing standards established in our market culture. Fromm (1947, p. 66) expands on this dynamic:

> In order that any society may function well, its members must acquire the kind of character which makes them want to act in the way they have to act as members of the society or of a special class within it. They have to desire what objectively is necessary for them to do. Outer force is replaced by inner compulsion . . . [the child] acquires that character which makes him want to do what he has to do and which he shares with most members of his class and culture.

As a student of Fromm's, sociologist David Riesman and others began to reflect on the consequences of the changing "agencies of socialization" in postwar America (Riesman, with Denney & Glazer, 1950, p. 37). Riesman's account of modern childrearing practices noted the expanding role that consumer goods, play, peers, and popular culture held in the middle-class American family at the time. Middle-class parents who privileged material well-being over self-control were unwittingly changing the lines of force in American culture, as the psychological need for approval became the dominant mode of conformity. Riesman went on to warn that peer pressure, the media, and popular culture were becoming powerful agencies of socialization that had the potential to supplant the inner-directed morality of the traditional American family. With parents no longer willing to enforce a work ethos, moral self-restraint, and delayed gratification, the other-directed child grew up in a field of peer culture whose modes of self-expression focused on the appropriate uses and pleasures of goods.

This new order of affluent, other-directed childrearing was dramatically intensified as commercial television brought a daily supply of marketplace discourses into the American household. The invisible hand of marketing was leaving fingerprints on the screen: the cereals it promoted were too sweet and the toys were too violent for many parents. As children's bedrooms began to fill up with the detritus of modern life promoted by paying sponsors selling Coonskin Caps, Burp Guns, and Barbies, alarm grew about an indulged and spoiled generation. As Lyn Spigel (1998) notes, parents and educators began to ask whether commercial TV was a magic kingdom or a vast commercialized wasteland cultivating a spoiled, aggressive, and uncivilized generation of young couch potatoes. Parents worried that their waning control over their children's moral and psychological maturation emanated from TV: "Worse still, parents may not even know how and where their children have acquired this information. With the mass commercial dissemination of ideas, the parent is so to speak left out of the mediation loop, and the child becomes the direct addressee of the message" (Spigel, 1998, p. 114).

Discussing the implications of changing socialization patterns for consumer behavior, David Riesman and Howard Roseborough (1955) noted an experiment done for the Kroger Food Foundation that documented a group of preteen boys and girls who were taken to a supermarket to choose twenty free items. The researchers were surprised to discover that children acted like adult consumers: they didn't pig out on candy, toys, chocolate, and ice cream, but acted like price-conscious adults, sometimes taking home large bags of flour and other consumer durables. Like adults, children in a mass-mediated society seemed to have acquired the social roles, norms, and values in which consumption of food and beverages, clothes, toys and games, appliances, tools, furniture, transportation, and leisure technologies all embodied a new lifestyle performative identity. From this experiment, the authors concluded that other-directed consumer socialization prepared the youthful consumers with an understanding of the roles, norms, and pleasures anticipated by their status in middle-class life.

These early studies did much to foster the market's embrace of child consumers. Encouraged by evidence of youthful interest in food, toys, and media, companies exponentially escalated their investments in promotions directed at these fledgling potential customers (McNeal, 1999). In department stores and supermarkets, in comics and the media, on buses, street corners, and even in the schools, merchants beckoned to children directly, tentatively at first, but with increasing conviction and confidence over time (Kline, 1993). With children watching television for three hours a day, consumer education had become a major part of children's informal learning from that medium. During the late 1960s, traditionalist parents grew alarmed by the materialist values that advertising seemed to promote to their children.

Under the Microscope: Consumer Socialization Research Becomes Politicized

The widening rift between the traditional values of the American family and the realities of living in a consumerist society reached a fever pitch in the mid-1970s. In 1977 sociologist Daniel Bell saw in the emerging consumer culture a reflection of the deeper "cultural contradiction" in advanced capitalism, in which people were caught between the opposing poles of contemporary economic and cultural dynamics: "The social structure today is ruled by an economic principle of rationality defined in terms of efficiency in the allocation of resources; the culture, in contrast, is prodigal, promiscuous, dominated by an anti-rational, anti-intellectual temper" of consumer profligacy (Bell, 1977, p. 432). Given the growing body of evidence about the effects of advertising on children, advocates increasingly lobbied governments arguing the need to protect young children from TV marketing. (See chapter 7 for a discussion of this research and chapter 2 for a history for the regulation of children's media.) And as the tug-of-war between family values and those of the marketplace mounted, the urgency of protecting the "innocent child" from marketing propelled consumer socialization research onto the policy agenda. However, a large question loomed: At what age can children be considered rational economic subjects under consumer law?

With these issues in mind, social scientists set out to put the dynamics of consumer socialization under the microscope. In a series of studies conducted during the 1970s and early 1980s, several researchers addressed this public controversy by asking (1) to what degree television marketing was contributing to or undermining parents' attempts at cultivating children's consumer skills, and (2) whether children's limited consumer experience merited legal protection in the marketplace.

Based on surveys, it became clear that television was contending with the family as an important agent of consumer socialization (Moschis & Moore, 1979). Even young children were aware of brands, and most made frequent requests to their parents for products they saw on TV, in addition to making requests in shops and supermarkets. There also was evidence that parents were playing a declining role in teen and adolescent acquisition of consumer competences, when measured by consumer affairs knowledge, money management skills, and brand preferences (Moschis & Moore, 1982). Nor did consumer-related courses at school have much positive impact on young people's knowledge and attitudes (Moschis & Churchill, 1978). Surveys indicated that when assessed for pricing accuracy, consumer affairs knowledge, and socially desirable consumer behaviors, children's consumer competences depended on developmental factors, but also differed by gender and social class. Youth from wealthy backgrounds had more opportunities to learn and practice consumerism. Surprisingly, parents and schools accounted for very little variance in the acquisition of basic economic knowledge, whereas the amount of television viewing did predict both consumer satisfaction and attitudes toward the marketplace, although it was negatively related to "puffery filtering" and advertising skepticism. George Moschis concluded that television seemed to be children's preferred source of effective consumer behavior roles (Moschis & Moore, 1979).

According to Scott Ward (1974, p. 2), "consumer socialization is the process by which young people acquire skills, knowledge, and attitudes relevant to their functioning as consumers in the marketplace." Adopting this definition, a team of researchers set out to map factors in domestic environments in which children learned to understand and perform economic transactions in a mediated marketplace. Although it is apparent that much consumer socialization takes place within the family before the child is three years of age, their studies focused on the older child's acquisition of information-processing skills required in the mass-mediated marketplace. The first was *advertising literacy*, which refers to the child's ability to understand and critically interpret the information about product claims made in branded television advertising, and the second was *economic literacy*, pertaining to the broader range of attitudes and skills associated with becoming rational economic subjects—that is, the cognitive capacity and money skills to shop effectively by comparing the relative attributes, uses, and benefits of competing goods along a standard yardstick of monetary value (Lunt & Furnham, 1996).

In a series of studies, these researchers (Ward et al., 1977) confirmed that many young children made requests for products that interested them (like food and toys) that they saw on television. Moreover, as children got older (eight years and up), these requests were more often branded—as were the older children's preferences for products. In general, younger children demonstrated little understanding of advertising and relied most on in-store experiences for their purchasing behaviors. Older children used media sources more and understood advertising's intent to persuade by age eight. They also exhibited a degree of skepticism when they watched ads, refusing to believe all the claims. Yet neither developmental competences (measured by age/grade) nor external influences of parents, schools, peers, and advertising (such as heavy media use, SES, parenting styles, materialist attitudes, and lifestyles) were sufficient in themselves to explain the acquisition of a child's consumer competence. Rather, Scott Ward, Daniel Wackman, and Ellen Wartella (1977) discovered a pattern of complex interactions between developmental and environmental factors that, over time, fostered children's money use, consumer norms, skills, and materialist attitudes. Cognitive skills like reasoning, the understanding of motives, and strategies for information gathering seemed most related to the child's development of information-processing and evaluation skills, whereas familial norms, training, and modeling of parents shaped saving and money use practices, brand orientation, skepticism, and lifestyle preferences. Based on these findings, the researchers suggested that increased regulation of advertising to children might be helpful in reducing family conflicts over lifestyle choices.

These consumer socialization studies added momentum to the "rancorous public policy" (John, 1999, p. 188) debate about whether children were being unduly influenced by advertising. As Deborah Roedder John (1999, p. 188) notes, the debate culminated "in a 1978 Federal Trade Commission proposal to ban television advertising to young children under the age of eight." But the growing research consensus that children under eight lacked sufficient consumer knowledge and were influenced by brand advertising was of little consequence when Ronald Reagan appointed a neoconservative, Mark Fowler, to the Federal Communications Commission (FCC), which, in 1981, deregulated children's commercial TV. Although policymakers ignored these first studies of consumer socialization, it must be said that these studies had mapped the key interacting factors influencing the acquisition of concepts and skills required for the child's competent functioning as an economic subject in the consumer marketplace (Ward, 1972). Over the following thirty years, others have continued to assess children's economic competences and consumer decision-making abilities in the deregulated marketplace of the United States.

Advertising Literacy

The research indicates that around seven or eight years of age, children learn to identify television commercials and distinguish them from other forms of programming based on perceived intent. At this age, they are able to describe ads not only as short and funny programs, but also as "trying to get people to buy something" (John, 1999, p. 188). Researchers also recognize that negative or mistrustful predispositions toward advertising are well established by the time children reach their eighth birthday (Boush et al., 1994; Obermiller & Spangenberg, 2000). But as Brian Young (Advertising Association, 2003) notes, twenty-five years of studying children's acquisition of customer competences has not ended the debate about their vulnerability in the marketplace. There are obvious reasons for this. As John (1999, p. 189) notes, based on the weight of evidence "there is little reason to believe that the vast majority of children younger than seven or eight years of age have a command of advertising's persuasive intent." Moreover, their choices are not fully informed if product awareness and preferences are limited to those brands that are heavily promoted on television (Buijzen & Valkenburg, 2000). Researchers also suggest that, although eight-year-old children distinguish ads from programming, recognize the intent of advertisers, and possess some critical skills, their understanding of the mediated marketplace remains incomplete. Indeed, as Thomas Robertson and John Rossiter (1974, p. 19) noted long ago, "Children's ability to recognize persuasive intent in commercials should not be taken as implying immunity to all commercials." Lynn Paine (1983) suggests that comprehending persuasive intent and forming a preference for a brand are less complex cognitive tasks than making informed consumer judgments. She goes on to argue that children cannot be regarded as sovereign consumers because they still lack an understanding of time, self, and money implied by the idea of consumer sovereignty. As Merrie Brucks, Gary Armstrong, and Marvin Goldberg (1988, pp. 480–481) point out, to be informed consumers, children (at least nine- to ten-year-olds) "need more than just a skeptical or critical attitude toward advertising. They also need a more detailed knowledge about the nature of advertising and how it works." In this respect, it is clear that children's comprehension of the tactics and appeals used by advertisers, and their understanding of the role that advertising plays in the broader media system, aren't consolidated until early adolescence (Boush et al., 1994; Obermiller & Spangenberg, 2000).

Moreover, given changes in the promotional environment over the last twenty years in which cross-promotion, guerrilla marketing, product placements, Web advertising, and synergistic strategies have come to dominate (McChesney, 2003), it is hardly surprising that very few seven-year-olds know the definition of a product placement. (See chapter 18 for a thorough discussion the growing hypercommercialism of children's culture.) Even twelve-year-olds have a hard time explaining who pays for and benefits from cross-promotion, or readily making the distinction between programming and advertising content in character programs. When it comes to the Internet, it is far from clear that the majority of children can avoid pop-ups and pornography, distinguish the commercial intent of sites such as Neopets.com, avoid cyber-lurkers, or understand how the information they input is being used by marketers (Media Awareness Network, 2005). Pointing to studies that suggest that young children do not have sufficient advertising and economic literacy to function as competent consumers in today's promotional culture (American Psychological Association, 2004), many researchers retain a "lingering suspicion and concern that corporate ingenuity, sophisticated market research, and the lure of the televisual can overwhelm even the most savvy child consumers" (Cook, 2004a, p. 148).

Economic Literacy

There is abundant evidence that most children are allowed to make purchases by age six, in large part because they have been coached on shopping trips with their parents. By age seven, most have become "active shoppers" in their own right, searching through toy catalogues, using pocket money for discretionary purchases, window shopping, chatting with sales personnel, carefully investigating their favorite products, while learning to influence their parents to buy them (McNeal, 1999). Eight- or nine-years-olds generally receive allowances that they are allowed to use freely. They know that products have prices, know where to look for price information, and know that there are price variations among products and stores (McNeal & McDaniel, 1981). They are also becoming aware of the availability of different information sources, many using a range of sources, and comparing across brands for price and quality (Turner & Brandt, 1979) on multiple attributes to evaluate them (Bahn, 1986; Capon & Kuhn, 1980).

Although it can be said that most eight-year-olds have become autonomous customers, their practical knowledge about branding, shopping scripts, and store pricing is no guarantee that they are rational consumer decision makers. Indeed, the lacuna of children's economic knowledge has recently attracted considerable attention in the literature. Economic psychologists argue that economic rationality implies more than a practical shopping script. Today's customers need a proactive shopping strategy that evaluates the risk-price-benefits of a product in a highly fluid pricing environment (Lunt & Furnham, 1996). As John (1999) also remarks, researchers have tried to isolate the age at which children acquire the cognitive abilities and understanding of complex marketplace transactions. Yet, the notion of informed decision-making sets a high bar for competence. It requires children to (1) learn about the places where goods are available (stores); (2) access and evaluate the information about goods that allows them to judge goods based on quality, usefulness, and price (product attributes, utility, and brands); (3) understand competitive pricing, choice, and the protocols of social transactions in shops (shopping scripts); and (4) be able to acquire and exchange money for products (economic skills). To fulfill these tasks, children must be able to search out information in order to compare various goods available to them for a price. Secondly, they must be able to critically evaluate information about product utility, cognitively weighing the various benefits offered by the whole range of products. Finally, they must be able to assess product utility and performance characteristics before considering them competent.

Few researchers have found that adults, let alone children, meet these stringent criteria proposed by the theory of market choice. The sparse literature suggests that economic literacy for children under the age of twelve is partial at best and shaped as much by social circumstance and parental coaching. Their decision strategies tend to use fewer attributes in forming preferences and comparing products. Moreover, their information searches for competitive products and prices may be limited by their lack of economic knowledge about the marketplace more generally. Given the developing cognitive skills of young children, there is limited evidence that they possess the ability to perform the complex price-benefits-risk calculation involved in exercising rational choice—especially in relationship to goods that have long-term risks associated with them, such as cigarettes or violent video games. To say that children under the age of eight have been empowered by their parents to define themselves and their lifestyles, relative to earlier generations, does not imply that they are fully rational economic subjects (Furnham, 1996). As such, I must conclude, with others who have looked at this question, that children still need to be regarded as neither victims nor savvy—but rather as consumers-in-training, *learning to behave willingly* in accordance with the prevailing standards established in our market culture.

Coda: Returning to the Familial

I'm 14 years old and have been a vegetarian for five months. Originally, I just cut out meat, but I have now extended that to fish and gelatin. I'm also a picky eater, and my Mum says that she doesn't know what to feed me anymore. Could you please give me some recipe ideas that a teenager would like—before my mum has a heart attack?

—Anonymous posting on VegCooking.com

I am 17 years old and recently decided to go vegetarian. I saw PETA's "Meet Your Meat" video in class, and it changed me forever. Unfortunately, my Mother does-n't support my decision. She cooks meat almost every night, and I have told her I don't want to eat it, but she gets mad. What can I make for myself using foods that my Mum most likely has in the kitchen already? I want to eventually become a vegan, but I think that I need to ease into it and start with not eating meat.

—Anonymous posting on VegCooking.com

Propelled by the conflict between parents and marketers over who gets to influence kids' consumer behaviors, the study of consumer socialization has largely focused on the older child's cognitive competences in the face of mediated promotions. In so doing, it has gen-erated a lively debate about whether the child is a "victim" of the market or an "empow-ered consumer." The weight of evidence, of course, has long indicated that, at least until age eight, and perhaps until age twelve, young consumers do not have either full advertis-ing or economic literacy. In this respect, I agree with Patti Valkenburg and Joanne Cantor (2001) that our concern about marketing has, to some degree, overlooked the important ways that parents continue to influence many aspects of the child's maturation as a self-regulating and self-expressive consumer—especially in the first five years of life. In a series of recent studies, it has been demonstrated that parenting style and guidance, familial nego-tiations, and restrictions on children's discretionary consumption can influence the course of maturation (Boush et al., 1994; Dickerson, 2000; Page & Ridgway, 2001).

Recognizing that families, media, peers, and schools all contribute to consumer social-ization, I suggest that it is time to put the agentive child consumer back in the context of the complex social communication matrix in which they "become consumers," recogniz-ing that *children come to make their own choices, but not in contexts of their own choosing.* Consumer socialization in many ways parallels learning to understand and speak a language, the ultimate goal of which is a self-regulating subject who is learning to express his or her own ideas, feelings, preferences, and values. Guided by social norms, most parents will become deeply involved in helping their children acquire language competence by talk-ing, singing, and reading to the child, modeling the production of sound, rewarding the child's efforts, playing games that associate sounds and actions, and ultimately sending them to school to be formally instructed as competent members of their language community. When, at age two, their child masters the word *no*, most parents realize that socialization is not about compliance but also about helping the child to express himself or herself effec-tively in the native tongue. The word *no* exemplifies the paradox of socialization—the obligation of the parent both to shape and guide the child's behavior, and at the same time its opposite—to help the child become autonomous, self-defining subject.

Consumer socialization in the first few years, I would argue, parallels linguistic socialization, taking the form of an unfolding "negotiation" through which the child becomes versed in consumer knowledge and skills through a growing experience of the material world. Although it may all start with a nursing dependency, the feeding relationship quickly becomes an intimate marketing experiment in taste, as modern parents offer a variety of flavors and textures, experimenting with what the child likes within the edicts of nutritional requirements. Feeding lays the pattern of an intimate strategic dialogue in which the parent looks to the child's face to decode the child's emotional experiences of consumption. If the child smiles and eats, the parent feels successful. If the child frowns and spits out the food, the experiment continues or conflict ensues. Like all games, this one consists of strategic negotiation. Children are learning to influence their parents about their preferences as much as the parents are finding ways of both pleasing and nurturing their children. Long before they learn to say, "No, I don't like that spinach," children have become engaged in a complex negotiation over consumption that generalizes to other objects including activities, toys, and clothes. The strategies each player uses gets more complex as children make requests for toys, friends, and snacks, and, on the other side, parents become concerned about children's sedentary lifestyles and snacking habits (Marquis, 2004). Since much of their exposure to consumer products comes from the media and shops, it should not be surprising that, increasingly, these negotiations are influenced by marketplace experiences to such a degree that conflicts over consumption seem endemic in family life. Consumerism thus exists as an agonic family game. But rather than see such conflicts as "normal," I have tried to show above that they also reflect a grand realignment in power and influence in our market-based society.

In raising two children, I have become well acquainted with the way media can accentuate the familial conflicts that arise in families over consumer socialization. In my daughter Meghan's case it wasn't sex, drugs, and rock and roll, but a radio program about dolphins being caught in tuna fishing nets, which, at age three and a half, precipitated her decision to become a vegetarian. Meghan loved animals and was so traumatized by stories about living creatures being killed or captured that she couldn't watch *Bambi* or *Free Willy* until she was ten years old. A few days after hearing the radio program, she asked me to explain where the tuna in her sandwich came from. We discussed at length the various foods that came from animals—tuna, meat, eggs, and cheese. These discussions had a profound effect on her. She decided then and there never to eat anything that had to die for her pleasure. Not surprisingly, her lifestyle choice was rather disruptive, as the whole family gradually adapted to her vegetarian diet. We learned to shop and cook differently, and now we talk about and practice consumption differently as well.

The autonomous lifestyle decisions and consumer empowerment of the young brings with it new tensions within families. In our case, Meghan's vegetarianism was experienced as a disruption at first because we had to realign our shopping and cooking to accommodate her tastes and ideals. The fact that many families make such accommodations indicates the new politics of contemporary families in which consumption styles, values, and personal tastes are constantly being negotiated in the family. To some degree, this may be evidence of a power shift in the family in which the provisioning role of the parent and their implicit control over children's consumption practices is gradually loosened until the point of self-sufficiency (which gets later and later in our society).

The letters cited at the start of this section were found on a Web site, indicating that our family is not alone in finding that children and young people are making lifestyle choices on their own—often at a very young age. As we have seen, most analyses of the agents of consumer socialization outside the family have narrowly focused on children's exposure to television advertising in children's programming. Given the billions of dollars invested in promoting fast food, sugary soft drinks, and toys, the investigation of their role in children's preference formation and attitudes seems reasonable. But it should not be surprising that other media are also a source of knowledge that interests them. In a media-saturated world, children are exposed to both programming and advertising in diverse media. In my daughter Meghan's case, it was a news report on dolphin-safe tuna that got her thinking about the consequences of her eating habits. In the letter above, it is PETA's "Meet Your Meat" video shown in class that revealed the processes and risks associated with meat production. In this, I find hope that the effort invested in broadening children's awareness of lifestyle choices in families, schools, and media is not always drowned in sea of happy meals and fun foods.

DISCUSSION QUESTIONS

1   In this chapter I argue that children are consumers-in-training from birth and that parents participate both consciously and unconsciously in the formations of "taste" and "cultural capital" that children require in a consumer society. Have you seen evidence of this in your own lives? In the lives of your younger siblings? Provide specific examples.

2   Using the example of my own daughter's vegetarianism I identify a new politics of contemporary families in which consumption styles, values, and personal tastes are constantly being negotiated in the family. Have you seen evidence of this in your experiences with your own family? Provide specific examples.

REFERENCES

Advertising Association: Food Advertising Unit. (2003). *Advertising and food choice in children: A review of the literature*. London: Brian Young.

American Psychological Association. (2004). APA *task force report on advertising and children: Psychological issues in the increasing commercialization of childhood*. Washington, D.C.: Dale Kunkel, Brian L. Wilcox, Joanne Cantor, Edward Palmer, Susan Linn, & Peter Dowrick.

Bahn, K. D. (1986). How and when do brand perceptions and preferences first form? A cognitive developmental investigation. *Journal of Consumer Research, 13*, 382–393.

Bell, D. (1977). The cultural contradictions of capitalism. Replicated in P. Murray, *Reflections on Commercial Life* (pp. 429–446). New York: Basic.

Boush, D., Friestad, M., & Rose, G. (1994). Adolescent skepticism toward TV advertising and knowledge of advertiser tactics. *Journal of Consumer Research, 21*, 165–175.

Brucks, M., Armstrong, G. M., & Goldberg, M. (1988). Children's use of cognitive defenses against television advertising: A cognitive response approach. *Journal of Consumer Research, 14*, 471–482.

Buijzen, M., & Valkenburg, P. M. (2000). The impact of television on children's Christmas wishes. *Journal of Broadcasting & Electronic Media, 44*(3), 456–470.

Campaign for a Commercial-Free Childhood. (2006). Retrieved March 26, 2006, from http://www.commercialfreechildhood.org.

Capon, N., & Kuhn, D. (1980). A developmental study of consumer information processing strategies. *Journal of Consumer Research, 7*, 225–233.

Cook, D. T. (2004a). Beyond either/or. *Journal of Consumer Culture, 4*, 147–152.

Cook, D. T. (2004b). *The commodification of childhood: The children's clothing industry and the rise of the child consumer.* Durham, NC: Duke University Press.

Cook, D. T. (2005). The dichotomous child in and of commercial culture. *Childhood, 12*, 155–159.

Cross, G. (2004). Wondrous innocence: Print advertising and the origins of permissive child rearing in the U.S. *Journal of Consumer Culture, 4*, 183–201.

Cultures of Consumption, and the ESRC-AHRB Research Programme. (2004). *Fast food, sluggish kids: Moral panics and risky lifestyles* (working paper no. 9). London: Stephen Kline.

Davies, H., Buckingham, D., & Kelley, P. (2000). In the worst possible taste: Children, television and cultural value. *European Journal of Cultural Studies, 3*(1), 5–25.

DeMause, L. (1974). *The history of childhood.* New York: Psychohistory Press.

Dickerson, E. B. (2000). The impact of mother-child interactions and narrative style on a child's recall, recognition, and comprehension of advertising messages. *Proquest Dissertations and Theses 2000.* AAT 3003001.

Dotson, M. J., & Hyatt, E. M. (2005). Major influence factors in children's consumer socialization. *Journal of Consumer Marketing, 22*, 35–42.

Fromm, E. (1947). *Man for himself: An inquiry into the psychology of ethics.* New York: Holt, Rinehart and Winston.

Frones, I. (1995). *Among peers: On the meaning of peers in the process of socialization.* Oslo: Scandinavian University Press.

Furnham, A. (1996). The economic socialization of children. In P. Lunt & A. Furnham (Eds.), *Economic socialization: The economic beliefs and behaviours of young people* (pp. 11–34). Cheltenham: Edward Elgar.

Halsall, P. (1998). John Locke (1632–1704): Some thoughts concerning education, 1692. *Internet modern history sourcebook.* Reprinted from J. Locke & C. W. Eliot (Ed.), *English philosophers of the seventeenth and eighteenth centuries: Locke, Berkeley, Hume* (Harvard Classics, Part 37). New York: P. F. Collier & Son. Retrieved April 14, 2006, from http://www.fordham.edu/Halsall/mod/169210cke-education.html.

Jenks, C. (1996). *Childhood.* London: Routledge.

John, D. R. (1999). Consumer socialization of children: A retrospective look at twenty-five years of research. *Consumer Research, 26*, 183–213.

Klein, M. (1950). *Contributions to psycho-analysis*. London: London Press.

Kline, S. (1993). *Out of the garden: Toys, TV and children's culture in the age of marketing*. London: Verso.

Kline, S. (2006). A becoming subject: Consumer socialization in the mediated marketplace. In F. Trentmann (Ed.), *The making of the consumer: Knowledge, power and identity in the modern world* (pp. 176–199). New York: Berg.

Linn, S. E. (2004). *Consuming kids: The hostile takeover of childhood*. New York: New Press.

Lunt, P., & Furnham, A. (1996). *Economic socialization*. Cheltenham: Edward Elgar.

Marchand, R. (1985). *Advertising the American dream: Making way for modernity, 1920–1940*. Berkeley: University of California Press.

Marquis, M. (2004). Strategies for influencing parental decisions on food purchasing. *Journal of Consumer Marketing, 21*, 134–143.

McChesney, R. W. (2003). Theses on media regulation. *Media, Culture & Society, 25*, 125–133.

McNeal, J. (1999). *The kids' market: Myths and realities*. Ithaca, NY: Paramount.

McNeal, J. U., & McDaniel, S. W. (1981). Children's perceptions of retail stores: An exploratory study. *Akron Business and Economics Review, 12*, 39–42.

Media Awareness Network. (2005). Young Canadians in a wired world II. Retrieved March 26, 2006, from http://www.media-awareness.ca/.

Moschis, G. P., & Churchill, G. A. (1978). Consumer socialization: A theoretical and empirical analysis. *Journal of Marketing Research* 15: 599–609.

Moschis, G. P., & Moore, R. L. (1979). Decision making among the young: A socialization perspective. *Journal of Consumer Research, 6*, 101–12.

Moschis, G. P., & Moore, R. L. (1982), A longitudinal study of television advertising effects. *Journal of Consumer Research, 9*, 279–86.

Obermiller, C., & Spangenberg, E. R. (2000). On the origin and distinctness of skepticism toward advertising. *Marketing Letters, 11*, 311–322.

Page, C., & Ridgway, N. (2001). The impact of consumer environments on consumption patterns of children from disparate socioeconomic backgrounds. *Journal of Consumer Marketing, 18*, 21–40.

Paine, L. S. (1983). Children as consumers: An ethical evaluation of children's advertising. *Business and Professional Ethics Journal, 3*, 119–146.

Preston, C. (2004). Children's advertising: The ethics of economic socialization. *International Journal of Consumer Studies, 28*, 364–370.

Research interviews conducted in Simon Fraser School, Vancouver, B.C. (April 2004). www.sfu.ca/media-lab/risk/.

Riesman, D., with Denney, R., & Glazer, N. (1950). *The lonely crowd: A study of the changing American character*. New Haven, CT: Yale University Press.

Riesman, D., & Roseborough, H. (1955). Careers in consumer behavior. In L. Clark (Ed.), *Consumer behaviour II: The life cycle and consumer behavior*. New York: New York University Press.

Robertson, T. S., & Rossiter, J. R. (1974). Children and commercial persuasion: An attribution theory analysis. *Journal of Consumer Research, 1*, 13–20.

Schor, J. B. (2004). *Born to buy*. New York: Scribner.

Spigel, L. (1998). Seducing the innocent: Childhood and television in postwar America. In H. Jenkins (Ed.), *The children's culture reader* (pp. 110–135). New York: New York University Press.

Spock, B. (1964). *Baby and child care*. New York: Pocket Books.

Sutton-Smith, B. (1986). *Toys as culture*. New York: Gardner.

Turner, J., & Brandt, J. (1979). Development and validation of a simulated market to test children for selected consumer skills. *Journal of Consumer Affairs, 12*, 266–276.

Valkenburg, P. M., & Cantor, J. (2001). The development of a child into a consumer. *Journal of Applied Developmental Psychology, 22*, 61–72.

VegCooking.com. (n.d.). Retrieved March 26, 2006, from http://www.vegcooking.com/askVeganChef1.aspx?Category=Young%20Vegans.

Ward, S. (1972). *Children and promotion: New consumer battleground?* Cambridge, MA: Marketing Science Institute.

Ward, S. (1974). Consumer socialization. *Journal of Consumer Research, 1*, 1–14.

Ward, S., Wackman, D., & Wartella, E. A. (1977). *How children learn to buy: The development of consumer information processing skills*. Beverly Hills, CA: Sage.

CHAPTER TWENTY

Do We All Live in
a Shared World Culture?

KATALIN LUSTYIK

Approximately one third of the world's population is made up of people under the age of eighteen. While these 2 billion young people make up half the population in many developing countries in Asia and Africa, they account for only less than a quarter in most western European countries. For these youths, the media are the primary source of entertainment and information, which in myriad ways serve to shape and define their lives. Young people in many parts of the world spend vast amounts of their free time in front of the television and computer screens watching similar programs, playing similar games, wearing (or dreaming about wearing) similar clothes, and humming similar pop tunes. Does this mean that American, European, and Asian teenagers today are much more similar to each other than their parents' and grandparents' generations were?

The globalization of media technologies and services is a key factor influencing the lives, attitudes, and perspectives of youth worldwide. As Joseph Man Chan (2005, p. 24) points out, "There is no doubt that cultures have become more connected as their development becomes more and more integrated globally." This might suggest that as cultural exchange intensifies, young people today live in a "shared world culture" (Lemish et al., p. 540), but how do the youth themselves feel about this?

The internationalization of youth culture is a highly uneven and multidimensional process that involves contradictions, resistances, and countervailing forces. But are there winners and losers? There is a growing asymmetrical relationship between youth cultures in different parts of the world, giving rise to a certain paradox. The use of computers and the Internet has gained popularity among young people in many parts of the world, and such technologies can facilitate a global social place for them, and offer direct contact across national borders. Computer and Web access, however, is the source of the greatest cultural divide, both between countries (affluent countries versus less affluent countries), and also within countries (better educated and wealthier urban or suburban youth compared to less educated, poorer and rural youth). (See, for example, chapter 14 of this book.) According to Francis B. Nyamnjoh (2002, p. 43), "If globalization is a process of accelerated flow of media content, to most African cultures and children it is also a process of accelerated exclusion." We must ask, of course, the question: How can such imbalances be addressed?

In this chapter, I attempt to address the broad issue of the internationalization of youth culture by focusing on a number of related subjects: (1) youth cultures and globalization, (2) media conglomerations aimed at kids, and (3) young people's appropriation of and engagement with global media. I will conclude the chapter by briefly addressing current international debates concerning the promotion of cultural diversity in the twenty-first century.

Youth Cultures and Globalization

In the twenty-first century, the world media landscape presents two seemingly opposite themes: increased opportunities and increased risks (Gigli, 2004). On the one hand, there is increasing access to information and ideas from more diverse sources than ever before, and opportunities to broaden our outlooks on the world, as well as to encourage awareness of others. The potentially positive influences of the media also include destroying stereotypes and social prejudice, promoting critical thinking, and participating in social and political life within and beyond national borders. The media today also can facilitate a certain level of interconnectedness among young people in various parts of the world.

Our current media landscape, on the other hand, also can threaten traditional cultural identifications and values. National and local forms of media production for young people, especially in the fields of television, film, computing, music, and sports, are increasingly influenced and shaped by a handful of transnational media giants. The tension between global forces and local cultural heritage presents a major challenge for many societies to maintain what is perceived as their unique cultural identity in the world today. English, for instance, is the most pervasive language of television programming, films, popular music, computing, video games, and the World Wide Web. The dominance of the Hollywood film industry means that, even in the case of relatively big and affluent nations in Europe, U.S. films earn up to 90 percent of the annual box office revenue (Will, 2005). If you live in Europe, finding French, German, or other foreign films—besides those from the United States—on the big screens can be challenging.

What do we mean by the globalization of youth cultures? Would playing online computer games with kids from China, Brazil, and Madagascar be an accurate example? Or would most people identify the process with products, symbols, celebrities, brands, and organizations that are easily recognized and often adored by young people in many parts of the world, such as Pepsi, Mickey Mouse, Madonna, CNN, Sony, or Nike? What about the globally synchronized release of each Harry Potter book and film as a shared experience?

There are different views on what constitutes cultural globalization and how it is envisioned from diverse geographical and cultural locales. *Global* is a highly contested term despite its wide use in corporate, academic, and public discourses. As Annabelle Sreberny (2005. p. 13) explains, sometimes "global" "is used to describe a phenomenon that is not nation-specific; sometimes to signify anything that involves more than one country; sometimes it alludes to general processes and sometimes to purportedly 'universal values.'" *Globalization* is an even more contested and complex concept. John Tomlinson (1999, p. 2) suggests that "globalization" refers to "the rapidly developing and densening network of *interconnections* and *interdependences* that characterize modern social life." There seems to be a general agreement that it is a continuously unfolding multidimensional and dynamic process with no end. "There is no point in assuming that we will ever reach a stage where there is a stable and enduring globality" (Chan, 2005, p. 24). For the purpose of this chapter, we could simply refer to globalization as a "process that opens nations, states and societies to many influences that originate beyond their borders . . . affecting the everyday context in which children grow up and interact with the rest of society" (Rizzini & Bush, 2002, p. 371).

Views on Media Globalization

There are two basic perspectives on media globalization within the field of communication research. The top-down, or macro-level, political-economy approach focuses on issues related to the unequal global distribution of media products and services and the regulation of various aspects of the global media—ownership, trade, global media governance. The other perspective on media globalization represents a more bottom-up, culturalist approach based on more empirical research of globalizing processes (for example, Ferguson, 1992).

The international flow of information, news, television programs, and films between various parts of the world have been documented and analyzed for decades (for example, Herman & McChesney, 1997; Nordenstreng & Varis, 1974). While the global dissemination of media and communication products has been growing dramatically, its general direction can still be described as a *one-way flow* from a handful of regional production centers (for example, the United States, the U.K., Brazil, India, Hong Kong, Japan) to the rest of the world. You have probably heard the terms *Westernization, Americanization,* and *McDonaldization*, which refer to the processes by which Western or American ideas and products are being exported and "imposed" on other cultures. These processes are often viewed as a form of *cultural imperialism*. This argument is based on the notion that the importation of media products extends to specific ways of defining the world, standards of knowledge, values and norms, even behavior patterns (for example, individualism, consumerism), which often occurs at the considerable expense of the importing cultures and populations (Schiller, 1991; Tomlinson, 1991, 1999).

The conventional model of cultural imperialism, critics insist, "presumes the existence of a pure internally homogeneous, authentic, indigenous culture, which then becomes subverted or corrupted by foreign influence" (Morley, 1994, p. 151). Others, critical of the Westernization thesis, call attention to reverse processes in which the "peripheries" influence the "centers." Roland Robertson (1994), for instance, examines how "Third World" ideas and styles concerning art, music, and religion frequently impregnate global cultural products.

Media Giants Targeting Kids

The transformation of youth cultures in contemporary society is often associated with processes such as *hypercommercialism*, *conglomeration*, and *consumerism* (Herman & McChesney, 1997; McChesney, 2002). (See, for example, the discussion of these topics in chapter 18.) Edward Herman and Robert McChesney (1997, p. 76) argue that the high level of commercialization in the media and the formation of large conglomerates gave rise to mass production and distribution of films, television programs, magazines, newspapers, books, sports, toys, and fashion, "each of which has been distilled into increasingly centralized, coordinated multinational corporate enterprises that conceivably operate on a global scale." Media conglomerates are considered to be among "the primary agents of cultural globalization" (Chan, 2005, p. 25). As Chan (2005, p. 25) explains, "they run operations across national boundaries, they thrive on the economy of scale, and obtain an ever increasing portion of their revenues from foreign markets." For example, the Walt Disney Company and Viacom's Nickelodeon and Music Television (MTV) are among the most successful media companies targeting children and adolescents worldwide.

Is it possible that in this day and age there are still some who have not heard about Disney? With its globally recognized Mickey Mouse logo, Disney is certainly among the most significant media and cultural institutions of our time (Wasko, 2001). Disney's world-famous theme parks are advertised as the most magical and exciting places on Earth. Five such amusement parks operate today in vastly different geographical locations: Disneyland in California (which opened in 1955), the Walt Disney World Resort in Florida (1971), Tokyo Disneyland (1983), Disneyland Paris/Euro Disney (1992), and Hong Kong Disney (2005). The parks are designed primarily for middle-class families and for "children of all ages" who can get married, or even organize business meetings in any of the parks. They not only represent state-of-the-art technology but, according to a devoted fan, they "seem to embody all that is good . . . [they are] the happiest place on earth" (quoted by Wasko, 2001, p. 207).

Nickelodeon, launched forty years after Disney, in 1979, has also grown to be an "important cultural phenomenon" with an impact that "far exceeds its status as a successful operator in the children's media marketplace" (Hendershot, 2004, p. 2). Nickelodeon promotes itself as "the world's only multi-media entertainment brand dedicated exclusively to kids," reaching close to 700 million households in over 160 territories worldwide today. Nick U.K., the first Nickelodeon channel outside the United States, was launched in 1993, followed by dozens of others in different parts of the globe. Animation generally tends to cross national borders easily, making *Rugrats*, *Dora the Explorer*, and *SpongeBob SquarePants* among the most popular programs targeting kids worldwide.

MTV: Music as a Global Language?

Is popular music a "common denominator of youth" in all countries? Young people seem to easily accept diverse musical styles often spiced up with ethnic flavors, innovative, exotic appearances, and ideas originating from diverse locations. For the world's youth, music often provides a "sense of a joint culture" (Lemish et al., 1998, p. 549). Music Television (MTV) is the world's largest television network and most valuable multimedia brand for youth, and considers itself an integral part of "an emerging international youth culture that transcends any national cultural identity" (Banks, 1997, p. 50). Have MTV's attempts to create an international youth culture been successful? "The global rock 'n' roll village" today consists of more than 430 million households in 167 territories covering North and South America, Europe, Africa, Asia, and the South Pacific. MTV's ultimate goal, "to be in every home in the world" and "to connect with viewers across every screen in the house," is coming closer to reality year by year (Banks, 1997, p. 44).

The company's rapid global expansion has raised concerns about the impact of U.S. and Western cultural influence on indigenous music in many parts of the world. The majority of music played on MTV in various parts of the world consists of artists from the United States and the U.K., "often giving scant attention to indigenous music and only showing local artists if they mimic American-style rock" (Banks, 1997, p. 43). Today, in parts of Asia, MTV claims to provide over 70 percent of regionally produced music content. This certainly helps the company attract larger local audiences and gain access to Asia's highly regulated media markets (Weber, 2003, p. 288). In 2004 MTV was the "Most Watched Music Channel in the Asia Pacific," viewed by more young adults than any other music channel in the region. The operation of ten separate twenty-four-hour MTV channels throughout the Asia-Pacific region provides an example of how media giants can convert into transnational networks of local and regional channels. While sharing the brand, part of the programming, and library titles, the channels rely on mainly local staff who create the local schedules, which are mixtures of network and local content (Chalaby, 2005, p. 31).

There still are concerns, however, regarding the ways that "MTV increases the clout and cultural power of major transnational record companies by largely limiting its playlist to artists affiliated with these labels" (Banks, 1997, p. 56). Jack Banks (1997, p. 51) has argued that this practice essentially prevents local producers from getting any airplay on MTV and encourages "young people around the world to embrace a consumerist way of life, reject-ing alternative values, traits or traditions as a part of their self-identity." According to Banks, "MTV's plans to develop an international youth culture based on consumerism provide a receptive audience to advertisers seeking to sell their products to upscale youth everywhere" (p. 58). Essentially, media conglomerates in general are primarily in the business of creat-ing new niche markets, and then delivering these audiences to the advertisers who are sell-ing not only Western goods but also Western cultural identities and values.

Kids Appropriating Global Media

To what extent are young people today being subjected to the same music, the same media products, and the same cultural values? What happens when children in many parts of the developing world "are moving from local radio to Disney or Fox without having any tele-vision which is specific to them and their culture" (Home, 1997)? According to Arjun Appadurai (1996, p. 17), "globalization does not necessarily or even frequently imply homogenization or Americanization, and to the extent that different societies appropriate the materials of modernity differently, there is still ample room for the deeper study of spe-cific geographies, histories, and languages." The key concept is "active cultural appropri-ation," which implies that there is a dialectic and complex relationship between the receiver and receiving culture and the cultural import.

Communication scholars have traced not only the global proliferation of media prod-ucts but also their influence on and reception by local and national cultures and audiences. The "effects" of American media on national culture and identity, and the adaptation of Western values by media audiences in different countries, have been the focus of a signif-icant amount of academic research over the decades (Ang, 1985; Liebes & Katz, 1990). There is a strong trend in audience studies that supports the idea of the "active audience" constructing its own meanings via processes such as selection, negotiation, interpretation, and discussion. To give a brief example, young people in South Africa used global media products (for example, American television programs such as *Ally McBeal*) as cultural resources to make sense of their own lives (Strelitz, 2004).

Disney Audiences

While research on young people and the media constitutes a major area of audience research, relatively few cross-cultural and comparative studies have focused on their expe-rience of cultural globalization and how they view and appropriate foreign media products. The Global Disney Audience Project looked at what roles Disney products and characters played in the popular culture of eighteen different countries on four continents (Wasko et al., 2001). The study concluded that Disney, for the majority of respondents, was associated with well-made entertainment and high-quality products. Whether or not respondents liked Disney, most agreed that "Disney promoted fun, fantasy, happiness, magic and good over evil" (Wasko & Meehan, 2001, p. 334). While the familiarity and popularity of Disney varied in different countries, 98 percent of the respondents had seen a Disney film, and 79 percent had watched Disney television programs and experienced Disney merchandise.

As the case studies revealed, many countries had incorporated Disney into diverse cultural rituals. For example, visiting Disney World in Florida had become a "right of passage" for the great majority of middle- and upper-class Brazilian teenagers (Reis, 2001, p. 92), especially Brazilian girls, many of whom wanted to celebrate their fifteenth birthday there "in lieu of the traditional, and often lavish 'festa de 15 anos' (15th birthday party)" (Reis, 2001, p. 92). Those who could not afford this Disney experience often reported feeling socially alienated and were considered "uncool" by their peers (Reis, 2001, p. 92). David Buckingham (2001, p. 294) concludes that British "children today are Disney children; and parents are Disney parents." He argues further that "We may all be consuming Disney in complex and ambivalent ways; but in the end we are all still consuming the same thing. The space for alternative childhoods, for alternative stories to be told, may be steadily reducing" (p. 294).

Global Culture in Practice

Audience and reception studies also focus on how media globalization becomes embedded into the lives of young people in various parts of the world. Questions could include whether children and teens distinguish between local and foreign programs, and, if so, do they prefer one to the other group? A preliminary study conducted in Denmark, France, and Israel revealed that respondents could easily adapt a global perspective on social life and enjoy a "hybrid coexistence of multi-cultures in their lives" (Lemish et al., 1998, p. 540). It also stressed that an important aspect of youth cultures today was the peaceful coexistence of often seemingly clashing cultures, values and beliefs. While a group of twelve-year-old Israeli girls who participated in the study expressed strict religious beliefs, they talked about their admiration of foreign female music performers "characterized by exaggerated sexual appearances" and their appreciation of American action movies packed with violent scenes (Lemish et al., 1998, p. 550). The researchers concluded that while respondents often consumed the same media content and used the same communication technologies, it had not necessarily resulted in cultural homogenization: "Conversely, the world is becoming ever more culturally diverse despite what seems like a common culture of consumption and style" (Lemish et al., 1998, p. 554).

The general tendency for audiences around the world to often identify imported media content, particularly products from the United States, with high production quality, creativity, innovation, and "coolness," and their own media products with a lack of technical and narrative professionalism, bad acting, and poor marketing, was supported in this study as well. Research, however, has also taught us that viewers, young and old, usually prefer familiar settings and context, and their native language if the story is good and done well (Sepstrup, 1990; Lemish et al., 1998). A recent essay competition in which nearly one thousand New Zealand youngsters participated led to the conclusion that "teenagers care passionately about seeing themselves on air, and have shown they want to see even more" (Teenagers Love, 2005). As one of the winners wrote, New Zealand programs "give us a chance to enjoy what's special about our country—our different peoples and our Kiwi culture" (School Competition, 2005).

Promoting the Diversity of Cultural Expressions

While young people would often like to see more of themselves and their cultures in the media, the majority of media content targeting them, with the exception of a few countries such as the United States, comes from abroad. In many parts of the world, where resources limit domestic productions, the general concern is that a great deal of exported media contain characters and messages that, at best, are not relevant to local cultures, or, at worst, convey violent images and mass-marketed messages. Nyamnjoh (2002, p. 43) goes further when he argues that children in Africa mainly consume global media content that is often "conceived and produced without their particular interest in mind." Thus, they are "victims of second-hand consumption . . . since the media content at their disposal seldom reflects their immediate cultural contexts." According to Nyamnjoh, it follows, then, that "they must attune their palates to the diktats of undomesticated foreign media dishes" (p. 43).

While there seems to be a "universal" desire to create a balance between the protection of local cultural production and the cross-border flow of cultural products that are increasingly controlled by a handful of media conglomerations today, there is a significant debate about how such balance could be created and sustained (Magner, 2004). The Convention on the Protection and Promotion of the Diversity of Cultural Expressions represented a recent attempt by UNESCO, the cultural branch of the United Nations, to accomplish precisely this. The convention declared that "cultural diversity is a 'common heritage of humanity'" that needs to be defended. The document addressed a broad range of issues, including supporting governments in their insistence that media industries are vital to the construction and maintenance of national cultural identity, and that it is the right and duty of governments to protect their cultures by applying subsidies and quotas to these industries (General Conference, 2005).

The majority of UNESCO members supported the document, which was declared in the French press as a "buffer against U.S. cultural domination," and "a vital tool for combating English-speaking standardization" (U.S. Isolated, 2005). The convention's key opponent, the United States, did not consider the document as a force for cultural diversity but rather as one that could potentially suppress the free flow of information and empower governments to put up new barriers to cultural trade. The U.S. ambassador to

UNESCO argued that "nations should have the right to 'protect' culture if to protect means to nurture it, but not if to protect means to shield it behind barriers to competition from cultural imports" (Will, 2005, p. A17).

Do We All Live in a Shared World Culture?

As we can conclude, the internationalization of youth culture is a dynamic and multidimensional process that cannot be discussed without addressing issues of media globalization, cultural imperialism, national culture and identity, media conglomerations targeting kids, and young audiences consuming media products originating from various parts of the globe. There is negotiation and appropriation, conglomeration and commercialization. There are contradictions, resistances, and countervailing forces.

Did we all grow up as Disney children and will we all become Disney parents? Do young people live in a shared world culture constructed for them by Coke, MTV, Nickelodeon, and other corporate giants? Do contemporary youth cultures offer more diversity and encourage more awareness of other cultures than previous ones did? These questions are more complex than they might seem at first glance. They need to be investigated with a proper regard for the specific historical and social contexts of each particular situation, and understood in terms of simultaneous, complexly related processes in the realms of economy, politics, culture, and technology. It is also fundamental to recognize the uneven, asymmetrical character of the globalization of youth cultures in order to critically and meaningfully engage with the topic.

DISCUSSION QUESTIONS

1   British media scholar David Buckingham (2001, p. 294) concludes in his Disney chapter that "We may all be consuming Disney in complex and ambivalent ways; but in the end we are all still consuming the same thing. The space for alternative childhoods, for alternative stories to be told, may be steadily reducing." Do you agree with his statement and prediction? What did he mean by "alternative childhoods" and "alternative stories"?

2   Do you think governments today should have the right to protect their national cultures by applying subsidies and quotas? If so, why? If not, why not?

3   What is your opinion of South African scholar Nyamnjoh's argument that children in many parts of the world are often victims of second-hand media consumption? Is it possible that children in the United States could also be victims of second-hand media consumption? If so, who, and for what reasons? If not, why not?

EXERCISES

1   Design and conduct your own Disney audience research. Design a short survey and look for five to ten respondents who represent different age groups and nationalities, if possible. Your questions could be similar to those in the Global Disney Audience Project: How old were you when you first came into contact with Disney products? What values does Disney represent to you? Do you own Disney books, videos, or DVDs? How would you explain Disney's global popularity? Have you visited a Disney theme park? If so, how would you describe your experience? When your data collection is complete, write up a one-page summary report about your findings.

2   Nickelodeon offers more than twenty country-specific Web sites for its global audiences. Are these Web sites "customized" in any ways to address the specific needs and interests of kids in various parts of the world? Visit several of them and compare and contrast their content as well as their visual features. You can even drop into some chat rooms to find out what Nick fans in Australia or Europe like to talk about. I recommend four English-language Web sites in case you do not speak other languages yet: Nick U.K. (www.nick.co.uk), Nickelodeon Australia (www.nickelodeon.com.au), the "original" Nickelodeon in the United States (www.nick.com), and the Nick Asia Pacific regional Web site (www.nicksplat.com).

3   What is your opinion of the argument that the global distribution of television programs is uneven and U.S. television programs tend to dominate other countries' TV programming? Perform your own content analysis by selecting two popular television channels from two different countries and compare their TV schedules for a given week. You could examine, for instance, New Zealand's TV3 (www.tv3.co.nz) and one of the U.S. network stations (for example, www.abc.go.com). What will you look for? How will you categorize the programs in the schedule?

REFERENCES

Ang, I. (1985). *Watching* Dallas: *Soap operas and the melodramatic imagination.* London: Methuen.

Appadurai, A. (1996). Modernity at large: Cultural dimensions of globalization. Minneapolis: University of Minnesota Press.

Banks, J. (1997). MTV and the globalization of popular culture. *Gazette,* 59(1), 43–60.

Buckingham, D. (2001). United Kingdom: Disney dialectics: Debating the politics of children's media culture. In J. Wasko, J. M. Phillips, & E. R. Meehan (Eds.), *Dazzled by Disney? The global Disney audiences project* (pp. 269–296). London: Leicester University Press.

Chalaby, J. K. (2005). From internationalization to transnationalization. *Global Media and Communication,* 1(1), 28–33.

Chan, J. M. (2005). Global media and the dialectics of the global. *Global Media and Communication,* 1(1), 24–28.

Ferguson, M. (1992) The mythology of globalization. *European Journal of Communication, 7,* 69–93.

General Conference adopts convention on the protection and promotion of the diversity of cultural expressions. (2005). Bureau of Public Information/Press Release No. 2005-128. Retrieved October 25, 2005, from http://www.portal.unesco.org.

Gigli, S. (2004). Children, youth and media around the world: An overview of trends and issues. Intermedia Survey Institute. Retrieved October 12, 2004, from http://www.riosummit2004.com.br.

Hendershot, H. (2004). Introduction: Nickelodeon and the business of fun. In H. Hendershot (Ed.), *Nickelodeon nation: The history, politics and economics of America's only TV channel for kids* (pp. 1–14). New York: New York University Press.

Herman, E. S., & McChesney, R. W. (1997). *The global media: The new missionaries of corporate capitalism*. London: Cassell.

Home, A. (1997, October 12). The not so magic roundabout [electronic version]. *The Independent* (London). Retrieved September 12, 2001, from Lexis-Nexis database.

Lemish, D., Drotner, K., Liebes, T., Maigret, E., & Stad, G. (1998). Global culture in practice. *European Journal of Communication, 13*(4), 539–556.

Liebes, T., & Katz, E. (1990). *The export of meaning: Cross-cultural readings of* Dallas. New York: Oxford University Press.

Magner, T. (2004). Transnational media, international trade and the idea of cultural diversity. *Continuum: Journal of Media and Cultural Studies, 18*(3), 380–397.

McChesney, R. (2002). Children, globalization, and media policy. In C. von Feilitzen & U. Carlsson (Eds.), *Children, young people and media globalisation* (pp. 23–32). Göteborg: UNICEF International Clearinghouse on Children, Youth and Media.

Morley, D. (1994). Postmodernism: The highest stage of cultural imperialism. In M. Perryman (Ed.), *Altered states: Postmodernism, politics, culture*. London: Lawrence and Wishart.

Nordenstreng, K., & Varis, T. (1974). Television traffic: A one-way street. *Reports and Papers on Mass Communication*, no. 70. Paris: UNESCO.

Nyamnjoh, F. B. (2002). Children, media and globalisation: A research agenda for Africa. In C. Von Feiltitzen & U. Carlsson (Eds.), *Children, young people and media globalisation* (pp. 43–52). Göteborg: UNICEF International Clearinghouse on Children, Youth and Media.

Reis, R. (2001). Brazil: Love it and hate it: Brazilians' ambiguous relationship with Disney. In J. Wasko, M. Phillips, & E. R. Meehan (Eds.), *Dazzled by Disney? The global Disney audiences project* (pp. 88–101). London: Leicester University Press.

Rizzini, I., & Bush, M. (2002). Editorial. Globalization and children. *Childhood, 9*(4), 371–374.

Robertson, R. (1994). Globalization or glocalization? *Journal of International Communication, 1*(1), 33–52.

Schiller, H. I. (1991). Not yet the post-imperialist era. *Critical Studies in Mass Communication, 8*, 12–18.

School competition. (2005). *New Zealand on Air*, August. Retrieved August 5, 2005, from http://www.nzoa.gov.nz.

Sepstrup, P. (1990). *Transnationalization of television in western Europe*. London: John Libbey.

Sreberny, A. (2005). Contradictions of the globalization moment. *Global Media and Communication, 1*(1), 11–15.

Strelitz, L. (2004). Against cultural essentialism: Media reception among South African youth. *Media, Culture and Society, 26*(5), 625–641.

Teenagers love seeing Kiwi culture on screen. (2005). *New Zealand on Air*, August 4. Retrieved August 5, 2005, from http://www.nzonair.govt.nz.

Tomlinson, J. (1991). *Cultural imperialism: A critical introduction.* Baltimore: Johns Hopkins University Press.

Tomlinson, J. (1999). *Globalization and culture.* Chicago: University of Chicago Press.

U.S. isolated over "protectionist" UN culture convention. (2005, October 20). *Agence France Press.* Retrieved October 25, 2005, from Lexis-Nexis database.

Wasko, J. (2001). *Understanding Disney:* The manufacture of fantasy. Cambridge: Polity.

Wasko, J., & Meehan, E. R. (2001). Dazzled by Disney? Ambiguity in ubiquity. In J. Wasko, M. Phillips, & E. R. Meehan (Eds.), *Dazzled by Disney? The global Disney audiences project* (pp. 329–344). London: Leicester University Press.

Wasko, J., Phillips, M., & Meehan, E. R. (Eds.). (2001). *Dazzled by Disney? The global Disney audiences project.* London: Leicester University Press.

Weber, I. (2003). Localizing the global: Successful strategies for selling television programmes to China. *Gazette, 65*(3), 273–290.

Will, G. F. (2005). Dimwitted nod to "diversity." *Washington Post*, October 12, p. A1.

Contributors

ALISON ALEXANDER (Ph.D., Ohio State University) is professor and associate dean for academic affairs at the Grady College of Journalism and Mass Communication at the University of Georgia. She was editor of the *Journal of Broadcasting & Electronic Media*, and is past president of the Association for Communication Administration and the Eastern Communication Association. Her work focuses on media and the family. She is the author of over forty book chapters or journal articles and the co-editor of four books. She was named the 1998 Frank Stanton Fellow by the International Radio & Television Society for "outstanding contribution to broadcast education."

CHRISTINE M. BACHEN (Ph.D., Stanford University) is associate professor of communication at Santa Clara University. Her research interests center around young people's use of media within the context of the family and how their use of various media shapes their perceptions of politics and romance. Her current research analyzes the civic content of youth-oriented Web sites and computer games and its implications for new media designers. Dr. Bachen offers courses in youth and media, media audience studies, and research methodology. Some of her journal articles include "Bridging the Gender Gap in

Computing: An Integrative Approach to Content Design for Girls," "*Channel One* and the Education of American Youths," "Imagining Romance: Young People's Cultural Models of Romance and Love," and "Portrayals of Information and Communication Technology on World Wide Web Sites for Girls."

J. ALISON BRYANT (Ph.D., University of Southern California) is research director for Nickelodeon's Consumer Insights group. Her current research focuses on the role of digital media in kids' lives and the changing relationship between parents, kids, and the media. She is the editor of *The Children's Television Community* (2007, Lawrence Erlbaum) and co-editor of *Television and the American Family* (2nd ed., 2001, Lawrence Erlbaum).

SAHARA BYRNE is a doctoral candidate in communication at the University of California, Santa Barbara. She has been the principal investigator on many in-school field experiments investigating child development and media literacy and has several years of experience as a production executive and writer in the entertainment industry.

JOELLEN FISHERKELLER (Ph.D., University of California at Berkeley) is associate professor in the Department of Culture and Communication at New York University. Her research and teaching interests focus on young people's everyday experiences with popular media and communication technologies, identity negotiation and cultural learning in context, and media education principles and practices. She is author of *Growing up with Television: Everyday Learning among Young Adolescents* (2002, Temple University Press) and has published book chapters and articles in journals such as the *Communication Review*, *Anthropology and Education Quarterly*, *Journal of Adult and Adolescent Literacy*, *Journal of Educational Media*, and *Television and New Media*.

KATHARINE E. HEINTZ-KNOWLES (Ph.D., University of Illinois) is a media analyst, researcher, and consultant specializing in the impact of electronic media on children and families. She has conducted research on media messages targeted to children and teens for groups such as Children Now, the Kaiser Family Foundation, and the National Partnership for Women and Families. Her work has been featured in over a hundred newspapers nationwide, including the *New York Times*, the *Los Angeles Times*, the *Chicago Tribune*, and *U.S.A. Today*, as well as national magazines such as *Parents Magazine*, *Parenting*, and *TV Guide*. In addition to her research and consulting, Dr. Heintz-Knowles conducts workshops for parents and educators and teaches media studies at the University of Southern Maine.

KEISHA L. HOERRNER (Ph.D., University of Georgia) is associate professor of communication in the Department of University Studies at Kennesaw State University. She directs the KSU 1102 learning communities program for first-year students, a program that *U.S. News & World Report* lists as one of the top twenty-five in the country. Prior to joining University Studies, Dr. Hoerrner taught in the Department of Communication, where she specialized in mass-media law, contemporary issues in mass communication, and children and media courses. Her research interests include congressional regulation of media content, advertising directed to children, and higher education.

NANCY A. JENNINGS (Ph.D., University of Texas at Austin) is assistant professor of communication at the University of Cincinnati. In addition to her doctorate, Dr. Jennings also has an M.B.A. in marketing. Her research interests focus on the impact of media on cognitive, social, and behavioral outcomes, particularly for children and their families. She currently is examining the nature of advertising during children's programs and evaluating the impact of outreach media literacy programs for parents and educators of preschoolers. Her work has appeared in the *Handbook of Children and the Media* and the *Handbook of Family Communication*. She also has published in the *Journal of Family Communication*, *Schizophrenia Bulletin*, and *Sex Roles*.

STEPHEN KLINE (Ph.D., London School of Economics) is professor of communication at Simon Fraser University. His areas of scholarship include the social communication of advertising, children's culture (including play, media, technology, and marketing to children), and interactive media. He is the author of *Out of the Garden: Toys, TV, and Children's Culture in the Age of Marketing* (1995, Verso), co-author of *Digital Play* (2003, McGill-Queens), *Research Audiences* (2003, Hargrave) and *Social Communication in Advertising* (2005, Routledge) as well as numerous book chapters and journal articles on children's culture.

DAFNA LEMISH (Ph.D., Ohio State University) is chair of the Department of Communication, Tel Aviv University, and editor of the *Journal of Children and Media*. Her research, teaching, and activism interests include children, media, and leisure, as well as gender-related issues of media representations and consumption. She has published extensively in academic journals and books on these and other topics. Her books include *Children and Television: A Global Perspective* (2006, Blackwell), *Children and Media in Times of War and Conflict* (co-edited, forthcoming, Hampton), *The Make-Believe Worlds of Children: When Harry Potter met Pokémon in Disneyland* (co-authored, 2005, Lawrence Erlbaum), and *Media Education around the Globe: Policies and Practices* (co-edited, 2003, Hampton). In addition, she guest edited a special issue of *Feminist Media Studies* on the media gendering of war and conflict (November 2005).

DEBORAH L. LINEBARGER (Ph.D., University of Texas at Austin) is assistant professor of communication in the Annenberg School for Communication at the University of Pennsylvania. Her research focuses on the relationships between children's developmental status, their use of media, and their larger social worlds. Her research combines descriptive work evaluating relationships between children's media use and their cognitive and social development; micro-level experimental work to detect the features used in media that elicit attention and contribute to comprehension of content; and macro-level program evaluation and intervention work that combines the knowledge gained through both descriptive and basic research and applies it in various real-world contexts. Her research has been presented at numerous conferences and published in psychology, communication, education, and pediatric medicine books and journals.

KATALIN LUSTYIK (Ph.D., University of Colorado), a native of Hungary, is assistant professor of television-radio at Ithaca College. She is the author of several book chapters related to the transformation of children's media culture in central and eastern Europe and the international and multicultural aspects of Disney and Nickelodeon animated programs. Her research and teaching interests include media globalization, media conglomerations and youth media, children's television, and European media content and policy, especially related to children and cultural trade.

SHARON R. MAZZARELLA (Ph.D., University of Illinois) is associate professor in the Department of Communication Studies at Clemson University. Her research interests are in girls' studies and the representational politics of mediated portrayals of youth. She is founding and lead co-editor of the journal *Popular Communication* (Lawrence Erlbaum Associates) and has published articles in *Popular Music and Society*, the *Journal of Broadcasting & Electronic Media*, the *Journal of Children and Media*, the *Journal of Communication Inquiry*, and *Communication Research*. She is editor of *Girl Wide Web: Girls, the Internet, and the Negotiation of Identity* (2005, Peter Lang) and co-editor of *Growing Up Girls: Popular Culture and the Construction of Identity* (1999, Peter Lang). In addition, she is editor of the new book series "Mediated Youth" (Peter Lang).

MATTHEW P. MCALLISTER (Ph.D., University of Illinois) is associate professor of film/video and media studies at Penn State. His research interests include advertising criticism, popular culture, and the political economy of the mass media. He is the author of *The Commercialization of American Culture* (1996, Sage), and the co-editor of *Comics and Ideology* (2001, Peter Lang). He has also published in such outlets as *Critical Studies in Media Communication*, *Journal of Communication*, *Journal of Broadcasting & Electronic Media*, and *Popular Communication*.

MICHAEL MORGAN (Ph.D., University of Pennsylvania) is professor and chair of the Department of Communication at the University of Massachusetts, Amherst. He has authored or co-authored many national and international studies on the effects of television on images of violence, sex roles, aging, health, science, academic achievement, the family, political orientations, and other issues. He was a Fulbright Research Scholar in Argentina and he has directed or collaborated on numerous international comparative research projects. He is co-author of *Television and Its Viewers: Cultivation Theory and Research* (1999, Cambridge) and *Democracy Tango: Television, Adolescents, and Authoritarian Tensions in Argentina* (1995, Hampton) (both with James Shanahan), and editor of *Against the Mainstream: Selected Writings of George Gerbner* (2002, Peter Lang). He teaches courses on media programming and institutions, media and the family, cultivation analysis, and other topics. In 2002 he received the University of Massachusetts Distinguished Teaching Award.

JOHN P. MURRAY (Ph.D., Catholic University of America) is professor of developmental psychology in the School of Family Studies and Human Services at Kansas State University, where he teaches adolescent development and conducts research on media violence and youth. He is also a senior scientist and visiting scholar at the Center on Media and Child Health at Children's Hospital Boston, Harvard Medical School, where he conducts research on children's brain activations in response to viewing video violence. A report on his initial studies of brainmapping violence was published in the February 2006 issue of the journal *Media Psychology* and are reviewed in his book, *Children and Television: Fifty Years of Research* (with Pecora, and Wartella, 2006, Lawrence Erlbaum).

W. JAMES POTTER (Ph.D., Florida State University, Ph.D., Indiana University) is professor of communication at the University of California at Santa Barbara. He is the author of a dozen books concerned with the media and how they affect us, including *Media Literacy* (2005, 3rd ed., Sage) and *Theory of Media Literacy: A Cognitive Approach* (2004, Sage).

ERICA SCHARRER (Ph.D., Syracuse University) is associate professor of communication at the University of Massachusetts, Amherst. She is co-author (with George Comstock) of *Television: What's on, Who's Watching, and What It Means* (1999, Academic Press) and *The Psychology of Media and Politics* (2004, Academic Press). Her research and teaching interests include media content, opinions about media influence, and media effects, especially regarding gender and violence. She has published her studies on those topics in *Mass Communication & Society, Journal of Broadcasting & Electronic Media, Communication Research,* and *Media Psychology*.

CYNDY SCHEIBE (Ph.D., Cornell University) is associate professor of psychology at Ithaca College, where she teaches courses in developmental psychology, media literacy, and television research. While at Cornell University, she and John Condry founded the Center for Research on the Effects of Television (CRETV). Dr. Scheibe currently serves as the director of the CRETV lab and television archive housed at Ithaca College in the psychology department. She is also the executive director and founder of Project Look Sharp, an award-winning media literacy education initiative. She has been conducting research on television content and children's understanding of media messages for more than twenty years and was a founding board member of the Alliance for a Media Literate America. Her recent publications include "A Deeper Sense of Literacy: Integrating Media Literacy in the K-12 Classroom" (*American Behavioral Scientist*, 2004).

NANCY SIGNORIELLI (Ph.D., University of Pennsylvania) is professor of communication and director of the M.A. program in communication at the University of Delaware. Beginning with her dissertation research, an in-depth methodological examination of television characters, she has conducted research on images in the media and how these images are related to people's conceptions of social reality (cultivation analysis) for the past forty years. An original member of the Cultural Indicators Research Team, she has published extensively on gender-role images, television violence, and health-related images on television. She has written several books, including *Violence in the Media: A Reference Handbook* (2005, ABC-Clio). Her research has appeared in numerous journals as well as in edited books on mass communication.

SUSANNAH R. STERN (Ph.D., University of North Carolina at Chapel Hill) is assistant professor of communication studies at the University of San Diego. Her research is situated at the intersection of electronic media and youth culture. She focuses on how young people experience the mediated world, how they use media to navigate through adolescence, and how they construct media messages to meet their own needs and fantasies. Her work has appeared in a variety of peer-reviewed journals such as the *Journal of Broadcasting & Electronic Media, Women's Studies in Communication*, and *New Media & Society*, as well as in several edited collections.

DEBORAH K. WAINWRIGHT is a Ph.D. student at the Annenberg School for Communication at the University of Pennsylvania. Before moving to Philadelphia, she worked in the Canadian television industry for nineteen years. Her experience spans the genres from cartoons and game shows to documentaries and music specials. But her passion for children's programming and its potential as an educational tool began as she produced and directed segments for Canadian *Sesame Street* and grew ever more fervent under the tutelage of Shari Lewis while working on *Lambchop's Play-Along*. She has a master of arts degree in educational psychology.

ELLEN WARTELLA (Ph.D., University of Minnesota) is executive vice chancellor and provost and distinguished professor of psychology at the University of California, Riverside. She was a co-principal investigator on the National TV Violence Study (1995–98) and is currently co-principal investigator of the Children's Digital Media Center project funded by the National Science Foundation (2001–2006). She is the author or co-author of eleven books, including *Children and Television: Fifty Years of Research* (with Pecora and Murray, 2006, Lawrence Erlbaum). She has authored or co-authored nearly fifty journal articles and numerous book chapters. Dr. Wartella is a member of the National Academy of Sciences Board on Children Youth and Families and recently served on the Institute of Medicine's Panel Study on Food Marketing and the Diets of Children and Youth (2006).

TAYLOR J. WILLIS is a University of San Diego graduate with a B.A. in communication studies with a media studies emphasis and a minor in psychology. His aspirations include cultural criticism and video production. This is his first published work.